7error7error7error7error7
777777777777777777777777
7ube 7ube 7ube 7ube7
7error7error 7error 7error7
on the on the on the on the
7ube 7ube 7ube 7ube7
7error7error 7error 7error7
7777777777777777724/7
7ube 7ube 7ube 7ube7

7/07/2005 =

7 7 7

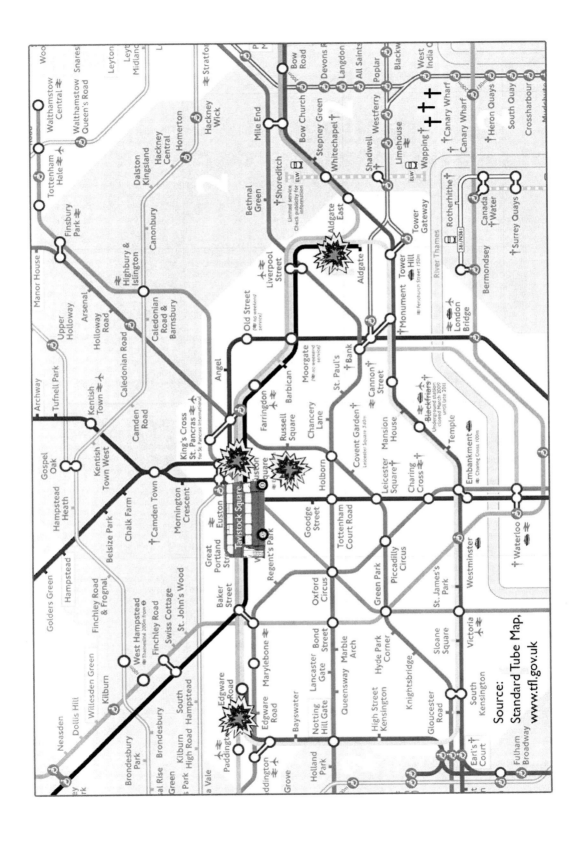

Source:
Standard Tube Map,
www.tfl.gov.uk

TERROR ON THE TUBE

Behind the Veil of 7/7

– an Investigation

by Nick Kollerstrom

2011

TERROR ON THE TUBE

Behind the Veil of 7/7 – an Investigation

Published by Progressive Press
PO Box 126, Joshua Tree, Calif. 92252,
www.ProgressivePress.com
ISBN 1-61577-737-7, EAN 978-1-61577-737-2
Length: 160,000 words plus index
The Author wishes to express deep gratitude to Kevin Boyle for all his assistance over Part II of this opus, i.e. the new material for this edition, and to Ian Fantom for his assistance in correcting and indexing the text.

BIC Subject area codes:

JFHC	Conspiracy theories
JPWL2	Terrorist attack
HBLX	21st century history: from c. 2000–
IDBK	United Kingdom, Great Britain
JKVM	Organized crime / JWXK War crimes
HRH	Islam
YXN	Personal and social issues: racism and multiculturalism

Library of CongressCatalog No. 2010292644.
LOC subject areas:
London Terrorist Bombings, London, England, 2005.
State-sponsored terrorism-- Great Britain.
Terrorism -- Political aspects -- Great Britain.
Terrorism -- Religious aspects -- Islam.

Synopsis: Independent research on the July 7, 2005 bombings in the London Underground uncovering wide discrepancies in the official narrative of the 7/7 London Tube explosions. This, on the author's analysis, is revealed as a Big Lie resting on the thinnest web of fabricated evidence, and unthinking repetition of unsupported and illogical allegations by the media. Kollerstrom's findings point overwhelmingly to State-Sponsored False-Flag Terror as the modus operandi of the wanton killings. The entrapment and demonization of four innocent Muslim youths as "suicide bombers" serves policies of US-UK-Israeli military aggression, and a British Police State. This new edition includes an index and a critique of the recent alleged "Inquest" by that state into its own dark crimes.

Printed in Great Britain, the United States and Australia

TERROR ON THE TUBE

Behind the Veil of 7/7 – an Investigation

Contents

Foreword

This present book deals with a very controversial issue, and the author, Dr. Nick Kollerstrom, is therefore well-suited to the undertaking. For all of his adult life he has taken such issues to heart and, in writing and other forms of activism, has prevailed to bring about much needed change against a tide of apathy. In the early 1980s he took the UK government to task on the issue of protecting children, and society in general, from lead. His book, *Lead on the Brain: A Plain Guide to Britain's No. 1 Pollutant,* forced many hesitant MPs to take action, which subsequently led to a safer environment. It is no surprise therefore that in the same decade he challenged the way in which the Thatcher government handled the Falklands War. As part of the Belgrano Action Group, he co-authored the title *The Unnecessary War*. Other causes of his have been somewhat more pedestrian, such as the treatises on lunar gardening, and works on the history of science.

The picture emerges of an activist and a scientist, and these two facets of his personality merge beautifully into a character that can reveal what is referred to in the Bible as the 'hidden things of darkness.' Light is hardly welcome in some quarters, especially when global criminals have set themselves up as leaders. Wickedness in high places reigns, and we the people are expected to close our eyes to it all.

Kollerstrom strives to open our eyes with facts. For years he campaigned for a truthful inquiry into 9/11, often working to support the likes of Cynthia McKinney and William Rodriguez. The former was for many terms a US Congresswoman, and the latter is the heroic figure who was the last man out of the North Tower on 9/11. When the terrible tragedy of 7/7 occurred, partly in his London Borough of Camden, and also not far from his alma mater, University College London, Kollerstrom was quick to save reports, and later he personally attended court hearings. He played a key role in ascertaining the time of the Luton to King's Cross train, after which the then Home Office Secretary John Reid publicly restated the time as per his research. Too often reports are changed, and court proceedings are kept secret from the public, so we do not really have at hand the true and honest record of what occurred. As time went on, initial reports, such as the one on the Guardian Internet pages by Mark Honigsbaum, were changed. Key evidence can be missed in the twinkling of an eye as the perpetrators of false flag terror activities, like some able magicians, exercise *leger de main* and keep the public from seeing the nature of their work.

This was what happened in 1933, when a certain madman gained power from the *Reichstagbrand* – the burning of the German House of Parliament. Many then were suspicious of it all, so much so that the International Investigative Committee in 1934 concluded that it was an inside job. That same year a German lawyer admitted to having knowledge of this, and in 1946 the whole dastardly plot was revealed by a former Nazi agent who gave his testimony at the Nuremberg trials. 20 million people had to die because the German press was manipulated, some of it owned outright, by Hitler. The left caved in then, much as it has done today. Reports of concentration camp atrocities were also conveniently ignored, both by government officials and journalists. Often those trying to bring to light the facts were ridiculed, vilified, imprisoned or killed. History today is in a repeat mode, and it sends chills up my spine to hear the likes of former US Congressman Joe Scarborough and his co-anchor at MSNBC urge that 9/11 truthers be arrested, tasered, and then sent to secret camps in Eastern Europe where they would not be heard from again.

Relatives of mine were, in fact, arrested and sent to just such camps, and their fate is what the MSNBC people were exhorting. Their exhortations are quite against morality, but serve to turn people against the truth, so that the guilty may avoid a real inquiry.

To be sure, however, there are those in the '9/11 truth movement' who, by their own actions, turn people against the truth. Indeed, the perception exists that some of these could be deliberate saboteurs and infiltrators, especially when they are former, if not active, agents of the intelligence services. It is a journalistic trick to single them out and use them as an example of the movement as a whole, conveniently ignoring the basic facts which are being put forth. There will always be those who blame things on aliens or the paranormal, or, as occurred in the last century, on a racial minority. Both Islamophobia and anti-Semitism are occurring today, and it is vital that we do not accept either. A small clique in the truth movement has been guilty of some rather absurd anti-Jewish theories, but the more observant ignore these red herrings, or, rather, question their validity, as it may well be part of the plan to have more than one scapegoat, blaming first Moslems, but strewing on the scene of the crime various other pointers so as to incite anti-Jewish speculation; in such an atmosphere it is hard to create a clear indictment. Kollerstrom differentiates red herrings from real clues. We are not here led to conclude that the perpetrators are all of any one ethnicity or religion. Whatever conspiracy exists, the common denominator is one of spiritual evil, coupled with the means to carry out such attacks: greedy, lusty and powerful figures, to whom Her Majesty, the Queen of England, simply and succinctly refers to as 'dark forces.' Kollerstrom's tone is in line with his regent's, rather than the shrill voices we often hear screeching about particular groups and societies. The reader is not burdened with speculations and rants, but is rather given, in a scholarly manner, the body of evidence which is ignored by the mainstream press – as it was ignored in the 1930s.

With these facts before us, let me close with my own exhortation, and urge on the reader the necessity of taking calm but determined action before we are led down the path any further towards a militarized and controlled society.

Ari Silverman

Introduction

by Kevin Barrett

It is often said that knowledge is power. But this simple three-word sentence can mean different things to different people.

For the followers of Malcolm X, it means empowerment through self-education. For the followers of Foucault, on the other hand, there is no such thing as knowledge *per se*. Apart from the workings of power, what we take to be knowledge is simply a shadow on the wall of our cave, cast by an infernal blaze of power that is always hidden somewhere behind us, just out of view.

The conflict between these two positions is what is really at stake in today's terror wars. The first position is the foundation not just of Islam, but of all true religions—and all true philosophy as well. Religion, after all, teaches us that (metaphysical) truth is indeed available to those who strive for it; while philosophy means "love of wisdom" and likewise involves the quest for truth, restricting itself (as religion does not) to critical methods.

The other position, that knowledge is an illusion created by the play of power, derives from Nietzche and reaches its absurd extreme in the judeo-nazism of Leo Strauss. Strauss, the top student of leading Nazi philosopher Carl Schmidt, taught Paul Wolfowitz, Richard Perle and the rest of the neocons that there is no truth, no good—and of course no God—and that justice is simply what the strong seize for themselves. According to Strauss, the elite—that is, the neocons—are exempt from morality, and ought to take power covertly and rule by foisting big lies upon the masses.

The first position—that truth is real and available to those who sincerely seek knowledge—is a torch being carried today by many people of diverse outlooks—and also by the religion of Islam, the core of a (re)-expanding civilization. (In Islam, God is also known as *al-haqq*, "the Truth," and the Prophet Muhammad has famously urged us to "seek knowledge even unto China.")

The second position—that there is no truth, just power—is a dark message being broadcast not just by the neocons and postmodernists, but also by universities, think tanks, and the controlled corporate media, which all unabashedly shy away from truths that cut too sharply against the grain of power. This situation reflects a decadent civilization's loss of faith in truth, in knowledge, even in existence itself.

The masters of illusion who fabricated the "clash of civilizations" often frame this alleged event as a clash of civilization *per se*, identified with the West, against the uncivilized barbarism of non-Western peoples, especially Muslims. The reality is rather the reverse. Civilization rests on a bedrock faith in truth and knowledge. When that bedrock is shaken, civilization collapses. Those who have fabricated the Big Lie known as the "war on terror" are the real barbarians. Like termites, they are gnawing away at the foundations of civilization. The civilized people, the defenders of civilization, are those who seek knowledge and proclaim the truth.

Nick Kollerstrom is one of the planet's courageous defenders of civilization, and his book on the London bombings is exemplary in its willingness to follow the truth wherever it leads. And here, as in the case of 9/11, it leads very quickly to a very uncomfortable place.

As Kollerstrom shows us, with regard to the 7/7 London bombings, knowledge is indeed Power—first name Peter. By simply googling "Peter Power 7/7" any bright twelve-year-old can quickly learn, beyond any reasonable doubt, that the 7/7 bombings were an obvious, bald-faced inside job.

Peter Power, for those who have not yet googled him, is the Scotland Yard terror chief who, on July 7th, 2005, was head of the British security firm Visor Consultants. In the evening of July 7th, 2005, Peter Power appeared on television and stated that on that very morning he and Visor Consultants had been running a "terror drill" that perfectly mimicked the actual terror attacks, including the exact times and locations where the bombs went off. Unfortunately Power did not reveal the name of the agency that hired him to run the drill. Subsequently, Power apparently realized his mistake, and began offering a series of ludicrously unconvincing retractions.

For the benefit of those unable to see that two and two make four, Kollerstrom painstakingly calculates that the odds of a terror attack randomly matching an exercise of this kind are about one in a billion.

Unlike Nafeez Ahmed, the author of the only other critical work on the London bombings, Kollerstrom follows the ugly truth exposed by Power's revelation (and by reams upon reams of other evidence) to its logical conclusion. We now *know* that 7/7 was an inside job designed to frame Muslims and hype the bogus "war on terror."

But what good is it to know something like that? Isn't it more advantageous to simply "raise questions about the official version of events" as Ahmed pretends to be doing—even as the questions he raises, and the information he presents, blow the official story out of the water and reveal the event as an obvious false-flag operation? After all, by pretending to be simply raising questions, Ahmed has been able to undermine the "war on terror" while keeping his university teaching position. Some of us who have spoken more plainly have not been so lucky.

Despite its pecuniary drawbacks, plain speaking has the advantage of enabling action in a way that "simply raising questions" does not. In ordinary life, when we know something, we are prepared to take action. For example, if mere questions have been raised about the likelihood of rain, we may not yet feel compelled to find an umbrella before venturing outside. When we finally conclude that we *know* it is raining—perhaps by looking for ourselves—we take appropriate action.

Likewise, it is fairly easy to question the official version of 9/11 or 7/7 without feeling the need to act. "It will turn out to be like the JFK case," such people often say. "We will never really know what happened." The unspoken corollary to this position is: *If I knew it was an inside job, I would have to take action. Taking action would be uncomfortable, even painful. Therefore I must ensure that I don't really know that it was an inside job. I had better not learn too much about this case. And I had better use every available psychological defense mechanism to remain unconvinced by those who claim they do know. I will begin by believing that anyone who knows something like this must be a "conspiracy theorist." That way I can dismiss the whole argument without even having to consider it, simply by mindlessly accepting a pejorative portrayal of the person who advances it. And if anyone tells me I'm falling for the ad hominem fallacy, I'll just say I don't speak Latin.*

Kollerstrom's book is not for that kind of person. Only those brave enough to risk their easy equanimity will dare approach it.

The knowledge that we have been lied to so horribly is heartbreaking. So are all the horrors that grew from the lie: The mass murder of more than a million innocent people in Iraq and Afghanistan, the assault on freedom, the torture and persecution of tens of thousands of people whose only crime is to profess the religion of Islam. The only way to even begin to atone for such horrors is to confront the lies that produced them. And we must confront those lies head on, with no equivocation or blathering excuses.

Kollerstrom's forthright discussion of 7/7 is followed by an equally acerbic look at the fake terror show trials that followed. As a science historian, Kollerstrom is in a good position to know that even Muslims, with all the power of Allah behind them, cannot turn drugstore hydrogen peroxide into a high explosive by fiddling with it in the lavatory of an airliner. Everyone who has been inconvenienced by the insane "no liquids or gels" so-called security measures imposed in the wake of the liquid bomb hoax needs to read Kollerstrom and weep—whether with grief, laughter, or some combination thereof.

In the end, the reader of this book will understand that the post-Cold War West is being terrorized not by Muslims, but by the Western state apparatus itself. This is hardly surprising, since we now know that it was NATO (under the command of the Pentagon) that was carrying out the worst "terrorist attacks" against Europeans during the Cold War, which we now remember as 'Gladio'. What makes it even less surprising, for those capable of independent thought, is that the very definition of the state is "that bureaucracy which can plausibly claim a monopoly of violence in a given territory."

How can we make the transition to a form of civilization not based on violence? That is the question that must be answered, and soon, if humanity is to succeed in its role as God's vice-regent on earth, preserving our planetary home as a garden paradise, and venturing forth to explore other worlds.

By exposing the fact that the expression "state terror" is redundant—virtually all mass terror is inflicted by states—Nick Kollerstrom and his colleagues in the truth movement are laying the foundations of a Copernican revolution in consciousness and social organization. Once we find that we can do without the terror of the state, and that we can live together in joy rather than apart in fear, we will look back at the so called war on terror as the last gasp of a psychopathic elite. And we will look back on Nick Kollerstrom as one of the brave pioneers who first stepped outside the fear-mongerers' illusion into the light of truth...and beckoned for us to join him.

Kevin Barrett is the founder of MUJCA, Muslims, Jews and Christians for 9/11 Truth, author of the book 9/11 Truth Jihad, *and hosts a talk radio show on GCNLive.*

PART I.

1. Need for an Independent Inquiry

The case for an independent inquiry into the attacks of July 2005 is now overwhelming.

— David Davis, Shadow Home Secretary, May 2007

The British people have been denied anything resembling a fair inquiry into the events of July 7th, 2005 – the London Bombings, which were the biggest attack on London since the Blitz. Instead, there has been an 'Inquest,' which was a massive, five-month event: it heard evidence concerning *how* people died. It may have *looked a bit like* a public inquiry – but, it wasn't one. It gave to the Metropolitan police one more opportunity to tell their story. We heard no intelligent mind evaluating it or asking any questions about it.

Londoners have been exposed to a series of things which vaguely resemble some sort of inquiry into 7/7, and which have elaborated the received story line of the London bombings in considerable detail – not always consistently. The Inquest did not allow any lawyers to be present on behalf of the four young men who died that day, who are alleged to have planted the bombs, and in fact did not include their four bodies: it continually presupposed that it knew how they had died, permitting no flicker or tremor of doubt concerning the official narrative. Large numbers of witnesses were summoned, who described in morbid detail who died where – but no speculation as to the cause of death, or what kind of bomb would have caused such mayhem, could be allowed.

This book seeks to remedy that defect. This is the only book you can read which tells you the truth about the London bombings. In this third edition I strive to tell you what *really* happened on that day – and, I even venture some comments about who did it, who was responsible.

The earlier editions of this book, published in 2009, argued for Islamic innocence, but did not claim to be able to say what had really happened on the day of July 7th. The new material, resulting from Inquest hearings, coming from the Old Bailey, Britain's High Court of Justice, appears in Part II of this book. This fresh evidence, together with fresh evaluations and perspectives on that evidence, enable a closer focus on the sequence of events. This book has the single aim, of stimulating informed debate. I claim that the primary axiom of Islamic guilt has now disintegrated, is no longer tenable.

Few are the people in the UK who are willing to discuss this matter. A notable exception here is Mr John Anthony Hill, recently released by the authorities from Wandsworth jail. He was kept in jail over most of the Inquest, and released once it was over. Could this be because of his video *7/7: The Ripple Effect* , is probably the most watched of 7/7 videos? Surely not. But, his initial arrest was early in 2009, just as a three-month so-called 'July 7th' trial was starting, and he was then released when it was over.

I have been God knows heavily vilified by the British media once it became known in 2008 that I was researching the present book on the subject, and furthermore being interviewed by the BBC in connection with it. I was unceremoniously ejected from the college where I had taken my PhD – and been an honorary member of staff for 11 years, in the Science and Technology Studies Department at University College London –the first time a staff member has been removed from UCL for ideological reasons. But, there are limits to the freedom of academic discourse, and surmising that one's own government might be complicit in a mass murder exercise of its own citizens may exceed that limit. Yet any self-pity to which I might be entitled has dissolved upon meeting this just and innocent man, held in Wandsworth jail.

I dedicate this book to my good friend Keith Mothersson, who was a guide for me, helping me with many steps of the argument and avoiding blunders in its text. He was a peacemaker and helped different factions of the '911 truth' movement in the UK remain on speaking terms, and see each other's point of view. As the first edition came out on the summer of 2009, he had been leading a fit and healthy life as a gardener-Buddhist, and 60-year old grandfather. Suddenly he was taken into his local mental hospital, and sedated with anti-psychotic drugs. I phoned him up and indeed, he could hardly remember who he was. No, the nurse explained, they could not figure what had hyappened, as dementia was normally a gradual process. Then after three weeks in the hospital his heart stopped beating. Just like that. No, the nurse said, they didn't know why. The police saw nothing suspicious about the death, while his family saw his funny 'conspiracy theories' as evidence of his loss of mental balance. Uh-huh. Years ago, Keith and I had been co-founders of Inlap, the Institute for Law and Peace, about legal arguments used by peace-activists. How suddenly a mighty tree may fall...

I had been enjoying a comfy perch in académe, researching a suitably obscure topic (how Neptune had been discovered) — and don't I wish I had stuck to that, concerned friends ask me? Instead of being thrown out of college and abused on all sides. I was accused of having a 'ghoulish' interest in the dead'— that seemed to be a favourite media term of abuse, as well as 'consorting with terrorists' which can apparently be hurled at anyone trying to question alleged Islamic guilt – could I not have just applied for one more research grant? Yet – or so it seems to me – everything we value as an open liberal democracy could fade away and become a mere memory, if we permit politicians to operate with a fabric of untruth as is described and analysed in this book. Are we not drifting towards a crypto-fascist, hierarchical, robotic total-surveillance police-state which is dedicated, exactly as Orwell described, to perpetual war against enemies that keep changing? I suggest that this country now needs, more than anything else, young women and men of vision who are capable of seeing though the fear-engendering untruths used by politicians, and who will stand up and say, 'That's not the way its got to be!' -and who will do so, as Keith Mothersson taught us, with a total commitment to nonviolence.

There is not a politician in the UK who is prepared to stand up in public and question whether the collapse of the Towers on 9/11 was caused by 19 hijackers crashing planes into them. Each tower was built of solid steel and concrete, with 5,000 times the mass of a Boeing 767, yet each one fell straight downwards in the path of greatest resistance, at the very speed of a fall through thin air — vanished as if by magic, but in fact exactly as in a controlled demolition.Not a single UK politician will *publicly* admit these glaringly obvious and widely propagated facts about the Twin Towers and WTC 7. We have in the UK no one like Cynthia McKinney, the glorious Cynthia McKinney, who is able to 'speak truth to power' and discuss 'false-flag terror' – that key, all-important political concept for our new millennium. Her black and feminist political background does help her here. There are deep connections in the logic and in the event-construction between the London bombings and 9/11 — two crucial psychological warfare operations based on false-flag terror — which will I hope slowly dawn upon the reader. They were both wonderfully designed, with extraordinary skill, to create the fearful image of Islamic suicide-terror.

At the time of preparing this third edition, the UK's 'threat assessment level' has been up to maximum for a whole year – without anything resembling a terror-scare materializing (the 'toner-cartridge of death' from Yemen – don't make me laugh). Euro-statistics given here in Appendix 11 show that the chance of being killed by a terrorist this century in Europe is comparable to that of being struck by an asteroid – *if* we exclude what seem to be government-staged events, viz. the bombings of Madrid 2004 and London 2005. Fear has to be generated, the politician *needs your fear*. This whole book is about a phantom image conjured up of four 'terrorists' in London one morning, and the efforts made by the Government to sustain that phantom, fear-creating image.

In a startling manner, in a way one had not experienced before, the ability to distinguish between what is real and what is not becomes of central relevance to contemporary politics. Traditionally that was the domain of the philosopher. Good, socialist, peace-activists never had to bother about such things, did they? But now we have to ask, were there *really* 19 hijackers on board the planes, on the fateful morning of 9/11 – or was something more in the nature of robotic control going on? Were there *really* four terrorists on the coaches and a bus on the morning of July 7th —or were the explosions arranged in some other way? My endeavor here is to show you that such discussions are *stimulating* and *enjoyable:* no expert is going to tell you the answer, so you might as well mull them over with your friends. Plato in his *Republic* described how the multitudes were doomed to watch flickering shadows on the wall, in a cave, without ever being able to see the fire behind them which was their source. As Webster Tarpley has pointed out, this famous metaphor has acquired a frightening new relevance in our new millennium.

The figure of Emmanuel Goldstein in George Orwell's *1984* is an all-purpose villain, and in this 21st century the figure of Osama bin Laden has functioned likewise. As the bogeyman he could be invoked by any politician who wished to stand up on his hind legs and bray about the Islamic 'terror threat.' In fact, Bin Laden was reported dead of kidney failure in December of 2001, in the Tora Bora mountains: if he's never been seen since, it's because he's DEAD. How many politicians in the UK would agree with this? Not many, but that only shows the magnitude of the problem and the challenge. If he died shortly after being given the blame for 9/11, then *several dozen* videos and tapes allegedly by or about him have been faked. That is an important realization – which never alas dawns upon Robert Fisk. Nor is it without relevance to the study of 7/7, where two dubious 'confession videos' appeared posthumously in the months after the event. The interface between the ISI (Pakistani intelligence) and the CIA which has been producing the from-beyond-the-grave Bin Laden videos could well have contributed to Siddique Khan's jihad-confession, which someone mysteriously gave to Al-Jazeera in Qatar two months after his death — the channel of choice for disinformation stemming from the secret services.

No Public Inquiry

The Government had to resist the clamour for a public inquiry. The Inquest reminds one of the extensive 'hearings' which the Greater London Assembly held in 2006, a year after the event. Harrowing testimonies were given, by one survivor after another, but to what end? I heard that one person involved in organizing it had been shocked by the sheer number of accounts of people having feet and legs blown off — hardly what one would expect had the blasts been caused by a 'terrorist' wearing a rucksack, but exactly what would happen if bombs were planted by insiders beneath the carriages. They were basically told to *get over it,* to forget it. (Again and again we heard that story from Inquest testimonies, the implications of which have been totally ignored by the British media) No discernable lesson or conclusion came from that extended series of 'hearings.'

Then there was the so-called 'July 7th trial' in 2008, an opportunity for a lot of new 7/7 material to be 'leaked' without anyone being concerned to evaluate it or challenge it. Do you want to believe in doubtful-looking closed-circuit TV (CCTV) images, first released three years after the event and without a timestamp? Chapter 13 describes this four-month trial, which began in April of 2008 at Kingston Crown Court, accusing three young friends of the four alleged suicide bombers. The day before it started, counsel for the prosecution Neil Flewitt informed a group of over a hundred potential jurors that 'As you know, Mohammed Siddique Khan, Shehzad Tanweer, Germaine Lindsay and Hasib Hussain were responsible for causing a series of explosions on the London Underground…' Then, a few days into the trial, he reiterated this view: "There is *no doubt* those four men were responsible for that appalling act of terrorism" (10th April). The trial was conducted within that context, that there was 'no doubt' of presumed Islamic guilt. There were two of these trials, lasting at least six months in all, of these three young men – after which the jury still could not find the three lads on trial guilty of participating in the London bombings!

Most calls for a public inquiry do not question Islamic guilt, but focus on the topic of the 2008 Intelligence and Security Committee's Report "Could 7/7 have been prevented?" and particularly, the alleged early detection of two of the Four in the so-called 'Crevice' case, tried in 2004. ('Crevice' has no particular meaning, being only a code word). Should not British intelligence have known more about these lads, if there had been such a police record? Not a lot came out of the Inquest on this matter. The so-called 'Crevice' trial, entirely based on what a disparate group of people had allegedly been intending, comes into the category of what is here called *phantom terror,* where nothing actually happens, no bombs have been made nor does anyone get hurt or killed – but, Muslims go to jail for what anti-terror police allege they were "intending." Nobody gets to hear the viewpoint of the convicted Muslims. Phantom terror becomes credible *in the wake of* real terror.

On May 1, 2007, survivors and relatives of those killed on July 7, 2005 delivered a letter to the Home Office calling for an "independent and impartial public inquiry" into the attack, following which on May 28th the Greater London Council passed a motion supporting this call; both brusquely rejected by the UK Government. The people of London still really need such a visible inquiry, as a way of working through their collective trauma. Members of the police, parliament and intelligence services ought to be public servants answerable to the public. It is not adequate that a pervasive ethic of secrecy should pass under the rubric of 'national security.' The legal case here rests upon Article Two of the European Convention on Human Rights,[1] which requires the state not only to protect life but to undertake an independent and effective investigation of the issue if the article is breached.

The United Nations Human Rights Commission adopted, in 2005 in Geneva an updated set of principles affirming that citizens had a 'Right to Know':

> Principle 2: The Inalienable Right to the Truth
>
> Every people has the inalienable right to know the truth about past events concerning the perpetration of heinous crimes and about the circumstances and reasons that led, through massive or systematic violations, to the perpetration of those crimes. Full and effective exercise of the right to the truth provides a vital safeguard against the recurrence of violations.
>
> Principle 5: Guarantees to give effect to the right to know
>
> States must take appropriate action, including measures necessary, to ensure the independent and effective operation of the judiciary, to give effect to the right to know... Societies that have experienced heinous crimes perpetrated on a massive or systematic basis may benefit in particular from the creation of a truth commission or other commission of inquiry to establish the facts surrounding those violations so that the truth may be ascertained and to prevent the disappearance of evidence.[2]

The European court of human rights has on several occasions confirmed *that failure to effectively investigate* arbitrary killings by the state is itself a violation of human rights. Let's note the criteria it marked out to denote the effectiveness of an investigation, namely: **promptness, thoroughness, impartiality, independence** and **transparency**. In this context, it has repeatedly insisted that 'the persons responsible for and carrying out the investigation to be independent from those implicated in the events,' adding: 'This means not only a lack of hierarchical or institutional connection but also a practical independence.'

Impartiality, the Court explained, requires that investigators examine with an open mind all relevant evidence, even including that which contradicts their 'firm conviction', and including in the scope of their investigation the possibility of official involvement in the crime, particularly when they are put on notice about suspicious activities by official entities. In order to ensure the impartiality of an investigation, witnesses 'shall be protected from ... any ... form of intimidation', particularly by state officials.

Clearly, the British people have been denied such an inquiry. Rachel North, a survivor of the King's Cross-Russell Square underground explosion – who has over the years functioned as the chief media spokesperson for the Government's view of what happened on that day – made a speech on this subject at a CAMPACC (Campaign Against Criminalising Communities) meeting in July 2006 calling for such an inquiry where she said,[3]

> I have met both Mr Clarke, the previous Home Secretary, and Dr Reid, the current one – and Ms Tessa Jowell, who is the Secretary of State with special care of the victims of atrocities and disasters. I have asked all of them the same

question. Why has there been no public inquiry into the 7 July bombings? In each case I have had the same answer: it will cost too much, it will take too long, it will only tell us what we already know. This is almost word for word what Mr Blair said in December 2005. It has been repeated ever since by his representatives. It is not truthful, and it is not good enough.

Dr Reid only last night made an unexpected announcement that the train time that the bombers took to Kings Cross was the 7.25am, not the 7.40am, and this has led to more speculation as to how much of the Home Office's anonymous official narrative is flawed. It is to me, and many others I have spoken to, an insult that two slim pamphlets, each containing fewer pages than the number of the dead – with their inconsistencies and contradictions and downright inaccuracies – are the sum total of all that this Government has to offer its people.

Ten months after the event, on 11 May 2006, the Government produced its anonymous 'official narrative'.[4] This anonymous account of what had supposedly happened on that day largely depended upon various CCTV images, which could not however be shown.

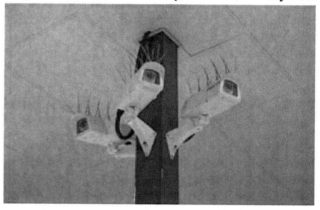

Two years later, at the 'July 7th' Kingston trial, four of these image-sequences were produced, in a rather questionable manner. So why could they not have been shown earlier? Whatever the answer, such a cavalier attitude is a far cry from the EU's requirement for 'impartiality, independence and transparency.'

We quote from Rachel North's book, *Out of the Tunnel*:

> I could not guess the reasons why the Government was refusing to have an inquiry into the worst terrorist attack on English soil, and the first suicide bombings in Europe. They normally had public enquiries into all sorts of things,

I could have told her. To this she added, very pertinently:

> If the terrorist threat was so important that we had to change the constitution and carry ID cards and make draconian new laws, then an independent review of what happened before, during and afterwards, with all the information in one place, conducted by someone independent of the Government with the power to compel witnesses and make recommendations seemed to me not just useful, but downright essential.[5]

Instead, 'as if we were children to be placated,' Britons were only given a narrative, a year after the event.

Within a month of that Official Report emerging, the Government had to admit that it had been mistaken on a very central issue: the train it had alleged the Four had caught into London had not run on that day. It was the research of myself and a colleague which established those train times that morning, and discovered this unexpected anomaly – a flaw in the perfect crime, as it were. That discovery gradually pulled me into a position of investigating the entire narrative of the event.

Here is another British voice calling for a public inquiry, the prolific author Nafeez Ahmed (of Sussex University). He yearns for that which can never happen:

> There is no doubt that an independent public inquiry into the events of 7/7, and the associated events of 21/7 and 22/7, is urgently required. This inquiry must be independent in the sense that it must be free of state influence or pressure. It must also be public in the sense that its objectives, procedures, and processes are entirely transparent and accountable, and moreover that rather than being conducted in secret meetings behind closed doors where information can be manipulated, it must be chaired by genuinely independent experts in an open forum. These factors, however, cannot mean anything in the absence of the legal authority to compel the state to release information on the London bombings and related issues.

If only! With a fine, youthful idealism he added,

> Given the complexity, multi-dimensionality and international nature of the relevant issues, an independent public inquiry into the London bombings should have a broad remit to examine not merely those terrorist attacks, but a host of related domestic and foreign policies pursued by the British state over the last decade in alliance with the United States and several European states.'[6]

Much as one wishes that we lived in a world where this could happen, the basis for it is lacking. Such hopes are like the story told to children: "To catch a bird, sprinkle salt on its tail." If our society and government had the autonomous capacity for an independent public inquiry into these matters, and if we had a really independent media, then the bird would already be caught: these crimes would not occur, as they could not be engineered with impunity.

The police operation embracing both the 7/7 and the 21/7 events was called 'Operation Theseus.' This alludes to the archetypal Greek hero Theseus, who was able successfully to penetrate into a dangerous labyrinth and return still alive, because he clung onto the 'Ariadne's thread' he had been given. Perhaps this thread represents the right use of our intuition, in following though a bewildering variety of false trails and real dangers. Sherlock Holmes would exclaim 'The game's afoot!' when he felt that there was a case to be solved, and would often enough have cause to rebuke the rather plodding Inspector Lastrade of Scotland Yard, who tended to miss the vital clues. The reader is here invited to be Sherlock Holmes, and exercise her or his intuition to try and discern the guilty culprits, which Scotland Yard may, just possibly, have missed. Operation Theseus has cost the taxpayer over seventy million pounds, over a three-month period, and was thereafter running at £0.3 million per day – the UK's biggest ever police operation. [7] A small fraction of this sum would have sufficed for an independent inquiry, which would help bring the subject into the public domain where it ought to belong.

The state will never arrange such a public inquiry – for reasons which will become evident in the present treatise – and, instead, a people's inquiry of some kind is necessary. A mosaic of testimonies informs our picture of what happened on the tube that morning, and they are far from being compatible. We need to hear witnesses giving their testimony in a form where two adversarial lawyers are able to grill them, which is the traditional British approach for finding out the truth. Were they really present, do they recall clearly? Such an inquiry should *not presuppose Muslim guilt,* nor indeed British-Asian or British-Caribbean guilt, that is the crux of the matter, and it is within the best tradition of British justice that guilt is not presupposed, but has to be established. A Channel 4 survey of British Muslims found that 59% believed that the Government had not told the whole story about July 7th, while 24% of them answered 'No' concerning whether the alleged bombers were indeed responsible. There are questions which our society needs to try and resolve, if civilised values are to remain intact.

Witness Testimony

At the Inquest, key witnesses do not turn up, indeed are not summoned: Peter Power, Ephraim Halevi, Sir Ian Blair. 'Skulking behind the Official Secrets Act', persons with vital information are liable to say they are not allowed to divulge it. Scotland Yard's terror chief Peter Power was running his game-simulation on the very morning, shadowing the terror-event as it happened, with his company that puts on such drills, Visor Consultants. Speaking shortly after the event, he averred that his client *helped to choose* the exact scenario, that is, the mock terror drill involving the three tube stations where the blasts actually occurred. All the world would like to see an Inquiry where he could be properly grilled on this topic – under oath.

To what extent do different testimonies support each other? I was impressed by the testimony of Australian Tania Calibrese, who had been sitting with her boyfriend on the top deck of the Number 30 bus in Tavistock Square. She recalled how she noticed police putting up tape to block off the street just *before* the blast (see Chapter 9).[8] In the film 'The Matrix', fabricated events can sometimes be recognised because their time-sequences are a bit out of joint.

Rachel North's book describes the unexpected half-hour closure of much of the Piccadilly line around her station on that morning, before the bombs went off. Indeed, half a dozen books written by survivors have appeared, giving their testimony of what happened that morning, which is in itself quite remarkable. These books spend not an instant pondering who might be guilty of the crimes in question, but they tend to spend quite a while wondering whether they can ever forgive the alleged perpetrators, whose guilt has never been proven. Do these authors believe that there was anyone in London who saw these dark-skinned lads on that morning, or even that any photos exist of these lads in London on July 7th? Well, the Inquest did come out with Louise French who finally after five years remembered that she had seen Hasib Hussain on the top deck of the 30 bus, and Mr Danny Biddle was recalling that he had seen 'Khan,' however I will venture to suggest that these may be 'false memory' syndrome. Clearly, readers must make up their own mind on such matters.

There is quite a bit of evidence that more than three trains were involved that morning – this is especially so for the Aldgate blast area, where both the Circle and Metropolitan & City lines were afflicted. A startling number of testimonies violate the primary hypothesis concerning the tube train blasts, namely that the explosions took place on trains travelling *away* from King's Cross. What if someone was injured, or killed, on a train travelling *towards* King's Cross? Would that be just a confused report, to be ignored? Unless a properly independent inquiry comes into existence, with broad civil-society support of non-governmental organisations, and able to give moral support and protection to whistleblowers, these matters are not going to be resolved.

Testimonies are reported in newspapers and on the BBC archives, from persons such as Eamon Spellman, Zeyned Basci, Mandy Yu, Aaron Roche and Grassiere Homiguez, to name only those involved with the Piccadilly line blast. The Indian Mr Kurush Anklesaria recalled that,

> I was on the train going from Bayswater station sitting in the first compartment of the train and after passing Paddington station at about 08:50 there was a huge blast just at the side of my feet and part of the floor was ripped open. (news24.com)[9]

On an *eastbound* Circle Line train, traveling towards King's Cross, could such a thing have happened? How likely could a blast from below be caused by an impact from the side, from a train passing in the other direction?

The testimony of 'Yotty Toda' from the BBC archives of July 7th, sounds as if she might have been in the same train, but an adjacent carriage:

> I was in the train when the blast occurred between Edgware Road and Paddington… I was in the second carriage so I had to go through the first one in order to evacuate. When I reached the end of the first carriage, I thought I would see the driver's compartment, but it was totally blown off. I saw parts of the compartment — such as the doors and the roof — scattered around the track. I was helped down to the track by underground staff and we walked all the way to the Edgware Road station in the dark tunnel.

Her train appears as travelling Eastbound, towards King's Cross, and just about to enter Edgware Road station. We are left rather concerned as to the well-being of the driver from her account. When people have been through unforgettable trauma, should we suppose they would forget what train they were on, and in which direction they were travelling? Moreover, this was the rush hour when many would be commuting to work.

The Harrods carpet salesman Eamon Spellman in the second carriage of the Piccadilly train kindly gave an interview with the author, which corroborated Rachel North's testimony. By contrast, the 'official witness' for the No.30 bus explosion was a Mr Richard Jones, who gave a thrice-changing testimony, claiming to recall the bus bomber at Tavistock Square.[10]

Without a public inquiry, there is a grave danger we will go down the US path of responding to terror-events with ever more funding to the intelligence and security services – who may be the very people who perpetrated them in the first place. Such a failure would place this country in the same situation as America, where ten years on no one has been convicted arrested for the crime of 9/11, let alone arrested and tried for it.[11] Persons who should be held suspect have been promoted. Once that happens, the terrible thing will have taken place, and we will no longer be living in a democracy, but in something else.

My Perspective

As a member of what used to be Britain's 9/11 truth movement, I take the view that 7/7 may fruitfully be interpreted in the light of 9/11. There are over a dozen 'truth' books about 9/11, and I'm puzzled that in this third edition, my book still remains the only one about the truth of 7/7. Detractors will label us as conspiracy theorists, but this is only name-calling; the government's July 7th narrative also is a theory about a conspiracy. In *Conspiracies, Theories and the Secrets of 9/11*, Matthias Bröckers has shown how mundane conspiracy is to everyday life, occurring any time two people share information privately, and not only by whispering together, the original Latin meaning. By currently politically correct usage, you're *not* a conspiracy theorist if your theory is that brown-skinned persons conspired to perpetrate the events of July 7th or 9/11, whereas you *are* one if you believe that white-skinned persons did.[12] You're not one if you believe the perpetrators are dead, but you are one if you suspect that they may be still among us.

The present work draws from the insights and researches of many people, whom it may be impossible to thank or acknowledge, and it brings web-insights onto the printed page. The videos *Ludicrous Diversion* and *Mind the Gap* draw from their expertise (Prime Minister Tony Blair averred that a public inquiry into the events of that day would be a 'ludicrous diversion' that would divert resources away from the War on Terror, hence the video's title). The July 7th Truth Campaign will dig out, discuss

> Any crime or secret activity involving more than one person is a conspiracy. And any attempt to solve it requires a theory. For example, the Government's claim that four young Muslim conspirators blew up Tube trains is no more nor less than a theory about a conspiracy. But is it a credible theory? And why are those — and only those — who *question* this particular conspiracy theory labelled pejoratively as — "conspiracy theorists"?

and evaluate the evidence in impressive detail, but are not keen on giving 'answers', as they are concerned not to appear as 'conspiracy theorists'. Yet the enemies of democracy have rushed to draw conclusions, with malice aforethought, and to force them on the public. Therefore our present approach necessarily does seek answers, coloured inevitably by perspectives and skills developed through investigating the grand event of 9/11.

The author visited the Luton train platform with James Stewart in the weeks after July 7th, and ascertained the computer records of trains that morning together with commuter testimonies. Thereby it was definitively ascertained that the alleged bombers could not have been present both in the Luton CCTV images and the King's Cross CCTV images as presented for that morning at the times stated. All the trains were delayed that morning, and the key train we were all told they had taken, the 07.40, was actually cancelled. A year later, the Home Secretary John Reid in fact admitted this to the House of Commons. 7/7 may have been planned as the perfect crime, but this delay had not been foreseen. This became a major focal point of unravelling of the official story. Even newspapers have sometimes been allowed to discuss, albeit quite nervously, this aspect of the narrative.

The train times discovery (Ch. 5) and the timeline (Ch. 3) are the main contributions that I made to the J7 website whilst I was a member of that group. Our viewpoints subsequently diverged. The J7 site comprises a vast encyclopaedia of information concerning the London bombings, with everything you ever wanted to know, such that anyone writing about the topic is more or less obliged to use material contained or reproduced on it. However, their site does not ever express an opinion as to who might have done it, or how or why — whereas in contrast the present work does have such an ambition. Let's quote their own words:

> J7 have been researching the events of 7/7 since the day itself and we can confidently state, based on the evidence that has been released, that we have no idea a) what happened, b) how it happened, and c) who made it happen. After over five years of continuous research, J7 has very few answers. Instead we have considerably more questions than we started out with that have hitherto not been satisfactorily answered. (J7 blog, 1.10.10)

Socrates debated with the Sophists, and these were very learned folk who doubted that definite conclusions could be reached about things, and I feel the J7 team have got themselves into that position. The Socratic method is based on asking questions, in order to arrive at answers — not to remain forever with unanswered questions. The vital question in a criminal case is, "Who did it?"

You are about to read an account of the biggest attack upon Londoners since the Blitz, treated as an unsolved murder mystery. Where does one begin such a narrative? A good deal of information has been left to the appendices. The new Inquest material comes in an updated Chapter 9, in the middle section. There is a special chapter about what I call 'phantom terror', which is a kind of echo-effect or propaganda booster. It can only take work after the real terror has been perpetrated. No one is hurt, but the police allege that someone may have been intending to do something. It has a vital role in enhancing the fear: which is after all the aim of the exercise. One of the phantom-terror stories (Heathrow) used the comic-book theme of 'binary munitions,' involving the same explosive as was allegedly found up in a bath in Leeds a week after July 7th. Or at least it was until a couple of years ago: the deadly explosive found in the bath in Leeds/ in the blown-up carriages/ in the car in Luton car-park does change now and then; that is part of the charm of this epic tale. It's why we need a historical sequence of the unfolding of the story, which is done in the opening chapters. Appendix 9 gives the background chemistry to the binary munitions story, where Hollywood fantasy has to a disturbing extent prevailed in the public mind over chemical fact — all the more so when no forensic report of the police investigation is available.

Let us embark then upon this inquiry: will it soon become outdated, once a proper, independent, people's inquiry takes place?

References

[1] Legal Challenge to Government as Pressure Grows for Independent 7/7 Enquiry, Letter requesting judicial review, 15.8.07: www.blairwatch.co.uk/node/1869

[2] Elias Davidson, *The Events of 11 September 2001 and the Right to Truth,* Reykjavik, 2007. pp. 6-7; www.aldeilis.net/english/images/stories/911/rightttotruth.pdf.

[3] CAMPACC (Campaign Against Criminalising Communities) has called for such an Inquiry, in which it is supported by the Human Rights & Social Justice Research Institute, Stop Political Terror, 1990 Trust, and The Muslim Parliament. See Appendix I.

[4] Anon, *Report of the Official Account of the Bombings in London on 7th July 2005*, HMSO, May 2006.

[5] Rachel North, *Out of the Tunnel*, 2007, p.253.

[6] Nafeez Ahmed, *The London Bombings*, 2006, p.268. See Appendix X book review.

[7] www.mpa.gov.uk/committees/f/2005/050915/07.htm — Financing Operation Theseus, Metropolitan Police Authority. No documents concerning Operation Theseus are (2008) publicly available.

[8] D. Obachike, *The 4th Bomb, Inside London's Terror Storm* p.23; *Daily Mail*, 'The real Faces of 7/7,' 7.7.06, for Tania Calabrese's testimony.

[9] News24.com home, Passengers 'ignored warning' 8.7.05, www.news24.com/News24/World/News/0,,2-10-1462_1733932,00.html.

[10] The Number 30 bus witness 'Richard Jones' claimed to be an IT salesman linked to the Scottish Ardossan Academy: a character named Richard Blood would seem to exist with these qualifications.

[11] The mentally-disturbed Zacarias Moussaoui, the alleged '20th hijacker,' has been arrested, and given life imprisonment, but not for facilitating 9/11.

[12] A pertinent comment on 'conspiracy theory' attributed to 'Jamey Hecht': "This phrase is among the tireless workhorses of establishment discourse. Without it, disinformation would be much harder than it is. 'Conspiracy theory' is a trigger phrase, saturated with intellectual contempt and deeply anti-intellectual resentment. It makes little sense on its own, and while it's a priceless tool of propaganda, it is worse than useless as an explanatory category." Here is a more laid-back comment by Len Bracken: 'Merely by broaching the subject of the state indirectly attacking, or allowing an attack, on citizens it should defend, we stand accused of being conspiracy theorists, a label we neither accept nor reject because we are independent historians and strategic theorists who do not share the widespread academic prejudice against conspiracies.' (Bracken, *The Shadow Government, 9/11 and State Terror*, 2002, p.34).

2. False-Flag Terror

Whoever constructed and carried out the event of July 7th, 2005 in London must have been fiendishly wicked by any standards. How can such depth of moral depravity exist? Who can deliberately wish to sow terror? We here attempt to develop a historical perspective on such matters. Perhaps the thesis here argued is a logical development of what Niccolò Machiavelli argued concerning the danger of having standing armies, kept in time of peace. His 1521 *Art of War* warned the Italian princes of his day that unemployed mercenaries and professional soldiers would inevitably stir up coups and conflicts in order to procure jobs and glory for themselves:

> I say … that … governments should fear those persons who make war their only business … no one can be called a good man who, in order to support himself, takes up a profession that obliges him at all times to be rapacious, fraudulent, and cruel, as of course must be all those who – no matter what their rank – make a trade of war.[1]

Here we will be especially concerned with the second of those three, dire adjectives: "fraudulent". Amongst New Yorkers, a sizeable proportion would concur with some degree of complicity by the US military in the event of 9/11,[2] and thus a British MP Michael Meacher is able to express such views on the topic and be listened to.[3] In the UK the figure for such sceptics may be around 40%, whereas only a much smaller proportion of the British public would accept the thesis here propounded about July 7th – viz, that the terrorists who constructed and perpetrated the event were persons of white skin, not brown.

The hypothesis here put forward is that the events of July 7th were an example of a phenomenon characterised as 'false-flag' by the veteran American analyst Webster Tarpley. Such events are not the work of their seeming perpetrators *but have been made to look as if they are*. Who, then, might be guilty? The unthinkable happens when the State itself conspires to inflict death and terror upon its own citizens. Only a few works of fiction seem able to guide us – Orwell's *1984* or Alan Moore's *V for Vendetta*. Surely this is not the world we live in? Can we not wake up from this as from a bad dream?

Here we wish to argue that, not only is this reality, but that the peace movement will remain powerless until and unless it apprehends what is going on here. Within our lifetime, the most fundamental axiom of politics has been: *the people have to live in fear*. The image of 'the Enemy' has to be there. Within the last couple of decades we have seen that image metamorphose, from 'the commies' to 'radical Islam'. The latter – or so we here argue – are no more a threat to the British way of life than were the communists of an earlier age. Long prefigured in the 1993 bombing of the World Trade Centre, for which the FBI kindly provided the explosives,[4] September 11th fully actualised that new enemy image, and gave a new rationale as to what a couple of hundred US military bases were doing all around the world. 9/11 was state terror, a visible message to all the world as to why the US military needed to devour some $400 billion a year.

As Webster Tarpley has argued,

the starting point for realistic appraisal of 9/11 is not primarily the sociology of the Middle East, but rather the historical record of NATO and CIA state-sponsored terrorism in Western Europe and elsewhere in the post world-War II period.[5]

We are here suggesting that July 7th can be seen in the tradition of that rather apocalyptic event, and more specifically within the framework of the 1980 Bologna railway station bombing and the Madrid 2004 railway bombing. July 7th, was, of course, also a train bombing; a Gladio speciality.These atrocities were 'false-flag' in that the perpetrators were contriving to have blame fall upon an innocent group. The actual perpetrators of false-flag terror always remain unknown; but somebody has to be blamed when terrible and innocent deaths ensue.

An understanding of the Tarpley thesis may be essential if civilisation is to endure. Something has gone horribly wrong with institutions which you thought you could trust. Now what our culture needs *more than anything else*, are persons who can tell the difference between what is real and what is illusory, persons who can discern the illusion that comes through their TV screen with such brief finality. *The Towers were mined* – that message passes by word of mouth, unmentionable in the media. The Twin Towers (and their triplet, building WTC 7) indeed fell on that day of doom, but not due to any airplane impact. Thus cause and effect appear differently. Your whole world-view will change, according to whether you believe: that fiendish terrorists commandeered Boeing aeroplanes and flew them into the Towers, *causing* the collapse

- or, whether you take the more scientific view that this is physically impossible, and that the cause of their sudden destruction lay more within them, within the Three Towers of the World Trade Centre (numbers 1, 2 and 7) that collapsed on that day.[6]

Thus the event of 9/11 does give us certain perspectives whereby the London bombings can be interpreted. If you believe that 19 Islamic fanatics took over those aircraft, and caused the destruction, then you are also quite likely to believe that four young Muslims also perpetrated the biggest attack upon London since the Blitz. But in either case, you ought to be perplexed as to why the respective governments saw no need for any inquiry to ascertain guilt for these events.

Let us see how the Tarpley thesis develops:

> The principle directly at stake here is that state terrorists wishing to conduct an illegal terror operation often find it highly advantageous to conduit or bootleg that illegal operation through the government military/security bureaucracy with the help of an exercise or drill that closely resembles or mimics the illegal operation. Once the entire apparatus is set up, it is only necessary to make apparently small changes to have the exercise go live… (Tarpley, xi)

War games suddenly become a bit too real – that is a notion we are going to have to get used to:

> We must stress the idea, unfamiliar and suppressed as it is, that the vast majority of international terrorism conducted on a spectacular scale is indeed state-sponsored terrorism. This does not mean that such terrorism is sponsored by the entire government, down to the last GS-4 clerical worker doing data entry for the Social Security Administration. It does mean that a faction or network of the

government uses its access to the levers of power to promote the terrorist action in various ways. In Europe in the 1960s and 1970s, and in the Arab and Islamic world today, there have been deluded and naïve individuals and institutions who have somehow associated large-scale international terrorism with revolutionary or progressive change, or with the establishment of international justice. Nothing could be further from the truth. If the Italian left of the 1970s and the German left of the same period sympathized with the Red brigades or the Baader-Meinhof group/Red Army faction, they only showed their own gullibility, since both of these terrorist operations were created by and controlled by NATO intelligence. Similarly, the Arab who feels sympathy for al-Qaeda needs to be forcefully reminded that al-Qaeda was created by the CIA and continues to be steered by the CIA, through various intermediaries and cut-outs, or discreet go-betweens... Terrorism in the modern era is the means by which oligarchies wage secret war against the people which it would be politically impossible to wage openly.

The naïve view of terrorism is that it grows up directly out of oppression, economic misery, and political despair. Oppressed and exploited people, or those who have been exploited by a foreign power, supposedly come together spontaneously in ones and twos, create an organization, and after a certain time of preparation go over to armed struggle against their oppressors or occupiers. But this is the rarest of exceptions.

This naïve view is blind to the most important institutional actors in the world of terrorism – secret intelligence agencies like CIA, FBI, NSA, KGB, Stasi, MI-6, and the rest. Secret intelligence agencies are institutions in which the very essence of oligarchy is at work: as the enjoyment of oligarchical privileges comes inevitably at the expense of the people, covert methods of control become indispensable.... Terrorism generally starts within these secret agencies, or nowadays more likely their privatized tentacles – such as the intelligence community in the United States has had since President Reagan's Executive Order 12333.

The world of secret intelligence agencies is a world of falsehood, camouflage, deception, violence, unspeakable cruelty, treachery, and betrayal. It is the most desolate and grim sector of human endeavour, where no human values can subsist. It knows neither hope nor mercy nor redemption. It is the one area of human life where Hobbes' maxim holds true – it is the war of all against all. But not as chaos – rather as an ultimately controlled phenomenon upholding the state power the intelligence agencies serve. During the cold War, the conflict of CIA, MI-6, SDECE, KGB, BND, Stasi and the rest was called the wilderness of mirrors, a desert populated by agents, double agents, triple agents, multiple agents, their case officers, their counterintelligence opponents, and the omnipresent specialists in *mokrie dela* – wetwork, as the KGB describes assassinations.

We start from the strong presumption that terrorism is intrinsically an activity which is controlled by a faction of government, probably acting under the influence of financier factions, which are generally the ultimate source of authority in the globalised universe after 1991.... It should also be clear that state-sponsored terrorism cannot call itself by its own real name. It must necessarily masquerade as an authentic voice of the oppressed – be they Arabs, Muslims, workers, national minorities, or whatever…. The false flag and false ideology allows the terror group to pretend to be something it is not, and to convince billions of naïve viewers of CNN or Al-Jazeera that the false dumb-show is reality (pp. 60-62).

You had never wanted to look into the sordid question of 'Who plants the bombs?' but had hoped to spend your life on happier and more edifying issues. After all, one could surely trust the police to find out that sort of thing? Let's here quote the US Secretary of State Colin Powell:

Terrorism is a part of the dark side of globalisation. However sadly, it is part of doing business in the world of business we as Americans are not going to stop doing.[7]

We wonder, can the world not live together in peace and harmony? A traitor is one who betrays his country. The traitor moves slyly, abusing the trust of the people. His acts may be done in the pursuit of an agenda of world-domination or whatever, and the anti-Muslim sentiment created may be viewed as necessary. For obvious reasons the military are going to prefer a War of Civilisations agenda. I believe and will argue that a CIA-Mossad-MI6 *'Axis of Evil'* was probably involved in perpetrating these events, as it was also very likely involved with the assassination of Diana and Dodi in 1997.[8] In both cases we never get to know exactly which part of it is responsible. War is the agenda, war is the reason. Pentagon document Field Manual FM 30-31B explicitly discusses launching terrorist attacks in nations that "do not react with sufficient effectiveness" to the geopolitical demands of the Globalists.[9] Donald Rumsfeld's 'Proactive, Preemptive Operations Group' (P2OG) within the Pentagon was authorized to stimulate terror events pre-emptively; its elite members were authorized to carry out secret missions designed to "stimulate reactions" among terrorist groups, provoking them into committing violent acts which would then expose them to "counterattack" by U.S. forces. This group emerged into the light of day in 2002, with an annual budget of $100 million. A British intelligence agent who works with such an agenda is going to be, in effect, a traitor to his country.

Seeing is no longer believing in this new millennium, as digital fabrications can be made to appear. Whom do you trust? If there is a message of this book, it is that 'Military Intelligence,' as in MI-5 or MI-6, is something in the nature of tactical deception.[10] The military operate on a need-to-know basis, for the projection of power: as in, we take your raw materials. That's the axiom. What is our oil doing under your sand? The world rather needs *civilian intelligence* to prevent the fabrications of war-makers from influencing politicians. The illusions created by the war-makers may always be exposed in the end, after they have worked – when little remains at stake. But, that is far too late! Society needs to be based on truth and justice, which means a network of civilian intelligence agencies prepared to look at state-sponsored terror and seek out those who wish to use terror as an agency of global change.

Here is Tarpley writing just four days after the event of July 7th:

Last week's London explosions carry the characteristic features of state-sponsored, false-flag, synthetic terror provocation by networks within the British intelligence services MI-5, MI-6, the Home Office, and the Metropolitan Police

Special Branch who are favourable to a wider Anglo-American aggressive war in the middle East, featuring especially an early pre-emptive attack upon Iran, with a separate option on North Korea also included. With the London attacks, the Anglo-American invisible government adds another horrendous crime to its own dossier. (P. 461)

The fabrication of the terror event involves war games and terror drills:

Operations like these are generally conducted through the government bureaucracies under the cover of a drill or exercise which closely resembles the terror operation itself. So it was with Amalgam Virgo and the multiple exercise held of 9/11.... So it was with the Hinckley attempt to assassinate Ronald Reagan, when a presidential succession exercise was scheduled for the next day.... An uncannily similar manoeuvre allows the necessary work to be done on official computers and on company time, while warding off the inquisitive glances and questions of curious co-workers at adjoining computer consoles.

Such a parallel drill was not lacking in the London case. On the evening of July 7th, BBC Five, a news and sports radio program, carried an interview with a certain former Scotland Yard official named Peter Power who related that his firm, Visor Consultants, had been doing an anti-terror bombing drill in precisely the Underground stations and at the precise times when the real explosions went off. Peter Power and consultants had been subcontractors for the drill; Power declined to name the prime contractors. (p.463; see Appendix 4b).

A dire modern version of Plato's cave is here apparent, where most people watch the flickering shadows on the wall and believe that this is real. The populace clamour to surrender their hard-won democratic freedoms for the sake of National Security, as surges of fear are endlessly transmitted through a strangely compliant media:

The Bush campaign [2004] presented the 9/11 myth as a new compulsory pagan civic mystery cult of which their candidate was the high priest. Bush unwaveringly built his entire campaign on the demagogic ethos of 9/11 and its related chauvinistic and racist themes. (Tarpley p.440).

Coincidence versus Intent

How far can coincidence go? What does your real world include? Can it include for example Peter Power doing a *Panorama* program the year before about how terror strikes central London, with four bombs going off in the morning rush-hour, three on the Underground and one in an above-ground vehicle, and Peter Power as the program's main consultant concerning the event-simulation? Will you allow that to be mere coincidence? Here we will attempt to give you the evidence and allow you to make up your own mind on the topic, as far as possible. If we here endorse something, the likelihood of which sounds remote to you, then we hope we shall do so in a responsible manner. Brandon Lee, son of Bruce Lee, made martial arts films and was killed in one act when a gun turned out to have a live bullet in it. So who was to blame? Somebody was responsible. Thus, game-theatre tumbles out into the real world as real, live, 'outright terror, bold and brilliant,' as the exploded No.30 bus advert proclaimed (for the film, 'The Descent,' opening that week). Would the police, if they did put up their yellow tape in Tavistock Square rather early, have assumed they were part of that morning's terror-drill, and be as startled as the rest of us when the event went live, so to speak?

Our fairly detailed accounts of the Terror will keep coming up against *trains going the wrong way*, and a larger number than three being afflicted. The mysterious delays in announcing the events to the public, which we'll come across in the Timeline, may have this cause. Trains blown up had to be travelling away from King's Cross and should have preferably left King's Cross within minutes of each other, on the official story. Then the three blow up synchronously just as they enter tunnels. It is best to start off without a hypothesis, with no explanation in our minds, as we try to access this primary data, on which everything depends, from human testimonies, and prevent it disappearing down the Memory-Hole.

Certain proofs may be viewed as conclusive, for example it is mathematically impossible for the police to have identified three of the four 'bombers' by Tuesday, 12th July as they claimed, when they had identified *in toto* a mere five out of the 56 persons killed. That is too improbable; the laws of probability do not allow this. As likewise – and indeed even more so – may be Mr Power's position, that he 'just happened' to be running a terror-drill exercise on that morning, at the same underground stations, etc.

You may find that this book has too much evidence on the subject, details and names that may not lead anywhere, testimonies that cannot easily be put together to make sense. Central components of the drama remain mysterious. In an unsolved murder, a detective has a lot of vaguely-disconnected fragments, and hunches as to whether they are related. Our story will unfold, of what some would call a New World Order Event, with conflicting testimonies and beliefs, and yet which, I propose, does have an over-arching purpose. However we may express that its effect was to extinguish Hope. Can you remember the euphoria in the days before, with the Make Poverty History campaign backed by elders and sages of the planet such as Nelson Mandela? Did we not all just for once believe that something was going to happen? Global concordance, the upbeat music, London winning the Olympic Games …

Then Bush and Blair met, and terror broke out again exactly as it had done on the previous occasion when they had met in the UK,[11] and finally the G8 leaders had to start listening again to the dubiously elected President. Thus were the world's hopes for G8 aborted. Debt was not forgiven for Africa; the rich continued to get richer and the poor, poorer. Normal life continued, as the people learned to live in fear. Transparent rucksacks came on sale.

TerrorStorm by Alex Jones is a documentary which logged up ten million viewings before Google Video re-set the count to zero, as if such mass appeal were unseemly! Despite several minor factual inaccuracies, its thesis is comparable to ours, in centering on July 7th, which is interpreted in the light of other major acts of false-flag terror. The film starts off with the attack upon the *USS Liberty* off Israeli waters in 1967. Israeli gunships started to attack it and would have sunk it (with LBJ's connivance) had not a Russian spy ship turned up, and the whole episode was suddenly cancelled. The plan was for a sunk US warship to be blamed upon Egypt, leading to a US attack upon Egypt. The ship staggered home and Israel and those in the Pentagon who either commissioned this attack or facilitated it, were simply *let off.* Hard to believe, yes, but this is the world we live in. Insights into these matters are spreading more widely through web articles and DVDs than through published volumes, as the latter are more readily censored. Books can be burnt, bookshops sued merely for selling an allegedly defamatory volume. What is calling itself the Truth movement is about *the history we need to know.* To quote John-Paul Leonard[12] in his blog for 8 July, 2005, the day after:

> O lovers of peace and opponents of war: never shall you see an end of calamities instigated by the war party, until the people see through the false flag trick!

Is another book needed? The collective view of the mainstream peace movement was expressed by Milan Rai in his book *7/7: The London bombings, Islam and the Iraq war.* According to this, the event was 'blowback,' i.e. revenge for Britain's involvement in the Iraq war, by alienated Muslim youth. Many of us valued Rai's ARROW leaflets, 'Active Resistance to the Roots Of War', however his book on this topic may not have got very far in this vitally important direction, in our view.[13]

The books by persons who were there on the day include *Out of the Tunnel* by Rachel North, *The 4th Bomb* by Daniel Obachike, *One Day in July* by Professor John Tulloch, *One Morning in July – The Man Who Was First on the Scene Tells His Story* by Aaron Debnam, *Into the Darkness, the Story of 7/7* by Peter Zimonjic, *One Unknown, A Powerful Account of Survival* by Gill Hicks; plus, there is *7/7 – The London Bombings, What went wrong* by Lt. Col. Crispin Black. Pressure for an official Inquiry is presently coming primarily from Rachel 'North' (originally Rachel of North London, she took and is widely known by this pseudonym). She had some shards of glass impact into her wrist as a consequence of being in a Piccadilly line carriage where the explosion happened. Her group of July 7th survivors is presently considering legal action against government agencies for failing to initiate any such inquiry. It is fair to say that, despite her frustrations with the Government, she is the *one person* who will stand up in public and defend and expound the official view; which is curious. It may not be ethical to own any of the above books (except for Mr Obachike's), as they do not for an instant doubt the hypothesis of Islamic guilt, nor do they offer evidence in support of such.

The most significant work on the subject is that by Nafeez Ahmed, *The London Bombs.* Ostensibly Ahmed's thesis is not so different from that of Rai and Stop the War: '7/7 was blowback' he writes, and concludes

The evidence discussed in this book demonstrates decisively that the London bombers had operated as part of a well established al-Qaeda terrorist network in Britain, whose key leadership is well known to British authorities.

Had he indeed shown this?[14] For the present we'll merely note that Ahmed's book makes *no mention* of what we here argue was fairly central, namely the terror-drill closely emulating the real thing, that morning. Ahmed's view is in general fluid concerning what he is suggesting may or may not have happened on that fateful day, but this may be appropriate given the level of disinformation that has been put out by the media on the topic. He has a scholarly way of writing upon the great question of 'Al-Qaeda' and the extent to which it may exist, and his writings will here be alluded to with respect. He has a pan-global perspective on the manner in which the CIA, FBI and MI6 sustain and fabricate the perceived Al-Qaeda menace. His books have drawn high praise from persons such as John Pilger and Gore Vidal.

On a quite pragmatic level, Ahmed had his book published by a mainstream company, which he would not have been able to do had he pointed a finger of accusation at MI5. His manuscript had 'alleged bombers' throughout; this had to be changed to 'bombers,' his publisher informed him. On websites where no such limitations are operating, he expresses considerably more doubts, for example as to whether there were any suicide bombers.

In his book, Ahmed concludes concerning the location of the tube bombs, that, although experts had confirmed they had been placed at floor-level:

> However reports from survivors and witnesses in the public record largely suggest to the contrary that the bombs exploded from underneath the carriages, rather than from bags placed upon the floor. These accounts emerged in the earliest aftermath of the atrocities…

But, if he is going to have the bombs placed somehow under the train carriages, how can he possibly sustain any Al-Qaeda authorship of the deed? Thus the reader's view ricochets back and forward in a way that Ahmed will not resolve. Rather the contrary, he likes the agnostic position! Were train carriages blasted off the rails by bombs underneath them, or not? In due time we will be coming onto how the GLC heard the terrible testimonies of survivors. The simplest possible statement one can make concerning those testimonies is that *many lost legs and feet, but not arms.* This primal, central fact has been greatly glossed over.

The story of July 7th seems to involve continued contradictions. For example, Ahmed has well described how, in the aftermath of the event, experts were in agreement that high-power, military-grade explosives had been used, remotely detonated just after the trains left the stations. Then the story switched over a week later to home-made explosives *brewed up in a bath*, in Leeds – with no attempt to explain how one story had metamorphosed into another (we examine this theme in Chapter 8). How could alleged findings in Leeds invalidate the conclusions of forensic experts in London? Ahmed tries to avoid drawing any conclusion here, except that the public have been lied to, and that the press have displayed undue credulity in believing the change of story. We may respect his position here as a lecturer in political science at the University of Sussex, as one who might wish in some degree to maintain an ambiguous position.

As you read, I hope to convey to you the power of truth and its relevance to change our modern world. It's a truth that hurts. We are all hurt by it in one way or another. Ingrained into the British national psyche is the assurance that 'we' are the good guys, in a manner that requires The Enemy, and can you imagine living without that? In films, 'The Enemy' has to get blasted to bits, after it has provided the action and excitement of the story. Does your enemy have a darker skin colour? Will you rally round the Prime Minister if he invokes the Blitz, Dunkirk, etc? This book is going to suggest that there may be *no Islamic terror-menace* as such in the UK, or none worth speaking of (see Appendix 11), and furthermore that the English and other peoples of these islands *do not collectively need* an Enemy.

References

[1] Machiavelli, *Art of War*, quoted in Tarpley *9/11 Synthetic Terror (2005-2007)*, p. 378.

[2] A NYT-CBS poll found in October 2006 that a mere 16% of New Yorkers believed the official story of 9/11.

[3] Michael Meacher, *The Guardian*, 'This War on Terrorism is Bogus,' 6th June 2003.

[4] Len Bracken, *The Shadow Government , 9/11 and State Terror (2002)*.

[5] Webster Tarpley, *9/11 Synthetic Terror (2005-2007)*.

[6] David Ray Griffin, *The New Pearl Harbour, Disturbing questions about the Bush Administration and 9/11 (2004)*, pp. 20-23; Tarpley, p.224.

[7] May 2001 'Remarks before the State Appropriations Subcommittee on Commerce, Justice, State and the Judiciary'; quoted in Ahmed *The London Bombings (2006)* p.10.

[8] Noel Botham, *The Murder of Princess Diana (2004)*.

[9] Daniele Ganser, *NATO's Secret Armies*, pp. 234, 297. Ahmed has characterized this document as 'the only smoking gun Pentagon memo which proves that state-sponsored self-terrorism is standard strategy for elements of Western military-intelligence services;' in 'Interrogating 9/11 Five Years on', New Dawn Magazine. But there is also the P2OG document, whereby Rumsfeld authorized terror attacks to be provoked in a 'pre-emptive' manner.

[10] We are here happily in accord with Groucho Marx's dictum, 'Military intelligence is a contradiction in terms'.

[11] Bush arrived in London 18th November 2003; the Istanbul bomb in the British Embassy went off on 20th (see Ch. 15).

[12] http://usa.mediamonitors.net/content/view/full/16539 John-Paul Leonard is the publisher of both Nafeez Ahmed's *The War on Freedom (2002)* (advocated by Gore Vidal as the best book about 9/11) and Tarpley's *9/11 Synthetic Terror: Made in USA (2005-2007)*, Progressive Press, Joshua Tree, Calif., as well as a number of other 9/11 Truth books, including Kevin Barrett's *Truth Jihad: My Epic Struggle Against the 9/11 Big Lie*. The first hour of Alex Jones' 'TerrorStorm' video may be recommended unreservedly, while the latter part may be mainly of interest to US viewers.

[13] A review in *Notes from the Borderland* Ed. Larry O'Hara, July 2006, compared the Black and Osborne books, pp.40-2.

[14] A more recent and extensive argument of this case appears in Ahmed's *Inside the Crevice, Islamist Terror Networks and the 7/7 Intelligence Failure,* 2007, a UK parliamentary briefing paper. His argument may here depend unduly upon official post-7/7 statements to infer alleged terror involvements of Khan. The moments of doubt he experienced over this matter in *The London Bombings* seem to have here disappeared (see Appendix 10b).

3. Some Preliminary Events

In this chapter we sketch in a few relevant themes by way of background information.

The Template?

The BBC Panorama program of Tuesday, 16th May, 2004, entitled 'London Under Attack' depicted a fictional terrorist attack involving four simultaneous suicide bombs.[1,2] It was presented in a documentary manner, as if it were really happening. To quote Webster Tarpley – in the context of US events:

> No terrorist attack would be complete without the advance airing of a scenario docudrama to provide the population with a conceptual scheme to help them understand the coming events in the sense intended by the oligarchy (p.408).

'The fictional day of terror unfolds through the immediacy of rolling news bringing the catastrophic attack into our living rooms,' helpfully explained the BBC's website. Viewers were treated to the sight of three trains on the London Underground being blown up between 8-9 am, plus one more explosion happening on a large street-vehicle an hour later, in central London. It reported that, on the day of the explosions:

> 'The Home Secretary has said the attacks bear the hallmark of Al-Qaeda...'

One year later, on July 7th at 7.40 pm, Britain's Foreign Secretary Jack Straw uttered the virtually identical words: 'The attacks bear the hallmarks of al-Qa'eda.'

> TUBE EXPLOSIONS – 3 blasts on London Underground
>
> The headlines at 9 o'clock. In the past hour there have been three major explosions on the London underground. The first occurred at 10 past 8 on the Piccadilly line between Knightsbridge and Hyde Park Corner. The second went off at 16 minutes past 8, on the Central Line between Tottenham Court Road and Oxford Circus, and the third at 27 minutes past 8 as a train was arriving at Vauxhall Station in Stockwell on the Victoria line. Emergency services have been called to all three scenes. There are no reports available yet on the number of casualties, and the police have said that it's too early to identify a possible cause. London underground is now closed and the police are asking people not to travel.

Peter Power was one of a small but select panel of advisors that helped create the BBC's *Panorama* programme 'London Under Attack' in May, 2004, and he was one of the commentators thoughout. He is Britain's best known crisis-management specialist and government adviser, managing director of Visor Consultants Limited (based in Piccadilly, London) since 1995, and a senior Officer of the Metropolitan Police 1971-1992. He made his comments within this programme as if describing a real and ongoing situation:

> Our research indicates that something like 350,000 people alone are making their way towards the city of London at this point, and if the access overload system has been triggered and they can't get onto their mobile telephones, this will have profound indications for them, the next of kin, and the very organizations they're hoping to go to work to.

Then, as if an hour later, at 10:10 –

BREAKING NEWS

We're just getting reports that there's been a further explosion in the region around Liverpool Street Station. We will of course bring you more news on that as soon as we can. Meanwhile traffic problems continue in central London as the full effects of the emergency police cordons are being felt.

As with July 7th, the road bomb in central London on a vehicle went off later, a little over one hour after the three tube bombs. Let's also note a judgement which Crispin Black, a former Intelligence Officer, made to the viewers within this program:

What we're seeing on film here today, isn't particularly complex or sophisticated. These are three bombs on the tube, we're not quite sure what kind of bombs but just three and a line in the city we're still not sure what's coming out of that. Now to organise these things isn't particularly difficult, remember Madrid had 10-13 bombs, so this is quite... this is quite a low scenario on the Islamist terrorist capability slide, and even with this I get a sense that... you know... we're being stretched.

Thus quite casually and almost subliminally was the concept of Muslim guilt introduced, as regards this fictional London terror event. The question of who had perpetrated the dreadful horror was not one the programme needed to discuss! There was no need for viewers to exercise their minds on this subject – they only had to listen to the programme's expert, who would tell them who to hate and fear. In this manner were the fundamental imaginations of the London bombings formulated.

Three years earlier, 9/11 appeared to involve four hijacked aircraft which exploded in one way or another, between a quarter to nine and ten o'clock in the morning.

The anti-terror drill 'Exercise Atlantic Blue' involved an (unexplained) collaboration between the Canadian, the US and the UK security services. It played out *terrorist attacks on UK transport networks that coincided with a major international summit.* It took place over five days, 4-8th April 2005, and aimed to ascertain 'how safe London Transport systems were from attack.' It included bombs being placed on buses and also explosives left on the London Underground. Over a thousand UK personnel were involved in planning and delivery of the exercise:

...based in Hendon, [it] involved 2,000 people from the Met [Metropolitan Police Service], City of London and British Transport police services, Ministry of Defence and 14 government departments and agencies, two London Borough councils, the fire and ambulance services and the NHS.[3]

Visor Consultants were involved, on contract to the British government, in the organization and conduct of the event, in coordination with the US Department of Homeland Security. Co-ordinated from Hendon, it was a 'command post' exercise, which meant that it worked on a strategic rather than an operational level and did not involve live action on the ground. The concurrent American exercise, which involved several times more personnel and did involve live action on the ground, was codenamed TopOff 3 (an acronym from 'Top Officials').

Details of this large-scale event are wholly unobtainable. There were brief announcements about it in the House of Commons and the like before the event, and a brief summary of the American operation, and one or two off-the-cuff statements by persons who were evidently involved in it (see Appendix 4). But not a word outlining or reviewing the UK operation after it had happened, except for the brief police-mag account from which we are here quoting. The business of it coinciding with a major international summit makes its timing, a few months prior to G8, hard to ignore. We note its focus upon the Northern line of London's Underground system. Did real alarms go off, were areas cordoned off, did ambulances turn up? The statements were ambiguous:

> It used mocked-up news reporting covering the events as they happened in the exercise. Ch. Supt. Webb said it played an important role in making the scenario real to the players in Hendon, and they were able to make it relate to a real event.

That same centre in Hendon, presumably its police station, was later used by the 'Gold Co-ordinating Group' set up at 10.30am on the morning of July 7th. That was an odd decision, Hendon being quite a way from central London, but it was made because that centre had convenient 'amenities,' owing to its prior use in the Atlantic Blue terror-drill.

A hint as to what might have been involved in Atlantic Blue comes from an Exercise NorthStar a year later, in Singapore, which Peter Power and his company assisted.[4] On 8th January, 2006, the government of Singapore conducted their own "standard exercise and briefing" called Operation Northstar V, a multi-agency civil emergency exercise. It was the largest scale exercise they had conducted to-date and was said to involve over 2,000 personnel. We learn about it through some questions and answers on the Singapore website:

Q. What is the exercise scenario?

A: The scenario for the exercise is similar to that of the London Bombings on 7 July 05, that is, near-simultaneous bomb blasts in the trains at the station platform and in the trains travelling into the tunnel. In addition, a new scenario has been introduced, that is, the release of chemical agents at the platform at one of the stations.

Q. Will bus and train services be disrupted during the exercise and what is the duration of such disruption?

A: While the exercise is confined to only 4 train stations operated by both SBS Transit and SMRT Corporation, however, due to the interconnected nature of the train network, temporarily disruption of train services will affect a total of 13 train stations. The 13 stations will be closed throughout the duration of the exercise that is from 6.25am to 9.30am.

Q. Why is there a need to disrupt train services during the exercise?

A: Simulations in the form of thunderflashes, smoke and fire simulators will be used to create simultaneous bomb attacks by terrorists so as to inject a realistic exercise scenario. Apart from dummy mannequins, 'live' casualties will also be deployed at stations' platforms and in the trains to portray injured commuters and fatalities. Trains will also be stalled within the tunnel and commuters will be evacuated through the tunnel to the nearest train station. To facilitate such an elaborate scenario and the conduct of the large-scale exercise, there is a need to temporarily disrupt train services and close 13 train stations.

Q. Will commuters who are caught in the exercise be trapped for a long period of time in the stalled train or in the train tunnel?

A: Upon the commencement of the exercise, no commuters will be trapped in the stations, trains or tunnels. All commuters who are in the 'exercised' trains and at the stations' platform will immediately be guided and evacuated out of the stations. For commuters who are in the 'exercised' train/s that are stalled in the tunnel, they will also be immediately guided to evacuate from the tunnel to the nearest train station.

As the safety of the commuters is critical to the conduct of the exercise, personnel from the SCDF and staff from SBS Transit and SMRT Corporation will be at hand to guide the commuters in the evacuation process and direct them to the alternative mode of transportation, i.e the *shuttle bus services*. Special attention will also be given to pregnant ladies, the elderly, young children and those who are in need of assistance during the evacuation process.

Q. Are the exercise sites accessible to members of the public?

A: While the commuters in transit are participating in the exercise as evacuees, the Police will be exercising strict cordon enforcement at the four train stations/exercise sites. Hence, members of the public who are outside these exercised train stations will not be allowed access into the stations.

Operation Northstar V must have appeared as alarmingly realistic for ordinary members of the public, what with thunderflashes, smoke and fire simulators used, plus about 500 simulated casualties with injuries who were also deployed to test emergency rescuers at the scene. To further invoke a sense of realism, the date, time and exact details of the exercise were not released until 15 minutes before the exercise, after which announcements on the exercise were carried by local broadcast media. This was a deliberate move to better gauge and test the exercise participants, *including the train commuters who were either in the trains or MRT stations when the exercise started*. If perchance something had happened during that game-simulation, it might have been hard to tell the difference between real injuries and its 'simulated casualties.'[5]

Each year the London Underground is meant to hold a terror-drill rehearsal, and the three that we the public got to hear about were held on a Sunday to minimize disturbance:

Bank,   September 2003

Lambeth, September 2004

Tower Hill,   June 2005

These events are an organic part of our post-9/11 culture, where terror has to be rehearsed and simulated. We notice that the 2005 event seems to have been brought forward by a few months, did something need to be rehearsed a bit earlier? In a BBC News Report following the 2003 Bank station exercise, Linda Smith of the Fire Brigades Union told BBC London of the controlled conditions under which the exercise was carried out: "The *cadets used as victims* had been fully briefed and of course *ordinary members of the public wouldn't have known what was going on*, " she said. "It was done on a Sunday, the area was cordoned off, there were no members of the public allowed even on the footpaths around the area." For the emergency exercise on

London's Underground of 12th June, 2005, the emergency services went into action at Tower Hill Tube station. It was already closed due to major track replacement work between Whitechapel and Earl's Court. Roland Murphy, from London Underground, said good safety procedures were in place "but we can always build and improve upon them." He added: "*All participants are unaware of the 'disaster' until the exercise starts, so they treat it as real as possible.*" A police cordon was erected around the station; nearby roads were closed.[6] We do not hear of any further such yearly tube exercises after 2005. Have any been held, since? It's hard to tell.[7]

Advice on conducting 'live' terror-drills in the UK suggests the inclusion of walking wounded and casualties to 'add to the realism', and was recommended to companies testing their emergency plans by the London Resilience website. Live exercises range from a small-scale test of one component of the response, like evacuation, through to a full-scale test of the whole organisation to an incident. Live exercises provide the best means of confirming the satisfactory operation of emergency communications, and the use of 'casualties' can add to the realism. Live exercises provide the only means for fully testing the crucial arrangements for handling the media.

We suggest that 'the media' may be in need of some training as regards how it is being 'handled' in this context. For example, how they are supposed to tell the difference between real walking-wounded and groups theatrically set up to appear as such; between theatrical flashes set up to look like bombs going off and a 'real' terror attack, between clusters of police cars and ambulances participating in a terror-drill and those really responding to an emergency? Otherwise they are likely to display inappropriate gullibility and credulity during such an event, in a way that may not be in the best interests of the British people. When reporters of the Trinity newspaper group (which manages about sixty titles in the South-East region) received an instruction to end their work and go home for supposed security reasons, as happened in London at noon on July 7th, the big news day of the decade, should they have obeyed that command?

There may be an analogy here with the foreshadowing of the event of 9/11 by war-gaming practices. The event kept being simulated until, finally, it happened. (Appendix 4d) Does the reader want these frighteningly-authentic terror-drills to take place on London streets, in a semi-covert manner, without prior warning? Were you consulted as to whether these exercises should happen, maybe in your neighbourhood? Do you feel safer as a result of knowing that they are going on?

After the 'terror attack' really happens, then the 'experts' use it to argue that their funding should be increased. We would like to suggest that very much to the contrary, such activities need to be eliminated if we ever want to have a world safe to live in. There is a subtle difference between terror-drills and war-games, but they share in common a defined enemy-image. Subtle powers and fiendish intent are attributed to this enemy by the Masters of War.

Let's step back from the scene and use a historical analogy. In 1949, the North Atlantic Treaty signed by various nations morphed into NATO, and this had the consequence that from then on, the collection of nations involved were continually wargaming—that is to say, they kept having war-practices. Such a thing had never previously happened in peacetime. What this meant was that a defined Enemy had to exist, and Russia became that. Initially Russia had asked if it could join NATO but was told it couldn't, because it was the Enemy. So it was obliged to form the Warsaw Pact a few years later. Peace could no longer really exist once NATO had come into being with its premise of regular wargaming exercises. Responsible citizens may accept the notion of an international military alliance, but should reject continual wargaming—whether national or international—with a defined enemy in time of peace. That activity generates an influential military elite, whose primitive imaginations will reverberate unduly through the fabric of civilised life, threatening its continued existence.

From 4th – 10th of March, 2004, NATO's annual get-together (codenamed CMX 04) involved anti-terror drills in European capital cities. We the public were told nothing about it; we don't have the 'clearance.' Preliminary press releases merely indicated that it would involve 'civil-military co-operation,' would practice 'crisis-management procedures,' and would war-game 'a widespread pattern of terrorist attacks,' involving 'weapons of mass destruction.' In the old days, NATO exercises used to involve ships milling about on the sea or troops in Germany, and we more or less knew what they were up to. But now they are in Europe's capital cities, and what were they doing there? Were they in uniform or plain clothes? Why were there no media reports about it? The point here is that *the Madrid train bombs happened in the immediate wake of this event*, i.e. on the 11th. That was, it will here be argued, no coincidence. The connection between wargame and terror event in Madrid needs to be apprehended in the light of the thesis argued in the previous chapter. Thereby we can in some degree understand who the perpetrators of this atrocity were. As is usual with these events, some hapless Muslims have been thrown in jail, however there are certain features about the explosives used and who supplied them which indicate that this may have been more of an inside job – see Chapter 14.

Warner Brothers were busy filming on the London underground between March and June of 2005, for their film 'V for Vendetta.' The authorities closed down Whitehall for three nights to shoot it, and various Government agencies, the MoD, police and Transport for London had to give permission. The plot concerned a London Underground train being designed to explode. It used the disused Aldwych tube station for some of its Underground scenes. One MP, David Davis, objected to the security access which had been granted to the filmmakers. Its photography was co-ordinated by cinematographer Adrian Biddle, who then died unexpectedly of a heart attack on December 7th, 2005. Its scheduled opening on November 5th was delayed, some say, owing to the event of 7/7, being postponed until March of the following year.

Israel, the CIA, and London Underground Security

Bob Kiley. Once elected, London's Mayor Ken Livingstone appointed Bob Kiley as supervisor for London's Transport Network in 2003. He may have done this in the ultimately frustrated hope of being able to issue New-York style bonds for financing London's Transport. From our point of view, it might have helped if more attention had been focussed upon Kiley's past involvement with the CIA, and his *present, continuing* membership of the US Council for Foreign Relations.[8]

The Council for Foreign Relations is America's elite policy-making group. It sorts out the staffing for successive administrations. On October 30, 1993, the *Washington Post* frankly described the CFR as 'the nearest thing we have to a ruling establishment in the United States', saying that its members were 'the people who, for more than half a century, have managed our international affairs and our military-industrial complex.' It noted that 24 top members of the Clinton administration – along with Clinton – were CFR members. The CFR is an American affiliate of the London-based Royal Institute for International Affairs.

The house journal of the CFR, *Foreign Affairs,* published in March/April 1994 an article by Anthony Lake, Carter's National Security Advisor, laying out a plan for 'dual containment' of Iraq and Iran. Because these were both 'outlaw states,' it explained that Iraq was first targeted for destruction, and then Iran would come later. It thus discussed the deeply-laid plans of the Neocons in America. It is relevant to us here that a high degree of demonisation of Muslims is required in the popular mind in order for such a policy to be implemented. (Piper, *The High Priests of War*, p.63)

Early in his career, Kiley had joined the CIA and was soon Manager of Intelligence Operations, and then Executive Assistant to the Director. He served under Richard Helms, the 'Man Who Kept the Secrets' (as his biography was called) and who was appointed CIA director in the wake of the Kennedy assassination. Helms was the only director to have been convicted of lying to Congress over CIA undercover activities, and he served time in prison for that. He was heavily involved in the cover up of the MK ULTRA project,[9] and therefore it may not be going too far to suggest that, as Helm's Executive Assistant, Kiley was also here involved. Mr Kiley may have averred that his CIA past was well behind him when he took on the job that Mayor Ken offered him, however the question of primary loyalty must here arise. "Graduates" of the CIA typically carry out the goals of the agency in their new careers.

In 1962 Richard Helms was appointed chief of the CIA's Clandestine Services, just before the Bay of Pigs invasion. Concerning Helms' skill in covering his tracks, we learn that:

> Years later a very senior CIA official would still speak in amazement of the fact that not a single piece of paper existed in the agency which linked Helms to either the planning or the actual execution of the Bay of Pigs. This senior official was not at all critical of Helms, who had been very much involved in the overall supervision of the operation. The official simply was impressed by Helm's bureaucratic skill and good judgement in keeping his signature off the documents concerning the invasion, even in the planning stage.[10]

Kiley became involved in infiltrating and presumably undermining radical student movements for the CIA in the 1960s.

A long-time alcoholic,[11] Kiley was one of Britain's highest-paid civil servants. He earned £3.9 million while Transport commissioner for London, and his house in Belgravia has recently sold for £2.7 million. He was given a £2 million 'golden handshake' on leaving his job. He would start drinking vodka in the afternoons, he has admitted, a habit which supposedly started decades ago when his wife and child died in a car crash.

Ken Livingstone was supposed to be a socialist. He won the Mayor of London election largely because of popular opposition to Tube privatisation. Against this, his alternative might have been labour movement democracy, especially for someone who professed a socialist ethic. Instead, he appointed Bob Kiley, because he admired the way Kiley had been Chief Executive of New York's Metropolitan Transportation Authority (Metro). As the *Daily Telegraph* reported, "He is credited with a transformation of the New York Subway after winning a political struggle to impose modern management methods that outraged the transport unions." Kiley brought in quite a pushy management team, increased the pace of work, tried to impose a two-tier pay structure, imposed lower pay for new employees, cut bonuses for night and weekend working, cut the number of hourly-paid workers by 10%, slashed revenue subsidies and increased fares, and brought in private companies to do maintenance work. Kiley had introduced 'concession bargaining', meaning that the unions gave up working conditions as part of each year's pay round.[12]

You might want to believe that Bob Kiley did do a fine job. After all, was not Britain awarded the Olympic Games contract partly because its tube system was seen to be running well? We are not concerned to argue such a political matter. But we do aim to show that Kiley's method of breaking up of traditional union structures and his introduction of private companies may well have deep relevance to the unthinkable acts which took place on July 7th, 2005.

A study of the secret powers developed by the CIA found that:

> The most remarkable development in the management of America's relations with other countries during the quarter-century since World War II has been the assumption of more and more control over military and diplomatic operations at home and abroad by men whose activities are secret, whose budget is secret, whose very identities are secret – in short a Secret team whose actions only those implicated in them are in a position to monitor and understand.[13]

Loyal penumbral companies have developed surrounding the Pentagon and CIA, whereby ex-members have become wealthy, and which facilitate plausible denial for covert operations.

Suspect 'Security' from Verint and Comverse

In September of 2004, nine months before the event, a new company, Verint Systems, was awarded a contract concerning London Underground's CCTV network by the now-bankrupt 'Metronet Rail.' Privatisation had been imposed against the wishes of elected Greater London Authority (GLA) by Gordon Brown's Treasury Department. Two-thirds of Verint's business consist of security products used by law enforcement and intelligence services to intercept voice, video and email traffic, while the other third is call-centre monitoring and employee evaluation software. It has approximately 1,000 employees worldwide.

No UK media discussed this matter. Here is how the decision was announced on Israeli news – which seems to have been the only place it was announced:

> An Israeli security firm has been chosen to provide security for London's Underground train network. Verint Systems, a subsidiary of Israel's Comverse Technology announced that Metronet Rail has selected Verint's Networked Video Solution to enhance security of the London Underground, according to an Israel21 report. After extensive testing of Verint's networked video system, including pilot installation on selected rail lines, Metronet Rail selected it to be

installed on the entire Underground. The system will enable security personnel to monitor passenger platforms and certain remote portions of the track. Verint president and CEO Dan Bodner told Israel21: "We have significant experience working with transportation authorities and are committed to delivering innovative networked video security solutions for the transportation industry." Metronet Rail, under a 30 year contract with the UK government, is responsible for maintaining parts of the London Underground's infrastructure. This includes ensuring security in trains, stations, tunnels and bridges.[14]

There was just this one press release concerning the London Undergound's involvement with this post-9/11 security-analysis company. I found that Transport for London would not comment on this matter, and MetroNet were at first reluctant to make any comment on the grounds that they could not discuss 'security,' but the latter did finally confirm that they were employing Verint Systems for their CCTV 'infrastructure'. Let's go back a few years, to some revelations made in a remarkable US news program in the wake of the cataclysmic events of 9/11. A four-part Fox News program, on December 2001, produced by Carl Cameron, argued that Israel had been in some degree involved in perpetrating the event of 9/11. He there stated that:

Two Israeli companies, Amdocs and Comverse InfoSys manage just about every aspect of the US telephone system,

'Comverse InfoSys' became Verint Systems in 2002 (see Appendix 2), and we therefore take note of Cameron's statement that:

Comverse Infosys provides the wiretapping equipment and software for US law enforcement agencies.

All activities of Verint Systems have been directed by Comverse Technology which owns 57% control of its stock. Comverse is involved in wiretapping, phone billing and mobile phone voicemail software developers. To quote from John-Paul Leonard's afterword in Ahmed's book,

All wiretapping in the US and virtually all telephone billing has been handled for years by two Israeli companies, Comverse and Amdocs – as approved by a somewhat reluctant Congress! Thus, "FOX News has learned that some American terrorist investigators fear certain suspects in the Sept. 11 attacks may have managed to stay ahead of them, by knowing who and when investigators are calling on the telephone."[15]

Cameron's program explained how:

Every time you make a call, it passes through the nation's elaborate network of switchers and routers run by phone companies. Custom computers and software, made by companies like Comverse, are tied into that network to intercept, record and store the wiretapped calls, and at the same time transmit them to investigators...

Comverse insists that the equipment it installs is secure. But the complaint about this system is that the wiretap computer programs made by Comverse have, in effect, a back door through which wiretaps themselves can be intercepted by unauthorized parties. Adding to the suspicions is the fact that in Israel, Comverse works closely with the Israeli government, and under special programs, gets reimbursed for up to 50% of its research and development costs by the Israeli Ministry of Industry and Trade. But investigators within the DEA, INS and FBI have all told Fox News that to pursue or even suggest Israeli spying through Comverse is considered career suicide.[16]

So the White House became nervous that its ultra-secure phone lines had a 'back door' to Israel, because that was how Comverse did things! It is rather remarkable that such a programme could be aired, and it soon came under fierce attack from America's Anti-Defamation League – which need not, however, detain us.

'Nextiva Transit' is Verint's networked hi-tech CCTV system now installed on London Underground platforms and remote portions of track. The system is programmed to automatically 'watch for people loitering on transit platforms or people wearing heavy coats on hot summer days'. The latter comment found on its website may remind one of the strange circumstances surrounding the shooting in cold blood of Jean Charles de Menezes at Stockwell Underground, apparently by the Metropolitan Police on 22nd July 2005. The allegation was made that he was wearing a coat that was bulging out unduly on a warm summer's say, which turned out not to be true at all …

Verint CEO Daniel Bodner is a former senior Israeli army officer who gets $4m annual benefits including salary. Verint Systems are currently being investigated by the Office of Fair Trading and the Securities and Exchange Commission over a proposed merger with Witness Systems Inc. for a possible phone monitoring technology monopoly. The parent company Comverse is presently at the centre of an $8bn fraud inquiry in New York. Comverse shares six directors with a wider network of linked companies also under investigation. It has been delisted from NASDAQ and suspended from stock trading on 1st February, 2007, because of financial mismanagement and non-filing of essential accounting information, along with Verint Systems who are now also NASDAQ-delisted.

Roughly three million people a day use the London Underground network. Since privatisation, contracts are shrouded in double walls of secrecy to protect both 'national security' and 'commercial confidentiality'. If secrecy were needed, it should come with a requirement of absolute 100% trust and clear loyalty to the people of London who use the tube network. Instead what we find is a company with 24-hour access to the entire tube network run by a senior ex-Israeli army officer, whose former employers are engaged in a largely covert war against Arabs for land. His present employers are wanted on 40-plus criminal counts, implicated in multi-million dollar fraud and conspiracy, and facing several long jail sentences.[17]

We here call for contracts with Verint Systems to be suspended by Metronet Rail, the GLA and the Government—for the safety of all Londoners—pending a transparent investigation into Verint and its parent company Comverse. Control of the London Underground CCTV network needs to be wrested from those with close ties to the Israeli armed forces, at least until the Middle East conflict is over. The European base of Verint Systems is located in Weybridge, Surrey.

There are close links between Verint and Comverse, not least because both Verint's Chair Kobi Alexander and its present Chief Executive Daniel Bodner are ex-Israeli Army officers. Robert Kaplan, a veteran of the Israeli Defence Force, argued in his recent *Warrior Politics* that a pagan ethic of war and cruelty was necessary to face the great crises of this age.

Rudolph Giuliani Comes to London

The former Mayor of New York Rudolph Giuliani is renowned for his decisive actions on the day of 9/11, by way of preventing journalists from gaining access to or photographing Ground Zero. The day before, on July 6th, he appeared up in Yorkshire, where he gave a rousing pro-War on Terror speech to a meeting of UK councillors at the Local Government Association conference in Harrogate. He spoke on the battle against terror, admiring Tony Blair, while deploring the way the world had allowed terrorists to "get out of control," through failing to take the problem seriously enough. Of Bush and Blair he said, "I have great respect for their setting a very determined policy as regard [sic] to terrorism, sticking with it when it became unpopular and I credit the fact we have been able to reduce terrorism to what they have done." After giving this speech he traveled down to London to be there at Liverpool Street next morning, one of the bomb-site locations.[18]

What was Rudolph Giuliani doing in London that morning, or indeed in the UK? No one has ever answered that. Maybe he was there because his company was providing security for the Great Eastern Hotel during July 7th, where the Tel Aviv Stock Exchange conference was happening. The profits of TASE had been soaring, with foreign investments going from $480 million in 2004 to $1.4 billion in the first five months of 2005, so it required decent security. Giuliani Security and Safety was a firm he had set up after retiring as New York's Mayor, and this would have been attractive for several reasons. Rudi is utterly pro-Israel in his politics, having been Israel's *most-favoured presidential candidate* for the 2008 Presidential elections.[19] He and Benjamin Netanyahu were old pals, as Rudi had welcomed the latter to New York during his tenure as mayor. Netanyahu was the keynote speaker for this TASE conference, the fourth held in London, so having Giuliani around would have been a pleasant bonus for him. That could also have been why Giuliani gave his tough, pro-War on Terror speech the day before to the councillors in Harrogate: he was in a mood to do that, being over here in his capacity of head of Giuliani Security. He could also have been there by way of wishing to attract investors, as the head of Giuliani Capital Advisors.

Euphoria

The world's biggest-ever free concert, 'Live 8', took place on the 20-year anniversary of Bob Geldorf's original 'Live Aid' concert for Africa. It was played simultaneously in South Africa and all of the G8 nations, being run in support of the 'Make Poverty History' campaign to Drop the Debt of Africa. It began on 2nd of July and ended on the 6th, the same day on which Londoners received the good news that their capital city was to be awarded the Olympic Games of 2012 instead of Paris, after Paris was halfway through the construction; and also, the same day on which the G8 summit of world leaders opened up North at Gleneagles.

One sensed in the streets of London an abnormal sense of Hope, in consequence of these tumultuous events. The exhilaration of Live 8 in Hyde Park still lingered and, only the day before on Wednesday 6th, thousands had sung and danced across Trafalgar Square, deliriously celebrating the news that London was to host the 2012 Olympics. It was an emotionally-draining roller-coaster, as Londoners were lifted up into euphoria by a combination of global events which were strangely synchronizing before disaster struck.

Something happened which turned everything around, back to the dreary grey Business as Usual; whereby G8 more resembled the annual general meeting of the multi-national mafia, continuing to fleece Africa.[20] As John Pilger noted, "The vaunted $50 billion of alleged debt cancellation is a complete fiction. In order for any of the eighteen theoretically eligible African countries to get their debt cancelled, they have to comply with so many conditions, that it will be a miracle if a single country actually benefits.' In return for alleged cancellation of debt, African countries would virtually have to hand over their governments to the West. The 'debt cancellation' is to be compared to the amount extracted from Africa by the multi-nationals: according to the IMF, at current prices, the value of the goods and services Africa produces in a year is $773 billion. The giant multinationals investing in Africa – Halliburton, Exxon Mobil, Coca-Cola, General Motors, Starbucks, Raytheon, Microsoft, Boeing, Cargill, Citigroup, Shell, etc – saw trouble looming, as the world looked towards the forthcoming G8 for steps of debt-relief in Africa.

To 'benefit' from the 'debt cancellation' offered, African nations would have to open their markets completely to Western capital; to guarantee that the 'free market' operates without let or hindrance; to reduce their governments to little more than branch offices for the multi-nationals in the name of fighting corruption; and to agree to become forward bases for US military penetration of Africa in the 'war on terror'. The bottom line has always been the raw materials that Africa possesses in abundance, especially oil, plus key minerals like manganese, cobalt, fluorspar, germanium, diamonds and gold. According to the World Bank, Africa offers "the highest returns on foreign direct investment of any region in the world".[21]

Ironically, the oppression of Africa by the West was mirrored in the marginalizing of African singers and bands: parked where Geldoff decreed, in an environmental theme park in Cornwall, they played in front of an audience of less than 50 people.[22]

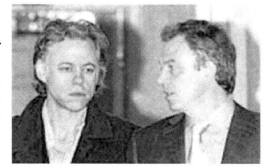

The Gentle Giant

Young Hasib Hussain had a life to look forward to – his successful exam results dropped though his letter-box only a day after the (presumed) termination of his life.

According to the *Yorkshire Evening Post*,

> he achieved GCSEs in English language, English literature, maths, science, Urdu, design technology and a GNVQ in business studies... Hussain's brother Imran,

25, said, "There was absolutely no sign of him becoming devoutly religious. He wore jeans and trainers."

Hasib was a soft-hearted 18-year-old with everything to live for.His father's view is here important. In letters to the author (see Appendix 5), Hasib's father Mohammed related:

> I am very grateful for your effort to find the real truth. I do not believe that my son is responsible for this.

> Hasib was waiting to hear about his university admission. He wanted to do 3 years business advance course. He said he had applied through his college and any university will take him because his marks and achievement will be very high. He was very keen and interested to go to University. As I know he has achieved his marks and level. So any University in the U.K. will welcome him.

> He was taking driving lessons from me just to learn basic things of driving.

> Yes he liked the buildings of London e.g. London Eye. He used to talk to his sisters about this! Or with my grandchildren. He only told us that he is going to London with his friends.

Mahmoud Hussain told the *Daily Mirror,*

> The boy I see on the TV news, the boy I see in the papers, is not the child I knew. He was the perfect son.... He was due to start university in September.. He had also agreed to an arranged marriage with a young woman from Pakistan... Hasib never did anything wrong. He was never a bit of bother to us... If a fly came into the house, he would catch it and take it outside. If there was a caterpillar in the garden, he would make sure it was safe... I keep thinking that this must be some kind of mistake. That it must have been someone else who did this. (2/8/05, 'My Hasib Must Have Been Brainwashed')

The education reporter of the *Yorkshire Evening Post* found some interesting material on Hasib Hussain:

> His tutors describe him as a "slow, gentle giant" who was "perfectly normal" ... "He was a perfectly normal student," said Colin Bell, headteacher of South Leeds High... In some ways that's been the difficult part for the school to deal with... There has been a lot of misinformation spread about this young man... he did not spread leaflets of hate mail around the school. It's just not true... We are as staggered as anyone else that this has happened and there was absolutely no indication during his time here that it would. There has been an element of disbelief and disappointment."

> (20/7/05: "'Slow gentle giant' who blew up the No. 30 bus and killed 13 others')

A *Guardian* reporter rather confirmed this, that Hasib's friends saw no sign of any radicalism, even a few days before the bombings:

> Hasib Hussain lay sprawled upon the short grass of Cross Flatt's Park, the ribbon of green that borders the red-bricked houses of Beeston. It was four days before the London bombings... Hussain betrayed none of the radicalism that would shortly immortalise the teenager... the patter never strayed from the norm: who was going out with whom, who was driving what, who'd found a job.

(17/7/05: Three cities, four killers)

Hasib was expressing confidence in his future, predicting a week before he died that he would achieve the results he needed for his place at Leeds Metropolitan University to do a Business Studies course. He may have been aspiring towards such a course partly because his role-model Mohammed 'Sid' Khan had also taken it. The day after the bombings, this was confirmed to his family – he had scored distinctions in four out of the five NVQ exams.

One friend remarked of him: "Hasib was someone I looked up to. He was a gentle giant." There were some remarkable virtues, commendable qualities, to these young men, cut down in their prime. Khan especially was renowned for his achievements in the local community. He was the local action-hero, who taught others by his example the way of nonviolent conflict-resolution. One thing they shared in common appears to have been that none of them had a wish to harm others.

A week earlier, Tanweer and Sid Khan had enjoyed a day-outing in London. They had met up with Lindsay at Luton, the latter having driven over from Aylesbury, and travelled by Thameslink to King's Cross. Our understanding is that Hasib may not have been acquainted with Lindsay, who lived in Aylesbury (fellow investigator James Stewart had a phone conversation with Hasib's brother Imram, see Appendix 5, and this was one of the facts which emerged). At 18 years of age, Hasib was quite a bit younger than the others.[23]

Two days before ....

On Tuesday, 5th July, 2005, 'controlled explosions' were carried out in the centre of Sheffield by the police, near to the city magistrate's court. The city centre came to a standstill during rush hour traffic, after a suspect bag was found outside an 'official building'. The whole area was cordoned off, and the bag was found to be empty.[24]

On that same day, the centre of Nottingham was evacuated due to a child leaving a toy in an office. Brave anti-terror police police performed a 'controlled explosion' after detecting this package, and alerted the whole town to a 'bomb scare.' Streets around the Mansfield Building Society were sealed off at 4 pm on Tuesday after a package was found in its reception area. The cordon around the town centre was lifted, after the 'controlled explosion'.[25] Nothing further was found.

On that same day, in the little Scottish village of Auchterarder, only a mile from Gleneagles in Scotland, a bomb scare was announced and the High Street was cordoned off for two hours. This served to focus the fear, sending the message to the world-leaders that the Sheffield and Nottingham bomb scares were somehow relevant to them. Nothing was found in that little village, where journalists, protestors and tourists had gathered, but the crowds of black-and-yellow anti-terror police swarming from morning to midday were enough to convey the message. A 'suspicious package' was finally found to be harmless.[26]

That triune concordance is no coincidence, but suggests an intention on the part of those responsible. Those responsible were the police. In three different locations in England and Scotland, bomb-scares were set off over nothing on the same day. On that day, the world was waiting to hear whether Paris or London would receive the 2012 Olympic

Games, so no such events could happen near London. Two days earlier in Cardiff, a high-street retail store had received a bomb-threat. Staff spotted a suspicious package, after which large areas around the city were evacuated and cordoned off. Army units put up blockades and investigated the package, and after several hours the scare turned out to be a hoax.[27] Thus in the days before July 7th, phantom terror moved across Britain, seeming to have a focus around the Gleneagles summit.

We'll see later how the whole of central Birmingham was evacuated a few days after July 7th, on the late evening of the 10th and night of the 11th, likewise due to nothing at all, as was a Sheffield music festival on the 11th and then the centre of Leeds on the 12th (see Chapter 8, & Appendix 7). Phantom terror events serve to amplify and promote fear, and require a genuine terror event at some point to validate them.

The Decision of July 6th: Where to House the Dead

A special room was set up to receive the dead, the contract for which was received on July 6th: July 6th, 2005, *the day before*. It was set up on a *military* site, in the grounds of the Honourable Artillery Company, near Moorgate in East-central London, quite near to Aldgate where one of the bombs went off:

> Based in Northamptonshire in the UK, the company [De Boer] had already completed several contracts for the Metropolitan Police ...The De Boer team spent months visiting permanent mortuaries and attending meetings with London Resilience to suggest a suitable structure and interior design... Six months later on July 6, 2005, a document arrived at De Boer's UK headquarters finalising what had been agreed for a future crisis response. Within 24 hours the plan was being realised .and implemented with the creation of a temporary mortuary in the grounds of the Honourable Artillery Company near Moorgate Underground Station in central London.'[28]

That's where the bodies were stored. In recognition of their fine work, the De Boer project manager was invited later on to meet Tony Blair at Downing Street. They surely did a fine job – at such short notice. They also helped by setting up structures at each of the four blast sites: 'Outside of the mortuary De Boer also provided structures and furniture at each of the Underground Stations affected, and refrigeration facilities at the site of the bus bombing.' This military participation starting *the day before the event* should not be ignored.

It was named the Resilience Mortuary, in the grounds of the Honourable Artillery Company. The concept of 'resilience' is part of the 21st-century vocabulary of 'drilling' for terror, whereby a company rehearses for the feared event. Peter Power's 'Visor Consultants' help companies to acquire 'resilience' by collectively rehearsing terror-attacks. It is the unfortunate message of this book that such drills are liable to have a more creative role in bringing about the terror event, than the public suppose.

A comparison with the events of 9/11 often helps in understanding the 7/7 catastrophe. Thus, one might be here reminded of the big FEMA vans (Federal Emergency Management Agency) that arrived to begin clearing up the damage in New York at Ground Zero on 9/11: they were proud of how quickly they arrived, in fact they turned up on Monday evening, the day before.

References

[1] http://news.bbc.co.uk/1/hi/programmes/panorama/3686201.stm BBC Panorama 5th May 2004 'London Under Attack' For the BBC transcript, http://news.bbc.co.uk/nol/shared/spl/hi/programmes/panorama/transcripts/londonunderattack.txt.

[2] These people were involved in making the Panorama program:
Anne Gallop, Deputy Chair London Fire & Emergency Planning Authority, Representative on London Fire & Civil Defence Authority 1997-2000.
David Gilbertson, Former Commander Metropolitan Police 1995-2001.
Crispin Black, Intelligence Assessment Staff 1999–2002, Major British Army 1996-1999.
Michael Portillo, Former Secretary of State for Defence, 1995-1997, Shadow Chancellor of the Exchequer 2000-2001.
Peter Power, Crisis management specialist & government adviser, Visor Consultants 1995-present, Director BET Group Security 1992-1994, Senior Officer Metropolitan Police 1971-1992. Lance Price, Former Deputy Director of Communications 10 Downing Street. Special Advisor to Prime Minister 1998-2000 BBC.

[3] www.met.police.uk/job/job951/live_files/2.htm The Job Vol. 38 April 15 2005 'Atlantic Blue tests International Readiness'.

[4] Visor's website states: 'We have specialist consultants who are regularly engaged on projects, ranging from running workshops in Singapore to helping...' It's hard to see what that Singapore workshop could have been for other than the Northstar V anti-terror drill.

[5] Source: Singapore Logon, 11.1.06, 'Singapore holds large-scale anti-terror drill by Minister for Home Affairs Wong Kan Seng', www.singaporelogon.com/index.php?option=com_content&task=view&id=102&Itemid=28.

[6] 'Live Emergency Exercise at Tower Hill,' 10.6.05, Transport for London http://www.tfl.gov.uk/corporate/media/newscentre/4027.aspx. See Appendix 4.

[7] A Transport for London (TfL) spokesman told me that an exercise had been held sometime during 2006 or 2007 in an undisclosed central London station, which was not however closed for the day—as it was during these 2003-5 drills—and no press releases were put out. One is startled by such secrecy.

[8] In 2000, Transport for London was established as part of the Greater London Authority by the Greater London Authority Act 1999, taking over functions from its predecessor London Regional Transport. But not until 2003 did it take over responsibility for the London Underground, after the controversial Public-Private Partnership (PPP) contract for maintenance had been agreed. This transferred the Underground – the track, signalling, bridges, tunnels, lifts, escalators, stations and trains – to three private companies, two of which were Tubelines and MetroNet. Prior to this, the London Underground had been state owned & controlled. Kiley was First Commissioner of TfL from 2001 to 2006.

[9] Wikipedia, Richard Helms, Career in Intelligence http://en.wikipedia.org/wiki/Richard_Helms.

[10] Marchetti and Marks, *The CIA and the Cult of Intelligence,* 1974, p.34.

[11] Daily Mail 28.3.07, '£3k-a-day Tube chief admits: I'm an alcoholic'.

[12] 'Tunnel Vision,' www.workersliberty.org/node/8049.

[13] Colonel Fletcher Prouty, *The Secret Team: The CIA and Its Allies in Control of the United States and the World,* 1973, p.381; available here: www.ratical.org/ ratville/JFK/ST/.

[14] Arutz Sheva, Israeli National News.com: 'Israeli Security to Protect London's Underground' 9th September 2004. www.israelnationalnews.com/news.php3?id=69208. Legally, Verint appears to be a US company, see Appendix 2.

[15] Ahmed and Leonard, *The War on Freedom* 2002, p.353.

[16] 14.12.01, Fox News Series on Israeli Spying on US Telecommunications: http://cryptome.org/fox-il-spy.htm (no longer available on Fox News). Quoted in *9/11: The Ultimate Truth*, L.K. Jadczyk 2006, p.111.

[17] It's a bit hard to follow these shadowy connections and still harder to tell what might be relevant. But, before a case is solved, it is quite normal for a detective to keep an eye open for all sorts of possible connections; see Appendix 2 for more.

[18] *Yorkshire Post*, 'Giuliani brings New York message to Region', July 7th. http://www.yorkshirepost.co.uk/news/Giuliani-brings-New-York-message.1077572.jp.

[19] www.haaretz.com/hasen/pages/rosnerPage.jhtml.

[20] John Pilger, 'From Iraq to the G8: The Polite Crushing Of Dissent And Truth', Global Outlook July 7, 2005 www.globalresearch.ca/index.php?context=va&aid=659.

[21] William Bowles, '"Jive 8" and Poverty in Africa: Bob Geldof does Damage Control for War Criminal', Global Research July 7th, 2005, www.globalresearch.ca/index.php?context=va&aid=656.

[22] Pilger, The Ghost at Gleneagles, 11.7.05, www.newstatesman.com/200507110004.

[23] I'm here grateful to the J7 team for use of material.

[24] BBC News, 'Bomb scare leads to city gridlock' http://news.bbc.co.uk/1/hi/england/south_yorkshire/4654289.stm. Here is another account of what happened that day in Sheffield: 'I live in the city, and witnessed chaotic traffic congestion. Sheffield is heavily congested at the best of times but this was something else. The city was gridlocked for two hours and no traffic was moving anywhere in the city centre. I noticed a higher than usual police presence. Other reports that I have gleaned from witnesses tell of police being present at several of the city's terminals tramway system. Did you get that? Sheffield was crawling with police acting on information regarding a bomb scare just 48 hours before the London bombings …The police clearly knew what they were looking for.' http://planetquo.com/7-7-The-London-Terror-Attack-Death-Of-A-Nation

[25] BBC News, 'Town bomb scare "genuine mistake"' http://news.bbc.co.uk/1/hi/england/nottinghamshire/6273968.stm, http://news.bbc.co.uk/2/hi/uk_news/england/nottinghamshire/6273968.stm).

[26] Ahmed, p.134. He also describes the evacuation of central Cardiff on 3rd July due to a hoax bomb-scare. 'Bomb scare ahead of G8 Summit', *Evening Telegraph*, 5.7.05.

[27] Ahmed, Ibid.

[28] London's response to 7/7 by David Donegan, Crisis Response Journal (no longer online, article archived on J7 site)

4. July 7th, London

Events were reported that fateful morning, but more vivid than these in the reader's memory are the *interpretations* of them given days later. These were designed to make sense of the cataclysm, and focussed around the twin notions of 'bombs' and 'terrorists.' Here we endeavour as far as possible not to impose interpretations upon the course of events, and to seek out the first reports before the official interpretations were imposed upon them. Thereby we may seek to access the *strangeness* of what may have happened. Early stories of power-surges morph into bomb stories, *after* the number 30 bus had blown up an hour later in Tavistock Square. That visible explosion catalysed perception, and then the notion that bombs had gone off in the underground started to be reported. It became the visible template to *explain* the carnage on the Underground. We here aspire to stay as closely as possible with what was reported.

For example, the trains caught by the four youths, from Luton Thameslink travelling south to King's Cross, appeared as one of the most concrete aspects of the official story, complete with reports of persons in the train in question as seeing this group, and CCTV footage with times to the second, allegedly catching the group at both ends of this journey. It then turned out that these train times simply were not feasible that day: to discuss this properly, we have shifted the whole train journey story into another section. The disintegration of that Government-Metropolitan police train-journey story impacts upon *all* of the CCTV footage which they allege to have for that morning, but cannot show anyone, and upon which they base their storyline. Science is about public knowledge; it concerns information which can be shared. It is *not* about secret film which some secret cabal claims to have, on which they base their narrative.

Inevitably, judgement and selection is involved in what to report as having happened. For example, the earthly remains of Mohammad 'Sid' Khan were supposedly scraped off the walls etc. of Aldgate East tube station, Edgware Road tube station, *and* Tavistock Square, presumably around the bus explosion. These were given to his widow in several packages (politely, she asked for an inquest). Conjecture is feasible where we will never have anything else, and maybe this story indicates some degree of disagreement between the persons who were concocting 'the plot.' Maybe at some early stage there was no consensus as to which explosive site had Khan designated as operating the bomb. Even the Official Narrative (anonymous) which HMSO started selling a year after the event maintained this absurd story, of identifiable remains of one individual being found in three different bomb-locations. As rationalists who seek to base our interpetations upon the evidence available, avoiding preconception and dogma, we see these stories more as indicating Khan's *absence* from any of the July 7th bombsites. From the account that will now unfold, the startled reader may fail to note any evidence showing that the four accused were together in London on that morning – or at least, any evidence that would stand up in a court of law for two minutes. Not only that, but even the concept of 'bombs' may come to appear as less than totally self-evident. What did happen, causing the terrible carnage?

The *London Bombings Dossier* is a well-researched study and analysis of the events of 7th July, 2005, compiled by David Minahan. It is the sort of compilation of evidence that would be an essential preliminary, if any serious enquiry into what really happened were to be attempted. As to his motivation and qualifications for making such a systematic compilation, Minahan explains:

> I was by occupation a claims investigator for an insurance company and later a leading firm of solicitors, so I have some experience of "forensic" matters. I was also some years ago the National President of a major Trade Union (MSF now merged with the AEEU to form Amicus). I am convinced that there has been a massive cover up and campaign of disinformation about this matter.[1]

There is a powerful contrast between Minahan's dossier and the anonymous 'Official Narrative' published a year later, which does the exact opposite: it cites no evidence at all, continually alludes to CCTV images which no one has seen, and gives the official Metropolitan Police line as if everyone were obliged to accept it.

Concerning the difficulty in describing What Really Happened, we cite from Minahan's conclusion—leaving in his impressive references, which allude to different folders in his dossier:

> The writer himself has come to the startling conclusion that there were in all probability eight explosions in the Capital on the 7th July in addition to the four publicly acknowledged; and that there is a possibility this figure may be as high as seventeen. The lower estimate would be correct if the blasts referred to in the following folders were one and the same, i.e. a single explosion at each group of sites (index numbers 1 & 2) (3, 4, 5 & 6) (7 & 8) (10 & 11) (22 & 25), and if there was a device on a train between Kings Cross and Euston Square; one additional bus bomb; and a single explosion at King's Cross Station!
>
> If, however, there were individual explosions at all the locations specified in the groups above, plus one at Old Street and a total of three bus explosions (as was originally reported) then the higher figure emerges. Conceivably the total could be even greater as there are some indications that there may have been an explosion on a Northern line train coming into Kings Cross; and in an unspecified building in the Euston area. There are also a number of 'second hand' accounts of a shooting at Canary Wharf. There is little doubt that (as outlined in the 'advance warnings' folders 12 & 13) the authorities knew in advance that something was going on. It is also beyond dispute that strenuous efforts were made to limit media reporting (28 & 29) not least in the case of the two Benton sisters from Kentucky (exhibit MR18).

While respecting Minahan's detailed research, we are not going to verify these complicated details. However, the reader should gain the general impression that the damage to the underground trains was a lot more spread out than can be accommodated by a 'four suicide bombers' story. Minahan's interpretation, if accepted, suggests that the perpetrators of the event had in some degree a different intention from that given by those weaving the story of the four suicide bombers; or, that redundant raw material was produced, the better to fit it to the scenario that would finally be chosen.

Timeline

06.26 The Northern line was "suspended between Morden and Stockwell from 06:29 due to a defective train at Balham," according to Transport for London.

07.10 A Northern Line train stops in tunnel for 15 mins between Tooting Bec and Balham. Passengers finally have to disembark at Balham (exiting via driver's carriage at front of train) and see many firemen around, scrutinising the bottom of another train already at the station.[2]

07.30 Tony Blair and George Bush go for a stroll in the gardens of the Gleneagles hotel that sunny morning, admiring the giant rhododendrons. US policy seemed to be shifting on the great, pressing issues of getting rid of trade subsidies to American firms, which would help Africa stand on its own feet, and also over taking climate change seriously.

07.57 The Piccadilly Line was "suspended between King's Cross St Pancras and Arnos Grove from 07:57 to 08:28 due to a defective train at Caledonian Road." Reports of a fire at the station exit, and fire engines were reported outside Caledonian Road station.

08.07 Bakerloo Line was "suspended between Paddington and Elephant and Castle in both directions from 08:07 due to a defective train in Piccadilly Circus."

08.25 A fire engine parks outside Caledonian Road station.

08.30 A notice at Arnos Grove Underground states: "Due to fire, Piccadilly Line suspended between Arnos Grove and King's Cross".

The yearly TASE Tel Aviv Stock Exchange conference opens in the Great Eastern Hotel at Liverpool Street.

08.35 The Eastbound Circle Line train No. 204 leaves King's Cross.

08.42 The Westbound Circle Line train No. 216 leaves King's Cross.

08.43 Mossad office in London was alerted to a pending terror strike six minutes before the first explosion.[3] Israeli Finance Minister Benjamin Netanyahu (who had been calling for war with Iran) happened to be staying in a Russell Square hotel, close to one of the bomb blasts, for the Deutsche Bank and Tel Aviv Stock Exchange conference. Around 08.43am he was warned not to go out due to a possible terrorist attack. He (and the Israeli Embassy) originally said that it was Scotland Yard who called in the warning, but the Yard later denied this. London's Mossad office has not clarified from whom they received this warning.[4]

08.48 The Westbound piccadilly Line train No. 311 leaves King's Cross.

08.49 The first report of a major incident at Liverpool Street station was received by the London ambulance service at 08.49, within a minute of the blast. [BMJ Diary of Major Incident][5]

08.50 Explosions are occurring on three London Underground trains: between Aldgate and Liverpool Street stations on the Circle Line, between Russell Square and King's Cross stations on the piccadilly Line, and at Edgware Road station on the Circle Line.

Originally police thought only the Aldgate/Liverpool Street train was hit at about this time. The Russell Square/King's Cross blast was first reported at 8:56, and the Edgware Road blast at 9:17; only two days later was it established that the three were more or less synchronous. It is possible that two piccadilly line trains exploded, with

streaming out from King's Cross and Russell Square. The cause of
at resembled a power-surge event. Let's quote Bruce Lait, survivor
speaking from his hospital bed: 'We'd been on there for a minute at
ing happened. It was like a huge electricity surge which knocked
eardrums. I can still hear that sound now'. Later, a policeman said
le, that's where the bomb was' and Lait recalled, 'The metal was
if the bomb was underneath the train' (reported in *Cambridge*
does sound like a bomb planted underneath the train, however all
s of the trains also appear as having been blown out and frazzled.

iuliani, who was mayor of New York City at the time of the 9/11
t the Great Eastern Hotel, close to Liverpool Street station, when
his was the same hotel where the TASE economic conference had
inance Minister Benjamin Netanyahu as keynote speaker.[6] Earlier,
ister back in 1996, Netanyahu had been officially welcomed to
uliani. After quitting as Mayor of New York, Giuliani had set up
curity and Safety,' which specialized in "mock terror drills" and
ness," rather like Peter Power's Visor Consultants. The two
usiness contacts in these areas.[7] After being told of the blasts,
his hotel to finish his breakfast.

a Metropolitan Line explosion between Liverpool Street and
reports of station power failures.

Edgware Road, report that train has hit the tunnel wall and significant
casualties. Call to London Fire Brigade and London Ambulance to attend three sites.

At Marble Arch, a No. 30 bus turned around and started its return route. It arrived at
Euston bus station at 09:35, where crowds of people had been evacuated from the tube
and were boarding buses. This bus then followed a diversion from its normal route,
reportedly because of road closures in the King's Cross area resulting from the earlier
tube bombings; travelling South, it visited Tavistock Square.

09.15 A Code Amber alert is issued by Network Control Centre, causing all
Underground trains to head for their nearest station, and the mass evacuation begins.

09.17 Report of explosion on train coming into Edgware Road underground station
100 yards in the tunnel. The explosion supposedly blew through a wall onto another
train on an adjoining platform.

09.18 The first ambulance call-out to Russell Square station was received.

09.24 British Transport Police say the incident was possibly caused by a collision
between two trains, a power cut or a power cable exploding. Police report 'walking
wounded.'[8] Camden Police arrive at Russell Square to find the injured lying on the
platform.[9]

09.30 COBRA, the Government's national crisis-management facility (Cabinet
Office Briefing Rooms), is activated in response to the explosions.[10]

09.35 The driver of the No. 30 bus at Euston, George Psaradakis was told to follow
'a safe alternative route.'

09.40 British Transport Police say power-surge incidents have occurred on the
Underground at Aldgate, Edgware Road, King's Cross, Old Street and Russell Square
stations.

09.40 (approx) The TASE conference at the Great Eastern Hotel terminates, on police instruction, before its keynote speaker Netanyahu had arrived.[11]

09.44 The diverted 30 bus stops after turning off Euston Road, to let some passengers dismount.

09.45 London Underground issues a Code Red alert, stopping all the trains. The diverted 30 bus stops a second time outside Tavistock House/BMA and the driver has a conversation with a traffic warden, as supposedly he needs to ask his way.

09.47 There is an explosion on the diverted 30 bus in Tavistock Square, in front of the headquarters of two Israeli-based security firms, Fortress GB and ICTS UK Ltd, one of which had Underground-line security contracts.[12] The British Transport Police had three officers driving behind the bus when the explosion occurred, and these were the first officers on the scene.[13]

09.50 (approx) A message is relayed to Tony Blair, towards the end of his meeting with Hu Jintao, the Chinese president, reporting that 'Explosions had been reported on the Underground and fatalities were feared.'[14]

09.49 Metronet announces the whole Tube network is being shut down.

10.00 COBRA meeting begins; in attendance are Dame Eliza Manningham-Buller, the head of MI5; John Scarlett, the head of MI6; and Sir Ian Blair, the Metropolitan Police Commissioner.

10.00 The number 30 bus driver George Psaradakis later avers that he helped wounded people after the blast, and then set off walking West for seven miles in fifty minutes (a fast walker?) and *"and sought help only once he reached the Central Middlesex Hospital in Acton, West London, at about 10.50am."*[15]

10.09 Witness Christina Lawrence, who had been on a train leaving King's Cross, tells BBC: "There was a loud bang in the tunnel and the train just stopped and all of a sudden it was filled with black, gassy smoke and we couldn't breathe."

10.15 After 28 minutes, Camden police arrived at Tavistock Square, and PC Walker described how he became suspicious of a 'microwave box on the lower deck of the exploded 30 bus.'[16]

10.20 Metropolitan police issue the following press release: "At approx 08:50 on 7.7.05 we were called to Aldgate LT station to assist the City of London police and British Transport Police regarding an incident on the underground system. All of the emergency services are on scene. This has been declared as a major incident. Too early to state what has happened at this stage. There have been further reports from multiple locations in London of explosions. It is too early to say what has caused these explosions. Police are responding to reports from: Edgware Rd, King's Cross, Liverpool St, Russell Sq, Aldgate East and Moorgate underground stations. Furthermore there has been a confirmed explosion on a bus in Tavistock Place."

10.24 Scotland Yard confirm explosion on bus at Tavistock Place, near Russell Square. "Union officials say there have been reports of explosions on three buses."

10.25 Transport union officials announce they have reports of explosions on *three* buses,[17] in Russell Square and in Tavistock Place. Witness Belinda Seabrook said of the Tavistock Place/Tavistock Square blast: "I was on the bus in front and heard an incredible bang. I turned round and half the double-decker bus was in the air."

10.30 Two or three 'suicide bombers' are reported to have been shot dead by police at Canary Wharf next to the HSBC tower.[18] Following the shooting, Reuters report that the 8,000 workers in the 44-storey tower were told to stay away from windows and remain in the building for at least six hours.[19]

10.30 The Gold Command centre (or Gold Coordinating Group) was set up at Hendon police station, not Scotland Yard. The Hendon site was well-equipped, having been used for the 'Atlantic Blue' terror drill three months earlier.

11.15 European Union commissioner for justice and security affairs Franco Frattini tells reporters in Rome that the blasts in London are terrorist attacks.

11.18 London's Metropolitan Police Commissioner Sir Ian Blair tells the BBC he knows of "about six explosions", one on a bus and the others at train stations.

11.38 Italian report by interior minister Giuseppe Pisanu, that at least 50 people had died in the London blasts, in Italian news agency ANSA. Until 3 pm, the UK media were only alluding to 'possible deaths'.

11.46 First confirmation of deaths. Police say two killed at Aldgate East.

11.56 Bus transport in central London is shut down, as well as the entire Underground, and people are advised to stay at home.

12.00 Mobile phone systems in and around London go dead for four hours. In early December 2005 it was revealed that the shutdown had been called by City of London police. Many reports place London phone difficulties or shutdown much earlier, from 10 am onwards.

12.05 pm British Prime Minister Tony Blair says there has been 'a series of terrorist attacks in London ... people have died and are seriously injured ... It is reasonably clear this is designed and timed to coincide with the opening of the G8' [summit]. (Actually it was the second day of three; if the bombings had happened 24-30 hours earlier they would have scuppered London's Olympic bid.) He says he will return to London within hours, and the summit will continue without him.

12.10 BBC News reported that a website known to be operated by associates of al-Qaeda had been located with a 200-word statement claiming responsibility for the attacks. BBC Monitoring reported that a group named "Secret Organisation — al-Qaeda in Europe" (or, the Group of al-Qaeda of Jihad Organization in Europe) had posted an announcement claiming responsibility on the al-Qalah ("The Castle") Internet forum. The announcement claims the attacks are a response to the British involvement in the invasion of Iraq and Afghanistan. A Saudi commentator in London noted that the statement was grammatically poor, and that a Qur'anic quotation was incorrect. The site, whose server was located in Houston, was later found to have connections with the Bush family.[20]

12.22 Instructions are given for *all* journalists of 60 weekly newspapers located in London and the South-East belonging to Trinity Mirror Southern titles, to return to their offices or go home, after which the offices were shut – for 'safety reasons'.[21]

12.51 Emergency services personnel tells CNN writer William Chamberlain that all survivors had been evacuated from King's Cross station, leaving the dead below ground 'in the double digits.'

12.55 The Home Secretary Charles Clarke makes a statement to Parliament. He says there have been four explosions and tells where they were located on the London Transport network.

1.33 Blair departs from Gleneagles, returning to London.

1.40 A debate on Italian state radio (RAI) about why the 50 deaths were not being confirmed or denied in Britain.[22]

03.30 Brian Paddick of the Metropolitan police stated that at 09.17 am there had been an explosion on a train coming into Edgware Road underground station approximately 100 yards into the tunnel. The explosion took place on a train and blew through a wall onto another train on an adjoining platform. Officials did not change this train time to 08.50 am until July 9th, two days later.

03.30 Israeli Army News avers that Scotland Yard warned the Israeli embassy re Netanyahu's visit: 'Israel was notified ahead of first blast,' 1.30 Israeli time.

04.00 Central London bus services restart.

04.30 There were five fatalities and others injured in the Edgware Road incident and three trains are believed to have been involved, according to a report issued by the Metropolitan Police Service.

4.51 U.S. law enforcement sources say the British government has said that at least 40 people have been killed. London hospitals report at least 300 wounded, the Associated Press reports.

5.43 After chairing a London meeting of the government's Emergency Committee 'COBRA' at Downing Street, Tony Blair made his first public statement, in which he averred of the bombers: 'We know that these people act in the name of Islam.'

5.49 The United Nations Security Council passes a resolution condemning the London attacks and expressing *"outrage and indignation at today's appalling terrorist attacks against the people of the United Kingdom that cost human life and caused injuries and immense human suffering."*

6.13 The BBC reports the number of people confirmed dead in the London bomb attacks has risen to 37, Deputy Assistant Police Commissioner Brian Paddick says. 21 were killed at Kings Cross/Russell Square, seven died at Edgware Road, seven died at Liverpool Street and two died on the bus at Upper Woburn Place/Tavistock Square. A further 700 were injured, 300 of whom were taken to various London hospitals by ambulance.

7.30 Statement by Peter Power on Radio 5 Live, about a terror drill he was rehearsing that morning, on behalf of an unnamed company, using the *same* underground stations as were attacked: 'At half past nine this morning we were actually running an exercise …'[23]

7.39 Jack Straw, Foreign Secretary, says attacks bear the hallmarks of al-Qaeda.

10.19 Amongst the many thousands of calls to the emergency Casualty Bureau, a call to the police emergency hotline comes from Hasib Hussain's family, reporting him missing.

11 pm Rachel North begins her daily blog about 7/7, which is soon copied onto the BBC's website. A shard of glass impacted into her wrist while supposedly in the Piccadilly Line coach which exploded, leading to a hospital visit that afternoon. That injury did not impede her blogging, and she is soon the best-known 'survivor.'

On October 2nd this image of Hussain was released to the public, allegedly showing him at Boots the chemist in King's Cross station at 9 am on July 7th. The time and date have been clipped off this CCTV image, and Hasib's figure appears suspended in space. He is supposedly pottering around King's Cross station before getting onto the 30 bus. This was for some years the only image of any of the four in London on that day released, and we suggest its dubious character speaks for itself — an obvious photomontage.[24] London is the undisputed world capital of CCTV cameras, and this obsessional degree of state surveillance would surely have provided a very thorough CCTV coverage of the four young men with rucksacks, not just this one derisory image without even a timestamp?

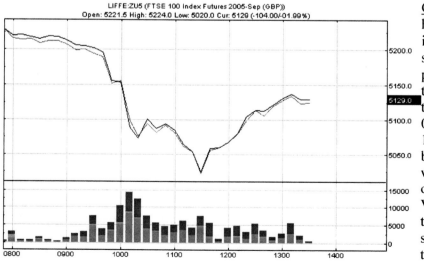

Graph: showing how the FTSE index fell by some 200 points in the two hours, in two stages after 09.40 and 10.00, when the bus explosion was announced on the news.[25] Volume of trading is shown along the baseline.

Notes and References

[1] Amicus, of which David Minahan was formerly the National President, is the UK's largest manufacturing Trade Union. See his article at: www.julyseventh.co.uk/J7-london-bombings-dossier/index.html.

[2] www.hof.org.uk/cgi-bin/newdisplaypost.pl?1:245801.cc (source withdrawn); See Appendix 6.

[3] Ahmed, p.132-4; Tarpley, p.461. On the day of July 7th, the US intelligence agency Strategic Forecasting made this statement about Israeli precognition of the event:

'Contrary to original claims that Israel was warned "minutes before" the first attack, unconfirmed rumors in intelligence circles indicate that the Israeli government actually warned London of the attacks "a couple of days" previous.'

It concluded that the British government had 'sat on this information for days and failed to respond': 'Israel warned United Kingdom about possible bomb attacks' Stratfor Consulting Agency, 7.7.05. http://fairuse.1accesshost.com/news2/stratfor-london.html. (There is an analogy here with 9/11, where the messenger firm Odigo in New York received information about the event about to happen, two hours earlier. As an Israeli-based firm, it received this mystery message from a branch of Odigo based in a village north of Tel Aviv, where Mossad was headquartered. Thus both of these events show evidence of Israeli precognition).

[4] 'Report: Israel was notified ahead of first blast' July 7, 13.30, IsraelNN.com. This story on Israeli Army Radio news made out that it was Scotland Yard which notified the Israeli Embassy in advance. www.conspiracyproof.org/london775/inncom001.jpg, www.conspiracyproof.org/london775/index.html, www.whatreallyhappened.com/londonarchive.html. Two weeks later, the head of the Israeli Mossad, General Meir Dagan, said that he had warned Benjamin Netanyahu at 08.40 AM, on 7/7/2005, ten minutes before the first blast occurred, not to go to his appointment. Later on, on July 7th, the Israeli news backpedaled, and claimed merely that: '"After the first explosion, our finance minister received a request not to go anywhere,' Finance Minister Silvan Shalom told Israel Army Radio" – Amy Teibel, Associated Press from Jerusalem. By July 8th, the story had changed again, with Netanyahu on his way to the TASE conference when he received the warning, from British security, after the blast (July 8th CNN interview, http://transcripts.cnn.com/TRANSCRIPTS/0507/08/ldt.01.html): the hotel he was heading for was 'right above that terminal' ie Liverpool street, so he never went there.

[5] The first blast, at Aldgate, occurred at 11 minutes to 9. Some of those involved in the 9/11 truth movement—who have observed other numerological oddities such as the 3/11 Madrid bombing 911 days after 9/11—consider that this could be significant.

[6] "The Tel Aviv Stock Exchange (TASE)'s annual conference for investment managers of international funds invested in Israel will be held in London this year, in July 7, 2005. This is the fourth time the TASE has held the annual event in London, as part of its activity aimed at encouraging foreign investments in Israel. This year's conference will be held in collaboration with the Israeli embassy in London and Deutsche Bank. Keynote speakers at the conference are Mr. Benjamin Netanyahu, Minister of Finance, and Mr. Moshe Tery, Chairman of the Israel Securities Authority... The increase in foreign investments in TASE stocks, from $480 million in 2004 to $1.4 billion in the first five months of 2005, is an expression of investors' highly positive view of the Israeli economy," explained Ronit Harel Ben-Ze'ev, Senior Vice President and Head of the Economic Department: 'Israel Opportunity 2005 Conference for International Investors in London', *Business Wire*, June 20, 2005, http://findarticles.com/p/ articles/mi_m0EIN/is_2005_June_20/ai_n13821222.

[7] Michel Chossudovsky, '7/7 Mock Terror Drill: What Relationship to the Real Time Terror Attacks?' www.prisonplanet.com/articles/august2005/110805mockterror.htm.

[8] BBC News, 7.7.05, London blasts: At a glance http://news.bbc.co.uk/1/hi/uk/4659331.stm.

[9] www.cbc.ca/MRL/clips/rm-lo/charles_disasters050711.rm.

[10] COBRA.

[11] TASE conference organizer Orna Goren told me that Netanyahu had been due to speak at 10.am, but that at 09.30 his security officer phoned and said that he would not be able to make it owing to 'an explosion near the conference venue'.

[12] See Appendix 2.

[13] www.timesonline.co.uk/article/0,,22989-1687566,00.html.

[14] *The Sunday Times*, 10.7.05 focus: 'Terror in London' www.timesonline.co.uk/article/0,,2087-1688489,00.html. This announcement was before news of the bus explosion had been reported, so we may conjecture that it could not have been later than 9.50 am. A differing account has this 'shortly before 10 am' as when Blair heard the first report, but believed it was merely a power surge or crash. Telegraph, 'We saw the best of things and the worst,' by Olga Craig, 11/07/2005.

[15] www.faulkingtruth.com/Articles/CommentaryToo/1037.html.

[16] On 17 February, 2006, PC Walker (Camden branch) described how he became suspicious of a 'microwave box' on the lower deck of the exploded 30 bus (Hampstead & Highgate Express, 17 February). According to his report the bomb squad was called and a second, controlled, explosion was conducted. This seems posthumously to confirm the initial and discrepant report of two explosions, by Richmal Oates-Whitehead, a New Zealand-born woman who worked for the British Medical Journal, also based in Tavistock Square.

[17] BBC News 7.7.05, 'London blasts: At a glance' http://news.bbc.co.uk/1/hi/uk/4659331.stm.

[18] TBR News, Rixon Stewart, 'Something Evil this way comes', 24.7.05, www.tbrnews.org/Archives/a1731.htm See Appendix 3.

[19] Some take the view (see Muad's Conjecture, Appendix 3) that these were three of the 'bombers,' who ended up at Canary Wharf (for whatever reason) and that is why reports of these shootings were excluded from the British media after the initial news announcement.

[20] See Ch. 7, note 12.

[21] www.pressgazette.co.uk/article/140705/tms_sends_journalists and www.spiked-online.com/Printable/0000000CAC6E.htm (both lost) "The email, which was sent to all TMS newsdesk staff at 12.22pm by editorial director Marc Reeves, said: 'Staff safety is the NUMBER ONE priority at this time. Please call back into the office anyone out in the field whether on bomb related stories or not. Alternatively, send them home if they are closer.'" See copy on: http://antagonise.blogspot.com/2005/08/ask-questions-and-you-shall-find.html.

[22] www.pittsburghlive.com/x/tribune-review/terrorism/s_351871.html.

[23] See Appendix 4. In New York, 'Earlier on Thursday morning there had actually been a security drill with armed officers entering the New York subway – although this was unrelated to the London attacks' (BBC News, July 7). This would have been about noon, London time. http://news.bbc.co.uk/1/hi/world/americas/4660939.stm.

[24] There was a story of exceptional absurdity attached to this image, whereby H.H. had attempted to blow himself up on a train, but failed, and concluded that the battery in his detonator must be flat; and so here he is in Boots, mulling over the purchase of a new 9-volt battery (*Official Account*, p.5).

[25] http://en.wikinews.org/wiki/Financial_markets_react_to_London_blasts.

5. The Impossible Journey

How the Perfect Crime Unravelled

At a Metropolitan Police press conference in the days after July 7th, it was announced that the alleged bombers caught the 7.40am Thameslink train from Luton to King's Cross. That the alleged bombers caught the 7.40am train was widely reported in television and newspaper reports the world over. This fact was also confirmed in the official Government narrative of events. Ten months to the day after the horrific events of July 7th, the Sunday Observer published 'The Real Story of 7/7' that claimed to be *the definitive account of how four friends from northern England changed the face of western terrorism*' in which the following claim is made: "7:40 am: The four bombers catch a Thameslink train, which winds through the affluent commuter belt of Hertfordshire towards King's Cross."

Thus, *The Times* on July 14th had described the newly-released image of one of the 'bombers': 'Hasib Hussain, an 18-year-old from Leeds, is shown in a CCTV image mounting the stairs at Luton station before taking the 7.40am train to King's Cross.' There was no timestamp or anything to identify this image (shown in Chapter 6), of the young man climbing a stairway.[1] Then a few days later, on 17th July it averred of the four young men at Luton station: 'A CCTV camera filmed them as they prepared to board the 7.40am train to King's Cross. Near them was another man who might or might not have been an accomplice or even a potential fifth bomber — but he disappeared into the crowd.' (*The Times*, 'The Web of Terror') We here notice the casual invocation of the 'objective' evidence of the CCTV camera images, which were however not viewable by anyone – a persistent theme of our story.

But, other media reports claimed that the four had caught the 7.48am from Luton, as the *Daily Telegraph* on the 14th July told its readers: "After two trains were cancelled, the eight-carriage 07:48 service was fuller than usual."

The well-known picture of the four 'bombers' entering Luton station on the morning of July 7th was released by the police on July 16th. Does it show them catching the 7.40am train, as was announced at the press conference? The image is time and date-stamped as 07.21:54, a few seconds shy of 7.22am. The Luton to King's Cross Thameslink service *normally* takes 36 minutes, and so the 7.40am from Luton would usually arrive into King's Cross at 8.16am. As we shall see, this would have fitted in neatly with the timed CCTV images alluded to, at Luton and King's Cross, by the police.

The present writer approached Customer relations at King's Cross and Marie Bernes replied, sending their computer database for the trains running that morning. Then I and James Stewart (a fellow- 9/11 Sceptic), agreed to visit Luton station and engage with the morning rush-hour commuters, on the platform bound to King's Cross. This was about six weeks after the event. We were stimulated to do this by the testimony of an African lady commuter who wished to remain anonymous (and was nervous of any publicity) who had averred that the train times as announced could not be true.[2] Would her story stand up? Commuters seemed quite glad to be interviewed, and a couple told us they knew the official story could not be true, because of the train delays they had experienced on that day. Perhaps fortunately the chief Communications Manager was absent from Luton station on that day, and instead we spoke to his deputy, a Mr Chris Hudson. He promised he would send us the database of Thameslink train times for that morning, and a week later this historic e-mail duly arrived (it's up now on the July 7th site). This confirmed the all-important fact that the 07.40 train had been cancelled for that morning. Moreover, all the other trains running had been severely delayed, due to an unforeseen factor, trouble with overhead power lines in the Mill Hill area.

That gave the following Luton to King's Cross timetable for the morning of July 7th:

Thameslink   Trains
Luton to King's Cross, 7-8 am on July 7, 2005

Booked Departure	Actual departure	Due in at King's X	Actual Arrival King's X	Delay (minutes)
07.16	07.21	07.48	08.19	31
07.20	07.20	08.08	08.15	7
07.24	07.25	08.00	08.23	23
07.30	07.42	08.04	08.39	35
07.40	Cancelled	Cancelled	Cancelled	Cancelled
07.48	07.56	08.20	08.42	22

Let's remind the reader of the timeframe available, of the constraints which are imposed by the official narrative.

07.22 Luton CCTV image of four entering station.

08.26 King's Cross main-station CCTV image of the four.

08.35 The Eastbound Circle Line train No. 204 leaves King's Cross.

08.42 The Westbound Circle Line train No. 216 leaves King's Cross.

08.48 The Westbound Piccadilly Line train No. 311 leaves King's Cross.

It is evident from this table, that the 07.48 train did not arrive in King's Cross until after two of the underground trains involved had already departed King's Cross underground station.

The numbers allude to the trains which blew up. Can you spot any Luton-King's Cross train which might satisfy these constraints? As we shall see, there are problems with any solution opted for.

Confronted by this problem, official sources often cited the 07.48 train as the one. To quote Ahmed, 'Essentially, the police have repeatedly asserted on the public record two different times for the train's departure from Luton.' Ahmed summarised the situation here as:

So, contrary to the police narrative that the bombers took the 7.40 train, this train was in fact cancelled. And contrary to the narrative that they took the 7.48am train, this too was delayed, such that that train arrived a total of 16 minutes after the bombers were, according to police, photographed by CCTV at King's Cross station at 8.26 am. Even if they had taken the train whose departure was delayed to 7.42am – very close to the first train time asserted by the police – they would have arrived at King's Cross 13 minutes too late to be caught on the Station's CCTV camera.

On 11th July, 2006, a year after the event, Britain's Home Secretary Dr John Reid confirmed before Parliament, that the just-published official Home Office report about 7/7 — a report that took ten months to produce and publish anonymously – had been mistaken with regard to its allegation about which Thameslink train from Luton to King's Cross the alleged perpetrators caught: 'The train in fact left Luton station at 7.25 am. It did, however, arrive at Kings Cross at 8.23 am, as recorded in the official account.'

If that major plank of the official story was mistaken, then what about the rest of it? Scotland Yard responded by claiming that the official account had been produced by the Home Office, and that the police had never given it the time for the train. That seems unlikely. After all, the police were supposed to be conducting what Ian Blair called the 'largest criminal inquiry in English history.'

Cyber-debate seethed as to whether the casual-looking group entering at 07.22 could have got through the Luton ticket office at rush hour in time to get onto the station platform and catch the London train at 07.25. This writer and James Stewart had argued against this: that it would take, say, five minutes. One would have to believe that they were not intending to catch this train, as they would surely have missed it had it not been delayed. Evidently the police had decided against this view in the beginning by deciding to go for the 07.40 train. The train which left Luton station at 07.25, arrived into King's Cross Thameslink at 08.23 am, taking 58 minutes, which would have given the four young men barely three minutes to walk up the stairs at Luton, buy their tickets in the morning rush-hour and then get to the platform. Some have suggested that Germaine Lindsay from Aylesbury had arrived early and bought the four tickets in advance (day-returns at £22 each), to make this feasible. But, from King's Cross Thameslink, it took a good seven minutes to walk through the long Underground tube passage—which includes a ticket barrier—to reach the main King's Cross station, in the morning rush-hour with large rucksacks – in no way could they have been captured on the 08.26am alleged CCTV picture. Had they been running, they would surely have attracted attention to themselves.

As if to cope with this problem, the Government's Official Account which emerged a year later had the four lads entering Luton train station entrance at 07.15 am, and one must admit this would have given them plenty of time to catch the train. Indeed it would have given them plenty of time to catch the 7.24; however they apparently let that go and waited for a nonexistent 7.40. This Narrative would seem to be trying to forget about the timestamp of 07.22 on the CCTV image released of the four entering the station! Here one can only quote Ahmed, 'Even minor details of the official account remain absurdly impossible.'[3] Thameslink itself ceased to be around this time, as if its demise were timed to be within a month of the Official Account, morphing into First Capital Connect.

Arguments continued about how long it took to walk from King's Cross Thameslink to the main King's Cross station and its Underground, with large rucksacks, in the morning rush hour. The police had committed themselves to having the crucial CCTV footage of the four together at King's Cross in the main station, by the underground, at 08.26 am, and that is quite a way from the separate Thameslink station.

By way of resolving this 'impossible journey' the Met or whoever composed the Official Narrative quietly moved the alleged 08.26 CCTV image onto the King's Cross Thameslink platform.[4] As no one was ever likely to see this CCTV image – which may not even exist – the Home Office felt it could safely rely upon journalistic amnesia to get through. It then added, that *four minutes later* the men were seen at King's Cross mainline, where they proceeded to split up in different directions, giving the impression that each man was off to board a tube train. Given that 'were seen' here alludes to CCTV images which no-one is ever likely to see, it is difficult to see why the public should take very much notice of this 'official' version. The Transport For London official journey planner recommends six minutes for making this journey in rush-hour, which seems a bare minimum. The 'Official Narrative' has them on the Thameslink station heading along the subway towards the Underground: "The 4 are captured on CCTV at 08.26am on the concourse close to the Thameslink platform and heading in the direction of the London Underground system." Yet in 2005 this passageway led to the Northern, Piccadilly and Victoria lines, but not the Circle Line, which required a rather different route. So, as noted by 'Kier,' the young men would not have reached the Circle Line platform in time.

No train that morning was capable of getting a passenger into both of the CCTV images, Luton and King's Cross. This could be partly why the police have not released the images they claim to have of the four at King's Cross. A month or two before John Reid's announcement concerning the 7.40 train, Thameslink itself dissolved, as if the strain were all too much: conspiracy theorists are now disappointed to find that they can no longer check over details at the Thameslink station at King's Cross, because everything has now been altered, with 'First Capital Connect' now running the show.

The Government's Official Report has the four splitting up at 08.30 am, supposedly captured on CCTV. That puts the Piccadilly-line bomber waiting on his platform for some fifteen minutes at rush-hour, as several trains went by, and finally catching the 08.48. The public might not find this very credible. The explosion at Aldgate is initially reported as having taken place at 08.50 with the other blasts coming *later,* thus the Piccadilly line train was reported as having blown up at around 08.56 (and indeed it still does so, in Rachel North's book). That happened immediately upon leaving King's Cross station, when the packed train had just entered the tunnel.

Journalists were fed up at only being informed of the synchronous nature of the three tube bombs *two days* after the event. If a tube train stops dead in a tunnel, the tube authorities *have to know this at once*, especially at rush hour – or else trains would start piling up. The blast-times initially reported were 08.50, 08.56 and 09.17, the first of these being Aldgate. There is no way in which London Underground could have received primary information about the blasts being thus spread out over twenty-seven minutes. No one has tried to explain this. Was the story from the *Panorama* program of the previous year (Chapter 3) somehow feeding into the construction of the narrative?

That version had its three rush-hour tube bomb blasts spread out over half an hour. For a suicide-bomber story of this nature, one would tend to expect the Aldgate blast to go off later than that on the Piccadilly line, given that the bombers were alleged to be 'huddled' together at 08.30 in the Official Narrative. The journey to Aldgate takes 15 minutes and is five stops away, whereas the Piccadilly line blast was immediately adjacent to King's Cross. The strangely-divergent times as initially reported tend to endorse the view that the Met was not initially working with a story of suicide bombers.

References

[1] The public were informed that this first picture released of Hasib Hussain mounting the stairs inside Luton station had been taken at 07.20 am (eg, ABC News, 14.7.05 'London Bombers Tied to Al Qaeda Plot in Pakistan' http://abcnews.go.com/WNT/LondonBlasts/story?id=940198&page=1); whereas days later, the picture of 'the four' released *entering* the station showed a timestamp of 07.22 am.

[2] Her testimony was that she arrived at Luton station that morning at 7.25am, and had no train to catch until 7.58am, because the 7.30am and 7.40am trains from Luton were cancelled on July 7th. She could only get a slow train at 7.58am from platform 3 to King's Cross, which didn't arrive there until 8.43am. It was so packed that many could not get onto the train at Luton. The 07.30, delayed in arriving into Luton that morning, came into platform 4, whereas the London trains normally come to platforms 1 or 3, which is why she believed it had been cancelled.

[3] Ahmed, *The London Bombs*, p.277.

[4] Anon, *Official Account*, p.4.

6. The Illusion Fabricated

Do these two pictures look similar to you? Can you spot the difference? The sharp one is of Mohammed Siddique Khan, teacher in Beeston's primary school,

while the other is supposedly a picture of him taken at Luton railway station on the morning of July 7th. It remained for almost three years the only picture of him allegedly taken anywhere on that day.[1] Not a single British newspaper ever suggested that there was anything odd about this photo, not a single radio or TV show about the subject ever seems to have doubted that it was evidence of his real presence in London on that day, nor has a single book published on the subject cast doubt upon this. In it, the railing behind him passes in front of his head...

Two images of the June 28th visit by three of them are here shown (one above right, and the other over the page). Comparing these two with the somewhat adjusted July 7th image, here shown on the right, let us first notice that 'Lindsay' is wearing the *same* dark

baseball cap, the *same* white trainers and carrying the *same* Tesco's plastic bag in his right hand! (Germaine Lindsay, or sometimes Lindsay Jamal). It is suggested that the reader follow him on the King's Cross platform CCTV images for that morning as well as those at Luton. One may wish to pause a while to reflect upon the equipment which these young men were alleged to have been carrying – capable of blowing up and maybe derailing several trains, using the rather unstable 'TATP' which can be prone to detonate spontaneously. Bombs with nails sticking out of them have been depicted in the tabloids, in this context. This young man looks more as if he is carrying his sandwich lunch prepared by his Mom. A sequence of fourteen images at 1-2 second intervals shows the three of them at Luton on June 28th, meeting up outside the station

and then entering it.[2] A similar sequence shows them walking down the platform at King's Cross. A majority of the British public came to believe that CCTV coverage exists of the four on July 7th at Kings Cross, on account of the way this CCTV sequence has shamelessly been shown and re-shown on British television with the date stamps removed. This happened especially over rolling news coverage during the first anniversary of the event. In order to arm ourselves against such wilful deception, it is rather important to go over these really-existing CCTV images, and contrast them with the single and 'photoshopped' one released, from July 7th.

Khan, Lindsay and Tanweer entered Luton station on June 28th, in the morning after 8 o'clock, on their way to London, as depicted in the first of these images. The second, eight days later on the morning of July 7th, about fifty minutes earlier, supposedly shows the same three also accompanied by the young Hasib Hussain, taken by the same unmoving camera outside the car-park entrance to Luton station. Hussain, absent from the earlier images of the 28th, leads the way into the station on the July 7th image. The mirror (or rather, darkened glass which acts as a mirror) in the background shows the figure of Lindsay reversed in the first image, as a mirror image ought to be, but the right way round in the second! Only two of the three on the 28th were carrying rucksacks so it's a bit hard to see how it could have been a 'dummy run' for the July 7th event as alleged by the press.

It had been raining on the morning of July 7th at Luton, and an impossible boundary between wet and dry appears in the photo – there is *no awning above the pavement* that could give that 'dry' boundary. The pavement does turn to a slightly darker shade of cement which the lads are shown crossing over, and those producing the July 7th image were somehow able to make this darker cement appear as if it were wet with puddles from the earlier rain. Everything gives one the impression that one or two of the stills of the June 28th CCTV were used or combined to make this clearly tampered-with composite image. Keen readers may wish to print out some of these images, and even visit the Luton station entrance in question. For 'concrete proof' of tampering, we suggest noting the pavement boundary by the two shades of concrete: the real thing does not look as depicted in the 'July 7th' image, whereas it is exactly as depicted in the July 28th images.

The bar in the image ought of course to be *behind* 'Khan's' head, as likewise the lower bar should go behind his body, and not in front of it as it does in this image! Standing in front of those railings – by the ground-floor entrance to Luton railway station – Khan would have to be very short, less than five feet tall, for the photograph taken by the single CCTV camera, 9 feet above the ground, to show this bar as passing behind his head. There is no reason to suppose that Khan, a busy family man, came down to London on the 7th, a mere ten days after his earlier visit. The image of him here appears to be a rough Photoshopped insertion, presumably scaled down in its tone to make him appear as in the background, which has had the effect of making the railing bars appear to pass in front of him! Khan is the one wearing the white baseball cap in all these pictures.

A professional image-analyst scrutinised the single CCTV image released from Luton Thameslink station on 7.7.05, and commented as follows,[3] about how the railing appears to pass through the head of 'Khan' ('PS' here means 'Photoshop'), and in addition the lower railing-bar, at the rear of the picture, passes in front of the arm. He used the image from the Metropolitan Police site which is the link here given (reference 2, below), this being the best version available, and presumably the original: it will help to view that colour image using Photoshop, to follow his evaluation. He first assumed the picture was genuine, however that was 'not what I found when I fired up PS and had a really good look. It is a fake and I'm still a bit in shock.' He noted that 'the jpeg compression was set to 30. At that level compression artefacts will have crept in making the alleged fakery easy to cover up.' Concerning the 'Khan' figure in the background:

> The railing error is really peculiar. The strength of the line is way too much to be attributed to compression artefacts, that much I know. It is very typical of a PS mistake too. What really bothers me about the railing though is that it should be a couple of pixels higher in order to meet the corresponding piece to the left of the shot. I can't work out why this mistake was made – it probably was a rush job. Still for me I would be prepared to give it the benefit of the doubt. It could be a marking on the man's jacket for instance.

> However when I looked at 'railing man's' head I realised it was a fake. The head has a black halo around it that has no reason to be there. The give away is the shade of black in the halo – quite unlike any other black anywhere else in the shot. The whole picture has a blue tint that is not present in this black halo. To me this is a smoking gun – it's so reminiscent of what happens when images are

pasted in – and I've seen it before many times[4]. Unless the outline of the pasted image is absolutely perfect something like this will always crop up when it's dropped in. The white baseball cap also has a missing pixel (upper right of the hat) which is very damning. It looks very obvious at 1000% zoom that someone cut into the hat when they were making the outline – the background halo disappears at this point too.

He then turned to the 'Tanweer' image on the extreme right of the group CCTV picture.

'I then looked to see if the fourth man's face had been blurred as I'd seen suggested here. Well, OMG!, it has been blurred. Very nice subtle job, just touching a few pixels but the colour is wrong. There's a shade of blue that doesn't match the rest of the picture that seems to have come from a PS brush. Also above his head something has been edited (it slightly breaks up the double yellow line on the road) – something may have been erased here I think. There's something about this blur that can't be put down to compression algorithms either – it is a blur with some tinting. Looking at the bus stop post it should have a straight line all the way up. As soon as it comes near the fourth man the line falls apart. It looks like his body is interacting with the post but he's far behind it. So I now think this fourth guy was pasted in too.

The more one studies this image the more you see the inconsistencies. There's a fair bit of blurring and the railing guy could also be missing a leg. It's weird what's happening with phone-box guy's left foot and the small post too. It's a strange shot though because when viewed at normal magnification it all looks fairly plausible – disregarding the railing anomaly and the odd composition. Zoom in and it's a different story.'

Shehzad Tanweer, whose father ran the Beeston fish and chip shop, hired a light blue Nissan Micra some days before July 7th, from 'First 24 Hour car rental' company in Leeds in his own name. His pal Hasib Hussain may have driven down with him on the early morning of July 7th, or possibly the night before. Tanweer visited London on both occasions, i.e twice within ten days. Did they get as far as Luton that fateful morning?

Something resembling Tanweer's car was caught on CCTV in Hyde Park Road, Leeds, prior to joining the M1 outside Leeds, at 03.58. Then at 4.54 am the Micra stops at Woodall Services on the M1 to fill up with petrol, and an image is here shown (released in May, 2008) of him wearing white Puma T-shirt, dark jacket, white tracksuit bottoms and a baseball cap. Tanweer is on the extreme right of the 'July 7th' image at Luton, so did he change his trousers during the drive down, and lose his baseball cap? The images of Tanweer on June 28th and July 7th are similar, except that his top and bottoms have reversed colours: white trousers and dark top on 28th, dark trousers and white top on July 7th.

The central figure, supposed to be Germaine Lindsay from Aylesbury holding the Tesco's white bag, has what looks like a 'broken foot.' A silhouette-enhanced version shows the bottom of his trainer-shoe turned upwards in an anatomically-impossible manner.[5] The whole of Lindsay's left leg looks as if it has been inserted, which accounts for the cut in its side just below the thigh. Its top is not covered by his coat as it should be, and there is a disturbing 'interaction' between this leg and the white plastic bag.[6]

Some have surmised from this image that none of the four suspected bombers were here present, owing to the strange artefacts around their images. Even the figure that appears as a rather skinny version of Hasib Hussain has his image glowing with artificial edge-effects (see the enlargement here) down his right-hand side, which an expert has judged to be indicative of artificial insertion.

The two images shown on the next page are meant to be of the same person, Hasib Hussain, just a few seconds apart. Are you happy to accept that? That on the right is him entering the car-park door of the station; that on the left is him mounting the stairs. The former looks rather thin for the beefy, 'gentle giant' Hasib.[7] Don't forget that Hasib has not been on this journey before while the other three have, so it is not at once clear why he, as the youngest member of the group, should want to lead the way into the station entrance – or, to be climbing up the stairs alone without the others.

The solo image of Hasib was released on the 14th and as such was the first image of the four to be released: we were told it showed him mounting the stairs inside Luton station at 07.20 am. Then a few days later the composite image of the Four was released, showing a timestamp of 07.21.54 for them entering the station. Clearly they have to enter the station before they can mount the stairs inside. Well, you may say, that is a mere few minutes' difference and does it matter? The whole point of CCTV images is that they have a timestamp on them. This kind of confusion would not be feasible, *if* the images were genuine.

Incidentally, one cannot confirm from the manager of Beeston's 'First 24 Hour car rental' as to which car was hired and when, as he has been instructed by the police not to talk. As we shall see, that tends to be the case with various key actors in this story.

The police have traditionally had the role of fighting crime, not evaluating guilt in the absence of a trial. Traditionally, they had the role of gathering and preparing evidence to be used at a trial. With the events of July 7th however, a new and rather questionable role appears: that of *telling a story*. There will never be any trial, and we the public have been asked to believe their self-referencing tale. Most of what we think of as the July 7th story has appeared first in newspapers, as supplied by unnamed police 'sources.' In this section we have noticed two CCTV images from the early morning of July 7th, which as it happened we were inclined to accept as valid – even though no one has seen them. A close symbiosis has existed between police and journalists, where the latter have just been printing as fact whatever unattributed police sources give them. There is no point at which a process of verification has taken place, and those giving the leaks have known this – *that they can say what they like*. Illusion is perpetrated, as the public's hazy memory is thus manipulated.

To assist you in recognising these characters, as there are so few pictures of them, here are a couple of images which made it onto newspaper front pages, taken from a Whitewater rafting expedition on 4 June, 2005, mere weeks before the event, featuring two of the lads. Khan is making a V-sign and Tanweer is just below him.

They were on an outing organised through the Hamara Healthy Living Centre in Beeston. The National White-water Rafting Centre at Canolfan Tryweryn in Wales is not a residential centre, and the lads would have been there a mere couple of hours. These images show I suggest young lads who have *not* got any dark shadow on their conscience. The purpose of this outing can be described as *having fun* (see also second picture), whereas it cannot reasonably be described as a bonding exercise prior to a group suicide, as the press with their usual docile unanimity did so describe it.

References

[1] www.officialconfusion.com/77/images/cctv/cctv%2077%20imgs/index.html
official confusion, 7/7, CCTV. For a discussion of CCTV images released later on, at the
Kingston trial, see Chapter 13.

[2] http://www.officialconfusion.com/77/cctv/cctv.html and choose 'video' – or, here:
http://z13.invisionfree.com/julyseventh/index.php?showtopic=1249.

[3] by 'Elephant', posted 7.8.05 on http://letsrollforums.com/cctv-footage-four-bombers-
t7121.html.

[4] For comment on this 'black halo' artefact, see 'Photo of 'Bombers' has been Doctored'
25.5.05 on http://prisonplanet.com/Pages/ Jul05/250705doctored.html.

[5] Posted by 'Brianv' 26.7.05 on 'Let's Roll!' 'CCTV footage of four "bombers" released'.

[6] '77 CCTV was faked' by Flashmp, www.youtube.com/watch?v=I3Z2ZaUD--A.

[7] Two months later a second picture of Hasib was released (shown here at end of Chapter 4),
appearing rather doubtfully in Boots the chemist at King's Cross.

7. The Phantom Menace

On the afternoon of July 7th, at 5.30 pm, emerging from the COBRA meeting,[1] Britain's Prime Minister Tony Blair told the British people:

"We know those who did this did so in the name of Islam."[2]

Thereby Britain's police were given a directive from above. Their business became, not to search for clues etc. in the normal manner, but to become part of a *war*. That war was open-ended. Magically, the Prime minister already knew and the British people were being asked, or rather told, to believe him. Newly-arrived back from Gleneagles, from the aborted Summit of world leaders, he needed no time to ponder who the perpetrators of this terrible event might be. His subsequent explanation as to why no enquiry into the biggest attack upon London since the Blitz would be necessary – that it would be a 'ludicrous diversion,' in his own words, from the fight against terror – was the very same as that which George Bush had given, concerning 9/11.

Likewise, it was in the immediate aftermath of 9/11 that George Bush informed the American people who had perpetrated 9/11. It had been masterminded by a faraway Arab from a cave in Afghanistan, he explained. Thereby the FBI received their instructions as to where to look, the American people received instructions as to what to believe, and the US army received instructions as to where the next war would be.

World War III?

An hour or two earlier in the day of July 7th, an informed source had claimed to know in general terms who had done it – and this was a published article! This astonishingly prescient informed source was a former head of Mossad, and the article appeared in Jerusalem.

Mr Efraim Halevi, ex-Mossad chief, Director of Israel's National Security Council, and formerly Israeli ambassador to the European Union, published an article in the Jerusalem Post.[3] Entitled 'Rules of Conflict for a World War,' it called for *a total world war*, where

> 'the only way to ensure our safety and security will be to obtain the destruction, the complete destruction, of the enemy.'[4]

He neglected to state who was the enemy, so perhaps we should have a guess. Could it be, perhaps, anyone who objected to Israel's expansion from the Euphrates to the Nile? Or, should it rather be defined in terms of persons having darker skin colour? Seeking for a hint, we quote further from this unhinged, psychotic text:

> We are in the throes of a world war, raging over the entire globe and characterized by the absence of lines of conflict and an easily identifiable enemy. There are sometimes long pauses between one attack and another, consequently creating the wrong impression that the battle is all over, or at least in the process of being won.

Curiously, the preceding sentence to this had commented on the place where the number 30 bus blew up on July 7th –

It was at 77 Great Russell Street that Dr. Chaim Weizmann, a renowned chemist, presided over the effort that culminated in the issuing of the Balfour Declaration, the first international recognition of the right of the Jewish people to a national home in what was then still a part of the Ottoman Empire.

That does seem an odd juxtaposition. And how very short a time for him to have had such ruminations. Great Russell Street is not far from the spot where the diverted number 30 bus blew up, after it had stopped at no bus stop nor traffic light. He surmised that 'I doubt whether the planners knew that one of the target areas, that in Russell Square, was within a stone's throw of a building that served as the first headquarters of the World Zionist Organization that preceded the State of Israel.' The contrary could well be the case.

We are startled and perplexed that an analysis of the London bombings and a discourse concerning who was responsible for them, with judgements concerning an allegedly-ongoing war of civilisation that would affect every one of us – should appear *on the very same day*. Normally one would expect an article about the implications of an event at least one day after. There is a two-hour time difference between Israel and the UK, so they would have heard of the London bombing around noon. As a daily paper, it did have an evening edition. Some have concluded that the article *had been already composed* before the bomb went off.

Mr Halevi showed remarkable precognition in describing the bombs, far away in London, as 'simultaneous.' He wrote: *The multiple, simultaneous explosions that took place today on the London transportation system were the work of perpetrators who had an operational capacity of considerable scope ...*' Through 7th and 8th of July, these explosions were being described as spread out over half an hour, and (to the consternation of journalists) only on the 9th did the police affirm that the explosions were simultaneous.

Halevi's remarks about how the Enemy behaves, could be viewed as a mirror-reflected account of Israel's treatment of its neighbours, whereby ordinary civilians have had to

> suffer the most cruel and wicked of punishments meted out by those who are not bound by any rules of conduct or any norms of structured society.

Thus, the former Israeli Prime minister Yitzhak Shamir described how Israel used terror as state policy:

> Neither Jewish morality nor Jewish tradition can be used to disallow terror as a means of war... We are very far from any moral hesitations when concerned with the national struggle. First and foremost, terror is for us a part of the political war appropriate for the circumstances of today...[5]

A judgement was made upon Mossad which just happened to appear on 10th September, 2001, a day before the attacks upon the Pentagon and WTC: 'Wildcard. Ruthless and cunning. Has capability to target U.S. forces and make it look like a Palestinian/Arab act' – as the *Washington Times* reported, in a paper issued by the Army School of Advanced Military Studies. Mossad's motto is, 'By way of deception shall you wage war.'

Halevi gave a clue concerning the war that had to be prosecuted – to the utter extermination of the Enemy – as follows:

> The executives must be empowered to act resolutely and to take every measure necessary to protect the citizens of their country and to carry the combat into whatever territory the perpetrators and their temporal and spiritual leaders are inhabiting.

A religious war was here being called for, insofar as it has 'spiritual leaders.' He thus placed the London terror-event into the context, of an *ongoing world war* of a religious-spiritual nature.

Halevi, when composing this article, had a seat on the advisory board of the UK company Quest, 'The Professional Intelligence Company' which specializes in risk management. Quest's website explains that it specialises in 'Technical surveillance operations, mobile, foot and static surveillance, close reconnaissance and covert and overt photography.' Should a UK company permit one of its members to indulge in implicitly racist warmongering? Efraim Halevi is a person who should face questioning, as to how he knew what he did.[6]

Portrait of the Killers

On the day after the event, London's police were uncertain as to where the evidence was pointing; Brian Paddick, the Met's Deputy Assistant Commissioner, said: 'we do not know whether suicide bombers carried out the attacks or whether bombs had been left in packages on the Underground or in buses' or 'whether the bombs were on the trains or in the tunnels.'[7] The CNN report which carried this added, that 'US law enforcement sources said investigators have discovered remnants of timing devices that may have been used in the train explosions.' Thus, all options were then open. 'Remnants of timing devices' were surely the first clue as regards the perpetrators to be discovered – all mention of which was to disappear, fairly soon – and these would argue *against* suicide bombers. Whether the bombs had been placed in the tunnels or in the trains could not as yet be ascertained.

Two days later, the first real portrait of 'the Enemy' responsible for the atrocity appeared in print. On July 10th in the Murdoch – owned *News of the World*, Sir John Stevens, Commissioner of the Metropolitan Police (2000-2005) and the most senior police officer in Great Britain, envisaged the perpetrators as

> apparently-ordinary British citizens... Highly computer literate, they will have used the internet to research explosives, chemicals and electronics.... willing to kill without mercy... They are painstaking, cautious, clever and very sophisticated.[8]

— and, of course, they were Islamic. That went without saying – why, readers did not even have to think about that. It was not even a question. Thereby the police acquired their 'profile' of the terrorists.

The previous year, a few days after the Madrid bombings (on 16th March), Sir John had warned that a terror attack on London was 'inevitable.' Then, soon after he had retired and a few months prior to the attack, he warned even more sombrely of how up to 200 Al-Qaeda 'terrorists' were operating in UK and a threat of attack from them was real.

He had backed proposed anti-terror legislation, saying that his critics were naive about the "brutal" threat posed by fanatics. His *News of the World* readers were assured that militants trained by Osama bin Laden 'fester' across the country.

Osama bin Laden (1957-2001) has featured as an all-purpose bogeyman for the new millennium, invoked by the military to ensure their budgets exactly as Emmanuel Goldstein was so alluded to in George Orwell's *1984*.[9] In that novel, we gather that this character might actually have died some years ago, but no one is too bothered.

Sir John's statement came days after the Prevention of Terrorism Bill was enacted. Among its proposals for terror suspects are house arrest, curfew, tagging, bans on internet and telephone use and detention without trial. Foreign terror suspects, almost entirely Muslim, are held at Belmarsh prison in London without trial, even though Law lords have ruled this breaches human rights legislation. Sir John's reply to critics was merely,

> The main opposition to the Bill, it seems to me, is from people who simply haven't understood the brutal reality of the world we live in. (6.3.05)

Helpfully entitled *Forget Human Rights. Kick Out The Fanatics,* Sir John's 'climate of fear' article conveniently appeared on the day when both the Conservative and Liberal Democrats were holding party conferences, and in the middle of the guillotined debate in the House of Lords on the Prevention of Terrorism Bill. '… But they would all commit devastating terror attacks against us if they could, even those born and brought up here.' And how did he know that? At no point did this article show a scrap of evidence to support these hate-engendering assertions. It explained how grateful we should be because 'even larger numbers of undercover agents, moles and special deep-cover surveillance teams risk their lives daily to track and monitor the evil in our midst.' The previous December, the Law Lords had ruled against detention without trial, which was why the Prevention of Terrorism Act had to be rushed through parliament without proper debate, he explained.

Suicide Bombers?

Initally, the British police and media were outrightly dismissing any notion of suicide bombers. On July 8th, Ian Blair stated emphatically:

> No, as I said earlier on, there is absolutely nothing to suggest this was a suicide bomb. There is nothing to suggest that. We can't rule it out. It may have been that. But it may also have been a bomb that was left on a seat. It may also be a bomb that went off in transit. These things are still open to the investigation. And I think the continuous reference to suicide bombing is unhelpful because it's completely unproven.

And then the next day, a 'senior government source' announced that they were investigating 'a foreign-based Islamic terrorist cell' (*The Telegraph*, July 10th). The themes then were that the tube detonations were synchronous, that military-grade explosives had been used, and that traces of detonators and their timers had been found.[10] That was the initial story, and not until July 13th did the papers propose or rather announce the notion of suicide bombers, British-born and from the Leeds area

...and make sure you've got your Identity Cards to be found after the bombs go off.

(eg, *The Telegraph*). At that point, the whole narrative started swinging round to a home-brewed explosive brewed up in a bath in Leeds – which could never be shown or photographed, nor even could a charge be pinned on the person whose house contained the bath. However, the earlier part of the story stuck — exactly synchronized train blasts within 50 seconds of each other, which strictly belonged to a more military, remote-detonation narrative — even after the perpetrators had become suicide bombers.

Did the suicide bomber idea originate in America? We turn now to ABC News Transcripts on July 7th, in the show, Good Morning America, at 7 am.

MARTHA RADDATZ, ABC NEWS

Charlie, just to reiterate, there is a senior US official telling ABC News that early reports indicate that the bomb on the double-decker bus was carried by a suicide bomber. It would not be hard for a suicide bomber to enter any of these buses to go into any city. As I think you know, Charlie, there have been over 500 suicide bombers in Iraq in the last couple of years.

(Voice Over) So, it's certainly not hard to recruit suicide bombers.

Again, this is a very early report that there is an indication that it was a suicide bomber who carried the bomb on to the bus. Also, this same US official saying that there was a power surge, again, these are early reports and they are getting these from British officials, there was a power surge after one of the explosions on the subway, and that explosion, and then the power surge, caused two trains to collide, making things all the more worse.

Americans heard it over their breakfast. For comparison, on the *morning* of 9/11, news announcements started commenting on Osama bin Laden.

Thus on the day of July 7th , three different components of the story emerge from three different continents: from the UK's Prime Minister that the crime was done 'in the name of Islam'; from Jerusalem, that it is part of an ongoing (and inevitable) War of Civilisation, and from America that it was done by suicide bombers. Thus from Britain, Israel and America there came the imagination of the Enemy for this event.

Meyssan's view

With such comments from the British media, marching in lockstep unanimity over the issue, we suggest heeding the words of a wise Frenchman. Thierry Meyssan runs Voltaire Network, an independent French intelligence service. Its enlightening comments stand in a powerful contrast with the military-based UK 'intelligence' which continually generates war-justifying illusions to produce fear and alarm – worshippers at the shrine of Phobos and Diemos, fear and terror. A mere nine days after Sir John's comments, Meyssan perceptively wrote:

The leaders of the Coalition took advantage of the terrorist attacks in London to denounce, once more, the existence of an Islamic conspiracy and make a call to fight terrorism. However, facts speak for themselves: the operation was organized in the guise of an anti-terrorist exercise in which British public order forces were supposed to participate. Like in the 1980s, when the Anglo-Saxon secret services would organize bloody attacks in Europe to instil fear for Communism in the population, an Anglo-Saxon military group activates the strategy of tension to cause the "clash of civilizations".[11]

Concerning the polar opposite views engendered, he remarks,

For some people, the attacks in London show, once again, that the Islamists want to destroy civilization and that, since the attacks in Madrid, they are attacking Europe... For other people, including me, they are just another operation in the tension strategy conducted by the Anglo-Saxon industrial-military complex.

Concerning perceptions of the 'Al-Qaeda' Enemy, Meyssan comments:

In the absence of material elements to prove the existence of Al-Qaida, certain leaders of the Coalition have decided to define it, not as a well structured organization but as an ideology around which dispersed groups move ... Unfortunately, this reasoning has a circular nature: this hypothesis can not be confirmed as in most of the cases it has been impossible to identify the authors of the attacks and nothing is known about them at all.

Some scholars, whose investigations are vastly financed by the States of the Coalition, aver that there is an international Jihadist movement in which it is possible to recruit the perpetrators of the attacks. However, it has not been possible to prove the existence of clear links between that movement and all the attacks.[12] The main difficulty is that the attacks have nothing in common, except for the unverified communiqués claiming responsibility.

In the case of July 7th, the claim came from the unlikely-sounding 'Secret Al-Qaeda in Europe' but little more was ever heard from it. It was posted up on a Houston message board having certain connections with the Bush family.[13] Meyssan well summarises the argument of Milan Rai's (somewhat dogmatic and naïve) book about July 7th:

For those who oppose the war, the attacks are a punishment for the invasion. The Spanish and the British took the war to Baghdad and the Iraqis responded in Madrid and London. Or, as there is no evidence of any Iraqi involvement in those attacks, those attacking the capitals of the countries of the Coalition are Muslims in solidarity with the Iraqis rather.

A French view of July 7th is indeed of value:

In effect, rather than the litany of deeds of Al-Qaida, the attacks in Madrid and London remind of those in Bologna in 1980. Then, the stay-behind networks of the Atlantic Alliance, jointly headed by the United States and Great Britain, organized an attack in a train station to create political tensions that would favor a toughening of the Italian government. Of course, the stay-behind network acted behind the back of Italian authorities, using agents within the Italian secret services and recruiting perpetrators among extremist political movements.

The attacks in London coincided, in time and place, with the carrying out of an anti-terrorist exercise organized by the firm Visor Consultants. According to the testimony of the director of the firm, Peter Power, recorded by ITV and which is available in our website, those heading the exercise from the headquarters realized that the script they had planned was "truly" taking place in front of their eyes. The deployment of firemen as part of the exercise, before the explosions, explains the speed and effectiveness of the aid actions.

In other words, if the surveillance cameras did not "see" those who planted the bombs it was because they were wearing uniforms. And NATO's stay-behind network is the only one that has agents within the public order forces. The tension strategy seeks to impose the "clash of civilizations" so that Europeans support the wars of the Coalition in the Muslim world.

And, in his broken English, Meyssan added:

> In addition, the synchronization of the attacks in London with the beginning of the G-8 meeting in Scotland should alter the agendas of the summit, thus relegating issues like global warming or assistance to the development of Africa and giving priority to others topics relating to security, as it effectively happened.[14]

Shallow minds will dismiss Meyssan's words as conspiracy theory, while persons of more philosophical outlook will reflect upon the mirror-like logic we have just been through. The logic of the intelligence community is often likened to a hall of mirrors. The webs of delusion are woven, and who can tell which is real and what is merely a fabricated terror image? A historical perspective is necessary and the opus on European synthetic terror – here alluded to by Meyssan as the 'Strategy of Tension' – is *NATO's Secret Armies, Operation Gladio and Terrorism in western Europe* by Daniele Ganser. The construction of postwar terror by NATO used undercover 'stay-behind' groups predicated on 'the Reds' as the menace, and its purpose was to explain why the public had to fund the huge NATO budgets – and refrain from electing leftwing governments. The present work touches upon two such events: the bombing of Bologna railway station in 1980, and the shooting of Belgian civilians in supermarkets in 1982, the latter by way of overcoming public reluctance in Belgium over accepting Cruise missiles. After all, we would not want our readers to suppose that Meyssan's comment here cited was unfounded:

> Like in the 1980s, when the Anglo-Saxon secret services would organise bloody attacks in Europe to instill fear of Communism in the population…

The Stevens Report

Had Sir John allowed himself a bit more time to reflect before going into print with his rabble-rousing prose in *News of the World,* he might possibly have found the conclusions of his own Stevens Report upon Northern Ireland (2003) to be relevant. The third installment of this report documented the murders of some 30 Roman Catholics in Northern Ireland 1989-1990, by a special branch of British Army Intelligence. His report had been started in 1989 but its publication was hindered until 2003. Sir John described his Report as 'the largest investigation undertaken in the United Kingdom.'

'The Stevens Investigation centred on the British Army intelligence's Force Research Unit (FRU), for working in collusion with Protestant Loyalist paramilitary groups to kill Catholics' (Tarpley p101)... Stevens concluded, 'Collusion is evidenced in many ways. This ranges from the willful failure to keep records, the absence of accountability, the withholding of intelligence and evidence, through to the extreme of agents being involved in murder.' Sir John might ponder whether anything like that was happening in the July 7th case, given the Government's adamant refusal to hold anything resembling a public enquiry. The report made it evident that the FRU could never have committed such atrocities on its own, but would have required "orders from the highest level" viz the Prime minister's office, i.e., Margaret Thatcher knew what was going on.

The Stevens investigation was launched in 1989, following the murder of top Catholic lawyer Pat Finucane. Finucane's family had always insisted that the security forces were involved in his murder, and dismissed the Stevens Report as inadequate. Alex Maskey, the Lord Mayor of Belfast, commented on the Stevens Report,

> This is not about rogue elements within the British system. It is about state policy sanctioned at the highest level. (Tarpley, p.102)

Indeed. Concluded Tarpley,

> The roles of the RUC, its Special Branch, the Force Research Unit, and British army agent Brian Nelson in the murder of human rights attorney Pat Finucane and others were revealed in McPhilemy's book. McPhilemy also provided evidence implicating British domestic intelligence (MI-5) and Secret Air Services (SAS) commandos in these operations. In spite of these revelations, opinion-makers persist in pointing to Northern Ireland as a prime example of spontaneous, religiously-inspired violence requiring a colonial police power to maintain order.

Tarpley's discussion of the Stevens Report was entitled 'Terrorist Murder as British State Policy.' The absence of due legal process in the wake of this report means that corrupted elements, guilty of conspiracy to commit murder, remain in power and are open to being manipulated by virtue of having these shady secrets.[15]

....

In 2006, Lord Stevens of Kirkwhelpton (formerly, Sir John) became Chairman of the security company *Quest,* where he could have chats with Halevi.[16] We may feel concerned at the influence such a firm is exerting, to the extent to which it is operating with overtly racist enemy-images.

References

[1] COBRA is the Government's most senior crisis-management committee. It meets in 'an ultra high-tech underground command and control centre beneath the cabinet office' where a national response to an emergency is co-ordinated: Crispin Black, *7/7 The London bombs, What went wrong?* p.11

[2] The BBC's website brazenly altered this key sentence, spoken by the Prime minister, into : 'In addition, I welcome the statement put out by the Muslim Council who know that those people acted in the name of Islam but who also know that the vast and overwhelming majority of Muslims, here and abroad, are decent and law-abiding people who abhor this act of terrorism every bit as much as we do' (BBC News 7 July 2005 'In full: Blair on bomb

blasts'). Those were not the words spoken! The correct version was formerly on Downing Street's website for that day www.number10.gov.uk/output/Page7858.asp (now removed).

[3] It appeared on the website of the *Jerusalem Post* at 18.10 hours (4 o'clock London time), and was taken down a week later after comments on how its author seemed to have known too much.

[4] http://www.chomsky.info/articles/199112--02.htm.

[5] Efraim Halevi 'Ex-Mossad Chief calls for World war after London Attack ' *Jerusalem Post* 7th July.

[6] Halevi heads the Center for Strategic and Policy Studies at the Hebrew University in Jerusalem, and also belongs to the Clove Club Old Boys Association for former pupils of Hackney Downs School.

[7] CNN.com International 8th July, 'Investigators pick through London carnage', http://edition.cnn.com/2005/WORLD/europe/07/07/london.tube/.

[8] Sunday times, 'Bombers may be British', John Stevens: http://www.timesonline.co.uk/tol/news/uk/article542405.ece.

[9] 'Messages to the World The Statements of Osama Bin Laden': Ed Bruce Lawrence, Book Review By N. K http://mujca.com/kollerstrom.htm; see also, 'The last days of Bin Laden' www.911action.org/the-last-days-of-bin-laden/.

[10] The 7th July *Washington Post* reported that timers were used in the bombings.

[11] For 'strategy of tension' as the NATO 'Gladio' policy, see p. 167.

[12] Some 150 pages of Ahmed's book are occupied with this theme, of very doubtful relevance as Meyssan here points out.

[13] 'The statement, under the name of the Secret Organisation of the al-Qaida Jihad in Europe, said: "The heroic mujahideen have carried out a blessed raid in London. Britain is now burning with fear, terror and panic in its northern, southern, eastern and western quarters." It was posted on an Arabic website, al-qal3ah.com, which is registered by Qalaah Qalaah in Abu Dhabi and hosted by a server in Houston, Texas. The server in Houston has intriguing connections. Everyone's Internet was founded by brothers Robert and Roy Marsh in 1998 and by 2002 had an income of more than $30m (now about £17m). Renowned for his charitable work, Roy Marsh counts among his friends President George Bush's former sister-in-law, Sharon Bush, and the president's navy secretary.' Everyone's Internet 'also hosts a number of pornographic sites.' *The Guardian*, 9.7.05: www.guardian.co.uk/attackonlondon/story/0,16132,1524813,00.html.

[14] http://www.voltairenet.org/article30617.html 19 July 2005. His three references are: (a) "1980: Massacre in Bologna, 85 dead", *Voltaire*, March 12, 2004; (b) «Stay-behind, les réseaux d'ingérence Américains», by Thierry Meyssan, *Voltaire*, August 20, 2001; and (c) Read *9/11 Synthetic Terror* by Webster Griffin Tarpley, Progressive Press, 2005.

[15] See also *Spies, Lies and Whistleblowers, MI5, MI6 and the Shayler Affair*, Annie Machon and David Shayler, 2005, p. 61, on army intelligence involvement, and how MI5 obstructed the Stevens enquiry by withholding crucial reports concerning agents involved in the collusion.

[16] As well as being the Chair of Quest Ltd, a firm which provides private security, investigations and risk management services (http://www.quest.co.uk/, media enquiries Shimon Cohen), Lord Stevens has been appointed by Prime Minister Gordon Brown as his International Security Advisor, thereby giving a high profile to the 'war on terror.'

8. The Trail up to Leeds

On Monday, 11th of July, Thameslink handed over all its stored CCTV images for the day of July 7th to the police – for *two stations only*. The Met had requested all of the data from King's Cross and Luton Thameslink. Somehow, the Met had decided that these were the two key stations (out of the nine stations that were serviced by Thameslink). It was acquiring terabytes of info from CCTV cameras all over London, but from Thameslink it requested data only from these two.[1] In that case the police must have asked for this data from Luton earlier, maybe on Saturday the 9th, two days after the event: for we surely cannot believe that they were given all the CCTV data on the very day they asked for it. How could the Met have decided so quickly, that it needed that data from right outside of London? We might here gain the impression that it had requested this data, even before the forensic evidence had been dug up from the sites, and before the rucksacks etc. had been identified.

Then on the night of that Monday, July 11th, the police made a breakthrough, we were told, in investigating this case. Sifting though the mass of CCTV images – and one does appreciate what a lot of these there were – they finally came across the crucial images – which alas they were not at liberty to show to us, the public – of four young men *carrying rucksacks* on King's Cross underground platform.

> "On Monday night came the breakthrough police were waiting for – when the CCTV at King's Cross showed the four young men setting off in different directions." Source: *The Guardian*

This supposedly happened at 8 pm, and was a day *before* the police say they found forensic evidence and property at three of the blast sites that identified three of the men. Somehow the police had created a rough 'profile' of the terrorists as 'young men, probably in their 20s and 30s, carrying rucksacks.'

Here is an account of this decisive eureka moment:

> Yet on Monday, astonished officers made an incredible discovery. Studying the footage from a camera located high above the dark, grubby station forecourt at King's Cross they noticed, at 8:30am, 20 minutes before the three tube bombs exploded, a man matching Hussain's description. And he was not alone. With him were three other men: 22-year-old Shehzad Tanweer, 30-year-old Mohammed Siddique Khan, and Germaine Lindsay, believed to be 19. All had large military-style rucksacks on their backs, as if preparing for a few days' backpacking. (Source: *The Scotsman*)

'It was like the infantry going off to war...' reported *The Telegraph* (13th), concerning the impression which the alarming sight of those four on the platform had, allegedly, conveyed. We need to emphasise this turning-point of the investigation, this breakthrough that would lead the police up to Leeds the very next day – because, a year later, the Official Narrative would backtrack on this claim and aver that nothing special happened to the police investigation, that Monday night .... Why? It's not really our business to speculate over that question. But, it could be that the police got fed up with being asked why no one could ever see their key bit of CCTV footage.

This breakthrough was announced the next morning (12th July). At a Metropolitan police press conference, Deputy Assistant Commissioner Peter Clarke said: "We have identified CCTV footage showing the four men at King's Cross station shortly before 8.30am on that morning of July 7th." (Source: Metropolitan Police) Pertinently, Nafeez Ahmed has asked

> This is difficult to explain – how did senior police officers know to look for young men wearing rucksacks? Given the extensive evidence available to police indicating the sophistication of the operation, the use of military-grade explosives, and timing devices, as well as the abundant eyewitness testimonials that the explosion occurred from underneath the carriages rather than from bags placed upon floors, it is difficult to understand what in particular could have prompted the police to conjure up this profile.

That was not all that happened on that memorable day. Tuesday 12th July was by far the most eventful in the whole police investigation.[2] Truly, it was their all-action day and it is hard to believe how much they then accomplished.[3] The other major events were –

* Police in Leeds visited homes of suspects: early on Tuesday morning, the police search premises in the West Yorkshire area, including the homes of Khan, Tanweer and Hussain and also 18, Alexandra Grove (the 'bomb factory'). How did they get there so quickly? From identifying the four on King's Cross platform on Monday evening, to visiting all three of the homes in Leeds the next day, seems a rather sudden jump.

* Also on that day, the police succeeded in identifying altogether five bodies from the blast sites, *three of which just happened to be the 'suicide bombers'*. On one version, no DNA tests were necessary to identify them, because the suspected bombers all happened to be carrying personal documents (source: *Boston Herald*), which survived the bomb blasts. On another story, the alleged bomber Tanweer was identified by "strong forensic evidence", despite the fact that only two victims had then been identified from all four blasts.

* That evening, police raided six properties in the Leeds area: two houses in Beeston, two in Thornhill, one in Holbeck and one in Alexandra Grove, Burley, with search warrants issued under the Terrorism Act of 2000. One man was arrested. West Yorkshire police stated that a significant amount of explosive material was found in the raids and a 'controlled explosion' was carried out at one of the properties. Officers sealed off an area around Alexandra Grove in the Burley area of Leeds and evacuated about 500 people after finding substantial quantities of explosives there. The police gained entrance to the flat by means of a controlled explosion. The Headingley area next to Burley was cordoned off and hundreds of its inhabitants were herded into the Kirkstall Leisure Centre, and not allowed home for three days and nights (*LookNorth News*).

* Explosions started to happen in Luton station car-park. [In the July 7th story, 'controlled explosions' seem to be a signal to us, the public, saying 'the story has now moved up to here'.] Luton railway station was sealed off from the public and 'controlled explosions' were performed there. Explosives were reportedly found in a car parked there, hired from Luton. A total of *three controlled explosions* were carried out as bomb disposal experts and forensic teams searched the rental car. Or, that was the early version. The 'Official Account' a year later had:

The Micra is found at Luton and examined. Nine controlled explosions were carried out on material found in it.

This sounds suspiciously like destruction of vital forensic evidence, or at least it would do if we believed that the car in question had been there (see Appendix 8). We would like an explanation from the police as to what these 'controlled explosions' consisted of.

* It was revealed late on Tuesday night how a vehicle had been recovered from Luton railway station hours after four bombers struck tube trains and a bus. It was towed off to a compound at Leighton Buzzard. By Tuesday evening, Bedforshire Police, working alongside the Metropolitan Police and British Transport Police, sealed off a 100 metre cordon around the depot and began a painstaking search for evidence and explosives – as had been found in the Luton car. Also reported on Tuesday was that 'A second car was also taken away from the railway station on the day of attacks as a matter of routine.' As time went by all sorts of variations would develop on the Luton car story, too fatiguing to narrate – whether one or the other was towed away or not, when the bombs were discovered inside them, how many bombs there were, in which car the explosives were contained, what colour the cars were, and which one of them had a day parking ticket. (Source: *Leighton Buzzard Online*)

The link from Luton to Leeds was established, then, by an explosive made in a supposed 'bomb factory' at 18, Alexandra Grove, Leeds (*The Telegraph*, 13th), a substantial amount of which was then found in a parked car at Luton station. If we are being asked to believe this, then there ought to be no doubt as to what kind of chemical was used to make the bombs.[4] Instead, senior police officers remained strangely clueless as regards the kind of explosive used, as the weeks went by. The chemist, Dr el-Nashar (a graduate at Leeds University), who owned the flat in question, was *released with no charges* (i.e. presumed innocent) by the Egyptian police, after he had flown to Egypt on 4th July; nor were any requests for extradition ever made by police in the UK.

Just as the CCTV evidence was meant to link together King's Cross and Luton in the story, so likewise were the explosives meant to link Leeds to Luton. These links had a certain insubstantial quality in common: the explosive could never be produced or identified, neither could the King's Cross CCTV images! Let's hear Ahmed's calm summary of this *incoherent and inconclusive case* – where the home-made explosive was supposedly 'TATP' (triacetone triperoxide – see Appendix 9 for its chemistry):

The actual finding of TATP at the Leeds property seems to remain … forensically unsubstantiated. This is also clear from the nature of the investigation into el-Nashar, whose house was where TATP was purported to have been found. Despite being detained by Egyptian authorities for three weeks as a suspected organizer of the London bombings, and apparently wanted by British police, he was eventually released by Egypt on the basis that they 'found no evidence to link' him to the attacks. Despite the huge media fanfare stirred up by British authorities about El-Nashar, he was never interviewed by Scotland Yard invest-igators throughout the duration of his custody in Egypt. Indeed it appears that early on in the investigation – that is one week after El-Nashar's arrest in Cairo – British police already knew that El-Nashar had nothing to do with the London bombings. A senior Egyptian security source anonymously told the state-owned Al-Ahram that 'British authorities have concluded that Egyptian biochemist

Magdy Nashar was not involved in the July 7 London bombings.' But how could they have been so certain of his innocence when days earlier police claim to have found incriminating traces of TATP explosives at his house? It seems the police did not take their own allegations seriously. Indeed, several weeks later in August 2005 when Al-Nashar was eventually freed, the Associated Press noted that, 'the reports linking TATP to el-Nashar were never confirmed.' (p35)

The homemade explosive story, with acetone and hydrogen peroxide brewed up in a bath (and, don't forget the sulphuric acid), was supposed to establish the link to Leeds. But this would involve rejecting the widespread view of experts expressed in the aftermath of the event, that military-grade explosive had been used, and found at the bomb sites. What is the status of police claims to have evidence for home-brewed explosives in a Leeds bathroom? It remains, to quote Ahmed, 'deeply questionable, for reasons that are difficult to uncover'.

The time sequence is a bit out of joint in this story. The car allegedly found in Luton car-park had no label on it saying, 'from Leeds.' If on Monday evening they had seen a CCTV image of four young men carrying rucksacks, how did that get them up to Leeds the next morning? They identified the car with bombs in it on Tuesday the 12th. So a car stacked with bombs of unstable 'Mother-of-Satan' TATP explosive was supposedly left in Luton car park for nearly a week of hot summer days until the police 'discovered' that it was full of bombs. Lindsay's car parked next to it, from Aylesbury, was even found to have a gun in it, phew! Should they not have arrived in Leeds – blowing up a house wall and terrifying local residents, cordoning off and evacuating areas and generally being tough on terror – a day or so *after* they had found the explosives in the car?

Rewriting the Script

But – and this is where the whole story starts to change – the Government's Official Narrative a year later has the police only recognize the fabled 'eureka' image at King's Cross, on Tuesday lunchtime – *after* police have been searching four different homes, of Khan, Tanweer, Hussain and of 18 Alexandra Grove with its fabled bath of explosives, on Tuesday morning:

> By lunchtime, police working on the theory that there is a King's Cross link to the 3 train bombs, all being broadly equidistant from there at the time of the explosions, identify a CCTV image of 4 men with rucksacks at King's Cross. They recognize Tanweer first from a DVLA photograph. The police identify CCTV images of the same 4 at Luton.

That is all very well, and let's grant for now the right of the police to re-write their history, as if they could simply erase their earlier testimony. The reasons for the police wanting to downplay their earlier story of a CCTV linkup – between an unseeable King's Cross image of the Four and a rather clearly Photoshopped Luton image of the same Four – are evident enough. But, how then did they get up to the four allegedly-crucial homes in Leeds, on Tuesday morning? The Official Narrative gives us this sequence; see if you reckon it's enough:

> Late on July 7th: 'Cash and membership cards in the name of Siddique Khan and Mr S Tanweer had been found at Aldgate'

After suicide-bombing a train, their cash and plastic cards remained intact. [This cannot but remind us of the fabled passport that fluttered down from the Twin Towers after they had turned into a raging inferno on September 11th. Conveniently found by the FBI, it turned out to belong to one of the hijackers. But, we digress].

> 9th July: 'Police searching for clues at the bomb sites find items linked to Tanweer and further items linked to Khan... In reviewing other records, it is also found that Khan has previously been picked up on the periphery of another investigation.
>
> 10th July: Driving license and other identifying documents in the name of Hussain found at Tavistock Square.

Hasib Hussain *did not have a driving license*. He was taking driving lessons. The present writer has corresponded with Hasib's father on this matter. (Appendix 5)

Police inquiries reveal that Hussain had traveled to London with Khan and Tanweer.

> 11th July: Further information provides a possible link between Hussain and 18 Alexandra Grove.

Here the Official Report is being rather reticent about how this link was established. Later on (Para 58), we learn about this flat: 'The factory was discovered on 12 July. It was left with much of the bomb-making equipment still in place.' Greeted by this shocking information, one can only wonder as to why the owner of the flat Dr al-Nashar was let off free after being declared innocent. We may sense a problem in the highly-efficient police discerning a link between Hasib Hussain and 18 Alexandra Grove on the 11th July, when the 'bomb factory' was not 'discovered' until the next day.

Did that convince you? The problem here is that the original chronology was all rather later in time than this 'Official Report.' Let's now come back to some originally-reported events over these crucial few days:

> 13th July: 22 blast victims have had their identity confirmed.
>
> 14th July: Police publicly confirm the identity of Tanweer and Hussain. They release a picture of a young man with a rucksack, said to be Hasib Hussain and to have been taken at 07.20 at Luton train station.
>
> 15th July: Property belonging to Lindsay allegedly found at Russell Square. The property at Russell Square is found two days after police searched Lindsay's house.
>
> 16th July: The police publicly confirm the names of Khan and Lindsay. *The Sun's* headline, 'Prove it': Pregnant Samantha Lewthwaite, 22, refused to accept that Jamaican-born Lindsay Jamal, father of her child, was the fourth London bomber. She sobbed, 'He wasn't the sort of person who'd do this. I won't believe it until I see proof'.
>
> 17th July: Photo released of the 4 'bombers' Mohammad Siddique Khan, 30; Germaine Lindsay, 19; Hasib Hussain, 18; and Shahzad Tanweer, 22, were pictured in Luton at 07.22.54 BST on Thursday, 7 July. How curious that it should have taken three days longer to publish this composite photo than the one of Hasib solo at the same station.

If the police were confirming the identities of the Four over these days and establishing their presence at Luton, would they really have been up in Leeds detonating house walls etc. on Tuesday 12th? We begin to sense why the Government cannot permit a public enquiry into this event: their whole story would just fall apart too rapidly. It would become laughable. It *can only be told* through a heavy reliance upon the amnesia and sheep-like docility of journalists.

Returning to Leeds, in Dewsbury the police raided addresses at Thornhill Park Avenue and Lees Holm, belonging to Mohammed Khan and members of his family. The distraught widow of Khan, Hasina Patel, and her child—and perhaps also her mother Farida Patel—were terrorized by the police attack and it seems that they have no longer lived in that house. Maybe there was a wish here to make them inaccessible to investigators.

On Friday, 15 July, police raided the Iqra Learning Centre, an Islamic bookshop in Beeston, Leeds. Offered the key by its owner, they preferred to batter the door down and seal off the shop. Its owner, Naveed Fiaz, was arrested under anti-terror laws and taken to ten days of solitary confinement at Paddington Green. The press averred that the shop was an 'unassuming front' used to 'recruit youngsters and fill them with anti-Western messages'. The *Daily Mirror*, citing unnamed 'insiders', declared that it was a 'bookshop of hate'. For locals however, Iqra was a respected community bookstore, and alleged 'anti-Western' material seized by police was in fact anti-war literature. The suspected 'bombers' of July 7th have had no links to the shop for several years. Mohammad Siddique Khan and Shehzad Tanweer had been volunteers at the shop, but had left in late 2001 around the time of the US attack on Afghanistan. It sold things like Stop the War leaflets and DVDs of George Galloway at the US senate. Tanveer Akhtar, who works as a community youth worker in the area, said the shop was there as a knowledge base: it sold books, but also had a library service, internet access, a creche, and meeting rooms. It was open to the public and fostered community activities to promote understanding and social cohesion. It had connections with Respect and the anti-war movement. It provided anti-war information there, with copies of Socialist Worker, books like John Pilger's *The New Rulers of the World* and films like Michael Moore's 'Fahrenheit 9/11'. 'It was anti-Bush, not anti-Western,' Tanveer recalled.[5]

Mohammed Afzal works as a volunteer at Iqra. He added, 'There was a magazine with an article by John Pilger inside. It had that picture of the Palestinian boy up against the wall with his father, the one who was shot dead by Israeli soldiers moments later. The police were saying how they could 'see how this could work someone up'. They're now talking about laws against indirect incitement of terrorism. Well that could be anything. If you criticise government policy, that's it you're working people up.' Locals believe the police raid on the bookshop was orchestrated for the media. 'They had the key to the shop, but they used a battering ram to break down the door anyway and pulled the shutters off', says Mohammed. 'The media were there waiting for them, it was all done in front of the cameras.' Tanveer added, 'The police just chose to raid that shop as a publicity stunt. A guy from the bookshop was saying, here's the key, take a look, it's not a problem, but they refused. The police went in there and blew the doors off.'[6]

The author visited Leeds after the event with James Stewart and heard a similar story, of how the owner of the local-community Iqra Book Centre had been placed in ten days of solitary confinement at Paddington Green, after the police raid that smashed up his shop. Its owner would sell Korans and try to help youths to stay off drugs, we heard. The Council of Europe's anti-torture committee has reported that conditions at Paddington Green were inadequate for prolonged periods of detention.

Bombs go off in London, where the police detonate at least two 'controlled explosions' which seem to somewhat contaminate the crime scenes; then four days later, the police detonate about three in Luton; and five days later, more go off in Leeds. Had one previously heard of this method of police investigation? After the Terror struck at Edgware Road on the 7th, the police arrived and performed a little-reported 'controlled explosion.' Why did they do that? It's hard to get details, but the effect has certainly been to prevent media access to the station, in the immediate aftermath. The story was that there 'might have been' an unexploded bomb. This startling tactic was the way to deal with such a threat. The bombs up North seemed to be more theatrical, and maybe the story of the Iqra bookshop gives us a clue as to what is going on here, where the police preferred to batter down the door rather than use a key offered to them.

On the 10th, the centre of Birmingham was evacuated, and many persons forbidden to return overnight, but nothing was ever found there to warrant this.[7] On the 11th July at 4 pm, 8,000 people were evacuated from the Abbeyfield Community Festival in Sheffield by the police, after a bomb scare, just before the main music act came on – again, nothing was found. Then on the 12th in Leeds, the Headingley area was cordoned off and maybe a thousand of its inhabitants were herded into the Kirkstall Leisure Centre, and not allowed home for three days and nights.[8] These background events, which may well have faded from the reader's memory as they are supposed to, were in a general sort of way supposed to prevent citizens from doubting the reality of the terror threat – and to reassure them that they could trust their Government to take tough actions against it. But also, in a general sort of way, these were clues to indicate that the main narrative was moving up North.

The Mathematics of Improbability

I. On 12th July, the police identified three of the 'bombers' by on-site remains, when in total just five bodies had been identified.[9] There were altogether 52 civilian fatalities, from the bombs of July 7, plus an alleged extra four of the 'bombers', so how likely was that? Let us assume that, after the event, forensic investigators were equally likely to identify a 'bomber' as a non-bomber. Most persons one talks to don't take that view, on the grounds that someone setting off an explosive on their person would be much *less* identifiable afterwards and their plastic ID would be much less likely to endure, than that of their victims, who could have been some distance away. However, for the purpose of calculation let us here make an *equal-probability assumption*.

To find the answer, one constructs a 'probability-tree' having five branches – one for each body discovered. Briefly, for the first body found, the chance of it being a bomber is 4/56 and the chance of it not being so is 52/56. Then, for the first of these options, the chance of a second body found also being a bomber is 3/55, and so forth. Then, the probability comes out at

$$P = 11 \times 4 \times 3 \times 2 \times 52 \times 51 / (56 \times 55 \times 54 \times 53 \times 52) = 1 \text{ in } 8,000, \text{ approx.}$$

So, the likelihood of this situation arising by chance is rather less than one in 8,000. From this we conclude that the police reported an impossible event. They could not have done what they claimed on Tuesday, 12th July – any more than they could have identified Hussain by his driving license before he had one.

....

II. Peter Power claimed to have been conducting anti-terror drills at the *same three* tube stations as actually got targeted – on the same day, at the same time, by chance. How likely is that? There are 275 tube stations in London, and if we start by assuming that any of these could have been involved, then the sum is

$$3/275 \times 2/274 \times 1/273$$

or around one in three million. Let us suppose, for the sake of argument, that around two anti-terror drills are conducted per annum relating to the London Underground;[10] and that the event would fall on one of the 260 working days in the year, i.e. a 'terrorist' would not pick a weekend or holiday.[11] If Power picked the correct day by chance for his exercise, that adds on a further 2/260 improbability factor, making a probability of chance occurrence of one in four hundred million. Here is how Power explained how he happened to be conducting the anti-terror drill *at the same time* of day:

> ...at half-past nine this morning we were actually running an exercise for, er, over, a company of over a thousand people in London based on *simultaneous bombs going off precisely at the railway stations where it happened this morning, so I still have the hairs on the back of my neck standing upright!*[12]

The Madrid bombs went off at 07.40 am and the 9/11 plane crashes happened at 08.45, while the Bologna train bomb of 1980 went off at 10.30 am, so one could take the view that 'terrorists' are likely to choose this rush-hour time of the morning. Morning rush-hour could appear as an 'expected' period for train bombs to go off.[13] Peter Power cited a time of 9.30, about half an hour after that which was being reported. Arbitrarily, we add in a very minimal factor of two for the likelihood of this time-of-day proximity.

This gives us an overall, best-estimate of *around one in a billion*. One could argue for a reduction of this value on the grounds that outer-London stations are less likely than the central London stations to be chosen. But, that's a slippery slope, because one ought then to add in, that it is *highly* unlikely that Muslims would have chosen Edgware Road and Aldgate stations, given that these areas are renowned for having high Muslim populations. If we leave our equal-probability assumption unaltered, that gives the likelihood of Peter Power's statement at *one in a billion*.

Or, if one wishes to suppose that, say, thirty of the London tube stations could realistically have been used for such a terror-drill practice, then that still gives a likelihood of somewhat less than one in a million.[14] By any standards it's impossibly unlikely. Probability theory is concerned with equally likely events, for example the throw of dice, and cannot work with unique events. Thus, Peter Power's directing and composing the script for a BBC *Panorama* program in May 2004 for a terror-on-London-Tube program, with a similar fourfold story of explosions in three tube stations plus one vehicle on a road in central London, cannot readily be factored into the above probability computation.

Likewise, as a parallel to Power's terror-drill, top experts of the London Ambulance Service were meeting that very morning of July 7th at its headquarters to discuss a simulation of 'four terrorist bombs going off at once in central London.'[15] One assumes it was the same game-simulation.

References

[1] Letters from First Capital Direct, March 2008. They would not reply to a further question as to when they received a request for this data.

[2] Channel 4 News, Breakthrough in bomb enquiry, 12.7.05, http://www.learning. channel4.co.uk/news/articles/uk/breakthrough%20in%20bomb%20enquiry/108865

[3] The police have various Forensic Explosives Laboratories dotted around the country, however they are not (I found) prepared to release any details as regards the alleged detection of TATP.

[4] I asked Luton CCTV department for the date on which they handed over their CCTV records to the police (which they did without retaining any copy). I was advised that indeed they did have that date and would be happy to advise me of it; but that first, I had to obtain permission from Customer Relations. Customer Relations gave that permission; then finally I was told that no such record from two years ago existed, owing to the changeover from Thameslink to 'First Direct.'

[5] Anindya Bhattacharyya, 'How police seized anti-war material in raid on Leeds bookshop,' *Socialist Worker,* 6.8.05: www.socialistworker.org.uk/art.php?id=7054.

[6] Iqra Centre and Free Speech Written by Abu Abdullah on 2005-08-22 12:11:09, http://www.mpacuk.org/content/view/947/105/

[7] See Appendix 7.

[8] Source: personal testimony, plus Look North news; see Ch. 3, n.20.

[9] On the 12th July (i.e., newspapers of 13th) the five named bodies were: Susan Levy, Jamie Gordon, Hasib Hussain, Mohammed Khan and Shahzad Tanweer – whereas they had no ID of the '4th bomber' of the Piccadilly line, later identified as Germaine Lindsay.

[10] Three such exercises actually happened in 2005: 'Atlantic Blue' in April, the yearly tube practice at Tower Hill in June, and then the Visor exercise in July. The second of these is excluded from our probability computation, being on a Sunday.

[11] This point is made in the (anonymous) skeptical critique posted at 'www.911myths.com/ html/7_7_exercise_probabilities.html

[12] For Power's three main statements on this topic, see Appendix 4b.

[13] Scotland Yard was able to foresee the July 21st London bombings, as regards the date and almost the time, reported *The Mirror* on July 22nd. (Ch. 11, Ahmed, p.104)

[14] Channel 4 news discussed allegations of a high improbability in Power's July 7th remarks, on 17th July, 'Coincidence of bomb exercises,'

[15] London Ambulance Service was meeting at their headquarters to discuss a previously held simulation of "*four terrorist bombs going off at once across London.*" 9.10 am as reported by Julia Dent, chief executive of the South West Strategic Health Authority, who was in charge of the response of the National Health Service to any major disaster. 'By an extraordinary coincidence, all the experts who formulate such plans are together in a meeting at the headquarters of the London Ambulance Service – and they are discussing an exercise they ran three months previously that involved simulating four terrorist bombs going off at once across London.' Source: *The Independent* 10 July 2005.

PART II

9. The Canary Wharf Executions and Muad'dib's Story

The best-known 7/7 video, '*7/7 Ripple Effect*',[1] made by the 60-year old John Anthony Hill, was released on November 5th 2007. It suggests what may have been the doom of the four young men, who were cut down in their prime: *three anonymous alleged suicide bombers* were executed outside Canary Wharf in the morning of July 7th – an event gaining a brief coverage on the morning ITV news but never repeated, and then airbrushed out of history, to be discussed in no UK national media. While the account here presented does differ in one fundamental respect from that of the *Ripple Effect,* as we'll see later, for now we follow the *Ripple* narrative.

The four young men, in Muad's narrative, had been inveigled into Peter Power's 'mock' terror drill. This simulation of a terror attack upon London, which involved a thousand employees (as Power stated) would have needed four persons acting as the mock terrorists. The 30-year old Mohammed Khan had come to have a certain trust for the police, as indeed he "was regularly called upon by them, to help them to sort out gang-rivalry problems. Mohammed was also taken on a tour of the House of Commons by a Leeds MP, who befriended him," to quote Muad'Dib. And so the four agreed.

The four are reported as having purchased *return* tickets from Luton to King's Cross that morning, for their day-outing: however, due to the delay of all trains that morning, plus the cancellation of the 7.40 train, they arrive in London *too late* to be on the tube trains they are supposed to be on. If we suppose they caught the delayed 07.30, which actually left at 07.42, they would arrive at King's Cross Thameslink at 08.39 — way behind its scheduled arrival time of 08.04. The three tube trains they had been told to catch left King's Cross at 8.35, 8.42 and 8.48 am (and there is a walk of not much less than ten minutes to get over to these platforms). Moreover, before they separate to fulfill their roles they get to hear of the bombs going off, as mass panic starts to swirl around them at King's Cross, and the horrible truth starts to dawn upon them: they have been set up, and therefore — not being familiar with London, and with the phones not working — they try to escape via Canary Wharf. This excludes Hasib Hussain: "Hasib Hussain splits off from the other three at King's Cross Thameslink station, because he still has time to catch the number 30 bus, as his part in the mock-terror exercise."

As the remaining three gradually apprehend their dire predicament, in a city with which they are not too familiar, they make the decision to flee eastwards. Then mobile phone networks around the City largely cease to function. The question has to be asked:

> The mobile phone networks did not work in the first hours after the bombings ... Were the networks deliberately closed down? [2]

That statement was made by Rachel North, and as such it is worth a great deal, as she has been in the thick of things, and is the last person who could be suspected of endorsing the views here expressed. For one answer to her question, we could turn to a discussion on the Mayor of London's forum, "Mobile Phone Networks Access Overload Control in the aftermath of the July 7th 2005 terrorist attacks in London":

What is not acceptable is the apparent lack of coordination between the Metropolitan Police "Gold Command" who were nominally in charge of the emergency, and the City of London Police (presumably one of the "Silver Commands"), who for their own understandable reasons got the O2 mobile phone network to implent Access Overload Control (ACCOLC) , in an area of about 1 kilometer around Aldgate Tube station i.e. covering much of the City of London, in spite of the decision by Gold Command not to impose ACCOLC in the same area at the request of the London Ambulance Service. [3]

One had gained the impression that, in the wake of the bombings, London's mobile phone systems soon crashed out due to general overload. But, we here learn that what happened was rather different. The City of London Police decided to implement a procedure around the City of London which closed down mobile networks, admittedly somewhat later than the time when (in Muad's story) three of the four young men apprehended what had happened and three of them decided to flee, going Eastwards. This probably had to last an hour or so, until they were liquidated. (See also testimony of Gareth, below, concerning blockage of mobile phones; this writer had his phone not working at about 9.30 that morning, in North London.)

They are reported shot at 10.30 am, which will just about fit in with the lads emerging from King's Cross Thameslink and missing their assignments. The journey to Canary Wharf from King's Cross normally takes around one hour, 15 minutes, by bus. As to why they chose to head out East, Muad'Dib explains: "At the Canary Wharf Docklands site there are media companies, for the Muslim patsies to have told their story to and cleared their names, if they could", as well as possible escape routes. The Independent newspaper was just around the corner.

On one of the early TV news broadcasts that day, a newsreader announced that a report has come in that three of the terrorists involved in the bombings have been shot and killed by the anti-terrorist branch of the police, at Canary Wharf, in the Docklands area of London's East End. Clearly the 'suicide bombers' could not have survived the tube-train bombings, and then been in the Docklands to be shot. A story appeared in the New Zealand Herald, concerning how two 'apparent suicide bombers' were shot outside the HSBC tower at Canary Wharf in London, and a further report appeared in the *South London News*, concerning the shooting of a 'terrorist.'

Until about 11 am, the story announced concerns a 'power surge' on the London Underground.[4] That is a whole hour *after* the bus has blown up in Tavistock Square. Why keep on reporting such an odd story? Here we conjecture that those controlling the operation were not willing to risk starting the 'bomber' story, until the four 'patsies" were terminated, and not liable to speak to anyone.

An 'Operation Kratos' killing?

Why dispose of them so dramatically and publicly? One answer here would be for the same reason that De Mendezes was murdered so publicly and not bundled away somewhere first, on the 22nd July – namely, the Operation Kratos protocol. It mandates certain members of the police to kill 'suspected suicide bombers,' but quickly, because the tactic is to shoot them before they have time to detonate their (alleged) strapped-on bomb. Operation Kratos was developed with guidance from Israeli Defence Force advisers, whereby "a senior officer is on standby 24 hours a day to authorise the deployment of special armed squads, who will track and if needs be shoot dead suspected suicide bombers." It was initiated without public consultation. The protocol mandates that "a police officer should not decide to open fire unless that officer is satisfied that nothing short of opening fire could protect the officer or another person from imminent danger to life or serious injury."[5] Preferably the head has to be targeted.

Quoting from the *NZ Herald* of July 9th, "The New Zealander, who did not want to be named, said the killing of the two men wearing bombs happened at 10.30 am on Thursday (London time). Following the shooting, the 8000 workers in the 44-storey tower were told to stay away from windows and remain in the building for at least six hours, the New Zealand man said. He was not prepared to give the names of his two English colleagues, who he said witnessed the shooting from a building across the road from the tower." That sounds like a considerable degree of intimidation, when even a Reuters correspondent Down Under has to write anonymously and withhold the name of his witnesses.

The story was that the men were 'wearing bombs' – one assumes they were no more doing so than was de Mendezes, 15 days later: but, the pretext is necessary for the 'Operation Kratos' method of killing. The 'tough talk' of 8000 workers being instructed to stay indoors for the next six hours indicates that it was not just your ordinary Metropolitan police at work here. The job might involve elite killers, such as the SRR, Special Reconnaissance Regiment, a newly-formed branch of the British Armed Forces concerned with counter-terrorism. This was, it would appear, an execution of the highest importance.

The story seems to be authentic: according to the *NZ Herald*, "Canada's *Globe and Mail* newspaper reported an unconfirmed incident of police shooting a bomber outside the HSBC tower. Canadian Brendan Spinks, who works on the 18th floor of the tower, said he saw a 'massive rush of policemen' outside the building after London was rocked by the bombings." Another newspaper report tells how the police shot a suicide bomber outside the Credit Suisse First Boston Bank, approximately 470 yards away from the HSBC building. Altogether four newspapers reported the Canary Wharf killings: the *New Zealand Herald, South London News* and Canada's *Globe and Mail* Newspapers.[6]

The erasure of this story from the UK media could suggest that it has considerable importance. Muad'Dib has here put together a plausible scenario. It predicts that Hasib Hussain was really on the 91 bus (for only one or two stops) coming from King's Cross Thameslink, having separated from the others:

> Hasib Hussain was the youngest of the four, only eighteen years old, and described, by those who knew him, as a gentle giant. Therefore he was possibly the least worldly-wise, and he was also on his own, in a strange city, and a long way from home. He might not have realized he was in danger of being framed as a patsy, believed all the chaos around that part of London was just part of the mock-terrorism exercise that he was part of, and so just continued with his assigned role, which was to board a certain double-decker bus, at an appointed time, and sit at the back of the top deck.

The Government's 'Official Report' on 7/7 has Hasib Hussain get onto the 91 bus outside King's Cross Thameslink, and then change when he gets to Euston onto the 30. Muad'dib continues:

> We are told that Hasib Hussain started from King's Cross Thameslink station, and was seen on a number 91 bus traveling West along Euston Road to Euston Station, where he caught the number 30 bus, that would have then traveled East, back along Euston Road retracing his steps, back to where he started from at King's Cross, if it had not been diverted into Tavistock Square. Why would someone carrying a large, heavy backpack do that, unless he was following a script, written by someone who knew, in advance, that that particular number 30 bus, registration LX03BUF, would be diverted into Tavistock Square, and that Hasib Hussain would therefore not be able to get on it at King's Cross Thameslink, which is where he had arrived at, on the train from Luton? Only someone who is a stranger to London would do that without asking why, because it is a totally illogical thing to do. Someone who knows London, and knows that the number 30 bus goes past King's Cross Thameslink station, could have caught it there, instead. It would be a complete waste, of time, energy, money, and an unnecessary risk to take.
>
> The 91 bus, that Hasib Hussain is reported to have taken from King's Cross, along Euston Road to Euston Station, to board the number 30 bus that got diverted into Tavistock Square, actually *goes to* Tavistock Square. So, if he wanted to get to Tavistock Square, he could just have stayed on the number 91 bus, and been sure of getting directly to Tavistock Square. The number 91 bus route goes from King's Cross to Tavistock Square. That is conclusive proof that that particular number 30 bus was part of Peter Power and his customer's mock-terrorist drill, pre-rigged with explosives, like the three tube-trains, and was pre-planned to be diverted into, and blown up in, Tavistock Square, rather than blown up by a backpack bomb. Whoever planned this, obviously planned to kill Hasib Hussain with that bus explosion, so he could not tell anyone what had happened.

Here Muad'dib seems to be arguing that Hasib might really have been on the 30 bus. His story has received corroboration from the Kingston Trial of 2008, which released footage showing Hasib at King's Cross station. Some have queried whether the other three could have got to Canary Wharf by 10.30, given that the Docklands Light Railway was closed. We suggest that British police did not shoot three people dead at a busy location, but were obliged to provide cover for the 'anti-terror' group who really did it, maybe the Special Reconnaissance Regiment.

The Testimony of 'Gareth' [7]

> I was working in the main Canary Wharf building on the morning of J7. I was contracted to a mailroom and worked in the same office as the facilities people. These are the people that have the responsibility for the health and safety for the bank's employees and every office throughout London has a team of these people.
>
> In these offices is an electronic wall panel linked directly to the government, through which they can send information in case of an emergency. On the morning of 7/7, every facilities office received a message that there had been a

power surge in the London underground. This was put out, but nothing was said about any explosions. Only Sky News and the other news broadcasters reported them.

A lot of people tried to call relatives, but the phones had been jammed. After hearing about the explosions and then bus explosion, our office caught wind of snipers having shot some people at ground level outside the building next to us. We heard that the HSBC staff were being told to stay away from their windows

As time passed the facilities people asked me and a colleague to go and prepare food and water at an evacuation site the bank were paying for, as well as set up a phone line and internet connection. That was at a church in Mile End, which was over a mile away. We took a small 5-man passenger lift down to the shopping precinct under the tower. We soon found out that a section of the shops had been marked off-limits by security. The main HSBC entrance is underground where the shops that had been blocked off were. As well as being blocked off by many security personnel, they had also cut the lights so no-one could see what was happening in the area they were guarding. I thought this was strange, because there were no reports of explosions at Canary Wharf on the news.

By this time there were a lot of people at the train station, but one could only get there by following certain routes because the CW security were blocking off areas to the public, so they were being led. Anyway, me and my colleague made our way to the street and soon noticed there weren't any cars on the roads, only emergency vehicles. This was also odd.

After we left the Isle of Dogs we noticed the police had set road-blocks denying anyone access, but never said why. At this point on our journey my colleague somehow received a phone call from a friend working in the city saying that someone had been shot and killed by a sniper at CW.[8]

The CNN news story

A news report on the day (09.48 Eastern Standard Time) from CNN reported the following question being put to Brian Paddick of the Metropolitan police, as follows:

Can you tell me -- the rumors that a police sniper shot dead a suicide bomber at Canary Wharf -- do you know anything about that?" Paddick responded: "We have no reports of any police sniper shooting at anybody today." The time stamp on the CNN report indicates that the news summary was posted at 13.48 GMT

There was *no such announcement* on the UK news channels. I'm here suggesting that Brian Paddick's reply was entirely correct, and that no Metropolitan police did gun down any young men at Canary Wharf that morning – somewhat as, no Metropolitan police shot dead De Menezes two weeks later. That theme will be discussed below. I suggest that the important article 'Theorising Truth. What Happened at Canary Wharf on 7th July 2005?' by Dr Rory Ridley-Duff, Sheffield Hallam University, is correct in giving a very central, indeed pivotal, relevance to whatever happened there. (The above quote came from it) That article is, one could argue, the one serious, intellectual analysis of what happened that morning yet to appear in the UK.

One could here add, that if the young men who had arrived *too late* at King's Cross, started to panic, especially once the bombs went off and huge crowds appeared on the concourse, what would they – being unfmailar with London – do? Why, they might very well have bolted back to the station they had just got off from, viz the southbound Thameslink bound for Gatwick. If we suppose they jumped onto such a train, without any very clear idea where they were going to – and let us further suppose that a general closure of the tube system started somewhere around 9.20 am (see Timeline): it would then be a fairly easy matter, for them to change at Liverpool Street – and in a few stops would arrive at Canary Wharf.

New Support for Canary Wharf shooting

On 11th October, 2010 (the day the 7/7 Inquest began), a blogger called 'Huggles' recalled how he had been at King's Cross station when it all happened:

> I was in Kings Cross right after the Piccadilly line blast and there was no problem calling into work to tell my boss that I would be late [a propos of whether mobile phones were working]. I then went into café to wait for the hubbub to die down. Over the radio we discovered that it was more than one bomb.

> Just over an hour and a half later, there was a report on Radio 5 that some of the bombers were shot by armed response units in the Docklands. When I got home that evening, the news reports said that all the bombers died in the explosions.

Asked whether he had personally heard that Radio 5 news announcement, 'Huggles' replied:

> I heard it on the radio but when I got home and I sat in front of the TV for the rest of that evening, it was not repeated. It was in the café I heard the news report.

I put up a report on this new corroboration of the Canary Wharf showing on my website, and was startled by the large number of comments sent in, corroborating it. I suggest there is no longer any room for doubt, that media reports *around the world* described three young men being shot as terrorists in the Canary Wharf area that morning: two at 10:30 and one more at an unspecified time, maybe before 11 am, because that was when the authorities started alluding to 'bombs' having gone off.

That appears as the first news-announcement of the shooting, on the 11 o'clock Radio 5 news that morning, of this shooting of three young men at Canary Wharf in the Docklands. We need to compare this with the no less than 17 accounts of the event, that were compiled by Professor Ridley-Duff at Sheffield University, Business Studies department. This was in the wake of the BBC's 2009 Conspiracy Files programme about 7/7, and Ridley-Duff was arguing that Muad'Dib's account was the more credible. This philosophy professor saw the Canary Wharf shootings as *pivotal to the 7/7 story*. We'll also include some comments he made, about my discovery of the train delays Luton to London that morning – it's not often one gets a professional academic philosopher commenting upon the matter! We appreciate the detached language he used:

> This paper uses three different theories of truth to consider claims broadcast in two documentaries about the London bombings of 7th July 2005: *7/7 Ripple Effect* and the BBC's *Conspiracy Files: 7/7*. *7/7 Ripple Effect* argues that the alleged bombers were not in central London when the bombs exploded, and supports this with press reports of shootings at Canary Wharf. To test this claim, press reports from Canary Wharf were retrieved using a search of the Nexis UK

News Database for the period 7th to 30th July 2005. Further searches were made using Google to locate blogs and discussion forum archives from 7th July 2005.

The theory presented in *7/7 Ripple Effect* is also plausible. When deploying a coherence theory of truth, the thesis put forward by the government and BBC collapses due to low probability that four men would choose the same targets, at the same time, and on the same day as a simulated crisis management exercise organised by Visor Consultants. The thesis put forward in *7/7 Ripple Effect* remains coherent with available evidence. The theory advanced in *7/7 Ripple Effect* is better able to explain anomalies in the official account as well as the evidence of a crisis at Canary Wharf on the same day.

Ridley-Duff *tested two hypotheses:* while a number of different hypotheses regarding the events of 7/7 have been put forward, the BBC documentary *Conspiracy Files* was closest to the view that the bombings constituted "homegrown and autonomous action by four British Muslims with no mastermind". Hill's documentary argued instead that "the four men were chosen or lured in to be patsies in a classic 'false flag operation' involving one or more of the intelligence services.

An inaccuracy in the House of Commons report has become central to Hill's alternative thesis. It was later established that the 07.40 train from Luton was cancelled on 7th July. An acknowledgement of the error was made by Dr John Reid in parliament (BBC, 2006). He amended the official account to claim that the four Muslims caught a train at 07.25, which arrived at King's Cross at 08.23:

This is a considerable contradiction as the official government report which states that a Micra arrived at Luton at 6.49 and parked next to a Brava. The men are then reported to have spent 25 minutes by their cars preparing before entering the station at 7.15:

The 4 men get out of their respective cars, look in the boots of both, and appear to move items between them. They each put on rucksacks which CCTV shows are large and full. The 4 are described as looking as if they were going on a camping holiday. The 'Official Account' (Anon), 2006, p.3

The question arises how the four men could have spent 25 minutes in the car park preparing for their journey and yet be recorded on a CCTV camera near the platform 2 minutes after the CCTV camera recorded them parking a car. The question becomes more urgent as a result of the BBC documentary showing two frames of CCTV footage of the men entering Luton station. The timestamp on the CCTV images is deliberately blurred out so the viewer cannot use these images to corroborate the time that the four men entered Luton station. (Ridley-Duff, *Theorising Truth, What happened at Canary Wharf on 7th July 2005?* web-article)

Muad'Dib Radio Interview

The author of the 7/7 Ripple Effect, the best-known 7/7 'truth' documentary, was put into Wandsworth jail for four months, after being extradited from Ireland. The distinguished US 9/11 expert Jim Fetzer, a retired philosopher-of-science professor and the founder and chairman of Scholars for 9/11 Truth, interviewed John Anthony Hill ('Muad'Dib'), in June 2009. He effused about the Ripple Effect:

> perhaps the most brilliant example of documentary film-making I have ever viewed in my entire life. Once you have studied this video, which runs for less than one hour, you will have a template for understanding 9/11.

That is praise indeed – coming from an author of about thirty books, about philosophy, and also 9/11 and the Kennedy assassination.

The author of *Ripple Effect* chose the Arabic name Muad'Dib from the novel by Frank Herbert, *Dune,* made into a film in 1984, whose lead character was called Muad'Dib. The interview starts with Muad'Dib saying how he watched the events of 9/11 as they happened, back in 2001, with the plane impacting into the second Tower, and its total collapse less than an hour later; and he and his friend found that they were sharing the same thought – that it had to be a controlled demolition, otherwise it could not have collapsed so quickly.

Some years later, Muad'Dib got the urge to make a video about the London bombings that, as he put it to his American audience, 'Joe Sixpack' would be able to follow. He had watched *Mind the Gap* and *Ludicrous Diversions*, both of which knocked holes in the official story, but he felt that neither were prepared to put the whole thing together in a way that the average person in the street could understand. He made *The Ripple Effect* at home, with his friends helping him to construct it.

Ripple was described by Jim Fetzer as

> A masterpiece, wonderfully constructed, using clearly public sources, its analysis is impeccable ,.. I've never seen anything I consider to be as good as this, for a documentary. It's just amazing! ..You have completely stripped away any illusion and if anyone had any lingering doubts over the close association between Blair and Bush, and their willingness to use acts of violence against their own population…This is such brilliant critique, that every citizen of the world needs to study this video… I'm just in awe of your accomplishment … A brilliant tutorial on the planning and execution of false-flag terror.

Hey, steady on Jim!

Muad'Dib explained, as part of his story, that Reuters and a lot of the main print media were located at Canary Wharf, where the young men could tell their story; or, there was a London airport in the same location. The three may have made a very hasty decision, maybe wishing to head for the Docklands to escape. He and Jim Fetzer discussed the 'Live-8' concerts around the world, so-called because eight cities were taking part, dedicated to the forgiving of third world debt; and how this was somewhat in opposition to the G-8 policies at Gleneagles a few days later: with 7/7 sandwiched strategically in-between.

Let's have one last, affirmative quote from Mr Fetzer:

> Your study is not only a documentary masterpiece, but… Since the manipulation of a population using acts of violence or threats of acts of violence, for political purposes, is the very definition of terrorism, you have proven that the British government is using terrorism against its own people… My hope is that the

supreme court of Ireland will not allow itself to be manipulated by the British intelligence apparatus, for the sake of a political trial that is attempting to punish you for bringing the truth, to the people of the United Kingdom.

That hope was denied. Muad'Dib has been sending out copies of his DVD to anyone who might be interested, and has sent a couple of copies to the Kingston 'July 7' Trial of 2008, addressed to The Court. In January of 2009 he was arrested for doing this, immediately prior to the 'July 7th' re-trial which began in February, then released once it finished three months later. As Fetzer observed, "This is a blatantly political prosecution."

As Kevin Barrett pointed out on his US 'No lies' radio station, what Hill did is traditionally allowed and indeed encouraged as a friend-of-the-court brief, called in the UK *Amicus Curiae*. One gathers that the Jury at the Kingston 7/7 trial jury did not ever see his video. He sent a copy of it c/o the Crown Court at Kingston – citizens have traditionally been at liberty to do this for any trial under the *'Amicus curiae'* legal concept. The charge against him was "Doing an act tending and intended to pervert the course of public justice contrary to common law." By suppressing his evidence, that is what the government has done.

Amicus curiae refers to someone, not a party to a case, who volunteers to offer information on a point of law or some other aspect of the case to assist the court in deciding a matter before it. The information may be a legal opinion in the form of a brief, a testimony that has not been solicited by any of the parties, or a learned treatise on a matter that bears on the case. The decision whether to admit the information lies with the discretion of the court.

A US view: An *Amicus Curiae* brief that brings to the attention of the Court relevant matter not already brought to its attention by the parties may be of considerable help to the Court. An *amicus curiae* brief that does not serve this purpose burdens the Court, and its filing is not favored (but nor is it punished). — Rule 37(1), Rules of the Supreme Court of the U.S.

Perverting the Course of Justice?

If there was a perversion of the course of justice at all, at the Kingston re-trial of the three 7/7 'suspects,' one should ask what right the state had to a re-trial? The three lads had already been tried, the year before, in the same courtroom, over three long months (See Chapter 13) – and the Jury did not find them guilty! The jurors were not unanimous, so it was a 'hung' jury. But, the legal concept of 'double jeopardy' surely forbade trying anyone twice for the same crime. One can't have a retrial just because you don't like the jury's verdict! Recently this axiom has been modified, with a re-trial only allowed if 'substantial' new evidence turns up. What was that supposed to have been? The July 7 trial of 2009 was simply a repeat of last year's trial – at the same place, but with a different jury! After three months of that second trial, the jury decided that the three on trial were 'innocent,' so what right did they have to lock two of those young men on trial away for seven years? What was the point of the jury sitting, and taking days to reach their verdict of innocence, if the defendants were going to be found guilty anyway? The 'guilty' charge, of allegedly intending to attend a terror training camp, was pulled like a rabbit out of a hat, merely to avoid the catastrophe of HMG's complete failure to prosecute anyone credibly over the 7/7 issue

The name Muad'Dib came from the science fiction classic *Dune* by Frank Herbert, eg here:

> *Muad'Dib's teachings have become the playground of scholastics, of the superstitious and corrupt. He taught a balanced way of life, a philosophy with which a human can meet problems arising from an ever-changing universe. He said humankind is still evolving, in a process which will never end. He said this evolution moves on changing principles which are known only to eternity. How can corrupted reasoning play with such an essence?* — Words of the Mentat, Duncan Idaho (*Children of Dune*, third book of trilogy, p. 5)

Muad'Dib has been interviewed on www.richplanet.net/, As Richard Hall there observed, 'Sending proof of someone's innocence should NEVER be a crime.' On Google video *Ripple* can be watched in one piece. He released it on November 5th ('for obvious reasons': Guy Fawkes Day) in 2007. It has been translated into German, Italian and Spanish.

Mossad's Warning

I asked Muad'Dib about an interview with a Mossad boss which is described 42 minutes into *Ripple Effect*. It had Meir Dagan a former head of Mossad clearly affirming that he

personally had given a ten-minute warning to Benjamin Netanyahu before the 7/7 event. Muad'Dib replied that the German newspaper *Bild am Sonntag* had reported it; the interview had also been on the web, but was since removed. He added, 'It was an interview with Meir Dagan, a fact which has since been changed by other newspapers who reported this story to: "according to the *Bild am Sonntag*, Mossad officials state that…etc".' He reckoned it was also on Alex Jones' film "Terrorstorm".

References

[1] http://jforjustice.co.uk/77/ 7/7 Ripple Effect

[2] *Timesonline* 18.12.05, Rachel North 'The July 7th Questions that Still Haunt victims.'

[3] www.mayor-of-London.co.uk/blog/2006/06/mobile_phones_networks_access_overload_control_london_july_7th_2005.html

[4] A 'power surge' was the official story for much of that morning. But, a power surge ought merely to have blown the fuses, which would (a) have stopped the trains and (b) brought on the emergency lighting. Here is an electrician's view: "During the first hour following the blasts, the 'official version' attributed the cause of the explosion to 'an electrical power surge'. Hmm....as a qualified and experienced electrician, I cannot quite figure how a 'power surge' can lead to an explosion. Electricity does not explode, and unless the laws of the physics have once again changed ... we have a serious flaw to contend with." http://planetquo.com/7-7-The-London-Terror-Attack-Death-Of-A-Nation

[5] Feb 2005, Ahmed, p.116.

[6] South London.co.uk, 'Hidden holdall bomb' causes carnage, by Ben Ashford; New Zealand Herald, 9.7.05 'Police shot bombers' reports New Zealander.

[7] Gareth (of the West Yorkshire 911-truth movement) only posted this account in 2007 (http://westyorkshiretruth.aceboard.com/225988-9331-5906-1-ripple-effect.htm). But, Muad'Dib told me he had heard it from Gareth very soon after the event, and that it guided his *Ripple* video.

[8] Web-reports on the Canary Wharf shootings:

The ICM Computer Group located at Canary Wharf reported a 'security lockdown' at Canary Wharf, plus a report about a 'police sniper' on the roof of a building in the wharf 'looking for a confirmed threat'. Posted at 12.54 on July 7th: 'I've just had a text message from Rachel (my little Rae of Sunshine). She's in London as was called in for holiday cover at Mirror Group where she works. She is locked in Canary Wharf Tower. The police have just shot a suicide bomber. She is safe but a bit freaked out.' (http://evildrem.livejournal.com/92416.html – found by Bridget Dunne).

From the blog of 'Neil Doyle': 'How reliable is it that SO19 did kill 2 bombers and if that was the case why wasn't it officially announced? Something did go on at Canary Wharf that day, my niece's friend works there and the security was extreme. They had to leave all their cars in the car park and find alternative ways to get home. Interesting point Jon about no news, maybe the SAS shot them in which case its understandable that this was covered up.'

10. Insights from the Inquest

What Really Happened

The perfect crime had been planned. It would make history, and be the British answer to 9/11. After years of planning, it was ready to go! No-one would ever guess…

7/7 was part of the *main sequence* of terror-events which have arced across our world in the New Millenium, *extinguishing the great hopes and dreams* which the world had for the new century: 9/11 in New York, the Bali bomb of 2002, the Istanbul bomb of 2003, Madrid railway station in 2004 and then London in 2005 – followed by the Mumbai train blasts of 2006. They have served to define the new Enemy — the phantom menace – and ratify Empire.

But, two things went badly wrong, for the July 7th operation. Both of these simply came out of the blue, and were totally unexpected – almost, one could say, acts of God. The selected 7.40 Luton to London train was cancelled, and the following trains that morning were also severely delayed – so that the Four just could not get to London in time. Secondly, Mohammed Khan's beloved young wife suddenly started having pregnancy complications, and by July 5th it was clear that Khan had to pull out.

The 'handler' of the Four faced a tricky moment, having to persuade the other three – the two young men in Leeds, Tanweer and Hussain, plus Lindsay in Aylesbury – to carry on with their agreed participation in the terror-drill *without Khan.* Normally Khan was the boss amongst them, almost their leader one could say. He was older. I have found *no evidence* that Khan participated in the events of 7/7: no-one ever saw him after he took his wife to the hospital for that checkup on the 5th. But, I could never figure out how to square this with the *Ripple Effect* story, in which the Four arrived in London on that morning, to participate in Peter Power's terror drill.

People in what is loosely called the 'truth movement' had been puzzled by the absence of any credible CCTV – or human witnesses – indicating that the Four had been in London on that morning. The police kept announcing that they had lots of CCTV, but why could they not show it? Why were all the bits of CCTV they released suspicious and clearly tampered with? If the problem was that the four had arrived too late, surely the police could have adjusted the timestamps?

I was ridiculed on the BBC's *Conspiracy Files* 7/7 film (June 2009), for scepticism that the Four had arrived in London at all on that morning. No doubt I deserved it – because I was wrong! Much CCTV of Hasib Hussain pottering around King's Cross station was shown at the Inquest on October 13th and fortunately I was in attendance. The public will *never be shown* that untampered-with CCTV. I for one was finally and totally convinced, of two things: firstly, that he really had been there, wandering around in a rather lost manner for 28 minutes: that CCTV started at 8.54 and ended at 9.22 am; and secondly, that the police had no CCTV of him there before six minutes to nine, *after* the bombs had gone off: he then abruptly appeared on their CCTV screens. And they also have none of him on the way to Tavistock Square.

What happened to the 18-year old Hasib Hussain? The three places we are told he went – the MacDonald's over the road, the 91 bus, the 30 bus – all mysteriously had their

CCTV switched off or the film went missing. The film shows Hasib Hussain at King's Cross spending a while trying to phone somebody: did he finally got through to his pals who told him they were on their way to Canary Wharf, and that he should come and join them? He left the station at 9.22 am and was he then the third young man to be shot down at Canary Wharf? That's an option.

The Inquest heard what I (and fellow-researcher Kevin Boyle) felt was a quite credible testimony, from a guard at King's Cross, who had seen Germaine Lindsay and spoken to him – and I noticed how careful the Inquest was to avoid defining the time when this happened: it was sometime before the bombs went off at ten to nine.

The police could never show all of their reams of CCTV, which it was intended would be shown. Why not? Only three lads were ever in those photos, whereas a fourfold story had to be imposed upon the British public, with four explosions. In the crush of rush-hour, lots of others were milling around in the background: timestamps of the too-late Three could not ever be adjusted, because of the unpredictable way in which other commuters in the pictures would be liable to come forward. That's why the only CCTV we have been shown is of dubious origin, with images of the four on that morning artfully contrived to have no one else around.

Was Khan travelling down with Hasib Hussain and Tanweer that morning? In CCTV photos released at the Woodall Service Station on the M1, just before 5 o'clock in the morning, can one see a glimpse of him in the car? I never managed to see this: there was one other person visible in the front of the car, identifiable as Hasib Hussain. The forecourt manager of the Service Station testified at the Inquest, after taking a solemn oath, that he had only seen *one other person* in the car, besides Tanweer, (Oct 13th pm 55:5-6. References in this format are to the Inquest transcript, http://7july inquests.independent.gov.uk/hearing_transcripts/index.htm.) and I suggest that is credible.

Tanweer at Woodall Services station, July 7th

That Woodall forecourt scene is important, I suggest, as being possibly the only CCTV sequence for that day which does not appear to have been tampered with, apart from the sequence at King's Cross of Hasib Hussain solo. Even though it was only released three years later, it seems genuine enough. We see a breezy, smartly-dressed Tanweer filling up with petrol, and the Inquest duly produced his receipt, for twenty pounds for petrol (and ten pounds for crisps and munchy sweets: Oct 13th pm, 54:12-15).

The Australian ex-policeman Andrew MacGregor has kindly contributed an article 'The Fate of Khan' to the author's website. He wrote:

Mohammed Khan and his 'co-conspirators' had been hired to take part in a drill by Visor Consultants. They had no idea that they were being set up to be 'suicide-bombers'. When Mohammed Khan informed his 'minder' that he was pulling out because of his wife's condition, Mohammed Khan sealed his own death warrant. Suicide bombers never survive, even if they change their minds.

Thus ended the life of the gentleman 'Sid' Khan, the Anglicised Muslim – aid to deprived children in a special school, and known for assisting local police in peacemaking between teenage gangs. We recall that, when his wife saw him on the posthumous 'suicide bomber' video, her immediate words were, "That's not my husband".

Message from the perps?

For five years we'd been told that I.D. of Khan was found at *three* different locations: the Edgware Road, Tavistock Square and Aldgate Station blast scenes. Could the story get any sillier? Those three 'clues' seemed comparable in *meaning* to the Khan image shown at Luton at 7.22 (Chapter 6), which it is inadequate merely to describe as a bad or blurred image: it is *so* bad – with two lots or railings passing in front of him that should be behind – as well as a whole lot of impossible artefacts inserted into the image – that it looks like a message from the perps: indicating Khan/s *absence* from Luton, rather than his presence.

The Inquest managed to add a *fourth* location where Khan's ID was located: Russell Square, the Piccadilly line blast. His mobile phone was located there by the blasted carriage – complete with the (faked) text-message sent from it that morning!

So we have Her Majesty's Inquest gravely listening to the *four* different sites where ID of Khan was located: all four of the blast sites. Nobody laughs, nor does a single newspaper journalist express doubt.

We are now reaching a stage, where the main outline of the story can begin to be told.

The Jaguar at Luton

The four alleged bombers had a 'minder' who looked after them.

The Four appear as being 'patsies' hired for the day to play the part (as they understood it) of stage-prop terrorists in the 'drills' that ran on 7/7. Patsies do need to have a 'minder' or 'handler' assigned to control their behavior in line with the pre-ordained scripted events.

A clue here comes from CCTV film from Luton station and its car-park, which the Metropolitan police released back in 2008. Since then they have withdrawn it but fortunately the 'J7 Truth Campaign' team made backup copies. The crucial film now only exists as excerpts stored on the J7 site – which is in itself a rather peculiar situation.

During the Inquest, a startling if not a brilliant insight has dawned upon that intrepid J7 team, in relation to this film. This re-casts the official narrative, and indeed subverts it, giving us a real glimpse into what probably happened at Luton.

Their disclosure concerns a Jaguar, that drove up and parked in Luton station car park beside the 'bomber's' car on the morning of 7/7, having also appeared on the morning of their so-called 'dry run' on June 28th 2005 – in just the same spot. J7 are to be congratulated on this high-quality video assembly, which clearly displays the sequence.

The Jaguar pulls in beside the bombers' car and ***on both days*** the CCTV footage has been edited to exclude what could be vital evidence relating to the role of the driver of this car in the 7/7 operation. The suspicion is, of course, that this driver would be seen greeting and conversing with Khan, Tanweer and Hussain.

Not many Britons will be ready to believe in an Al-Qaeda operative driving a Jaguar.

Over the years we've heard various stories of the 'fifth man' as the 'handler' or 'mastermind' of the Four and unlikely characters have here been named (eg, the Beeston-born Haroon Rashid Aswat, who turned out to be a MI6 double-agent). That whole debate needs to go back to square one, with this new evidence indicating that a handler (the man in the Jaguar) 'managed' the Luton stage of the operation.

Exact Synchrony

There was precision in the linkup between the cars. Lindsay arrived rather early (having driven over from Aylesbury), parked – and then *nodded off.* That's one relaxed suicide bomber! At 5.56 he was fast asleep when a parking attendant slapped a parking ticket onto the front window of his Fiat Brava. That's new information that has emerged from the Inquest (Oct 11 am, 70: 7-13) – and it presents us with something that hardly resembles a suicide bomber. Lindsay then woke up and may have wandered around inside the station, before re-parking his car in another bay when the Jaguar turned up.

6.49 On the video, we see Lindsay driving into that new bay of the car park, so he comes in from under the camera, and re-parks his car.

6.52 Then there is an 88-second gap in the CCTV sequence, during which the Jaguar drives in and parks fifty yards away in the same car-park. When the CCTV re-starts, we see it there. The Jaguar is parked in the *same spot* of the car-park as it had been on the 28th.

6.52.12 A car arrives at the far-end of the car-park, which turns out to be the Nissan Micra driven down by Tanweer from Leeds. *Five seconds later,* at 6.52.17 in the misty morning, the headlights of the Jaguar switch on. *Four seconds later* at 6.52.21 it starts moving, turning round to drive back towards where the two cars are parking next to each other. Tanweer's Nissan Micra' arrives and synchronously within seconds the Jaguar starts driving round, coming towards the Four. Just as the Nissan Micra parks next to the Brava – at 6.52.38 – the CCTV cuts out. The video stops, as the Jaguar is turning round to park by the two cars.

This is a key point in the whole narrative: the two cars, from Leeds and Aylesbury, park adjacent to each other – *and the CCTV cuts out.* Why? The only sensible conclusion is that the film would show that the Jaguar then parked beside the other two cars. (That's behind them as seen from the CCTV camera, so it's hard to spot once it's there). We could here surmise that the Jaguar would be carrying the rucksacks which the Four were required to carry into town.

The Jaguar could hardly have seen and recognised Tanweer's car enter the car-park from its back window in the dim morning light. We easily see both cars from the CCTV images. This is a matter for the reader to judge. In the circumstances it is surely reasonable to infer that there had been phone communication between the two cars, prior to the entrance of Tanweer's car, to get such a close accord.

Why has the Inquest not mentioned this? Why have the police not found the number-plate of this car? Did Peter Power then own a Jaguar? Once the CCTV cut out, did he then give the three young men their bulky rucksacks which they needed?

6.54 There is a 77-second gap in the narrative. The Jaguar may have parked next to the two cars, so the three cars are together in Luton car-park. At 07.19 the Four put on rucksacks and walk away from the cars.

For comparison, on June 28th, at 8.08 the Jaguar arrives and parks, then at 8.10 the three go into Luton station.

The Official Narrative is hugely undermined by the presence of this car on both occasions, as the editors of the CCTV images well understood.

Patsies need minders. They do not understand the situation in which they are involved and their behaviour must be strictly controlled in a completely predictable way. (For comparison you might want to check out the Christmas 'Crotch bomber' story, where a smartly-dressed 'minder' escorted a silent and clueless-looking 'Mr Mutallab' onto the plane at Amsterdam airport, in 2009, despite him not having a passport.)

These young men casually sauntered towards their personal doom… oblivious, at this point, of the dark agenda they were unknowingly serving (though, hearing of Lindsay's behavior in King's Cross station, it seems that they realised their terrible plight later in the morning).

They were at Luton to catch the 7:40 train, but may have caught an 'earlier' delayed train at 7:42. The delays that held up the arrival of this train in King's Cross acted like a knife through the heart of the carefully planned Official Narrative. Instead, other more compelling and realistic possibilities begin to demand our attention.

Last Glimpse of Germaine Lindsay

Germaine Lindsay begged to speak to the Duty Manager at King's Cross – minutes before the bombs started going off on the London Undergound that morning. 'It's something very important' he added – and that was the last we ever heard from him.

Mr. Fayad Patel was employed as a customer service assistant by London Underground and was on duty at a barrier at the end of a 'gate line' near the main ticket hall in King's Cross underground station, on July 7th. Mr Patel, sometime between 08:15 and 08:45 was approached by a man he later identified as being Germaine Lindsay.

According to Mr. Patel's evidence to the Inquest, Mr. Lindsay told Mr Patel that he "wanted to speak to the "duty Manager... then later "It's something very important." Patel had earlier given this testimony in 2006 under oath, and here repeated it without change. Patel gave an equally startling and unexpected reply to Lindsay: "***Well, we're quite busy at the moment because of, obviously, with the station control.***" – The *what?*

Mr Patel described to the Inquest how delays on the Northern Line, on National Rail and perhaps elsewhere that morning meant that "the entire Tube gate line area was congested and *we'd implemented a station control to try and minimise the flow of passengers.*" This involved shutting escalators off, shutting the main entrance and exit points and then periodically opening them as and when appropriate. Therefore unusual controls were being imposed on the main concourse at King's Cross. Passengers were being delayed and, as Mr Patel says later, getting angry and "abusing" staff.

In addition, various community-support police officers were coming into the station – as Mr Patel recalled:

> Q. Do you know why they were there?
>
> A. I believe they were just passing through or they were going to a training course or something, and they heard about — and they came to help.
>
> Q. What had they heard about?
>
> A. They had just heard that there's some kind of problem or some kind of power failure or — at King's Cross.

This could well have been related to the terror-drill that morning, alluded to by Peter Power. With extra police and lockdown controls, whatever was happening was 'obvious' – according to Mr Patel's reply given to Lindsay.

So, a rap is going back and forth between Lindsay and Mr Patel:

> I asked him also, is there any particular reason why he needs to speak to a duty manager, is it okay if he just speaks to a supervisor, and he seemed quite adamant to speak to a duty manager (Inquest transcript, Oct 14th am, 67:5-9).

That is the last we ever hear of Germaine Lindsay! There is an irony here, in that Patel is not willing to disturb the Duty Manager because of the 'controls' being imposed upon the station, whereas it was precisely these 'controls' *sensed by Lindsay* which led him to make this (we may imagine) rather desperate approach.

That is the scene confronting the alleged 'suicide bomber' Lindsay as he arrives at King's Cross underground station on the morning of 7/7.

We already know from Inquest evidence given previously during the week that he arrived early in the car park at Luton station, dozed off while waiting for the others in his car and got given a parking ticket while asleep (Oct 11th am 70:12-17).

Now, inside King's Cross, he sees hordes of angry people being prevented from moving around the station and he has something "very important" to say to the station Duty Manager. (Mr Patel found it very unusual that Lindsay would use this specific term for the man in charge. Normally people ask for 'the foreman' or 'the supervisor')

One wonders what it was about the unusual situation and the angry people that disturbed Mr. Lindsay.

Perhaps he was concerned for their health and safety?

The obvious point here is that the idea of a suicide bomber wanting to approach a station manager to sort out an issue, however serious, is utterly, utterly ridiculous.

To any reasonable person this fact alone should prove that Germaine Lindsay was definitely NOT a suicide bomber.

It surely does not take much imagination to realise that any man about to die on a suicide mission is bound to be locked into his own obsessed, prayerful, demented bubble. That Lindsay should have arrived at the point where he was about to do his killing and then had second thoughts of some kind is hard to imagine. That he would want to share his concerns with an employee of the London Underground, is simply insane.

However, there is an alternative narrative that does make sense.

Lindsay arrives at King's Cross – with or without the others – to play his particular (well-paid) role in a terrorism "drill". When he gets to the main concourse he sees mayhem. There is something very unusual (to him, at least) going on. Ghastly possibilities start to unfold in his mind.

The thought occurs, "what if we are being set up to take the rap for real bombs?" He wonders what to do. He decides he will not continue with the game until he is reassured by someone who is in on the drill that there is nothing to worry about. He speaks to Mr. Patel.

Mr. Patel goes to get the Duty Manager (Lindsay knows this title from the run-throughs he and his three pals have been through with their handler). He looks again at the chaos around him. While waiting for the Duty Manager to arrive he thinks to himself, "if we are being set up why should this person be looking out for my interest? Why should I trust him, whatever he tells me?"

Germaine Lindsay deserts the drill. Unfortunately for him and the others, the special mobile phones they have been given by their handlers to communicate with each other before and during the drill can be used to track their positions at all times. Lindsay does not realise this. Nor does Khan, nor Tanweer. Lindsay uses his phone to register his alarm to the others.

They were too late for their mission anyway.

They now know there have been real explosions. Something dreadful is going on. They use the phones to meet again. They go on the run.

The information they are transmitting is being used to hunt them down...

Summarising, we have two glimpses of Germaine Lindsay that morning, both destructive of the official story: one of him quite relaxed and nodding off in his car up at Luton, the other at King's Cross when the dreadful possibilities start to dawn upon him.

The evidence here referred to was heard on the morning of Thursday 14 October 2010 at the 7/7 Inquest (in the Old Bailey).

The June 28 visit to London

An insightful comment upon the so-called 'dummy run' made on 28th June, was posted by 'Graeme' upon my website, here it is:

Confirmation at the 7/7 Inquest that MSK, Tanweer, and Germaine Lindsay visited South Kensington Underground Station on their so-called "dummy run" on 28th June is – in my opinion – the final proof that these three young men thought they were going to be involved in a terror-drill on July 7th. Now, a terror-drill has to have a starting-point and an end-point. They were told by their "handlers" that Kings Cross was going to be the former, while South Kensington would be the end point. For those not familiar with the London Underground network, all three tube lines that the men were told they would be taking on July 7th leave Kings Cross in different directions, but within 40 minutes of leaving there, the trains all meet again at South Kensington.

The three men would be told to disembark there, safe and sound, and together they would head back to Kings Cross – either on the tube, or probably some sort of van or mini-bus that would be waiting for them outside South Ken. station. It is interesting to note that testimony given by Detective Inspector Kindness at the Inquest states that the three men arrived at South Kensington on a westbound District (or Circle) Line Train, and after disembarking they crossed over to the eastbound platform and paused for a short conversation. They then descended the escalators to the Piccadilly Line and there made even more observations.

So, these young men are not planning a suicide bomb attack. There would be no need for them to make such a careful study of South Kensington Station, knowing that they would be dead at least 15 minutes before their trains ever reached there!!

Thank you Graeme.

Practice Makes Perfect

Most of us who have been paying attention have known for some time that there were two 'drill'- type events associated with the 7/7 London bombings.

The first was the *Panorama* programme of May 2004 during which one overground and three underground explosions took place over a short space of time during the morning rush hour (Chapter 3).

The second was the famous 'drill' revealed by Peter Power on the day of 7/7 itself when he said that drills were taking place in the same three stations and at the same time as the bombs actually went off.

For many, including this author, these were coincidences beyond all reason.

However, astonishingly, it has been revealed to the 7/7 Inquest, in documents presented by J7 to the court, that there were *two other separate drills* in London prior to 7/7 that used as their template the same scenario of three underground bombs.

We now have a group of public services practicing *four times* for the exact circumstances that prevailed on the terrible morning itself. Does it not eventually become reasonable to suppose that those who organised all these very similar drills also organised THE IDENTICAL EVENT ITSELF?

The media, as usual, have failed to report these staggering facts, but let us appeal to them right now. All the anomalous evidence in this Inquest points in the direction of 7/7 being a classic 'false-flag' state-sponsored attack. The evidence that supports the official narrative is dubious and much of the evidence nailing the new (twice-altered) timeline has not been seen before this Inquest.

Here is a detailed run-down of the drills:

1. The Panorama Program

BBC's Panorama programme ran what looked like a management training exercise on screen fourteen months before 7/7 – as we described back in Chapter Three. Present round the studio table were various leaders of government, public and police services, including the Conservative ex-minister Michael Portillo and Peter Power, head of Visor Consultants.

The crisis scenario had three blasts on the central London underground, around 8.20 am, and one above ground an hour later. *Panorama* also used the memorable phrase, 'The fictional day of terror unfolds through the immediacy of rolling news bringing the catastrophic attack into our living rooms;' adding – a bit too knowledgeably – that the event was 'Set in the future – but only just.'

2. The contemporaneous 7/7 drill

On 7/7 itself Peter Power conducted a terror drill that shadowed the cataclysm as it happened – over the same three tube stations at more or less the same time. He was interviewed on the afternoon of 7/7 on Radio 5's Drivetime programme:

> Mr Power: At half-past nine this morning we were actually running an exercise for, er, over, a company of over a thousand people in London based on *simultaneous bombs going off precisely at the railway stations where it happened this morning, so I still have the hairs on the back of my neck standing upright!* ... And we had a room full of crisis managers, for the first time they'd met, and so *within five minutes* we made a pretty rapid decision, 'this is the real one' and so we went through the correct drills of activating crisis management procedures to jump from 'slow time' to 'quick time' thinking and so on.

We here note the exactness of the synchrony, within five minutes. A few days later, Power flew to Toronto to attend a world conference on disaster management! He there gave an interview with the Canadian Broadcasting Association. In the middle of his terror-drill, he explained, they had "to stop the exercise and go into real time." It worked very well, "although **there were a few seconds when the audience didn't realise whether it was real or not.**" Here the synchrony is given as being, to within seconds.

3. Atlantic Blue

The massive-but-totally-secret *Atlantic Blue* exercise was held over 5-8 April, 2005 (See Chapter Three). All echelons of government participated in this big, international terror-drill. Walking wounded were taken into hospitals etc, and it's difficult to ascertain how far this was really happening on the pavement, versus being on a video screen. Two thousand Met police were involved, plus 14 different government departments, such as the NHS. It involved terrorist attacks upon UK transport networks that *coincided with a major international summit.* Visor Consultants were involved, in co-ordination with the US department of Homeland Security. It was run from Hendon, the same place that

'Gold Command' police acted from once 7/7 started to happen (It thus had a connection with the Northern line of the London Underground). Total secrecy was imposed upon the British media. *The Observer* was able to publish a brief outline of what had happened in the UK's Atlantic Blue exercise, but only from Washington sources: it revealed that this had been the biggest transatlantic counter-terrorism exercise since 9/11, and that it included bombs being placed on buses and also explosives left on the London underground.

After July 7th, *the Independent,* carried out an hour-by-hour analysis of the catastrophe, and made the following comment upon what had happened at 9.10 am:

> By an extraordinary coincidence, all the experts who formulate such plans are together in a meeting at the headquarters of the London Ambulance Service – and they are discussing an exercise they ran three months ago that involved simulating four terrorist bombs going off at once across London.

What a surprise! The top London Ambulance Service experts were all gathered together on the morning of 7/7, and they just happened to be reminiscing about a game-simulation they had been involved in three months earlier – i.e., Atlantic Blue. We would like to be told exactly *when* the four mock-bombs went off, during the Atlantic Blue terror-game.

London's mayor Ken Livingstone was over in Singapore on the day of 7/7 – to celebrate Britain's being awarded the Olympic Games for 2012, the day before. In giving his evidence to the July 7th Review Committee, he recalled the *Atlantic Blue* exercise a few months earlier:

> I said from Singapore that we had actually done an exercise of multiple bomb attacks on the Underground as one of the exercises...

That is almost the only British statement about *Atlantic Blue*! America and Canada also participated in the event, which overall was called 'Global Shield.' The US exercise was called TOPOFF3. (alluding to Top Officers, and the third such event) The latter had an intriguing 'Red Team' which generated the 'enemy' simulation...

4. Operation Hanover

London's police hold a little-known yearly terror-drill practice, called *Operation Hanover.* In 2005 it just happened to be held on 1-2 July. Well, fancy that. Its game-plan was threefold: three 'simultaneous' bomb attacks on three underground stations. The police have been reticent about discussing this astounding precursor event, mere days before 7/7 – only revealing it in 2009:

> The Metropolitan Police Service told the Committee that they had, in the past, run exercises with scenarios similar to what actually happened on 7 July 2005. Since 2003, they have run an annual exercise known as Operation HANOVER which develops different scenarios for attacks on London and rehearses how the Metropolitan Police Service would respond. By coincidence, their 2005 exercise, run by the Security Co-ordinator's office in the Anti-Terrorist Branch, took place just a few days before the attacks – on 1–2 July. The office-based scenario for this exercise was simultaneous bomb attacks on three London Underground trains at Embankment, Waterloo and St James's Park stations. Once again, the scenario is

quite similar to what actually took place, and the fact that it took place so close to the actual attacks is an interesting coincidence.*

Questions: had the 7/7 Inquest wanted to find out the *cause of death* of 52 Londoners, then I suggest that the most important questions which Lady Justice Hallett could have asked the Met, concerned these four terror-drills:

1. Concerning the *Panorama* program, from where did the producers of the program get the idea?

2. Concerning the *Atlantic Blue* terror-drill: What were the times and locations of the four bombs in the 'game'? Were they three on tubes and one on a bus? We would also like full disclosure concerning the whole event.

3. Likewise for *Operation Hanover*, let the Met state times and locations of the tube bombs in the exercise.

4. Likewise Peter Power should be asked for the exact times and locations of the four bombs imagined in the Visor terror-drill that morning.

The 'coincidences' we have here looked at go astronomically beyond what is feasible. These impossible coincidences point to the startling fact that these terror-drill rehearsals **are *the design of the 7/7 event itself.*** Most of the participants were doubtless quite unaware of this. The gestation of the 7/7 event was via this sequence of drills we have just reviewed.

Peter Power and the "Gennifer Flowers" defence

There was much head-scratching as to why a participant at the very centre of the 7/7 drills would decide to 'go public' about these exercises, immediately, on that same day.

Gennifer Flowers came forward during Bill Clinton's 1992 presidential Campaign alleging that she had had a twelve-year relationship with him. There were rumours (at the very least) that some of Clinton's ex-lovers were proving to be very 'unlucky' young women. It was widely speculated that Flowers decided to 'get it out there' so that any future accident that might befall her would act against, rather than in favour of, the Clinton interests. She was, it seems, very interested in staying alive.

Likewise, this is the most obvious explanation for Power's seeming "faux-pas". He knew he held very dangerous information, and feared this made him a possible target of the dark forces of the state... and this is a man who really understands just how dark those forces can be... so he got the facts out there, pronto!

---

* From the Government's Intelligence & Security Committee 2009 Report, 'Could 7/7 have been Prevented?' That oddly enough went offline just after I posted this quote up on my website in October 2009. The sole online reference (I believe) is now the J7 submission to the Inquest. It is in the 5th volume or chapter of their submissions, scroll down to "Hanover series:"   www.julyseventh.co.uk/J7-Inquest-Submission/05. Explosions_Immediate_Aftermath.pdf

Role of the SRR: Perpetrators of the London bombings?

One month before the BBC's *Panorama* program, which scripted the first outline of what London would suffer a year later on 7/7, the British army formed its brand-new Special Reconnaissance Regiment, or at least announced it. On April 5th, 2004, Defence Secretary Geoff Hoon explained that, as part of the British army's 'Special Forces', it would focus on 'combating terrorism'. It would go 'deep undercover' for its reconnaissance, behind 'enemy' lines.

On April 6, 2005, the SRR came into existence, a mere three months before 7/7. It appears as a secretive organisation above the law, with a license to kill – and with bomb making skills. Its insignia shows a sword being shoved up through a helmeted head.

Let's take a closer look at the little that has come out. Our main areas of concern are:

- The assassination of Jean Charles de Menezes

- The gunning down of two young men as 'terrorists' at Canary Wharf at 10.30 am on July 7th

- The fabrication of bomb equipment in Basra

- The startling rescue of SRR agents once captured in Basra.

Here is an Irish view:

By May 2005 another of the British military intelligence units involved in the 'dirty war' in Northern Ireland – the 14th Intelligence Company – nicknamed the '14th' or 'the Det'- was renamed the Special Reconnaissance Regiment (SRR) responsible for 'counter-terrorism' operations in Iraq and the UK. Brigadier Gordon Kerr was appointed the head of the SRR. All retain immunity from prosecution – this time that held by all coalition troops in Iraq at the demand of the Bush administration as occupying power.

True to old form in Northern Ireland we now know that the SRR have already been involved in getting at least one more innocent person killed. On the day that the Brazilian Jean Charles De Menezes was killed by armed police in the London underground, at least one member of the Special Reconnaissance Regiment was the man who wrongly identified him as possibly being one of the July the 7th bombers. The government and the Metropolitan Police have refused to answer questions about whether more than one member of the SRR was involved in the surveillance team following Menezes. (source: duncanmcfarlane.org)

The Scotsman newspaper also reported that the two SAS men arrested by Iraqi police last August for allegedly driving around with automatic weapons and bomb-making equipment were also under the command of the SRR – which would also put them under the command of Brigadier Gordon Kerr as head of that unit.'

Here is a socialist view:

> Members of military intelligence from the Special Reconnaissance Regiment (SRR) carried out the flawed surveillance of Jean Charles de Menezes. The SRR ran death squads in Iraq, targeting supporters of the resistance to the US-British occupation of that country. When the SRR was formed in 2005, it incorporated a secret unit of the British army that had supplied names, addresses and photographs of Catholic targets to Loyalist paramilitaries in Northern Ireland.

So it employed trained killers and bomb-makers from its inception – three months before 7/7.

Those seconded into the SRR had *sophisticated bomb-making technology*:

> According to investigators examining past collusion between the security forces and paramilitaries in Northern Ireland, members of the shadowy army undercover outfit, the Force Research Unit, and officers from MI5 learned in the early 1990s that a senior IRA member in south Armagh was working to develop bombs triggered by light beams. They decided the risks would be diminished if they knew what technology was being used.

> "The thinking of the security forces was that if they were intimate with the technology, then they could develop counter-measures, thereby staying one step ahead of the IRA," a senior source close to the inquiry explained. "It may seem absurd that the security services were supplying technology to the IRA, but the strategy was sound."

The Identity of De Menezes' Assassins: Even *Wikipedia* comments on the involvement of the SRR in the Charles de Menezes assassination: "On 22 July 2005 Jean Charles de Menezes was shot dead by armed police officers on the London Underground rail system, at Stockwell tube station. Three media reports carry assertions by unattributed UK government sources that SRR personnel were involved in the intelligence collection effort leading to the shooting and on the tube train whilst the offensive action occurred."

We should doubt Wiki's view that police shot de Menezes. The Met were evidently distressed (I would say) at not being able to deny responsibility, even though such a mode of killing was quite foreign to their practice. The British police are not into shooting seven dum-dum bullets slowly into the back of the head of a totally innocent man pinned to the ground. But they had to shoulder the blame, because the killers were immune from public scrutiny.

Here is *The Times* drawing attention to the real assassins of De Menezes:-

> Press photographs of members of the armed response team taken in the immediate aftermath of the killing show at least one man carrying a special forces weapon that is not issued to SO19, the Metropolitan police firearms unit. The man, wearing civilian clothes with a blue cap marked "Police", was carrying a specially modified Heckler & Koch G3K rifle with a shortened barrel and a butt from a PSG-1 sniper rifle fitted to it — a combination used by the SAS. Another man, dressed in a T-shirt, jeans and trainers, was carrying a Heckler & Koch G36C. Although this weapon is used on occasion by SO19, it appears to be fitted

with a target illuminator purchased as an "urgent operational requirement" for UK special forces involved in the war on terror. (31 July 2005)

The Express made a similar comment, about a photo taken just after the event:

> The picture, along with several others, was taken outside Jean Charles's home in a block of flats in Scotia Road, Tulse Hill, and shows several men who appear to be carrying SAS weapons and wearing military issue clothing. The man in the blue check shirt wore a helmet with a green SSR tag on the side. It is believed this means he was part of the Special Reconnaissance Regiment, based next to the SAS HQ in Hereford.

Turning to the Canary Wharf shootings on July 7th 2005, at a press conference that afternoon, senior police officer Brian Paddick was asked, "Can you tell me — the rumors that a police sniper shot dead a suicide bomber at Canary Wharf. Do you know anything about that?" and he replied, "We have no reports of any police sniper shooting at anybody today." That was true, because it was a different group, not the police, who fired the shots: and we are surmising that it may have been the FRR.

Basra, September 19, 2005

"Iraqi police sources in Basra told the BBC the 'two British men were arrested after failing to stop at a checkpoint. There was an exchange of gunfire. The men were wearing traditional Arab clothing, and when the police eventually stopped them, they said they found explosives and weapons in their car. It's widely believed the two British servicemen were operating undercover."

"Iraqi leader, Fattah al-Sheikh said that police had 'caught two non-Iraqis, who seem to be Britons and were in a car of the Cressida type. It was a booby-trapped car laden with ammunition and was meant to explode in the centre of the city of Basra." (BBC Radio 4, 9/20/05) Who were these people? Quoting from *The Scotsman:*

> British defence sources told the Scotsman (9/20/05) that the soldiers were part of an "undercover special forces detachment" set up this year to "bridge the intelligence void" in Basra, drawing on "special forces" experience in Northern Ireland and Aden, where British troops went "deep" undercover in local communities to try to break the code of silence against foreign forces.

That *raison d'etre* is lacking in credibility, because the Northern Ireland and Aden operations ended long ago. The elite forces operating under the Special Reconnaissance Regiment were formed by then defence secretary, Geoff Hoon, "to gather human intelligence during counter-terrorist missions."

The Scotsman added, rather crucially: "This is the same Regiment that was involved in the unlawful July 22 execution – multiple head-shots – of the innocent Brazilian, Mr. Jean Charles de Menezes, after he boarded a tube train in Stockwell Underground station." That was a well-informed source speaking to *The Scotsman.*

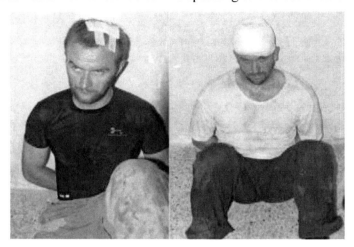

Nafeez Ahmed commented on the Basra episode,

> A glance at the Special Reconnaissance Regiment gives a more concrete idea of the sort of operations these two British soldiers were involved in. The Regiment, formed recently, is "modelled on an undercover unit that operated in Northern Ireland", according to Whitehall sources. The Regiment had "absorbed the 14th Intelligence Company, known as '14 Int,' a plainclothes unit set up to gather intelligence covertly on suspect terrorists in Northern Ireland. Its recruits are trained by the SAS." (Ahmed Blog 4.10.05, 'Caught red-handed: British Undercover operatives in Iraq')

After the SRR killers had their cover blown, what happened? They were rescued, in a spectacular manner, as British forces used *up to **10 tanks supported by helicopters** to smash through the walls of the jail* and free the two British Servicemen.

The SAS were made to shoulder the blame. Why was it so vital to rescue the guilty men *and* to cover their identity by blaming the SAS? Why have we since heard nothing, not even the names of the persons arrested? There must have been something awful that the two bomb-makers could have blurted out, had they not been rescued. Normally, undercover agents know that they will be abandoned to their fate if caught, and do not expect to be rescued.

Captain Ken Masters, commander of the Royal Military Police's Special Investigations Branch in Iraq, was charged with investigating allegations of mistreatment of Iraqi civilians by British soldiers. While attempting to investigate the "rescue" of the FRR members, he was found hung in his military accommodation in Basra on October 15. Reports indicate that he had displayed no signs of stress or illness and that no suicide notes were found at the scene. Following this, there was no government enquiry, no questions in the House, nor did anybody go to jail.

What bunch of killers could have such power?

Through the Looking-Glass

For the SRR to go 'deep undercover' behind the 'enemy' lines might have made a grain of sense in Northern Ireland (perhaps "the troubles" were a pretext contrived from London to hold onto the colony in the first place), but when applied to Al-Qaeda the situation is very different. Al-Qaeda does not as such exist, it is the 'phantom menace.' Its primary characteristic is *non-existence!* Its image has been nurtured and developed since the late '90s by the FBI and MI6. For an excellent treatment of this theme, see the "Power of Nightmares" video by Adam Curtis, that was broadcast on BBC4. If ethically challenged operatives, not so say killer thugs, are given a mandate to go 'deep undercover' etc, what is going to happen? Are they not going to go *right through the looking-glass* and end up as being themselves, 'the enemy'? It is the "anti-terror" militia who create the false-flag terror events: that is the frightful reality and paradox of our new millennium.

Look at Bali, in 2002, or at Madrid 2004 when the big NATO anti-terror drill of March 4-10th culminated so to speak in the railway-station explosions of 11th March. What NATO had drilled for in several European capital cities, then happened, on cue.

In the months prior to 7/7, Warner Brothers were filming in the London Underground for their smash hit, "V for Vendetta." We here hypothesize that the FRR were responsible for planting the bombs on the London Underground, in which they would have had assistance from US agents planted as film crew. That film featured a tube train primed to explode. It was due to open later in 2005, but its release had to be postponed as its theme was too similar to the 7/7 event. Its filming ended in June, 2005. Its photography coordinator died mysteriously and unexpectedly in December, prior to the release.

Acknowledgement: The case here presented has come about through discussions with retired Australian policeman Andrew McGregor. I have basically applied his suggestions and insights.

What Went Bang?

What ripped apart the train coaches on July 7th, leaving splattered blood, loose limbs, twisted steel and derailed coaches? Can the British public really be so gullible as to believe the government's story about peroxide (boiled up in a saucepan) and black pepper?

The 7/7 Inquest has been hearing from forensic experts who are prepared to swear on oath and keep a straight face while discussing how a hitherto unheard-of mix of black pepper and hydrogen peroxide blew up trains and a bus on July 7th, 2005. (Earlier, in 2008, senior government analyst Clifford Todd had previously told the Kingston July 7th trial that the devices were 'unique in the UK and possibly in the whole world' because no-one had heard of this explosive being used before[12] and he reiterated this at the Inquest (Feb 1,pm, 67:1-4). (Footnotes are numbered here in chronological order.)

Concerning the Tavistock Square blast, the Inquest was told:

Chemical analysis of the debris suggests that the main charge used did not consist of any previously seen compositions... In the absence of chemical traces of other high performance military explosives and based on the physical damage done to the bus, it is not unreasonable to reach the conclusion that the main explosive charge consisted of a novel, improvised material previously unseen by this laboratory. (Feb 2 am, 56:14-19)

by Kim Simpson, at the Government's Forensic Explosives Laboratory at Sevenoaks. Thus, after extensive laboratory analysis and detective-work, a professional forensic analyst could not say what exploded – it was something unknown to her laboratory. But, she did claim to have detected a trace of 'piperine' in the bus (found in black pepper), and she conjectured: "The main charge was most probably a novel mixture comprising concentrated hydrogen peroxide together with additional compounds, which may have included a piperine-containing ingredient." (2 Feb am 59:6-9)

At the Inquest, no government expert ever affirmed that a mix of black pepper and peroxide would go bang. Instead, five years after the event, we were merely told that the explosive was 'most probably a novel mixture.'

At Russell Square, 'none was found, no traces of HMTD or TATP or, indeed, any other explosive was found'. (48: 21-23 Feb 1st pm) (55:12-14) 'At Russell Square, no parts of an initiator were found and, as you said earlier, neither were any traces of HMTD' – barrister Hugo Keith.

At Edgware Road, 'the standard test for organic explosives proved to be negative (51:21-22)... and in no case did we find any (52:10-11) trace of conventional high explosives'.

At Aldgate: Q: There were analyses carried out as to whether or not the piperine substance could be found at the scene, but were your conclusions inconclusive in that regard? A: That's right, we tried to see if we could find that and, in the end, we weren't successful, so we couldn't draw any conclusion from that. (51:20-25)

We'd all been told – or thought we had – that the explosive brewed up by the 'suicide bombers' had been found in the car in Luton car-park, and also in the bath at Alexandra Grove, Beeston. If so, there would have been ample opportunity to analyse it. The Inquest did not hear of any chemical analysis here performed, which identified what had gone bang! Had those compounds really existed then we would surely have had their chemical composition analysed – and reported. The conjectured explosive used would not have kept mutating over the years as if new fashions could replace the old. If perchance a peroxide-based explosive had been found, then the one analytic detail we'd require to be told is its percent concentration.

The Inquest did hear Mr Todd affirm that: 'Our first analysis on some materials from Alexandra Grove showed us the presence of a material called piperine. It later transpires that that is simply something that is contained within black pepper.' So, they found some black pepper. But also, it heard of 'the detonator' as a white powder being identified:

Q: 'Did you undertake investigation of what that white powder was?

A. We did, and that was HMTD, which is a particular — a very sensitive high explosive, it can be manufactured relatively easily from readily available materials. – Cliffod Todd (Feb 1st pm, 40: 8-12)

HMTD is a very unstable explosive, detonated by many things including friction.

How TATP just faded away: 2005 – 2007

Within a week after event, experts were averring that a volatile substance called TATP had blown up the trains, and was therefore what the four young men had carried down south in their rucksacks. TATP (Tri-acetone tri-peroxide) is white. It was in the bath, newspapers reported[6]. Also, it had been left behind in the car park at Luton.

'Preliminary analysis' had found 'traces of TATP' both at the site in Leeds (reported the prestigious Jane's Defence Weekly, on 22nd July, 2005[8]) and at the sites of the explosions: that analysis linked together the London bombs with the Leeds plotters. Military experts around the world would have read this. On 26th July, ABC News from America released a sequence of images of what had, it claimed, been found in the Luton car-park. They clearly showed a white substance[9].

The TATP story lasted for three years. By the time of the 2008 Kingston trial, that story had vanished without a trace – just like TATP evaporating on a summer's day.

If we go back to the 'Official Report' of 2006 on the London bombings, the Home Office's official narrative, all it told us concerning the ingredients, one year after the event, was: 'Forensic analysis of material taken from Alexandra Grove continues' – i.e., it was not prepared to comment on what explosives might have been found there. Three years later, Andy Hayman's book *'The Terrorist Hunters'* – impounded upon publication on a High Court order, on the grounds that it disclosed 'too much' – merely said that on July 12th a 'thick bubbling yellow liquid' was found in the bath at Alexandra Grove with an 'unbearable rotting stench' and no hint as to what it was: pure school pantomime.

At the so-called 'bomb factory at 18, Alexandra Grove in Leeds, pictures of the bath has been shown, at the Inquest, containing some sandy compound.

Clifford Todd stated on oath, concerning the explosives found, that he there found two types of brown sludge, one darker and not explosive, and 'the lighter, sandy-coloured material, that was shown, in at least one specific case, to be a high explosive.' (39:25 Feb 1, pm) We waited for the barrister to ask him of what the high explosive was made – but, he didn't. He never said that his lab had analysed an explosive made of peroxide and black pepper.

Were kilograms of black pepper indeed purchased?

Q. Some of the witnesses who searched at the flat describe the smell and odour that was there, a bleach-like odour, is that right?

A. Yes.

Q. And a pepper smell from — clearly from the many bags of pepper that were used?

Does anyone really believe this?

The Early Story

The TATP story replaced the early accounts from real forensic experts who found that traces of military explosive 'C4' had been found at the crime scenes[2,3,4] plus evidence of timed detonators [1] – i.e there would have been no suicide bombers because the military explosive (made in NATO laboratories and definitely not in a bath in Leeds) was exploded by timed detonators. The latter would explain why the three tube blasts went off within 52 seconds of each other. That story lasted about a week, then unaccountably faded away once the Leeds suicide-bomber story developed[5].

Maybe the police got tired of being asked how four young men with no known interest in chemistry or bomb-making could have mixed together strong sulphuric acid, acetone and strong hydrogen peroxide very slowly in a refrigerated fume-cupboard, to make the TATP. The great advantage of TATP was that it transformed upon detonation entirely into gases without burning, so it left no residue, it was pure blast with no heat or light – so no-one could expect to find traces of it around the crime scenes.

Once the 7/7 trial came along in the summer of 2008, all trace of the TATP story had gone – to be replaced by the joke about black pepper. Like the zombie programmed characters in the film *The Matrix,* none of the British media objected. A proper detective agency would have wanted a chemical analysis of what was claimed as an explosive, whether in a car in Luton car-park or a bath in Alexandra grove – signed by a professional chemist, and stating what was found. That is what is here notably lacking. A proper detective agency would need info about the blast pressure ratio which experts infer from the crime scene, because different types of explosive create a more or less intense shock wave upon detonation. It's not rocket science.

We might at least have expected *The Observer* to register some perturbation, after all on July the 17th it had reported that 22 lbs of TATP (tri-acetone tri-peroxide) had been found in the said bath at Alexandra Grove[6]. Did that just fade away like a dream? It seems so. TATP is quite volatile, in the heat of the summer it would tend to evaporate, which was presumably the point of the ice cubes the Four were meant to have taken with them – so we would expect any TATP made to be stored in the fridge not left in a bath.

You don't need a degree in chemistry to figure out that buying 30% peroxide from a 'hydroponics' shop will not enable you to concentrate it to an explosive level. 90% peroxide may be rocket fuel, but can you make it? Only a British journalist would believe that boiling 'liquid oxygen growth promoter' in a saucepan will concentrate it up an explosive-blast level. Quite the contrary: in fact one is more likely to concentrate the peroxide by freezing, where water will freeze out before the peroxide –but, that has never been a part of the narrative: pans and heaters were shown scattered around at Alexandra Grove, not fridges. Even 50% peroxide is not explosive, it *won't go bang.*

Let's have a quote from the laugh-a-minute script:

> Clifford Todd (principal forensic investigator at the Forensic Explosives Laboratory, part of the Defence science and technology lab in Sevenoaks): so what you need to do is concentrate that hydrogen peroxide and you need a method to know when it's concentrated enough, and that's what I believe those

calculations referred to, how they were going to determine when they'd concentrated it sufficiently.

Hugo Keith: Hence the sensitivity of a revelation of that particular detail into the public domain?

Todd : Correct, yes. (para 42, pm 1st Feb)

Voila! The key, central issue where the entire government case would fall apart is – too sensitive, and cannot be discussed. The actual method of such concentration – low-pressure fractional distillation (which will work if you have a pure solution of hydrogen peroxide to start with) – and its total non-accessability to the young alleged bombers, and their incompetence to operate such a process, would indeed be a 'revelation' as Hugo Keith indicated, which would be against the interests of the state to release into the public domain. Moreover even if they had by some miracle managed to achieve it, they would have no way of knowing that they had done so: short of trial explosions – which not even the most mendacious neighbour of Alexandra Grove flat has claimed to have heard – there is no way the Four could have known whether the peroxide they had brewed up would go bang or just phut.

The above quote by Mr Todd continues, 'The calculations that we did see on a particular piece of paper appeared to relate to the density of hydrogen peroxide...' (Feb 1, 41:24-25)' Au contraire, to ascertain the strength of peroxide one has to find its specific gravity, an A-level chemistry operation involving exact weight and volume measurements, where no trace of the required apparatus was hinted at in the Alexandra Grove photographs.

Will it go bang?

Hugo Keith: 'Obviously the saucepans were used in the actual bomb-making process.' (18:2) I suggest British anti-terror prosecutions should first be obliged to show they can get a bang out of the unlikely shop-purchased materials they are alleging were used, before wasting tens of millions of taxpayers' money. Let them be given a saucepan, hair-bleach (or, more recently, 'liquid oxygen' from a hydroponics shop) and black pepper. If they can't get a decent bang, then they should stop wasting our time with any more huge fake-terror trials.

'The bombers used respirators because the hydrogen peroxide gave off noxious fumes as it was boiled down, blistering paint work and killing plants outside one of the ground-floor flat's windows,' explained Dc Richard Reynolds, of the Metropolitan Police's SO15 counter-terrorism command, to the Inquest No, Mr Reynolds: boiling peroxide may liberate oxygen, plus water vapour, but that is all. The 'noxious fumes' story is a hangover from the earlier TATP narrative which faded without a trace three years ago – its synthesis would indeed have produced frightful smells, requiring a fume cupboard and fridge.

The main identification of explosive at the Inquest, was of the 'detonator' HTMD which kept being found on clothing that supposedly belonged to the Four, and on the floor of the Nissan Micra car, Tanweer's wallet, etc.

It strains our credulity that the flat never exploded. TATP, HTMD, peroxide being boiled – any one of these blowing up would have detonated all the others.

We are being given an analogy with the 21/7 'bombers,' who two weeks after 7/7 mixed chappati flour with peroxide. But, those 'bombs' just went phut – they did not 'fail to explode' as reported through the British media, they did all they ever could have done. However effective the detonator, that is all those 'bombs' could have done. Government reports on that event never cite the one thing that matters namely the concentration of hydrogen peroxide mixed with the chappati flour. Optimistically we might suppose that it was say, 40% – that somehow, Muktar Said Abraham and his co-plotters managed to get that far by boiling their shop peroxide.

There can be no comparison between the bombs used on 21st July 2005 which went phut and created fear (not terror) within the small circles that noticed them – and, the terrible shattering blasts two weeks earlier. Nobody capable of rational thought could suppose that the bombs were similar. I do not claim to know what blew apart the coaches that morning; but,. I really wish the people of London would apply their considerable collective intelligence to answering the question. To do that they would first have to cease believing the government's Fairy Tale from Hell.

Is Magdy Al-Nashar still alive?

Egyptian chemist Al-Nashar was renting the flat at 18, Alexandra Grove from a housing co-op. He had just completed his biochemistry PhD at Leeds, and flew out to Cairo on 4th July 2005 – with a return ticket, booked for August 12th. The Met must be very confident that he is not going to return, or he might have some comments on the state of his flat as depicted at the Inquest. He was flying out to thank the Egyptian institution which had funded his PhD. When arrested in Cairo his laptop was found to be full of classical music. He suffered the nightmare of being held in captivity and grilled as to whether he was the 'mastermind' on the London bombings. He had indeed been a friend of Lindsey Jamal. He was released *with no charges;* which is indeed hard to square with all of the fiendish bomb-making equipment the Inquest has been shown, in his flat.

On 8th January 2007 the world was first shown pictures of the inside of his flat – oddly enough they were from a replica of his flat, constructed in Brooklyn, New Jersey![1] Well, fancy that. We would surely appreciate Mr al-Nashar's comments on what exactly is a replica of what in this situation, after all the world of clandestine intelligence is proverbially a hall of mirrors.

Where's the Fridge? A huge industrial fridge was present in the flat – or, so the New York Police Department explained, reported by *The Times* on August 4th, 2005:[7] "An expensive fridge was found in the otherwise rundown flat in Dewsbury … they had commercial grade refrigerators to keep the materials cool," said Michael Sheehan, the NYPD's Deputy Commissioner of Counter Terrorism." It would be essential to own such, if one were trying to brew up the liable-to-detonate substances such as TATP and HMTD. But, can you see one in the comprehensive map of the flat shown to the Inquest? Did these big 'industrial fridges' just fade away, along with the TATP? Perhaps we should re-launch the offer of the late 'Lord Patel', for a million pounds to anyone who can spot this fridge in the pictures!

No Post-Mortems

Not until the Inquest – five years later – did startled lawyers acting on behalf of the victim-families get to hear, that NO POST MORTEMS had been performed on the dead. We heard the bewilderment of pathologist Dr. Awani Choudhary at the Inquest, being one of the first doctors on the scene from the BMA at Tavistock Square. He testified about his attempts to save the life of Gladys Wundowa:

'I have not seen the post-mortem report, but I thought that she was bleeding from somewhere ... So if the post-mortem says that she was not bleeding from anywhere, just had a spinal injury, I will be surprised...

Q. Since you ask about the post-mortem, can I simply inform you that, *as with all the other casualties of the day, no internal post-mortem was conducted* into Gladys Wundowa, so unfortunately, much as we would like the answers to the questions that you've asked, they don't --

A. I... I'm absolutely sure that she had had internal injury as well as a spinal injury, and *I'm absolutely surprised that a post-mortem has not been done through and through.*

Q. Well, Mr Choudhary, that isn't a matter to concern you.

A. Sorry.

Q. ... we don't need to concern ourselves about that matter.   (Jan 20 am, 63:22-65:6)

No, of course not – 52 dead and no post-mortems, nothing to worry about.

What could possibly explain the astonishing decision not to carry out post mortems? The greatest modern act of mass-murder on British soil and no-one was interested in collecting precise evidence of cause of death? So much could have been learned about the explosions and the explosives from such medical examinations.

Is it unfair to suspect that the failure to collect this basic information was caused by fear (or worse) that post mortems would throw up scientific evidence to contradict a preordained narrative of suicide bomber terrorist attacks? Might the injuries have indicated the use of military-grade explosives to which the 'terrorists' could not possibly have had access?

The lawyer acting for the families expressed shock and outrage at the fact that 'cause of death' had not been definitely confirmed. Their clients would have to put up with 'brief, neutral and factual' statements over this most basic of issues – as *The Telegraph* reported from the Inquest:

'But the bereaved families said the coroner should be allowed to go into much greater detail about how the deaths came about. They do not want a "sterile" conclusion that their loved ones were unlawfully killed that fails to rule on whether the security agencies could have prevented the atrocities or whether the emergency services could have saved more lives, their lawyers said.

'Patrick O'Connor QC, for the relatives, told the inquest in a legal argument hearing: "Of course the bereaved interested persons would be very disappointed. But the public may well be quite astonished if that were the position and we were literally kept to the kind of one, one-and-a-half, two sentence verdict in the inquisition that is suggested by some." He added: "The statue of Justice is very often depicted blindfolded, but never gagged." (18 Feb., 2011)

An Inquest without post-mortems? By way of to trying to remedy this situation, the Inquest turned to the Ministry Of Defence. Why should it be their business? MOD experts had had to *construct a model* to show the probable fatal injuries and likely causes of death for those with no obviously fatal external injuries. Colonel Mahoney, Defence Professor of Anaesthesia and Critical Care at the Royal Centre for Defence Medicine in Birmingham, spent a couple of days at the Inquest explaining the situation, whereby 'virtual Underground carriages' had been constructed as models, but it all seemed rather vague:

> Q. But your approach must, overall, be read subject to a number of caveats?
>
> A. Yes.
>
> Q. Firstly, as you mentioned, there was no invasive post-mortem in any case.
>
> A. Yes.
>
> Q. Secondly, the X-ray examination was limited, as you've just said, to fluoroscopy?*
>
> A. Yes.
>
> Q. Thirdly, although you have photographic evidence, in some cases the photographs were difficult to interpret, for reasons I won't explore with you?
>
> A. Yes.   [Jan 31 pm 5:3-17]

Still Clueless about the Explosions: Colonel Mahoney was faced with not only an absence of post-mortems, but also with a weird absence of a coherent theory about the explosive that had been used ... We saw how earlier in February the Government's explosives experts at the Inquest had to tiptoe around the fact that none of them would endorse the government's peroxide-and-black pepper story. Asked to prepare a report for the Inquest, Colonel Mahoney did so. We note a couple of remarks he made there, from comments he had heard from Clifford Todd, the forensic expert.

His report alluded to 'Mr Todd's opinion that the devices were consistent with the use of high explosives.' In no way can peroxide and black pepper be called a high explosive. Secondly, he found 'There is little evidence from Mr Todd's evidence to suggest that the devices produced a significant heat output.' ('Blast waves and their effect on the Human Body', pp.18 & 19) Any peroxide bomb with back pepper as a base *is* a thermal bomb, because the heat comes from the rapid oxidation of the pepper. The more home-made the bomb the more it is going to be 'thermal' ie produce heat. Only the high-blast expertly made explosives of the military will yield a pure blast without heat.

Thus Colonel Mahoney's report nullifies the Inquest's silly joke about peroxide and black pepper – it points back to the first theories about the 7/7 blast, which emerged in the week after the event, when the real experts were averring that a military explosive had been used. Colonel Mahoney is the author of several books on this topic: Lady Justice Hallett alluded to 'the area in which you are most expert: namely, the effects of explosive devices.' (Jan 31 am, 66:3-4)

What happened to the Bodies? Why did the families have to wait for a week or sometimes even more, before they learned of the fate of their lost ones? A study by Jenny Edkins (University of Wales, Aberystwyth, author of 'Trauma and the Memory of Politics') about the way 7/7 victims were treated explained, 'This paper is motivated by a concern, an anger even, at the way in which people were treated by the authorities in the aftermath of the London bombings of July 2005. In particular, communication with those searching for missing relatives or friends was one-way or nonexistent. This treatment, it seems to me, provides an example of what Michael Dillon has called "governing terror..."'

'Families were plunged into a world of Disaster Victim Identification Forms, Police Liaison Officers, and stonewalling by officials.... In the aftermath of the explosions on the London underground and in Tavistock Square in Bloomsbury on Thursday 7 July 2005, relatives of the missing were kept waiting for up to or over a week for information about where their sons and daughters, friends and family members might be.'

We cite five examples:

*   Marie Fatayi-Williams was only allowed to see her son Anthony's body on July 14th a week later . A police officer was standing around. She had to make a great deal of fuss to obtain this, and she kept being advised against it. She tells this in her book, *For the love of Anthony.* She is never *given the body*, she cannot bury her own son.

*   A film by Benedetta Ciaccia's former boyfriend, Raj Babbra, called '7/7 – Life Without Benedetta', has her father and mother, speaking in Italian (in Part 3 at 3:58, with only a bit of it subtitled), say: 'It's an awful thing to lose your child … let alone not being able to see her dead … they didn't show her to me … I was advised not to see her … we were told it was better to remember her the way she used to be.' They never even got to see her body.

*   John Taylor, 60, whose 24-year-old daughter Carrie died in the Aldgate blast, described how it took 10 days for he and his wife to discover that their child had died.

*   In *A Song for Jenny* by Julie Nicholson (2010), the Reverend Julie Nicholson asks a policeman why it was taking so very long before she heard about her daughter Jenny (p287), her book gives the wierd reply: 'He confirmed four hundred body parts had been recovered and sent to a specialised laboratory in Bosnia for ID, which could take several weeks.' – no comment! She was dissuaded from wanting to see her daughter's body, but she insisted. She knew it was her daughter Jenny (she wrote) because of the hands.

*   Relatives of Samantha and Lee, a couple who both died as a result of the bombings, did not get a formal identification of Samantha until 16 July, nine days after she gave her full name to her rescuer at Russell Square. The parents complained, 'We were never asked if we could or would like to see her or be with her. We do not know where her body was kept.' Asked Jenny Edkins, 'Why was it not possible for this family to be with the body? Why was the information that she was dead withheld from them?'

The default position may have been, that families did not see the bodies of the deceased. Whatever was going on, the protocol seems quite macabre. Alison Anderson and Robert McNeil were the experts in body identification who organised the mortuary after the July 2005 London bombings, and they had worked for the United Nations in Bosnia and

Kosovo. Why did the families need to wait for so long? Why was there a military company coping with the bodies? We can only wonder what was written on the death certificates, as next to nothing seems to have been ascertained about how they died.

J7 have written what is arguably their most brilliant piece yet on this topic, and let's quote here from it:

> So, assumptions are piled upon presumptions and houses of cards are built on shifting sands. These are the openly-stated unknown unknowns from which the bereaved families are meant to learn how they lost their loved ones. (J7 Inquest blog, 'Colonel Mahoney, in Porton Down, with the flawed data')

Conclusion

'Its only bread' remarked Muktar Said Abraham (MSI) to a bystander when the 'bomb' in his rucksack, comprising Chapati flour and peroxide, 'went off', or rather dribbled down onto the floor of the 28 bus, at Hackney, on July 21st, 2005.

If the Four had made bombs as the Inquest wants us to believe, then they would have to be comparable to the chapati flour – bombs that somewhat alarmed Londoners two weeks later: with the same method of concentrating the peroxide plus pepper in place of chapati flour. The 'knowledge' of how to make these bombs is the sort of thing one might expect to hear discussed at some Mad Hatter's tea-party. No empirical verification has ever taken place – no real explosives expert has endorsed their feasibility – no bang is ever viewable on Youtube showing this mix.

There have been quite a few mega- fake-terror trials in London following 7/7, involving peroxide bombs. None of them gave us any hint as to how the alleged perpetrators could have known what concentration of peroxide they had ended up with – whether 30% or 50% eg. If the aim had been to make TATP, this would at least have had the advantage that one would be able to see if it was working, because white TATP would slowly appear. Would not the Four journeying down to London need to have some idea as to whether their bombs would blow up?

My impression is that detonators may have gone bang in the case of the 21/7 events, these supposedly being made of TATP. The Inquest has averred that detonators were made of an even more dangerous and unstable peroxide compound, HMTD.

Summarising, the Inquest has clarified that the Government could not find any forensic chemist, who would claim to have been able to identify the primary explosive mix – not at London, Luton or Leeds.

References (in Chronological sequence)

[1] 11th July, 2005, World Tribune.com: Advanced bombs so powerful that none of dead have been identified; timers were used.

[2] The Independent, 12 July 2005: Christophe Chaboud, 'On 12 July 2005, Superintendent Christophe Chaboud, chief of French anti-terrorism Coordination Unit who was in London assisting Scotland Yard with its investigation, confirmed to The Times that,'The nature of the explosives appears to be military, which is very worrying….the material used were not homemade but sophisticated military explosives …' (Nafeez Ahmed The London Bombs, p.24)

[3] The Times, July 13th: Christophe Chaboud informed The Times that 'traces of 'military plastic explosive, more deadly and efficient than commercial varieties, are understood to have been found in the debris of the wrecked underground carriages and the bus.' (Times, July 13th).

[4] 13th July Then on 13th July it was stated that these were of 'C4' explosive:

London explosives have military origin – Science Daily. London, July 13 (UPI):

Scotland Yard has asked for European cooperation in finding how last week's London subway and bus bombers obtained military plastic explosives. Traces of the explosive known as C4 were found at all four blast sites, and The Times of London said Scotland Yard considers it vital to determine if they were part of a terrorist stockpile. C4 is manufactured mostly in the United States, and is more deadly and efficient than commercial varieties. It is easy to hide, stable, and is often missed by traditional bomb-sniffing detection systems, the newspaper said. Forensic scientists told the newspaper the construction of the four devices detonated in London was very technically advanced, and unlike any instructions that can be found on the Internet.'

[5] The Independent 14 July 2005, 'A bath filled with explosives has been found at a house in Leeds that was the "operational base" for the London suicide bombers... The huge quantity of explosive found'

[6] 17th July The Observer 'London bombs: Three cities, Four Killers.' El-Nashar left for Egypt on 4th July; '22 lbs TATP in the bath.'

[7] The Times, 4 Aug 2005 July,7 bombs used Hair dye say NYPD (as alluded to by Lord Patel)

[8] Jane's Defence Weekly 22 July TATP links London & Leeds.

[9] Photographs of the material present in the Luton car-park appeared on 26th of July 2005, released by ABC News in America. It showed white explosive material.

[10] 4 Aug 2005 The Times 'July 7th bombs used hair dye, say NYPD'

[11] Daily Mirror 8 Jan 2007 'Exclusive – inside the 7/7 Terror house': shows replica of a flat in Brooklyn, made by NYPD! 'Mr Cordes revealed the bombs were made with triacetone triperoxide, or TATP'.

[12] On 14th April 2008, Neil Flewitt QC told the Kingston Crown Court that the mix of black pepper and peroxide was so 'unique' that the bombers must have had help designing and building them.

11. The Four Blast Scenes

In this chapter we focus entirely upon the four blast centres as described with many witnesses at the Inquest held at the Royal Courts of Justice, over the five winter months 2010-2011. Sometimes we will draw on highlights from earlier sources, such as the Greater London Assembly (GLA) hearings of 2006. For the first time detailed maps have become available, showing who was where at the terrible moment. The distribution of dead bodies helps to indicate where the explosion was. Quite a lot of material regarding the three tube blast scenes has been removed from this chapter in the earlier edition, to help us to focus upon the new evidence and what it shows. For reference purposes, most of that material is preserved in the following chapter, Eyewitness Reports from the Tube.

If the blast came from one single rucksack then we would expect its effect to be radial, and to have spread out from one single centre. Or if perchance we were to find several large holes blown in the floor of a tube coach, spread out over fifteen feet or so, we might want to look for some other explanation. Much of the energy of the Inquest is devoted to locating the four alleged 'suicide bombers,' and here we are concerned to ask the one, single and all-important question: can we reasonably place these four young man at what we ascertain to be the four blast centres — or not? Were they really there — or, is it a phantom image of 'terror' we are given, like some conjuring trick where our attention is diverted away from the real action? Did anybody see them? This is in London, the most densely CCTV'd area of planet Earth, so how come there are no pictures? You, the reader, are here invited to decide.

ALDGATE

The first blast on the morning of July 7th was at *11 minutes to 9*. It ripped apart the second coach of a Circle line train, shortly before it entered Aldgate station. Was it done by a suicide bomber or by explosives placed under the train? We now evaluate this central question, thanks to the detailed map of the coach provided at the Inquest.

The distribution of dead bodies is shown in red on the diagram. It is fairly symmetric around the long axis of the coach, and does not indicate one side of the carriage or the other as the source of the blast.

And yet, the Inquest was told that the deadly rucksack was in a corner, by the first set of double doors. The first comment available on this matter came a couple of hours after the event, recorded by a member of the British Transport Police:

> 10.37 BTP Master Log: From what I can see, the injuries are consistent with a bag device and not a person borne device. Appears the device was placed left by the walk through doors. This is the first indication from what I can see. Above relates to Aldgate.'

We note that, if the bag was 'left' there as stated, then it was *not* a suicide bomb.

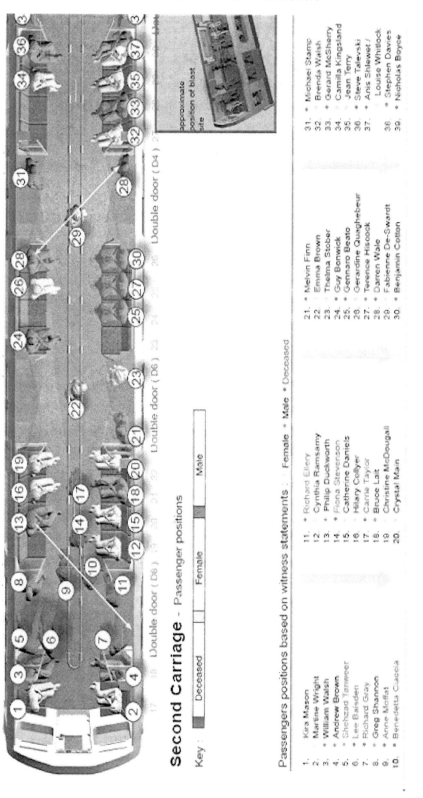

Second Carriage - Passenger positions

Key : Deceased | Female | * Male

Passengers positions based on witness statements : - Female * Male * Deceased

1. Kira Mason
2. Martine Wright
3. * William Walsh
4. * Andrew Brown
5. * Shehzzad Tanweer
6. * Lee Baisden
7. * Richard Gray
8. * Greg Shannon
9. * Anne Moffat
10. * Benedetta Ciaccia

11. Richard Ellery
12. Cynthia Ramsamy
13. * Philip Duckworth
14. Fiona Stevenson
15. Catherine Daniels
16. * Hilary Collyer
17. Carrie Taylor
18. * Bruce Lait
19. Christine McDougall
20. * Crystal Main

21. * Melvin Finn
22. Emma Brown
23. Thelma Stober
24. * Guy Bonwick
25. * Gennaro Beato
26. Gerardine Quaghebeur
27. * Terence Hiscock
28. Darren Wale
29. * Fabienne De-Swardt
30. * Benjamin Cotton

31. * Michael Stamp
32. Brenda Walsh
33. * Gerard McSherry
34. * Camilla Kingsland
35. Jean Terry
36. * Steve Talevski
37. * Anis Sklewel / Louise Whitlock
38. * Stephen Davies
39. * Nicholas Boyce

Part of the diagram submitted by the Metropolitan Police to the Inquest is here shown, of the front part of this second coach. All persons on the coach are numbered, and nearly all are named, with figures in red being the fatalities

The Three Testimonies

Here are three witnesses in that coach, whose testimonies are coherent, i.e. they are in accord with each other. They suggest that the blast came from under the floor. They were all given some years ago, i.e. not long after the event.

Had anyone on that coach recalled seeing the young Islamic terrorist (allegedly Shehzad Tanweer) lurking in the corner, then one might not feel at liberty to recall such evidence. However, that is not the case. There absolutely are no such witnesses: *not one.*

1. The 22-year old Emma Brown was standing holding the pole in between the second set of double doors. Have a look at position 22 in the diagram, where she was, it's a very key position:

> Emma was thrown from the pole she was holding, the vent under her feet exploded and flames shot up through the hole.

That is from the testimony which she gave to the London Assembly, in 2006, and it is a testimony that sums up all the questions that have not been raised about the horror which befell London.

Admittedly, she did not seem to recall it too well in her Inquest testimony (Oct 20th am, 89:21-25).

2. In the following chapter we see the report by Bruce Lait and his dancing-partner Crystal, who were sitting next to each other (positions 18 and 20 in the diagram). Their evidence, like that of Emma Brown, clearly indicates that the blast came from below, **under** the train — with not a Muslim or a rucksack in sight.

3. Police officer Lizzie Kenworthy came into the carriage where the blast had taken place, entering from the first carriage into immediate proximity of where the bomb had gone off. The gruesome sight confronted her, of people with feet blown off:

> I crawled through the interconnecting door, which had blood on the glass. One woman sitting on the seat was twisted round. She was trapped and there wasn't much left of her leg. The chap next to her had lost his leg and there was a woman to their left who was on her back trapped in the metal, which had twisted up through the middle of the carriage. The roof was still on, but the lining of the carriage had been blown off. The sides had also come off and there was a big hole in the floor. A guy was writhing around on a big sheet of metal a bit further up.

These accounts surely indicate a blast from below the centre of the floor — not from a bomb left in the corner. The Inquest also heard PC Kenworthy's testimony on how the hole in the floor of the carriage was 'like a ravine … as if the floor was cleaved' (Oct 20 am 10:15-20).

Hole in the floor

An account of a big hole in the floor comes from the testimony of Mr Terence Hiscock. He had previously given several sworn affidavits to the police about his experience, as well as being interviewed by an author for a July 7th book. We see him seated at position 27 on the diagram. Asked to locate the 'crater' he replied:

Well, it was below — it was in front of where Mr Brown was sitting, so it would have been, looking at that, somewhere between 18 and 15, but it wasn't so much a crater or a defined hole as just an area where the floor seemed to have gone... (Oct 20th am 10:8-14)

Checking out that area on the floor in front of the seats 18 and 15, we find it corroborates Emma Brown's testimony, being right in front of where she was standing.

The Wrong Eye?

William Walsh (number 3 in the diagram) was sitting immediately next to 'the bomb location' but was not killed, nor have we any record of him suffering injuries. Greg Shannon was standing right beside the spot and, incredibly, survived (there seems to be no record of his injuries), while Martine Wright (position 2) sitting opposite lost both legs, and Andrew Brown sitting next to her (position 4) lost one. Thelma Stober lost a leg but survived (position 23) — and she was rather far away from 'the bomb'.

Philip Duckworth, sitting more or less opposite Bruce Lait, was blinded in his left eye. If the blast had come from the corner shown in the diagram, should it not have been his right eye? The white arrow shows where he was hurled, right across the carriage: could a blast from the corner exert such an effect? If he was hurled any where it ought to have been *away* from the blast: it looks more as if the force that propelled him (there may have been two simultaneous explosions outside the carriage for all we know) came from *outside* the carriage. Two people were sent right across this carriage — shown in the diagram by the two arrows.

Newspapers have reported that Mr Duckworth was blinded by 'a piece of the bomber's shinbone.' For this to have happened in his left eye he would presumably have had to have turned right round to stare at 'Tanweer' in the corner before the bomb went off — in which case he would likely have had some memory of him being there, or of his appearance.

Naturally, the Inquest omitted all these matters, steering according to its dogmatically fixed conclusion. It heard the testimony of Bruce Lait and Lizzie Kenworthy on the afternoon of 19th October, with no questions relating to their previous statements suggesting a bomb blast from below, nor any questions that would permit them to broach this important issue.

An Electrifying Experience

For the five people sitting directly opposite the 'bomb', their accounts of what happened in that coach were *primarily electrical*. We can see their positions as 4, 12,15,18,20 in the diagram. They were all sitting next to each other, except that a door separated the first two. Did any of them tell the Inquest about the blast of the bomb?

No — what they described was rather more strange.

1. Andrew Brown (position 4, who lost one of his legs)

> When I regained consciousness, I was actually lying backwards, flat, with my back resting on the window frame through the broken window, and at the time I remember I was -- I had a sensation as if I was being electrocuted, because I was aware that I was unable to move and it was the electrocution that was making my

body rigid... within a few seconds of me regaining consciousness, the electrocution was seemed to reduce, and I was then gradually, over about -- it's difficult to estimate the time, but I would say, over 30 seconds to a minute, I was -- the electricity diminished and I was able to move and sit up. (Oct 20th am 23:1-6)

2. Cynthia Chetty (position 12 — next to Ms Daniels)

I remember, first of all, it was like a clicking sound and then there was just a bright white light that seemed to go on for quite a while and, during that white light, I thought it was only me affected, I don't know, maybe there was a power failure or something and I was being electrocuted, that's what I thought. And I could hear screaming and I could smell smoke. (19th am 4:4-9).

3. Ms Catherine Daniels was sitting right next to Bruce Lait, on his left (position 15), and here is what happened to her:

I suddenly felt a huge amount of pressure on my whole body. I felt as if I was being electrocuted. I thought I was dying and I think I shouted 'Lord, please forgive me'. This pressure lasted for about four seconds. It was then pitch black and I sat up. I had been pushed back in my seat. I think I said 'I'm alive, but I can't see'. Then the emergency lights came on. (Oct 20th am 29:2-9).

She was right next to the area of where 'the bomb' was supposed to be!

And two testimonies that are not from the Inquest, but from right after the event:

4. Bruce Lait (position 18):

We'd been on there for a minute at most and then something happened. It was like a huge electricity surge which knocked us out and burst our eardrums. I can still hear that sound now.

5. His dancing-partner Crystal (position 20):

I was really tired. I had my eyes closed for about 20 seconds and all of a sudden I felt as if I [was] having a fit and couldn't control myself. I slipped to the side. It was as if I had been electrocuted and thousands of volts were going through me. My face was really sore. I slowly opened my eyes and it was dusty and foggy and black.

From a bit further along the coach, we have Dr Gerardine Quaghebeur at position 26:

I think the first thing was that it went dark, and there was a very — like a whoosh, a very strong wind. It almost felt like something electrical, because my hair just went up on end, and that was the first thing I remember, was that everything seemed to be electric. There was a lot of -- it was very dark, but there was lots of like sparks, just funny feelings. (Oct. 20th pm 4:6-8)

These electrical experiences tend to suggest something *outside* the coach as having caused the blast, whereas they do not seem at all compatible with a 'suicide bomb' backpack going off. I guess that's why our credulous and servile media don't ever mention them. These experiences have been surgically removed from the story, although they are probably the most consistent thread coming from survivors of the Aldgate coach.

Aldgate testimonies also featured sparks and "orange flames" seen outside the coach — for example, Mustafa Kurtuldu in the adjacent coach recalled: 'It went white and there were flames outside the train, but they died down quickly.' Sarah Reid in the next carriage recalled, 'There was a fire beside me. I saw flames outside the window of my carriage' — and she claimed to have seen those flames *before* the blast went off. Derek Price told the *Daily Telegraph,* 'A flash of flame went down the side of the train.'

These Aldgate blast experiences are strangely different from what we are meant to believe. The reader should note that any fireballs or flames, especially when seen outside the carriage, are incompatible with use of the explosive TATP, see Appendix 9].

The Inquest heard of massive electrical failures that took place throughout much of the East London underground after the blasts, and these are surely quite relevant here.

Survivors have been placed under pressure from the media to 'remember' the suicide bomber — a person who, on the basis of the vast majority of witness testimony as well as the nature of the explosion evidence itself, *simply was not there.*

Three Trains, that Morning

For comparison, the Edgware Road blast derailed the coach, as became evident from Mark Honigsbaum's testimony (given in the next chapter). Would a detonation inside a coach do that? When survivors of the Piccadilly line blast emerged and gathered at Russell Square station, talking amongst themselves, they assumed it had been caused by something outside the coach — either a power surge or that the train had hit something (testimony of 'George' to London Assembly, 2006, in next chapter). Comparisons here could be useful.

The evidence we have looked at helps us to understand why no journalist or member of the public was allowed to inspect the blasted coach remains: they were kept in secret for a year and then destroyed.

There is however one obvious explanation as to why the scene of the crime could not be revealed.

The British media unanimously reject the position here argued, as beyond the pale of discussion. Whereas, if the evidence supported the accepted narrative, we can be sure that every last confirming detail would have been placed before us and anyone else that wished to look. Collectively, are we really unable to manage calm and informed debate on this terrible issue?

*The official time of the explosion is 08:49.00 — *exactly* 11 minutes to 9. (11 Oct., pm, 16:3-5) Likewise the Madrid bombs went off exactly 911 days after 9/11. Here we have identical 'false flag' fingerprints, and these kind of number-patterns keep turning up.

EDGWARE ROAD

The hole that moved

Over the years, the position of a huge hole in the floor of the 2nd carriage on an Edgware Road Circle line train, on the morning of July 7th, has seemed a mystery. It could apparently move about between the first and second set of double doors. Here is a letter from the Home Secretary John Reid to a group of Edgware Road survivors, putting it by the first set:

> My officials have made enquiries of the Metropolitan Police. The police have confirmed that the wording of the Official Account accurately reflects their initial conclusions following statements they took from witnesses and their early examination of the scene. This shows that the bomb probably exploded near to the first set of doors. But where <u>exactly</u> the bomb exploded has yet to be established. The police are currently awaiting the final report from the Forensic Explosives Laboratory. This will be vital in determining the precise location of the bomb at the time of its detonation.

They were waiting for a 'final report' from the Forensic Explosives Laboratory — to tell where the hole was! You couldn't make it up. There is no hint here that anyone at all would be able to look at the remains of the coach — the primary scene of the crime — and ascertain where a huge crater was located.[1]

This was also the view of the Government's Official Report of 2006, that the blast had been by the *first* set of double doors.

We are reminded of the Piccadilly line coach near Russell Square, where the Met first placed the blast centre by the first set of double doors (near the driver), then Rachel North started blogging away, averring that she had been standing right there and it wasn't there. So, they *moved the bomb location* over to the second set of double doors.[2] One might naively suppose that the blast location in a ruined coach was a fairly straightforward thing to ascertain.

Maybe the Met's 'Operation Theseus' (for investigating 7/7) is taking too far the words of the Lord, 'Let not thy left hand know what thy right hand doeth.'

At the 7/7 Inquest in November 2010 the curtain was at last drawn back to reveal (drum roll) the position of the big crater — it was at one side of the space between the *second* set of double doors, the side *away* from the driver. It cannot be moved any more because of the eminence of professor Tulloch, the Australian media studies professor, who was sitting right next to it. The Inquest did rather garble-up his account of where he was sitting — for a reason we will come to. The Met gave a diagram to the Inquest, that clearly showed where the hole was:

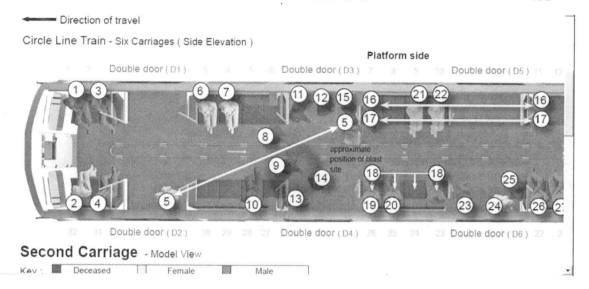

Number 10 is 'Khan', number 13 is Daniel Biddle, number 16 is John Tulloch.

Other holes were reported too, as one would expect from a blast that came from beneath, but not as big as the huge crater. Witnesses alluded to these other holes, but clearly the government's story cannot have this![3]

The phantom image of Khan

Khan is absent from *any* witness statements *or* CCTV images — for London or Luton — on that day, with one sole exception, as is becoming glaringly obvious from the present Inquest. The authorities have *only one testimony* that puts him in London — or indeed anywhere else — on that morning, to which we now turn.

Mr Daniel Biddle has given enormously divergent accounts to different newspapers, as to how he 'saw Khan' in the carriage — hardly surprising, considering the way he lost both legs and an eye, due to standing right next to what became the big crater, then being smashed out through the door onto the outer tube wall, spending two months in a coma in a hospital, where he teetered in between life and death *and* viewed the posthumous 'Khan' jihad video from a hospital bed — before making any public statement.[4]

His first statement to *The Mirror* had Khan sitting down on one of the four seats between the two sets of double doors, ten feet away from Mr Biddle, with a rucksack on his lap. He made eye-contact with Biddle just before his rucksack blew up. Then the next two interviews, with The Times (December) and *Guardian* (January) had Khan standing *packed right next to him* in the crowd, with his rucksack on his back and making eye contact just before 'pulling the cord.' Clearly that 'memory' is an expression of his primary awareness of where the bomb went off — that blew his legs off. Did he agree to take part in the Inquest on condition that these accounts were not attended to? At the Inquest Biddle came back to his initial *Mirror* story (except, that there is no longer any eye-contact). He answered 'Yes' when asked, would he confirm the distance of ten feet away? (Nov 8 am 42:23) So, inexorably, the police had to place Khan where Biddle said he was (Number '10' in the figure).

We are surprised that the Inquest did not break out laughing, at the extreme absurdity of the position, whereby 'Khan' is sitting nowhere near the blast epicentre, in fact a good ten feet away from it.

The person Biddle testifies to seeing cannot possibly be Khan:

> there was nothing about him that made me think he was dangerous in any way …
> he looked like a normal guy going to work within London, whatever he did, and
> there was nothing that he did that made him stand out different to anybody else at
> that particular moment in time. (Nov. 8, 30:18-25)

Khan was wearing a white baseball cap according to the (highly dubious) CCTV from Luton, and maybe from King's Cross — no way could he resemble an ordinary commuter. Maybe that hardly mattered, given the amnesiac and credulous attitude of the British media towards the 7/7 story that has been drip-fed to them by the Met.

Biddle will 'recall' Khan moving his hands over his rucksack just before the blast — and that will do. Never mind the various police judgements that the rucksack had to be on the floor; or that no-one else in the carriage noticed him.

Two people who had sat directly opposite where Khan was placed did give Inquest testimony: they were *not* asked whether they saw Khan. It seems unlikely that no-one else was sitting on that row of four chairs where Khan is located, given that five or six persons are here shown standing up in the adjacent space between the double doors. We must wonder if the Met would be reluctant to produce witnesses who had been sitting there, who (a) would not recall Khan, and (b) have no injuries.

Obfuscation

The Court responded to this impossible dilemma by obfuscating the positions of persons in the coach, especially Tulloch. It did this by having two diagrams of the coach: one with seats numbered consecutively, and the other which numbered people in the coach.[5] They needed some way of distinguishing seat-numbers from person-numbers. Eg, Tulloch was person 16 in one diagram, sitting in seat number 7 in the other. That shouldn't have been too hard. But, more than one barrister kept alluding to him as sitting in seat number 16, and so forth, and deep confusion resulted — I suspect that not many people browsing the Inquest-transcript (of November 8th, afternoon session) are going to follow what was going on. But, Tulloch did clearly identify his seat, as the one right next to the space by the double-doors, and he did locate the crater as being in front of him and immediately to his right.[6]

While perusing the two diagrams, we notice that one man numbered as '9' near the blast was killed by it *and* hurled right over to the other side of the first set of double doors, crumpling up in the corner by the door. That body flew straight past the seat where Khan was allegedly sitting!

The positions of the six or seven dead bodies at the moment of blast, as reconstructed by the Met, are clustered around a centre. That is the centre of the space between the second sets of double doors, very close to the blast location.

The Inquest should summon John Reid, to explain how he could have given the information as Home Secretary that the crater was by the first set of double doors. Was it because, it was near to where they believed that Biddle was placing Khan in his first testimony?

Mark Honigsbaum's Testimony

The Inquest should review evidence that the coach was lifted up from the rails by the mighty power of a blast below the coach, as described by the early testimony of *Guardian* journalist Mark Honigsbaum:

passengers had just left Edgware Road when they heard a massive explosion under the carriage of the train' he explained, which had caused all this mayhem. Just as their train left for Paddington, passengers felt the blast as 'tiles and covers on the floor of the train suddenly flew up, and then, the next thing they knew, there was an almighty crash which they now believe was from a train opposite hitting their train which had been derailed by the explosion. Then everything went black..

The Inquest heard the driver of the train, Ray Whitehurst, remembering what it felt like, as the bomb went off. He experienced a lift, as of the coach being 'raised' — and then as it came down again the train suddenly stopped and he was slammed against his front window:

Q. Do you recollect a movement or a physical sensation in the seat in which you were sitting or the train itself?

A. I felt the front of the carriage raise and it was as if I'd hit a brick wall. I went — the train just stopped dead in the air and came down with a thump, and I hit my head on the windscreen (Nov 16 pm, 45:20-25)

Maybe the Inquest needs a train engineer to ascertain if indeed the blast did tend to lift the train up?

We must surely feel glad that Mr Biddle has come through with a fairly optimistic outlook after the unspeakable horror he has been through. But, as regards how he lost his limbs, the following comment from blogger 'Jim' may be relevant:

Many of the survivors on the trains lost their lower limbs meaning the blast most likely came from underneath. This is probably the reason more people were not killed because the vector of the blast wave was partially dispersed by the floor of the train.

Three big holes in the floor

Staggering new evidence was presented at the Inquest, demonstrating that two or three major holes were blown in the floor of the Edgware road coach — and that each one had a man *fall into it*. Two of those men gave testimonies which we look at here, while the third slowly died after falling into the hole.

Clear maps provided by the police of the coach, enable us to locate them.

None of these holes are compatible with the alleged position of the suicide bomber. Indeed, we may doubt whether a suicide bomber sitting down with the rucksack on his lap, would make a hole in the floor at all. The holes we shall here examine, are some distance away from the seat where the bomber ('Khan') supposedly sat, spaced around the first and second set of double doors.

We here review *four* witness statements which describe the holes (plus a brief statement by barrister Hugo Young about them). The people who fell into holes are Daniel Belsten, John McDonald, and Mr Brewster who was killed. Earlier discussion of Professor John Tulloch's testimony located the position of the main 'crater' as right next to where he had sat.

For comparison, the Aldgate bomb testimony heard in October showed evidence of a blast effect down the central axis of the coach, more spread-out than one would expect from a single rucksack.

Four Testimonies

1. Ray Whitehurst the train driver of the Edgware Road Circle line train wanted to check out what had happened — after his train slammed abruptly to a halt in the tunnel, hurling him against the front window. He got out, and ushered out the passengers in the first two carriages, providing some steps for them to dismount from the middle of the first carriage. Then he re-entered, and walked down through the first carriage, trying thereby to enter into the second.

He couldn't, because of a body straddling the connecting passage between the two coaches.[7] Could he jump over this? Let's hear his own words:

> Q. You went inside the train, not down the outside?
>
> A. No, I wasn't down the outside then. And I thought — well, I tried to get across him, but I realised that, if I tried jumping across him, there was a hole in the floor that I could see, and I was probably going to go down that hole. So I decided against ...' (Nov 16 pm, 58:9-15)

Instead he had to dismount from the train at that point — he could not risk jumping into the hole in the floor, which he could dimly see.

Having been at the Inquest that afternoon, I have confidence in driver Ray Whitehust's testimony as being totally balanced and authoritative: if he says there was a large hole there, then it was there. His testimony is especially valuable because he was not in a state of deep trauma — like the other survivors.

2. Daniel Belsten was sitting right up by the front of the 2nd coach in seat 2, (Nov 11, 2:18-3:4) — and here is how he described his experience of *falling into* that hole:

> Q: What do you recollect of the explosion itself?
>
> A: I just felt a whack to the side of my head and just a big white flash, a big whack to the side of my head and — I don't know, just everything was in slow motion. I just felt everything was just going in slow motion and I just felt like I was falling through the floor of the carriage, and I could feel — you know, I could smell all hot metal burning and felt like I was being electrocuted, you know....

These accounts somehow never quite sound like a bomb going off...

So, this first hole was right up at the very front of the 2nd carriage.

Daniel Belsten is then rescued — being quite surprised to find he is still alive and that has his legs are working — and led out via the *first* carriage. It's not quite so bad there, he found, but:

Q. Did you stay in the first carriage for a bit or –

A. No, there was — all the manholes in the bottom of the carriage were blown out, but I couldn't stay on my feet, you know, I was falling on my feet, and Susanna and this other bloke, you know, helped me up and kept saying "Watch the holes in the floor", so we was like — but it was like other people all sat there, you know, knocked unconscious or whatever, I don't know, but we just got to the end of the carriage and there was, like, some ladders, wooden steps, to bring you onto the track.' (Nov 11 am, 9:13-22)

Driver Ray Whitehurst testified to setting up that ladder in the middle of the first carriage, where Daniel Belsten dismounts. So, the *first carriage* has its manholes blown out — and Mr Belsten is warned to watch out for holes in the floor!

3. <u>David Matthews</u> was an Underground train driver, who had walked through from Edgware Road station, entering the second carriage in an attempt to find the driver. He *described two holes* around the *second* set of double-doors of this 2nd carriage.

Q. You've mentioned somebody lying across some seats just a few moments ago.
A. That was Mr Brewster.
Q. That was?
A. Mr Brewster.
Q. Oh, that was Mr Brewster.
A. Yes.
Q. Because the crater extended into the seat area, didn't it, between 30 and 27? [NB, this area between 30 and 27 is where they are trying to put 'Khan']
A. There was two craters, wasn't there?
Q. We've heard some evidence there were two holes.
A. Yes.
Q. There was a huge crater caused by the bomb.
A. Yes, and another one further up.
Q. Possibly, and was that towards the rear, that's to say carriage 3, so between –
A. Yes.
Q. — seats 7 and 23?
A. Yes, between 26 and 23, yes.
Q. Right. Might that have been a manhole cover that had come up from the floor of the carriage?
A. It could have been, but it was — no, because the seats were missing, so it was definitely not a manhole cover. (Nov 17, am, 105:21-106:18)

Barrister Hugo Keith admitted the problem to Prof. Tulloch:

Q. Professor, don't worry about the X [where the blast was indicated on the diagram], because we have heard evidence from some witnesses which suggests that there's other disruption and potentially other holes in the floor as well as the bomb crater, so it may in fact be a different hole that you're referring to. (Nov 11 am 40:15-20)

4. John McDonald's testimony is especially powerful and informative, because he had previously given a detailed account of his experience to the London Assembly back in 2006, quoted in the next chapter. The present Inquest took little notice of the earlier testimony, and did not allow him to read from his prepared notes. That's an advantage for us, insofar as it gives two somewhat independent testimonies from the same person.

Going back a few years, his harrowing account of *at least* two large holes in the floor of the Edgware Road coach was given to the London Assembly's July 7th Review Committee back in 2006 (Vol.3, 'Views and Information from individuals.') 'John' fell into one hole, and thought he was going to die, then was helped out, and then describes another big hole, also with someone slipping into it. Around that second big hole he came across, 'the metal all around it was all jagged and bent from the explosion'.

At the Inquest, we learn that his full name is John McDonald, with a couple of allusions made to his earlier GLA testimony (Nov 9 pm, 27:23). Initially he is reading from his old notes. His account given back in 2006 was not very compatible with the official narrative — so, we wonder, how consistent would his story remain, over several years? Asked what he first experienced, he replied (Nov 9, 42:18 — 44:11)

> A. Just after the train left Edgware station, there was a small bang, and then there was a massive bang, followed by two smaller bangs. Then, there was an orange fireball.

Sitting at the far end of the coach he was surely in a fine position to experience what exactly did happen: a small bang, followed by a massive bang, then two smaller bangs — and then a fireball!. Hmm, well fancy that. Not surprisingly, he is soon interrupted by Lady Justice Hallett, who objects to his reading from notes, and wants him to reply to questions directly.

John Macdonald provided a diagram for the Inquest, on 9th November 2010. He was sitting right at the far end away from the blast (in seat no. 16, where he was person No.37) Going towards the front of the coach, the first hole in the floor on his diagram is that which, as we showed earlier was right in front of Professor Tulloch. (When Tulloch wanted to get up and move, he had to move diagonally to his left, and ended up by seat no. 23).

Wandering down the carriage, John McDonald *falls into* that hole:

> Q. Can you just tell us very roughly where you think the manhole was through which you fell?
>
> A. I think it was — it was just where David Gardner was at the side of it, just about where 26, 25, in front of there, in the centre.

The seat numbers 25,26, are right next to the 'Tulloch hole.'

He thought he was going to die, but was rescued and pulled out of the hole, then he comes across the second hole in his diagram, which someone else had fallen down:

> Q: With that in mind, tell us, please, how extensive the hole was, the crater, into which Mr Brewster had fallen.
>
> A. That was completely different.
>
> Q. It is, but I ask you because it's marked on your map.

A. Okay, is that the hole in which Mr Brewster had been blown into was massive. It occupied the whole of — the whole area where the double door platform was and it went into the area of the central aisle.

Q. So you're saying –

A. So, well, I would say perhaps it was about a third of the width of the carriage.

Q. Thank you, yes, and it obviously extended, as we can see from your diagram –

A. And the hole was — at the side where David Gardner was, there was a little ledge and that there was — it probably came inside about — let me think — about — just about the width of this box, a little bit wider at the side.

Q. All right.

A. The shape of it, as it got nearer the end, was a bit wider. At some parts, it was this width, and then it got wider towards the end of the — where the double door should have been. But, also, it had — parts of the floor were blown upwards and some of them were blown downwards.

The Inquest heard in detail about the slow death of Daniel Brewster. Then one person looked *under* the train after he had died, and saw: 'His legs just seemed to be very mangled up in the wreckage. You couldn't really see his legs.' (Nov 9th pm, 84:4-7) Now, an Inquest is supposed to be concerned with *cause of death.* That's what this multi-million pound, five-month extravaganza is about, isn't it? There were quite a few allusions to the relatives of Mr Brewster who were present: it is surely evident that he died from the whole lower half of his body becoming mangled up with wreckage *below the floor* — not from anything (eg a rucksack-bomb) above it. Should not the Inquest have some comment, on how this came about? What was happening, under the coach, that killed him?

John McDonald's two testimonies are concordant. The earlier one is more deeply imbued with horror ('I walked into an unknown hell') while his testimony at the Inquest is more schematic, with a helpful diagram. Both have him falling into the hole in front of Tulloch. That second hole in his diagram is basically the hole indicated in the Inquest's seat-diagram, prepared by the Met. It was enormous, John Mcdonald recalled.

This Inquest may be the first time we have heard of the name of the Edgware-Road train driver Ray Whitehurst: I could not find it when composing my book (one may find a comparable comment on the J7 site, that the names of the key train-drivers were unobtainable). His testimony is now on record, and knocks a big hole in the official story. The driver of the train saw a large hole by the very front of the 2nd coach — which Daniel Belsten fell into.

There seem to have been *three large holes* in the Edgware-Road circle line 2nd coach. Clearly, if there was more than one hole in the floor of the coach, that drives a stake right through the heart of the suicide-bomber theory. It cannot recover again after that. It may stagger around a bit like an undead zombie, but basically *it's finito.*

The authorities may be hoping that the media will not pick up on the complete refutation of the official story that has just emerged from the Edgware Road section of the Inquest. One fears that, alas, thatsuch a hope is quite justified.

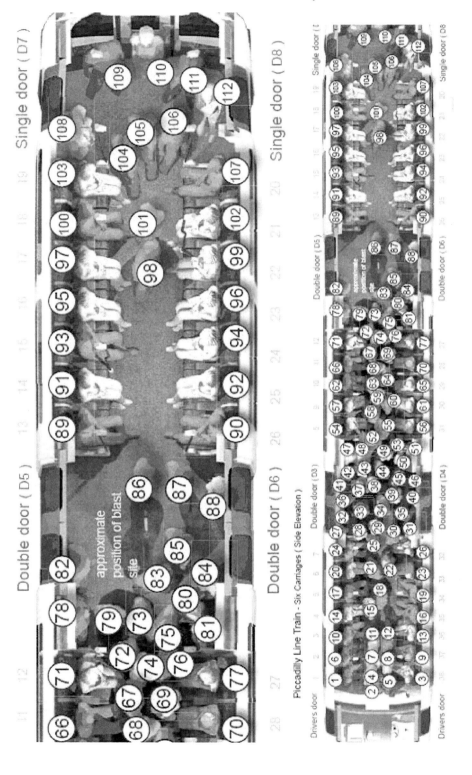

Piccadilly Line Train - Six Carriages (Side Elevation)

KING'S CROSS / RUSSELL SQUARE — 26 DEAD

The Piccadilly line train that pulled out of King's Cross at a quarter to nine was packed. The Met's diagram of its first coach numbers locates the 112 passengers who survived, and in addition there were 26 who died on that coach. The blast erupted in the last third of the coach away from the driver, with its 'centre' given as between the second set of double doors. However the damage and deaths went right to the end of the coach, and the door connecting that coach with the second coach was totally pulverised.

The distribution of dead bodies was shown in a second diagram given by the Met to the Inquest, and they cluster around the blast centre, by the double door (D5). The diagram puts 'Lindsay' in the far corner from the blast, between the single door (D7) and the end of the car. This second diagram is reproduced with the Notes at the end of this chapter.

As passenger Steve Lovegrove testified, 'The damage was concentrated in the rear third of the 1st carriage.' He stood at the front of the adjacent 2nd carriage.

The police officer Aaron Debnam arrived at the front carriage, having entered via the Russell Square station, and described his horror at seeing corpses scattered everywhere: 'There was **a huge hole in the floor three-quarters of the way along the carriage** and the ceiling was hanging down with all the wiring exposed' with hardly an intact window in sight. The far door of the first carriage was damaged beyond recognition, crumpled like a piece of paper. Blood was everywhere.'

As with Edgware Road, we hear accounts of the coach being lifted off the rails, and the injuries all seem to be of legs and feet.

- Teenager Joe Orr a few feet away from the blast (position 66) recalled how 'The carriage had been ripped apart. There was blood everywhere, and limbs blown away from bodies. He heard someone scream, 'My leg, where's my leg?'' Then a lady said to him "My foot's missing". (to The Mirror, 11th July)

- Gracia Hormugos, in that dreadful last third of the coach (position 92) recalled how: 'My whole body was shaking. I felt like I was being electrocuted. The guy next to me lost his leg. I could see the bone. I was trying to help him, trying to keep him awake:' (Telegraph 9 July).

- Gill Hicks right on top of the main blast (position 79) lost both of her legs.

The construction of Germaine Lindsay's position

As usual the Inquest faces the problem of no witnesses seeing a 'terrorist' nor any CCTV record of such. How to resolve this? The modern syntax of 'terror' involves hydrogen peroxide bottles being 'found.' Any 'terror cell' discovered by the police is going to have these, and any hapless Muslim marched off to jail on a 'terror' charge may well have had these 'discovered' in his house. Such bottles strangely served the purpose of helping to locate 'Lindsay' in the Piccadilly line carriage — as we'll see in the dialogue quoted below. After all, if the public will believe that black pepper and peroxide can blow apart tube coaches like a can of sardines, why not have a few peroxide bottles around, to be on the safe side?

Other 'clues' such as Germaine Lindsay's passport *and* his driving licence — such vital material for a jihad warrior to take with him on his final journey — (Inquest Dec 17th am, 133:8-134:2) were located next to his body by the 'anti-terror' squad on the 17th of July, a few days after they had been to his home in Aylesbury. One would here have appreciated his widow being allowed to make comments at the Inquest.

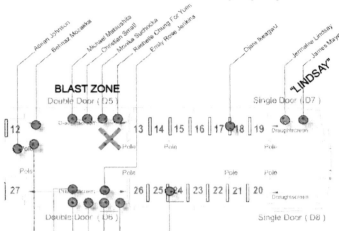

As well as his passport and driving licence, clever police also found his certificate of mobile phone insurance, with his name on — that really settles his identity beyond doubt, we may be sure. Is there some Jihad training manual with instructions on how to get to Paradise — don't forget to take your driving license and mobile phone insurance, otherwise how can they be sure who you are? Just your passport may not be enough these days.

We do not gather why all of these paper documents should have been so fireproof.

There was the slightly larger problem, that 'Lindsay's body with 'clues' such as peroxide bottles and ID such as mobile phone insurance were found right at the far end of the carriage, by the last single set of doors, whereas the blast centre was located about twelve to fifteen feet away, between the double doors. The story is not matching up. It didn't match up in the previous two coaches — the Aldgate and Edgware road coaches had alleged blast epicentres quite separate from the constructed 'terrorist' position. The Inquest has given maps of the blasted coaches where these two points just cannot coincide: the story falls apart. But, 'Lindsay' is a deal further away from the main or primary blast area, than were either of the other two.

Here is an extract from Detective Inspector John Brunsden's testimony to the Inquest: (Dec 17 am, 131:20-132:8)

Q. In that area, area Z, you did you find a plastic bottle which had been cut round an edge as opposed to simply destroyed in the blast?
A. Yes, that's what it looked like to me.
Q. Why did that bottle seem to you to be out of place?
A. Obviously in the Anti-terrorist Branch we learn a reasonable amount about explosives, and we were very conscious of the fact that explosives can be made from peroxide-based materials, and peroxide can be contained in plastic bottles, and so I was concerned that this may have something to do with that.
Q. Was that bottle found in the near vicinity of a male body to whom you formally gave the exhibit JB3?
A. Yes, that is correct, sir.
Q: When the body was moved, did you find a piece of circuit board attached to his body and also attached to his body another piece of plastic bottle which,

again, had had a segment cut from it?

A. Yes, that is correct, sir.

Q. So in very close proximity to his body?

He was later questioned by Mr Patterson: (136:1-7)

Q. Just one or two additional exhibits, please, Officer. I think there were other similar peroxide bottles that were found on the train that appeared to have the neck cut off them, rather like the one that you've already mentioned.

A. Yes, that is correct.

Q. I think there was one JB228, which was at area Y, so at that rear part of the carriage but –

A. On the other side.

Thus a peroxide bottle was 'found' on the other side of the coach at the far end.

Jude Obi walks away

We are interested in testimony from Lilly OKeefe or Jude Obi, who were both right next to the alleged position of 'Lindsay' and survived, as well as a few others in that crowded corner of the coach.

Mr Obi was right next to Lindsay — according to the Government's Fairy Tale from Hell. After the blast, *he gets up and walks away,* with no idea a bomb had gone off. He told the Inquest that he thought the carriage had derailed.

Gosh, fancy that.

Mr Obi clambered over people and left the wrecked carriage to walk along the track wih a group to Russell Square, where he then helped the injured onto the platform.

The Inquest should have been invited to answer the following question: was Lindsay a suicide bomber, or not? Are they saying he let off his rucksack which he was wearing — or, did he put it a safe distance away before it blew up? Can they please make up their mind on this matter? If he was wearing it, how come Mr Obi right next to him could just walk away and had no idea a bomb had gone off? If he was not wearing it, but had left it twelve feet away where the main blast centre appeared, then how come he was killed, could he not just have walked away like Mr Obi?

In the unfolding of this Inquest, there is no intelligent mind evaluating matters. No intelligent mind ever asks a question or makes a comment. The Inquest's narrative just unfolds, wallowing endlessly in grief and horror. Nothing in its story of the Piccadilly line blast make sense — but, it's *good enough for the British media.*

The police are keeping a huge 'Holmes' database on the 7/7 story. Let's just say that in Sherlock Holmes' day the police sought for clues — they did not plant them.

TAVISTOCK SQUARE

It would take a brave man – or a foolish one – to tell the story of what happened that fateful morning at Tavistock Square. The contradictions are too deep for a narrative, and rather few are the witnesses who have come forward. Any readers who wish to believe that Hasib Hussain got onto that bus, sat at the top in the back seat and released his bomb from there, must accept that there is very little meaningful testimony to support any one of those propositions.

A New Image of the Bus

This important new image of the blown-up bus was shown at the Inquest. As regards why it was not released for so long, we may note the very level cut along the top deck. Many have commented that it looks as if the top of the bus had been prepared to lift off: and not like the result of an explosion. We can compare this with the image above released earlier, where the neatness of the cut doesn't show:

It is fairly evident that the top of the 30 bus lifted clean off because it had been cut. We can see the cut-line along the base of the upper roof support, made with a power saw.(Thanks to Simon Shack for this picture).

The bus was packed as it pulled out of Euston, but then many dismounted when it stopped after turning into Upper Woburn Place. There were no standing passengers as it exploded, with most seats occupied.

The Last Journey of Hasib Hussain?

On the Government's story, Hasib Hussain left King's Cross station at 9.22 am to catch a 91 bus, and travelled one stop Westwards to Euston. It stopped at Euston station, where he dismounted: had he stayed on it, its next stop would have been in Upper Woburn Place, on its way into Tavistock Square! That 91 bus has its normal route through Tavistock Square. After dismounting at Euston, around 9.30 am he catches a 30 bus, which would then normally go back to exactly where he had just come from, viz King's Cross. Why would he want to do that? He could not have known that this bus — and no other 30 bus — was about to be diverted, maybe because of the large crowds, and drive straight into Tavistock Square. If we wished to assume that Hasib was on either or both of these buses that morning, then this switch of buses could be interpreted by saying that there was one bus designed to explode, and Hasib, who was a stranger to London, had been given a sequence of instructions to get him onto it. Otherwise, if perchance he had wanted to blow himself up in Tavistock Square — after all, that's where he supposedly went — then he could just have stayed on the 91 bus, and blown that one up.

Maybe the bus which blew up — we are conjecturing now — had to be the one with the words 'Outright terror, bold and brilliant' on its side, with a 7/7 code number: bus number 17758.

I suggest we are obliged here to accept the logic of 'Muad'Dib' (John Anthony Hill) the creator of '7/7: The Ripple Effect': if Hasib Hussain got onto both those buses, the 91 and then the 30, it can only have been because he had been told to do so. There is no conceivable way he could have intended to get onto those two, one after the other, of his own volition — for the reason we have just discussed, viz. that the second normally goes straight back to where the first one came from. The perps may have had their own reasons for being able to prime the 30 bus to explode and not the 91. But we cannot know this, all we know is, they have given us a sequence of events which cannot have been willed merely by a young 'suicide bomber,' supposing such existed.

After crossing over the Euston Road, the number 30 bus then stopped on Upper Woburn Place. Passengers are advised of a diversion, due to the crowds, and 30 or 40 (the Inquest was told) choose to disembark there and take the ten-minute walk to King's Cross station. On the side of the bus is an advert for a new film 'The Descent' opening on the 8th, proclaiming 'OUTRIGHT TERROR, BOLD AND BRILLIANT' on its side. It coasts up to the British Medical Association and stops a little way past its main front door, where there is no bus-stop or traffic light. Its driver gets out *in order to ask the way,* and is then startled to see his bus explode.

It is here that we enter what looks for all the world like some theatrical stage-set, where the top of a bus will neatly lift off, to reveal .. .what? Its top neatly blows off — bus roofs are only held on by the windows and the thin frames between them. A smooth, straight edge remains behind after the roof lifts off, and settles down across the street. The closing scene of the Beijing Olympics reminded some of this event: they started on 8.8.08, and, by way of promoting the forthcoming London Olympics of 2012, had a red London bus enter the stadium. Its top neatly lifted off, opening out to reveal some British celebs.

The opening of the British horror movie *The Descent,* a film about people dying trapped underground, had to be postponed from the 8th, on the grounds that people were still dying and trapped underground on that day (source: Wiki).

The photo shows the bus driver walking away from his bus. We see no dust on his clothes, no scratches on his face. On the top deck at the very front of the bus, a couple one has blood on his jersey, the other holds his bleeding nose. These are the shocked survivors, standing up.

Amongst the web-pictures of this scene, *the most permanent feature* is a 'Kingstar' van, adjacent to the ruined bus. We recognise its gold-star logo in the second image here shown. Kingstar is a firm based outside London, twelve miles away, with no offices in town, and one of its specialities is *controlled demolition:*

> 'Demolition in areas where minimal disruption and minimal noise requirements are paramount,'

Its website explains. It will undertake risk assessment and 'any aspect of controlled demolition and/or dismantling'.[8] Although travelling in the opposite direction, the van stopped only about six feet from the rear half of the bus, where the seat of the explosion is supposed to have been. A public inquiry would wish to ascertain just when the Kingstar van arrived, and how long it remained there. Shortly after the blast at 09.47, a Sky News helicopter was instructed to clear out from the area.

The BMA front door is at least ten yards away from where the bus stopped. Blood was

spattered all around it. 'Blood dripped from the walls of the headquarters of the British Medical Association,' *The Independent* assured its readers the next day. It was very dramatic — a bit too dramatic, maybe? It was rather far away from the bombed bus to be credible. A second image helps readers to decide on this matter, in which the top of the front portion of the bus peeps above the bushes of Tavistock Square. The bus halted in front of Tavistock House, where the security firms Fortress UK and ICTS Ltd are located on its first floor). Conspiracy-theories swirl around these two firms: are they Israeli-based, and do they have London Underground security contracts? (See Appendix 2) Next door, the Tavistock Clinic was started in the BMA in 1920. It is fair to say that the Tavistock has been quite involved in the developing concepts of psychological warfare, and the effect of war-trauma and 'terror.'[9]

One more picture of the bus taken from overhead shows the adjacent pavement. This view has to be a few minutes later because yellow-clad police and health workers from within the BMA building are now swarming around the scene. The police appear quickly, partly because three British Transport Police were driving *right behind the bus* at the time. As the Chief Constable wrote in a letter to the BMA, "Three of my officers were travelling behind the bus when the bomb exploded, and were the first officers on the scene. Whilst they began to rescue passengers from the bus, your staff immediately sprang into action assessing and treating the casualties."[10]

Camden police arrived at about 10.15, and on the front page of my local paper, PC Walker described how he became suspicious of a 'microwave box' on the lower deck of the exploded 30 bus (Hampstead & Highgate Express, 17 February). No one was in a hurry to explain what a 'microwave box' might be, or what it was doing there. It was demolished at the scene in a controlled explosion.

On some theories there are 'agents' to be seen in these photographs, who are helping to manage the crisis, with light blue shirts and short hair, such as the one in the lower right of this photo, on the phone. Obachike claims to have encountered various of these around the Square after the explosion, for example photographing the event, or directing people where to go.

Two Australians Tania Calabrese, 29, and her boyfriend Tony Cancellera, 34, were sitting on the top deck of the No. 30 double-decker bus when it exploded: Tania had just been idly noticing how the police were putting up yellow tape around the square, when disaster struck. Her account was printed on July 10th so it was soon after the event. It suggests that two of the perpetrators rushed off the bus shortly beforehand. It did not appear to her that a bomb had gone off, which may somewhat remind us of tube train testimonies.

> Ms Calabrese held on to the seat in front as the bus collapsed around her and debris flew. Her boyfriend was thrown by the blast and knocked unconscious. Ms Calabrese described the horror around the bus as she searched the street for her missing boyfriend.

> The couple were sitting in the middle of the top deck of the bus, opposite the stairs, when the explosion occurred. They had been travelling from their West London home to work in the City of London when the attacks took place. Ms

Calabrese said she had no idea the bus had been bombed, and initially thought they had been involved in a traffic accident. "I don't remember a bang," Ms Calabrese said. "I didn't hear anything. It was just like a violent shaking. It felt like a really bad car accident. I thought something had hit us from behind. Then the shaking was uncontrollable. I couldn't control my eyes. As soon as I felt the impact blood flew out of my nose metres in front of me. I remember grabbing on to the railing in front of me while the bus was shaking.

"I was thinking, 'OK this is going to stop', but then I could hear creaking metal and the floor around my seat started falling down. I just held on to the chair in front of me. The floor started slowly twisting and I ended up not that high off the ground. I couldn't walk down the stairs because the bus was flattened. I just jumped off. I landed on the floor and looked around. It was so quiet it was freaky. There was something like smog all around but it was actually fibres from the seats so there was like dust everywhere and black smoke.

"It was really quiet, and there were people lying all over the floor. There were people with cuts on their faces and everyone had nosebleeds. I was holding on to my face as well." Realising that a catastrophic event had happened, Ms Calabrese searched for her boyfriend. "I don't know how long it took to find Tony. It seemed like forever but it might have only been two minutes," she said. "I was screaming and calling out his name. I finally saw him on the road from a distance. When I got to him, his eyes were flickering and his body was convulsing. His head was in a puddle of blood.[11]

"He looked like he was in one piece but he was completely out of it. I was screaming for him to wake up and then a man showed up. I screamed, 'Please help me. This is my partner'. The man leant down with me to help Tony, and then I freaked out, and for some reason I decided I had to look for my handbag. I don't know why. I went running around and came back without it, and then Tony started to wake up. It was really quiet but maybe that was because I was deafened by the blast. I couldn't hear anything except screams.

"All my clothes were ripped and the hem on my pants was blown off by the blast as well as the buckles on my shoes. My jacket was ripped everywhere and my scarf had blood all over it. They put us in an ambulance because they were worried about Tony's back and his head. They wrapped him in padding and put him on a stretcher and took us to hospital."

They have been released from University College Hospital, but as they lay in beds there on Thursday night the couple were interviewed by police. Authorities were eager to glean any information the Sydney couple may have had about the events leading up to the explosion, especially as it was unclear whether the bomb was detonated remotely or was the work of a suicide attack. There were suspicions that a male and female couple had fled the bus moments before the explosion, indicating that two terrorists may have been sitting next to those they would murder moments later.

The mystery couple were originally sitting at the back of the top deck. They fled as it sat in the traffic around Kings Cross and Russell Square Underground stations, where a bomb had earlier exploded below the streets. "We saw two people run off the bus before the bomb went off," Mr Cancellera said.[12]

Later accounts try to make out that she saw a single suicide bomber, but she and her boyfriend do not say that here. Just before the event, she recalled the excitable atmosphere on the bus, and what the police were up to: 'We were talking to two ladies in front of us and the whole bus was buzzing — one of the ladies said she had heard something about a bomb and then I noticed there were police putting up tape to block off the street. There were a lot of people getting off just before it happened.'[13] Daniel Obachike's book reiterates this hard-to-believe notion, that the police were putting up yellow tape around the area *before* the bus blew up.

According to traffic warden Adesoji Adesi, the driver of the No.30 bus, George Psaradakis, had been asking two Camden council parking attendants for directions when the explosion occurred. He *had never driven that number 30 bus before*, but was recruited only the previous day to drive it. In an article entitled 'I can't forget my bus passengers' he states that he cannot recall anyone resembling Hasib Hussain boarding his bus. (*Daily Mail*, 11 Jan 2006). The Athens News Agency reported details about conversations that he had with his family in Greece in the aftermath of the bombing. "He told me that he was fine. He said that two passengers were killed and that a girl died in his arms," said Yiannis Paterakis, his uncle.[14] We are here informed, that the bus driver saw three dead bodies. The BBC initially reported three persons dead at Tavistock Square,[15] then the *Evening Standard* later that day had the figure had rise to ten. After seeing his bus blow up, the Greek driver 'walks' for seven miles across London, we were told. Although he lives in Stoke Newington, in North London, he walked *Westwards* and sought help only once he reached the Central Middlesex Hospital in Acton, at about 10.50am — still wearing his blood-spattered uniform. If we suppose that having 'a girl' dying in his arms took him up to ten o'clock, that would mean he travelled seven miles in fifty minutes. That sounds more like a car drive, maybe in a police car, than a walk. A bus driver has a duty of care towards his passengers, so his leaving the scene so quickly is surprising. His brother lives in west London and after being discharged from the hospital he was re-united with his family at his brother's house, rather than at his own home. He was then taken into police protection for the next week. He reappears and then will never talk to anyone about the incident, or at least not in any specific manner.

The 'Official' Witness

One and perhaps the first widely-publicised testimony seemed to place an Islamic suicide bomber on the bus at Tavistock Square, and that was by a Mr Richard Jones. On the 11th of July, the *Telegraph* reported his story, whereby,

> 'Several stops before it [the bus] exploded, Richard Jones, 61, an IT consultant, had noticed an agitated man constantly dipping into his bag. "He did it about a dozen times," Jones said. He alighted just one stop before the blast on board, still curious about the nervy passenger. If the "agitated man", said to be olive-skinned, about 25 and 6ft 2in, was carrying the bomb, it may have been because he was forced to leave the Tube before he had a chance to plant it.

This testimony of Richard Jones contained the very allusion to a 'suicide bomber' with a rucksack, he *seeded* this concept. His narrative began to appear on July 8th, the day after. Because it was so early, it appeared before the consensus had emerged that 'the bomb' was on the top deck. His testimony kept changing every time he told it, and bore no resemblance to others on the lower deck. On July 8th, Jones had told *The Sun* that he got off the bus because he had 'reached his destination'. The *Mail on Sunday* on July 10th reported that Richard Jones had 'served an apprenticeship at an explosives factory', in Ayrshire, which could raise some interesting issues. Jones alleged that Hasib Hussain got onto the 30 bus 'several stops' before it exploded. Jones' initial testimony has him and Hasib standing up on the lower deck, facing each other. A live interview which Jones gave on 15th of July described how 'the suspect' was constantly fiddling with his back-pack on the floor: 'he done this about twelve times in the nine or ten minutes we were on the bus together.' Jones was at one point claiming to have dismounted from the bus 'moments' before it blew up, which would have to mean on the corner of Woburn Place as it turned off Euston Road. The Inquest interviewed Jones, and 'tidied up' his story by emphatically stating that the mystery person whom Jones saw fiddling with a rucksack could not possibly have been Hasib Hussain, because Hussain was upstairs.

Richard Jones told the Inquest he was sitting in a seat, which was right next to the seat assigned to Mr Daniel Obachike (seats 6 and 9 in the Met's diagram prepared for the Inquest). Mr Obachike has argued in his book (*The 4th Bomb*) that Richard Jones was not on the bus at all, while others have doubted whether Mr Obachike was truly on the bus. Perhaps someone could arrange a debate between the two of them! Let's merely comment that the Inquest has (by virtue of accepting Richard Jones' story) *two* dark-skinned people, six foot tall and fiddling with large rucksacks, on this bus, one on the lower deck and one on the upper deck; we may doubt whether either were present.

The CCTV Blackout

Two days after the attacks, Scotland Yard put out a statement regretting that no CCTV images were available from the bus, loading the blame onto the bus company, 'Stagecoach:'

> It's a big blow and a disappointment. If the cameras had been running we would have had pin-sharp close-up pictures of the person who carried out this atrocity. We don't know if the driver forgot to switch them on or if there was a technical problem but there are no images.[16]

The bus management company Stagecoach (based at Stratford, East London) wasn't having this, and insisted that their cameras had been working. As they told one investigator:

The Route 30 Stagecoach bus did have CCTV equipment fitted and the hard drive was recovered from the vehicle and passed to the Metropolitan Police … The set up of the cameras also means they cannot be accessed or switched off by the vehicle driver.[17]

This suggests that Scotland Yard's statement about the CCTV was misleading: the cameras *were* working and no bus driver could have switched them off. The four were positioned at the entrance and exit doors, plus one on each deck scanning the length of the vehicle.

A week later, testimony from an anonymous employee of the 'Stagecoach' company appeared, averring that the 30 bus in question had received special treatment the previous weekend:

> CCTV gets maintained at least 2 or 3 times a week and can digitally store up to 2 whole weeks worth of footage. This is done by a private contractor....So when I heard that the CCTV wasn't working on a vehicle that's no more than 2 years old since last June.....I'm sorry that's rubbish, I work for the company I know different.
>
> Also a point of interest....last Saturday a contractor came to inspect the CCTV on the buses at the depot, according to my supervisor the person spent more than 20 hours over that weekend — 20 hours to see if the CCTV is working? Also that person who came was not a regular contractor, for security reasons the same few people always come to the depot to carry out work, this time it was different.[18]

So, the Saturday prior to July 7th, a maintenance group *previously unknown* to the depot crew spent *twenty hours* tinkering about with the bus — an unheard-of length of time for CCTV maintenance. Shades of Diana in Paris, where all the CCTV along the highway became strangely dysfunctional on the last drive which Dodi and she ever took? Shades of the De Mendezes shooting, where all the CCTV in Stockwell tube station was strangely unavailable that morning.

In January of 2011, the Met provided the 7/7 Inquest with a diagram showing all the people who were on the upper deck at the blast moment:

The dead (numbered 48-55 and 61) are all to the right of the collapse-point and 'Hasib Hussain' is shown at position number 53. The top deck of the bus collapsed between the 'thirties' (to the left) and 'forties' (to the right) using the numbers shown.

Upper deck of 30 bus at Tavistock Square, with Hasib Hussain as allegedly number 53.

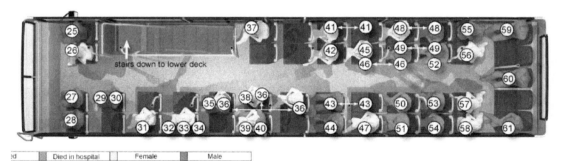

The Inquest heard the bus witness Lisa French seeming to recall the figure of Hasib Hussain on the top deck of the 30 bus, which had exploded in Tavistock Square: 'I made the decision not to go and sit next to him because I was aware we both had very big bags and that he, we, you know, would be taking up a lot of room.' She recalled him carrying 'probably a laptop rucksack … quite large, sort of square, so I think that's why I thought it was a laptop bag rather than a camping rucksack…and I also had a laptop bag.' It was a square-ish laptop bag like hers, only bigger, and he was carrying it in his hands and then wearing it over one shoulder (We could also note here the two young men with rucksacks at the front of the top deck, see: http://officialconfusion.com/77/images/bus/bus_large.jpg)

That announcement made headlines around the world — but, why had we never heard about this before? This is the first instance of the Inquest finding a witness who claimed to have seen something like one of 'the terrorists' where he was supposed to be. She suddenly became famous from what looks like a *new memory* she has acquired.

A moving account was given by Lisa French of the bomb blast at Tavistock Square in 2008 or early 2009 ('three and a half years' after the event). She had been diagnosed as having 'Post-traumatic stress disorder,' and given 'cognitive behaviour therapy' to try and cope with life. Her husband has suffered from nightmares, from what had happened to her. Her therapist advised her to try and fulfill an ambition — so, she decided to try and jump out of an airoplane, which she did, and also raised some money for charity. On this earlier account, she blacked out at the moment of blast, so doesn't remember anything, but when she came to people were talking about 'bomb' and bus:'

> I can remember I woke up feeling very confused, didn't really know what had happened, but I can remember hearing somebody say "bomb" and "bus" and realising, with the destruction around me, that something very serious had happened.

A year after this detailed account, which has no hint of 'seeing the terrorist,' she comes up with detailed memories of going up the stairs behind Hasib Hussain, implying she could recognise him, see him with his laptop-bag sitting down, etc. Did the therapist plant the 'memory' in her? She said:

> I went for quite a number of sessions, over 20, with my psychologist, and he performed some cognitive behavioural therapy with me, and also some rapid eye movement therapy, too. The CBT therapy involved some discussion around what had happened and how that made me feel, and also quite a lot of homework.

There is a parallel here with psychological counseling programmes offered 9/11 survivors, which reportedly were used to embed the official narrative in their memories, "curing" them of "cognitive dissonance" from inconvenient dissenting memories.

She gave another interview later in 2009 (*Journal Live,* Nov 2nd) entitled ' 7/7 bus blast survivor Lisa French meets her saviour.' He turned out to be 'Chris Symonds, the

British Transport Police worker who came to her aid and guided her from the wreckage of the red London Transport bus.' No hint was here given of her having any memory of seeing 'the terrorist' — as neither was there when she did the BBC interview (on that same date), where we learnt of the wonderful manner in which she overcame her terror — she had 'travelled across the world to help other victims of bombings, and also cleared mines in the former killing fields of Cambodia.' You can watch a brief intro to the BBC's programme, 'The remarkable story of the Tyneside woman who survived the 7/7 London bus bomb,' no longer available. It seems not to have hinted at the Inquest's story.

In June 2010, *Now* Magazine published her story, 'I sat two seats from the Suicide Bomber' where the text does not have her claiming sight of the 'terrorist' — and let's compare this with her position given in the 7/7 Inquest, where she is located five or six seats away from the designated position of 'Hasib Hussain' on the top deck, i.e. hardly near enough to notice him on a crowded bus.

There are earlier media accounts of her mainly concerned with 7/7 anniversaries, and how she has kept in touch with Louise Shepherd who was sitting next to her on the bus that morning. While admiring the brave and inspiring example she has given to the world of how to cope with trauma, we may have doubts over her most recent recollection of it.

Sitting next to the 'Terrorist'?

Ms Sapna Khimani was sitting immediately behind where the Met have placed 'Hasib Hussain' — number 57 in picture. This seat faced the rear, so her back was immediately next to 'the bomber' — she was as near to the alleged rucksack' as was Hasib Hussain. She is today quite alive and well, and gave testimony to the Inquest. (Jan 13th pm, para 26):

> Whilst seated on the bus, the next thing I knew is that suddenly there was a bright flash of white light from behind me from left to right. Simultaneously, I felt that on my left side and a fire cracker bang noise, all coming from my left....[She blacked out, then recovered soon after as a medic was taking care of her] I was not aware of any pain or injury at this time... The next thing was complaining that I was feeling really cold and someone gave me some blankets.

They took Ms Khimani to University College Hospital for a checkup. Unfortunately the barrister Andrew O'Connor cut off her written report here, from which he was reading. I inquired at the Inquest and was told there was no way the public could obtain the rest of the report — that is unfortunate. If anyone could get a further interview with her it would be of great value. In the meantime I suggest that her account conclusively disproves the notion that a devastating bomb went off immediately next to her. She showed no memory of pain, did not have her back broken or destroyed (or we would surely have heard about it) and after blacking out for a short while was well enough to give her husband's name to a medic who arrived to help her.

Mia Scott was sitting just across from where the Met have placed Hasib Hussain. I suggest that her testimony to the Inquest on Monday, 17th January was totally authentic and reliable. The position in which she was sitting on the upper deck of the 30 bus was clear, and dispels any idea that the 'suicide bomber' was sitting next to her. Consulting the map, she was in seat 56, and just to her right and behind her was allegedly 'Hasib Hussain.' Her right leg was somewhat damaged but is now better. Her only permanent damage is to her ears from the blast.

This bus was moving very slowly on a stop-start journey, and it stopped for a while before being able to turn into Upper Woburn Place. In addition the passengers have strange news to talk about, that morning, and they had all seen the huge crowds milling around. Various witnesses described an unusual, convivial atmosphere during the time from embarking at Euston to the dreadful blast. Mia Scott got up and looked around her, then looked out of the window. She could correctly identify from memory the various persons around her (her seat faced the back of the bus). She remembered the 'two girls' to her right (in positions 57 & 58) and how one of them used her mobile phone, and she recalled the 'Indian gentleman' at position 60. However, when she was asked if she recalled 'the bomber', 'Hasib Hussain' and told what seat he was supposed to be sitting in, *right next to her,* I watched carefully as she just looked worried and then replied, 'No I'm sorry I don't.' She described the 'muffled bang' and 'as if I was floating through air' (she had been blown onto the street, quite a distance behind the bus, as the barrister told her).

I suggest this testimony from Ms Scott makes the option of a 'terrorist' bomber sitting adjacent to her very unlikely. She claimed she did not lose consciousness and her memory seemed intact. There was surely no large six-foot high Asian-looking fellow, sweating profusely and with dark glasses (to quote earlier witnesses from the number 91 bus) with a huge rucksack next to her — *he wasn't there.*

Tavistock Square has a powerful aura of peace, with the Ghandi statue at its centre shedding an aura of holiness, plus the Hiroshima tree, and a large rock with an inscription praising those who refuse to fight in wars. The adjacent Bedford Square has a tree planted to commemorate the dead of July 7th. Tavistock Square provided the visible image of 'a bomb' that morning, and had a constructed witness Peter Jones who would testify to seeing the 'terrorist,' the only person to claim to do so that morning. It was in the light of this deeply ambiguous event that the tube-blasts could be at once interpreted, by the media, having hitherto been reported as power surges.

The bus ended up at Fort Halstead in Tonbridge Wells, the MOD's 'Royal Armament Research and Development Establishment': where the bombs are made. A flock of forensic-analysis experts from Fort Halstead appeared at the Inquest, to advise about traces of this and that detected in the bus: clearly, they must have had the bus there to do that; just as years earlier the remains of the plane that crashed at Lockerbie was taken there for analysis. I also had a source who delivered material to Fort Halstead on a regular basis, who was told this. Is it still there?

References

[1] The best account of the hole in the Edgware Road train comes from 'John' given to the London Assembly back in 2006, who actually fell into it.

[2] One week after the event, the Met placed the bomb-crater of the Piccadilly Line train in the first carriage by the first set of double doors, and has stuck with that story; while the BBC (and the Official Report) moved it to the second set of double doors.

[3] Evidence for other holes is described next.

[4] 'It can be inferred that there is no definitive account from Danny Biddle. His position and Khan's position in the train seem to alter each time he tells his story' — 'Official Confusion' website.

[5] The Inquest's diagram which gives consecutive seat numbers, also gives the positions of bodies after the blast.

[6] There is a sub-plot about whether Prof. Tulloch ever 'saw Khan' — which would be tricky as he was sitting on the *other side* of the blast-crater about fifteen feet away from 'Khan.' In an early interview he said: 'I don't know if I did see him...I'm still not sure.' (*The Sunday Telegraph* Australia 10th July, no longer online). Then a BBC interview has him locating the bomb crater and presuming Khan was there — but, not claiming to have seen him.

[7] The person whom the driver Ray came across was laid out in-between the two coaches 'with a hole the size of a tennis ball in his leg.' Had that bolt, or whatever blew though his leg, been blasted out from *below* the carriage floor?

[8] www.kingstar.co.uk/demoli.htm

[9] The Tavistock Clinic, founded in 1921, the Tavistock Institute of Medical Psychology pioneered research into psychological warfare. John Rawlings Rees was its Deputy Director and he developed the "Tavistock Method," which induces and controls stress via what Rees called "psychologically controlled environments." N.B., Do not confuse with the Tavistock Institute at Swiss Cottage with a bronze statue of Freud outside it.

[10] 8.9.05: http://bridgetdunnes.blogspot.com/2005/09/british-transport-police.html

[11] The figure in the top right-hand corner of figure 7, lying by the kerb with others huddled round, is believed to have been Tony Cancellara.

[12] Matthew Hall, 'Aussies tell of carnage', 10.6.05, www.pbase.com/image/45940965. Also at www.theage.com.au/news/war-on-terror/aussies-tell-of-carnage/2005/07/09/1120704597489.html

[13] Daily Mail, 'The real Faces of 7/7,' 7.7.2006, www.dailymail.co.uk/pages/live/articles/news/news.html?in_article_id=394473&in_page_id=1770

[14] Greek News, 11th July 2005, 'Greek Bus Driver Key Witness', www.greeknewsonline.com/modules.php?name=News&file=article&sid=3528

[15] Obachike, D., *The 4th Bomb* 2006: two dead initially reported, that morning, p.199.

[16] The Mirror, 13 July 2005, Jon Rappoport.

[17] Letter from Stagecoach to 'an independent J7 researcher': www.julyseventh.co.uk/7-7-cctv-evidence.html.

[18] Stagecoach: www.officialconfusion.com/77/witnesses/150705stagecoachwit.html (sent originally to Alex Jones' PrisonPlanet website)

12. Eyewitness Reports from the Tube Blasts

When extreme events take place, conflicting accounts are to be expected. However, the reader must here ascertain whether the sheer extent of the conflicting evidence is compatible with the official story. Our primary concern here has been to retrieve the *early* stories and reports, before the official line is overlaid upon them. In an investigation, one could say that the 'What?' needs to have a priority of coming before the 'Who?', the 'Why?' or the 'How?'. So many people assume they know what happened, when they have merely been given the pre-digested Home Office account.

This chapter contains more detailed eyewitness reports available before the Inquest testimonies focused on in the preceding chapter. The reports here used have been taken from the Greater London Assembly Report on the July 7th hearings, from BBC News websites, and from newspaper accounts, aided by the efforts of independent researchers such as the July 7th Truth Campaign.

I. ALDGATE

The first news reports came in at 09.17, of an explosion at Liverpool Street station. The adjacent Great Eastern Hotel was hosting the Tel Aviv Stock Exchange's yearly conference, in conjunction with Deutsche Bank, and this was the hotel where Rudi Giuliani, the Mayor of New York on September 11th, 2001, happened to be staying. Giuliani remarked, "I was right near Liverpool [Street] Station when the first bomb went off and was notified of it and it was just to me very eerie to be right there again when one of these attacks takes place."

Israel's Finance Minister and former Prime Minister, Benjamin Netanyahu – who had been busy banging the drums of war with Iran – was due at the Great Eastern Hotel for this conference. But, a mere six minutes before the blast went off, he was given a warning not to attend. The conference he was due to attend was right by the blast area, and the hotel where he was staying was adjacent to another! Netanyahu never got to his conference despite being its keynote speaker, but remained for that morning in the Russell Hotel – close to the sites of the Russell Square and 30 bus blast sites.

The Government's anonymous *Report of the Official Account* which appeared a year after these events, known as the 'Narrative,' affirmed that an Eastbound Circle Line train was by the platform of Liverpool Street 'seconds before it blew up,' i.e. it had only just entered the tunnel before it exploded, and that the bomber Tanweer had been sitting 'towards the back of the second carriage.' The tunnel between Aldgate and Liverpool Street is some 600 yards.

Aldgate and Aldgate East are two separate stations, the former on the Circle Line and the latter on the Metropolitan and City line. Reports leave room for debate whether the train was going Eastwards or Westwards, which of these two lines it was on, and relate to all four of these City of London stations: Moorgate, Liverpool Street, Aldgate East and Aldgate. The Government's story features trains travelling *away* from King's Cross that are attacked. Any blast on a train going the other direction – unless merely experienced as a result of two trains passing by each other at the instant of explosion – kills the official theory.

The London Ambulance Service (LAS) received its first emergency call about the incident at 08.51 from the British Transport Police requesting its attendance at Liverpool Street Station in response to reports of an explosion. It quickly became apparent that the location of the incident was closer to Aldgate Station, and emergency vehicles were re-deployed to this scene. Source: London Ambulance Response, report at 10.30 am.

An early ambulance record stated: "London Fire Brigade requested our attendance at Aldgate station. Following procedure, I called London Underground to check the details and ensure it was not a false alarm. Underground staff confirmed that an explosion had occurred and whilst I entered the details, they started to get more information about further incidents on the network at Liverpool Street and Edgware Road."[1]

They were first summoned to Aldgate station; then reports came in of a *further incident* at Liverpool Street. The Fire Brigade was summoned by the Metropolitan police service: "at 08.56 Metropolitan Police call the Brigade to a fire and explosion at Aldgate tube station".

The first travel report from Transport for London made at 09.55 informs the public that the network has been suspended and all stations evacuated following major incidents at Liverpool Street and Edgware Road on the Hammersmith & City Line. A web site update at 10.25 states that one of the trains involved was a Hammersmith & City Line travelling towards Liverpool Street: that is, towards King's Cross, rather than away from it! And the same report was given by Tube Lines on July 7th. The travel report stated that: "At 09:46, the London Underground was suspended and all stations commenced evacuation, following incidents at Aldgate station heading towards Liverpool Street station on the Hammersmith & City line."

The Met reported on July 7th at 4.30 pm that "At 08.51 on 7 July at Liverpool Street Station there was a confirmed explosion in a carriage 100 yards into the (Liverpool Street-bound station) tunnel," i.e. the train was entering the Liverpool Street station. This information was repeated the following day by Andy Hayman CBE, Assistant Commissioner of Metropolitan Police Specialist Operations, responsible for terrorist investigations. On 8th July, 2005 Andy Hayman told a press conference of the assembled world's media:

> In relation to the tube train in Aldgate travelling toward Liverpool Street, the explosion occurred in a carriage approximately 100 yards into the tunnel. The device was in the third carriage and unfortunately we can't be any more specific than that.

He is here reporting a Circle Line – not Hammersmith and City – travelling the wrong way, anticlockwise. That was an official announcement by the 'Assistant Commissioner of Metropolitan Police Specialist Operations, responsible for terrorist investigations.' One can view testimony in support of this on a 'Youtube' video.[2] Interviewed by CNN on the afternoon of July 7th, the survivor (whose name we don't quite catch) describes the explosion on a Circle Line train going anticlockwise, coming into Liverpool Street from Aldgate. She saw lights and sparks outside her coach and 'people in a horrendous state,' and attributed whatever had happened to a power surge. The traumatised passengers had to walk back via Aldgate where she saw 'at least a dozen' fire engines outside, as well as a crowd of paramedics. At the bottom of the CNN screen a banner proclaimed 'Police and witnesses report at least 6 explosions.'

These were the initial perceptions as received by London's *Evening Standard* David Taylor, the Executive News Editor:

> About 90 seconds after the first bomb, our Transport Editor received the first call about Aldgate – literally, 90 seconds after it occurred, from one of his contacts who had been on the train that was ahead. He said there had been a massive bang and people were running through Liverpool Street. Within a moment or two we had another call from a City source, who had offices above Aldgate, who told us of a huge explosion. By about 9.05am, we had a trusted and known union contact who was telling us that people on the ground were saying there had been three explosions on the network. To add to that, we had eyewitnesses by about 9.30am who were ringing up to say that they had been on the train and had seen bodies on the line at Aldgate.

Which way was the Circle Line train going? The July 7th Review Committee heard a lot of the stories, and here is its transcript of how Jonathan Richards of LBC News and Heart 106.2 received the story:

> From our perspective, we were having witnesses telling us that the Aldgate bomb had been on a train that was travelling from Kings Cross towards Tower Hill. However, the police and TfL, for 36 hours afterwards, were maintaining that the train was coming from Tower Hill towards Kings Cross. *Which as it turned out, was quite important.* That was a case of reporters specifically putting the point to the police and TfL, and them saying 'No, you've got it wrong; it was coming from Tower Hill.'[3]

For those not familiar with the geography of the London tubes, allow me to explain what will be obvious to Londoners: a train travelling from Tower Hill towards King's Cross would have had to have been on the Circle Line travelling anticlockwise, and Aldgate is the stop because Tower Hill in that direction. Thus 'the police and Transport for London, for 36 hours afterwards' were insisting on a train direction incompatible with the official story.

Michael Henning in his testimony to the GLA described how survivors emerged from Aldgate, not Liverpool Street, and how they walked down the tube line. Drivers from other trains came to the rescue:

> They helped us off the back of train. No criticism for them, but the decision was made to walk to Aldgate station, which meant that we had to walk past the train. I subsequently found out that those in the rear carriages did not know there had been an explosion. They had no idea what they were going to see in a matter of seconds.

Mr Henning here appears as concerned about the trauma which persons in the rear carriages would experience, as the wounded trooped past them on their way to Aldgate station, and surmised: 'whether perhaps we should have walked to Liverpool Street and spared them the views that were coming.' That indicates that the train was travelling *from* Aldgate *towards* Liverpool street.

The initial report of the Met at 10.20 am stated:

> At approx 08:50 on 7.7.05 we were called to Aldgate Station to assist the City of London police and British Transport Police regarding an incident on the underground system. All of the emergency services are on scene. This has been declared as a major incident. Too early to state what has happened at this stage. There have been further reports from multiple locations in London of explosions. It is too early to say what has caused these explosions. Police are responding to reports from: Edgware Road, Kings Cross, Liverpool Street, Russell Square, Aldgate East and Moorgate underground stations.

Then at 12.30, the Met issued a statement excluding Aldgate East as the site of an explosion: "There are four confirmed sites where police are dealing with reported explosions this morning. These are:

* Russell Square and King's Cross underground
* Moorgate, Aldgate, and Liverpool Street underground
* Edgware Road underground
* Tavistock Square, where there has been a confirmed explosion on a bus."

Aldgate East station (Hammersmith and City line) has changed to Aldgate (Circle Line), easy enough to confuse, maybe. Likewise, London's paper the *Evening Standard* of July 7th reported 'huge blasts' on 'packed tube trains' at Liverpool Street, Aldgate and Moorgate stations – as well as Edgware Road, King's Cross and Russell Square.

An early BBC London report that morning stated that, in the 20 minutes that had passed since 08:50, the Network Control Centre was now dealing with these separate issues: loss of power supply, derailment at Edgware Road / person under train, person under train at Liverpool Street, and loss of high tension power cable near Moorgate. That account could validate the 'power surge' hypothesis. Linked to the incidents at the three City stations, (Liverpool Street, Aldgate and Aldgate East) was a blown high-tension power cable at Moorgate. A power surge would not be localised to one specific station.

Many of the witnesses describe 'flames,' 'fire,' 'electrical surges' and 'crashes' while very few describe hearing an explosion. Michael Henning testified that: "There was no bang I heard; it was just a lot of noise. I had been twisted and thrown down to the ground". Bruce Lait and his dancing partner Crystal are the best-known witnesses, maybe because the Queen visited him in his hospital bed in Cambridge. From there, Lait recalled how the carriage had had about 20-25 people in it:

> I remember an Asian guy, there was a white guy with tracksuit trousers and a baseball cap, and there were two old ladies sitting opposite me…We'd been on there for a minute at most and then something happened. It was like a huge electricity surge which knocked us out and burst our eardrums. I can still hear that sound now…We were right in the carriage where the bomb was … The policeman said 'mind that hole, that's where the bomb was'. The metal was pushed upwards as if the bomb was underneath the train. They seem to think the bomb was left in a bag, but I don't remember anybody being where the bomb was, or any bag.

The blast came from below – with not a Muslim or a rucksack in sight. His local newspaper, the *Cambridge Evening News,* reported this on July 11th.[4] His testimony was given a mere day or two after the blast, which tends to make it reliable, in contrast with Mr Biddle's, which only came to him more than two months later, *after* seeing a suggestive video on the subject.

His dancing partner Crystal described an event with no blast but an eerie electrocution effect: "I sat next to the double doors where the glass panel was. Bruce was beside me on the left. A lady was standing in the middle of the carriage holding the pole and two older ladies were opposite me. I was really tired. I had my eyes closed for about 20 seconds and all of a sudden I felt as if I [was] having a fit and couldn't control myself. I slipped to the side. It was as if I had been electrocuted and thousands of volts were going through me. My face was really sore. I slowly opened my eyes and it was dusty and foggy and black. To start with I couldn't hear anything, I couldn't see anything. I must have been screaming: 'Help me, help me'... Directly in front of me was a big hole."[5]

The Times carried some eyewitness reports:[6]

* Joanna Myerson, 29, covered in black soot and shaking with shock, was travelling from West Hampstead on a Circle Line train at 8.56 from Farringdon to Aldgate (i.e., clockwise on the Circle Line). All of a sudden everything went white and we got thrown to the floor and there was smoke and fire outside. It sounded like an impact almost. You could see a sort of electrical fire outside the carriage, on the wall of the tunnel." In this train *going in the "right" direction*, it would seem that no bomb went off inside the carriage.

* Mustafa Kurtuldu, 24, from Hackney, said: "The train seemed to almost lift up off the rails. It sounded like an impact."

* At 8.50am, Manjit Dhanjal was sitting on a train between Aldgate East and Liverpool Street station (that is, heading toward King's Cross), on her way to work in the City. "There were a few sparks and I thought it was just a power surge." Ms Dhanjal, 26, said: "Then I saw this fireball a few carriages in front of me, and everything went black. She saw sparks and wondered about them, before the main fireball appeared.

* Sachin, another passenger travelling west from Aldgate East, gave a detailed account of how 'My train had just left Aldgate East station when I heard a huge explosion which shook the windows of our train. The lights dimmed and came back on again and the train came to a stand-still [....] Shortly afterwards though, the train driver told us that a fuse had blown (whatever that meant) and I was reassured by that.' The whole train came to a standstill in the tunnel and had to be evacuated, which took until about 11 am, walking out at Aldgate East station.'[7] Accounts describe walking wounded emerging from Aldgate East 'with cuts and soot and debris in their hair.'

* Ken Murphy in his report to the BBC describes being one of the paramedics on the scene. He enters a dark tunnel from Aldgate station and sees body parts *before* reaching the train or the affected carriage. The recovery team Manager for LU, Howard Collins, claims that train 204 travelled 80 to 90 metres after the actual explosion. Here we have a train number, with a description indicating that it was travelling *away* from Aldgate i.e. towards Liverpool Street and King's Cross.

A week after the blast, the Met put out a statement alluding to:

'the Circle Line train travelling from Liverpool Street to Aldgate station. The device was in the third carriage of a train approx. 100 yards into the tunnel...'[8]

Right after the blast, the Metropolitan police took over management of the whole crash site from MetroNet, who manage the Piccadilly line. They ought to know what was going on. But, the official 'Narrative' has the Aldgate blast happening in the *second* carriage (from the front). So the experts are here disagreeing over the carriage in which the bombs were located. How could that be? The police, having ownership of the crime scene for a couple of weeks after the blast, ought surely to be able to tell which carriage was cratered-out. This dilemma forms an analogy with what we saw in the case of the Piccadilly and Edgware Road blasts, where the experts were surprisingly unable to decide at which end of the carriage the blasts had occurred.

Whatever happened at Aldgate, it was more *non-localised* than has been made out by the British media. Perhaps those setting it off could not control its effect exactly, or it is even possible that they were not concerned with what the later-constructed story would involve, i.e. only trains travelling *away from* King's Cross. It was something very electrical. Pictures show electric wires and circuits blown, and strange fires often without the sound of a blast were experienced.[9] Turning away from these uncertain conjectures, we conclude with one clearly-described experience. If the best-known survivor testimony from this Aldgate incident was that of Bruce Lait and his dancing-partner Crystal, then this was because of their testimony that the blast seemed to have erupted from beneath the floor; and also because of his rather clear memory of the persons around him before the blast, which excluded any Muslim with rucksack. We may also note that, being a couple together, may have assisted them in hanging onto the integrity of their memories, which no one has questioned.

References

[1] Source: p.201 GLA July 7 Review Committee Report. For comparison, P.C. Aaron Debnam on duty that morning heard the announcement of an 'explosion at Liverpool Street' just before nine o'clock; later, the announcements were that it had been an 'electrical failure.' Later, he heard of the Edgware Road blast (*One Morning in July*, 2007, p.3).
[2] http://www.youtube.com/watch?v=gO67qqDl2fU.
[3] Source: 7 July Review Committee 11 January 2006 – transcript of agenda item 4, session one.
[4] www.cambridge-news.co.uk/news/region_wide/2005/07/11/83e33146-09af-4421-b2f4-17 79a86926f9.lpf.
[5] Source: *Sunday Mirror* 12th July 2005.
[6] http://www.timesonline.co.uk/tol/news/uk/article541312.ece Timesonline July 7th 'London Blast: Survivor's Tales'.
[7] p.247 GLA Review Committee report.
[8] Met Police Service Home, 'One week anniversary' bombings appeal' 14.7.05.
[9] Power surge hypothesis:
http://antagonise.blogspot.com/2005/08/77-london-bus-explosion-kicker.html.

II. EDGWARE ROAD

<u>Chris Stokes of Whitchurch:</u> 'The window behind me had exploded in, part of the ceiling was on the floor and there was a large hole in the floor … We broke through into the next carriage where it was even worse'.

<u>Danny Belsten from Manchester</u>: 'they walked me through the first carriage where the manholes in the carriage were blown out'.

<u>Hustin (a blogger)</u>: 'I boarded the train at King's Cross after a series of line closures forced me onto a Circle Line train …Travelling just past Edgware Road Station the train entered a tunnel. We shook like any usual tube train as it rattled down the tracks. It was then I heard a loud bang. The train left the tracks and started to rumble down the tunnel. It was incapable of stopping and just rolled on. A series of explosions followed as if tube electric motor after motor was exploding. Each explosion shook the train in the air and seems to make it land at a lower point…When the train came to a standstill people were screaming, but mainly due to panic as the carriage was rapidly filling with smoke and the smell of burning motors was giving clear clues of fire'.

<u>Sharan (Middlesex, London)</u>: 'I was in the last carriage of the Circle Line train that had just left Paddington. The tube had just left when there was a sudden explosion and the square marked area in the centre of the tube exploded…There was black smoke everywhere and a very strong smell as if the wiring in the carriage was burning… As I walked [down the tunnel] I began crying because I could not bear to see the state of the front 3 carriages. There was smashed glass everywhere, the carriage had almost melted.' Sharan was on an Eastbound train that had just left Paddington.

The testimonies repeatedly fail to sound like bombs going off inside carriages. The bombed carriages were destroyed by Metronet and Tubelines a year after the event, after no one had seen them: or, no one who would communicate anything to the public.

Mark Honigsbaum's audio report

Guardian columnist Mark Honigsbaum was outside Edgware Road during the morning of July 7th. He had been speaking all morning to survivors as they were evacuated, and his phone call put through from the Hilton Hotel opposite the Edgware Road tube was made around noon to *The Guardian's* newsdesk. He first filed this audio report, after speaking to a good eyewitness source at Marks and Spencers who believed the Edgware Road bomb was under the train, and then he later composed and sent off a written account.[1] His written account did *not* make it into the next day's edition of the paper, despite his vivid, first-hand accounts of the terrible event.

His audio report has a *Guardian* URL but is not indexed in the Guardian's audio-report library, www.guardian.co.uk/audio/.[2] It thus hovers in a limbo condition, where it could not be deleted because too many people had copied it, yet remained unpublished and un-archived. What was the problem?

If there was a problem, it was just that of a journalist telling the truth.

The shattered survivors filed into the nearby Marks and Spencers, and then into the London Hilton opposite, to be treated for shock and burns. 'What seems to have happened is that … passengers had just left Edgware Road travelling Westwards towards

Paddington, when they heard a massive explosion under the carriage of the train' he explained, which had caused all this mayhem. Just as their train left for Paddington, passengers felt the blast as 'tiles and covers on the floor of the train suddenly flew up, and then, the next thing they knew, there was an almighty crash which they now believe was from a train opposite hitting their train which had been derailed by the explosion. Then everything went black and the carriage filled with smoke. A man caught by the blast had "very, very bad injuries to his legs".[3]

On Saturday, *The Guardian* published an anodyne, chopped-up version of the Honigsbaum report.[4] 'Davinia', Mark reported on the audio, experienced a massive fireball coming towards her, and the next thing she knew, she was burned all over. That is the *only* part of the above story which got into print. Otherwise, the printed account gave more space to a witness in the eastwards-travelling circle-line train. In seven paragraphs it described how the train slammed to a halt after the blast, and then on the track ahead 'There were huge pieces of metal which had been ripped out of their rivets lying about.' It tells of windows being broken, but gave *no* indication as to what caused the train to stop – as did Mark's initial report, so clearly.[5] It stated that Davinia was on her way to Canary Wharf, but did not trouble its readers with the fact that this Circle Line train would have had to be travelling East, not West.

The log of the Duty Operations Manager at Edgware station merely stated 'Edgware Rd 216 – Leading 2 cars derailed & badly damaged- 5 confirmed dead, many injured' The damaged vehicles of the Edgware Road train were 5505 and 6505, the latter being the one lifted out by crane (source Clive Davros). Thus we do have confirmation of a specific train which suffered derailment, in accord with Honigsbaum's story. A year later he tried to back out from this early report of his, but without suggesting what was wrong with it – or that confirmation via other testimonies was available.[6]

Where was it?

One week after the bombings, the Met issued an appeal for witnesses, and described the Edgware Road locus as

> Westbound Circle Line train *coming into Edgware Road station*, approx. 100 yards into the tunnel. The explosion blew a hole through a wall onto another train on an adjoining platform. The device was in the second carriage, in the standing area near the first set of double doors.[7] [italics mine]

Westbound and Eastbound Circle and District lines run adjacently from that station with no wall between them: so somebody just dreamed up a hole being blown in a wall! It later transpired that damage to the tunnel had been confined to cabling that carries signalling information, communications and power, i.e. to electrical apparatus.

Was the train just entering the Edgware Road station, as the Met reported? Professor John Tulloch, travelling on a Circle Line train from Euston Square to Paddington, having just composed a paper on 'Risk in everyday Life,' clearly recalls that the blast came just *after* the train had left Edgware Road, entering the tunnel.[9] Likewise, most testimonies as in that above-quoted by Mark Honigsbaum have the train – indeed all three of the trains normally focused on – just pulling *out from* the station when the blast occurred. The Transport for London website on 9th July had the bomb going off on

'Circle Line train number 216 travelling Westbound, heading from Edgware Road station to Paddington station.'

Here is a picture, the only one, of the floor of the Edgware Road tube after the blast. Indeed this is the *only image in the public domain* of a train carriage at Edgware road (strangely appearing from America – see Appendix 8). It again fails to clarify anything much. As with the earlier image, the whole side of the carriage is missing and one sees merely the wall of the underground. All the CCTV images and photos taken were quickly classified as national security items – somewhat as, after 9/11, Mayor Giuliani quickly forbade the taking of photos at 'Ground Zero'. The first and second cars from the front were wrecked.

The London Assembly Hears Evidence

Personal testimonies were heard in 2006 by the '7 July Review Committee' of the London Assembly. It was given a mandate 'to review some of the lessons to be learned from the 7 July bomb attacks on London'. No one commented on the striking corroboration of the Honigsbaum thesis that here appeared.[10] We may pity this Review Committee for the way it had to ignore all the central themes emerging from the testimonies which it heard: that considerably more than three trains were affected, that the blasts were not confined to single locations, that there were rather few accounts which sounded like bombs going off and certainly no reliable accounts of Muslim terrorists, that serious injuries were all of the lower body, legs and feet, never arms; and that trains travelling towards King's Cross were plainly also involved. Testimonies involved carriages imploding and parts of the floor being blown upwards.

Here is the disturbing testimony of 'John' [McDonald]:

> Just after the train left Edgware [Road] station, there was a massive bang followed by two smaller bangs and then an orange fireball. I put my hands and

arms over my ears and head as the windows and the doors of the carriage shattered from the blast. Splintered and broken glass flew through the air towards me and other passengers. I was pushed sideways as the train came to a sudden halt. ... Shouting and screaming were now coming from the train that had stopped next to us ... Passengers left by the trackside door, that had been blown away.[11]

I walked into an unknown hell... I got to the centre of the carriage and my foot slipped beneath me, and I fell into a hole in the floor. My arm stopped me going right through and on to the live rail beneath. My bag, which I had been carrying on one side, jammed me to a standstill. My other arm was resting on what I thought was a soft bag. My forearms were keeping me from falling through the hole. I could not see a thing. I thought I was going to die; there was no one there; they had all left the carriage. I put my knees into the foetal position to stop them from touching the live rail beneath me. I tried to swing my legs to see if I could find a ledge or a bracket underneath the carriage to rest my shoes on, but there was not any. [He is rescued from the hole] I could not see anything below my waist, but managed not to fall into any of the holes...

Jason asked me to look after another man, who I will call Stan, who was halfway through a hole in the floor. This is where the double doors of the carriage should have been. There was a massive hole in the floor and the roof; the metal all around it was all jagged and bent from the explosion. Parts of the metal were covered in blood. I went to a little ledge – all that was left of the floor – to see if I could get close to Stan to give him some water from my bottle, but I could not because of the jagged pieces of metal. I went inside the hole and tried to reach Stan, but I slipped on a blood-coated sheet of metal. I thought that I might try to jump into the hole, but decided that, if I did, I would get impaled on the large, jagged, pointed piece of metal that was protruding from the hole.

The maintenance light from the Tube wall threw a soft beam of light on to Stan's face. All the other areas of the floor were dark with no light. I told him and Stan that I would go and get help. I could not get out of the train from that side, so I had to return back the way I came. I could not see anything below my waist, but managed not to fall in any of the holes.

His rescuer had just finished putting a tourniquet on a man's leg. Another person asked for help in putting a tourniquet on 'David's leg' .... 'There had been screaming in the carriage alongside, which I had ignored, but now the screaming was coming from the end of our carriage ... After all the death and destruction in the carriage, we had to get a result: he must not die. The screams were getting louder, 'We are all going to die. It is a waste of time. Al-Qaeda planted bombs in each carriage,' they screamed. I walked alongside the track to find Jason with two women. He said their feet had been severely injured by the blast. The women continued screaming, 'It is all a waste of time. We are all going to die.' I said, 'That might be the case, but you still have your legs. Other people have lost their legs down the carriage, and are in a far worse state than you.'

Let us try to summarise. People have legs or feet blown off, never their arms: that is a recurrent theme. No hint appears of any Muslim with a bomb – that is common to all witnesses in this sixty-page report. There is a huge hole in the floor between two doors, with jagged, blood-coated metal sticking *upwards* everywhere. And, there was more than one hole: after being rescued from one, 'John' then managed to avoid falling into 'any of the holes.' More than one blast was experienced, with people screaming about multiple bombs. More than one *train* was involved – and, it may not be our business to fathom exactly how this event was arranged.

Moving on to other testimony from the London Assembly hearings: 'Ben' was in the approaching train, travelling from Paddington towards Edgware road, when at 08.51 there was a very loud bang, and 'Our train came to a very sudden stop, as did the train travelling in the opposite direction. I initially thought the two trains had struck each other... 'Tim' was likewise in the approaching train at Edgware Road: 'When the explosion occurred, the noise was both vast and quiet. Darkness came immediately,' He was able to get through into the damaged Circle Line train where he could use his medical skills: 'So many questions flooded my brain as I worked to tie up leaking blood supplies, observe the dead and move swiftly to those who showed signs of life. A man already referred to by John this morning, half in and half out of the floor, was still breathing. He had no shirt, just a charred torso....' He saw 'Alison,' 'a person blown out of the doors and into the wall of the tunnel .... Her right leg was not the right shape.'

Mr Biddle remembers

These are real and vivid human testimonies. We now return to a different case, not included in that London Assembly testimony, which may show the condition of 'False Memory Syndrome'. Danny Biddle was in a coma for six weeks after losing an eye and both legs in the Edgware Road blast that morning. As he lay recovering, he watched the 'Khan' video of 5th September and it exerted a deep effect upon him.[12] From being in that vulnerable state, he had placed before him the powerful images of this terror-video. Then, three weeks after watching that video, he was finally ready to share his memories of the event.

The first version of Biddle's story (24th September) had him standing in the tube and seeing Khan, who was ten feet away and sitting down, fiddle in his rucksack and then 'pull a cord.' Biddle 'was then hurled out of the carriage and left lying with the carriage doors crushing his legs.' A South African Army officer rescued him by prising the train doors off his legs. The doors had fallen onto him and chopped them off. It sounds as if 'Khan' had got on the crowded train before him, as he was sitting down while Biddle was standing up. (*The Mirror*, 24th September)

Two months later his story appeared in *The Sunday Times,* and now we hear of Biddle getting on the Circle Line train at Liverpool Street station that morning. He found himself standing right next to 'Khan': 'That morning I got on the front of the train, which was closest to the stairs, and stood next to the bomber, Mohammad Siddique Khan. I looked at him, as you do. He seemed quite calm. Nothing, in retrospect, made me think: "This guy's got a bomb." He looked at me, and as he did so he put his hand inside his rucksack, looked at me again, looked away, and pulled back his hand.' Biddle is now claiming to have survived being right next to the bomb – which supposedly splattered 'Khan' all over the walls! [13]

> Next, 'I was slammed straight out of the train by the force of the blast, bounced off the wall of the tunnel — that's how I got the big scar on my head — and skidded along like a rag doll. As I landed, the train came to a halt and the doors,

opened out by the blast, closed violently — guillotining my legs.' The blast caused the doors of a moving train to open, so Mr Biddle could be thrown against the wall of the tunnel – then have his legs chopped off by a tube door? Tube doors in their normal motion are rubber, gentle, and unable to cut anything, least of all a leg.[14]

Mr Biddle recalled how his large, South African rescuer (Adrian Heili) climbed under the train, and while doing so checked as to whether the 'live rail' was still live by laying his hand upon it. This has to be a dream-hallucination, as such things do not happen in the real world. We respectfully suggest that Mr Biddle may not as yet have fathomed the unbearable memories, of what blew his legs off that terrible morning.

It is of interest to compare Biddle's memory with that of another who was sitting fairly close to him, and who likewise lost a leg. Mr David Gardiner recalls being blown *upwards* and hitting his head on the roof of the coach; his testimony only occurred a year after the event: he was a mere three feet away from the bomb when it went off, the *Evening Standard* revealed – '... three feet from Mohammed Siddique Khan' – but gave no evidence of Khan being there (June 21, p.2). Sitting next to the perspex barrier, Gardiner reckons this helped to save his life: 'Everything went black. I remember being lifted, floating through the air, hitting my head. Next thing I was sprawled on the floor. It was dark and murky, people were moaning.' His left leg had to be amputated above the knee. Mr Gardner described his sensation as the blast went off: 'I was floating through air, wondering if I'd be alive when I came down.'[15]

Seeing Khan?

'Tell Tony he's Right' blared the *Sun's* headline for November 8th with a horrific picture of Professor John Tulloch, who was slowly recovering from his wounds, having been not far from Mr Biddle when the blast occurred. Mr Tulloch had not been consulted over this front-page exposure. He had been sitting directly opposite where the media and police were placing Khan the supposed (but curiously unseen) master-bomber, and no shortage of people had asked him if he could remember this. Was he not sitting just three feet away from Khan?[16] The image of the bomber failed to trigger his memory, and he remains unconvinced whether he saw the man who may have been sitting opposite him. 'I don't know if I did see him,' he said. 'I'm still not sure.'

Going back to his very first interview on July 13th, he had there stated: 'I don't remember hearing any noise or blast. But I could see a strange nasty yellow light and then it all went black ... Then I saw another train next to us. I assumed it must have been a train crash.'[17] Three months later, an interview with the *Western Mail* proclaimed 'Survivor may have seen bomber moments before explosion', and gave a detailed account of the events – but with no hint of him seeing Khan.[18] He merely described a gruesome bright yellow colour, by which everything had seemed distorted, a sudden yellow snapshot of the carriage.

Commendably, Prof. Tulloch protested at the *Sun's* 'using my image to push through draconian and utterly unnecessary terrorism legislation.'[19] The comment he made about Blair's initial response to the news of July 7th, from his bed in Paddington Hospital, remains of deep interest:

I saw those photos of Blair at Gleneagles. I saw his performative act, the way he put his head down and held his hands. Of course he was ready for it. Of course he had his performance all ready for it. I was very angry about that.

As a professor of media studies, he should know (*One Day in July*, p.49).

Two Trains, or Three?

'Transport for London' counted six fatalities from the Edgware Road blast. It added: 'A Hammersmith & City Line train at Edgware Road sustained damage, while passing Circle Line train 216 when the device exploded. No fatalities or injuries were recorded on the Hammersmith & City Line train.'[20] The status of this damaged Hammersmith and City Line train remains a bit of a mystery.

The anonymous 'Official Account' or 'narrative' of May 2006 concerning the events of July 7th had *no comment* on which trains were involved in the Edgware Road event, while the London Assembly's report of June, 2006 just stated, 'At 9.07 am, Fire Control received a call alerting them to the location of the incident on the Hammermith and City Line at Edgware Road.' – and that was all![21] The main blast cannot however have been on this line.

Jenny Nicholson, 26, who died that morning, seems to have been on the *eastbound* Circle Line service which she had boarded at Paddington station, and she had phoned her boyfriend, James White, only minutes earlier.[22] This situation turned out to have theological implications, as the mother of the young lady, the Rev Julie Nicholson, found herself unable to celebrate communion for her parishioners, and announced that she was resigning from her parish, because the 'wound within' had to heal! The Bishop of Bristol commented that 'These situations in life shake the faith of everybody, because they immediately bring into focus the "why" question.' This 'why' question did not, alas, allude to how someone could be killed in a train going in the *opposite direction* to that on which a suicide bomb is said to have exploded – but was solely addressed to the Deity!

Kurush Anklesaria testified:

'I was on the train going from Bayswater station sitting in the first compartment of the train and after passing Paddington station at about 08:50 there was a huge blast just at the side of my feet and part of the floor was ripped open.'[23] Other reports do not have an Eastbound-train getting its floor ripped open! A young man from Oxford, Simon Corvett, recalls being on an Eastbound train around Edgware Road Tube station when there was a deafening, huge bang which broke all the windows and brought the train to a halt, with passengers all screaming. Clearly one would like to re-contact these people and see if they still stick by their testimonies, especially concerning where they had come from and where they were going to. Simon Corvett's testimony was in the *Evening Standard* for July 7th i.e. it was given right away, and since then has appeared on various other sites. Are their testimonies to be flushed down the Memory Hole just because they recall going the 'wrong' way? Let's just say that it is hard to avoid the conclusion that Jenny Nicholson did really die in an Eastbound train, around Edgware Road.

An Eastbound Circle Line train was just passing by the Westbound train and coming into Edgware Road, when its driver Geoff Porter experienced 'a bright yellow glow' (he mentioned no sound) and 'My first thought was that the other train had derailed and hit me.' He jammed on the brakes, and then allowed his passengers to disembark out from his driver's compartment. Later, he walked through his train to check that everyone was OK. Passengers had soot on their faces but he saw no injuries. Thus the death of Jenny Nicholson *could not have been* on this train.[24] Mr Porter added, curiously, 'Two guys had gas masks on, I don't know where they got them from.'[25] – one regrets that this throwaway remark was not followed up, instead of being forgotten, for it surely points to the perpetrators, or at least to unwitting exercise personnel whom the perpetrators had pre-positioned. This is the *only* testimony we have, from a train driver, in the whole July 7th saga.

It would appear that several trains were involved, and that the rush to pin the blame on a single (unseen, unphotographed) suicide bomber has led to the marginalizing of debate over how the explosions really took place. The dossier prepared by David Minahan[26] (*A Forensic Analysis of the 7/7 London Bombings*) concluded: 'There were at least four trains involved in the Edgware Road incidents. One of these was at a platform whilst travelling east...Another was in the tunnel, travelling east between Paddington and Edgware Road. ...There was at least one fatality on this. It is a matter of record that Jenny Nicholson had boarded a train at Paddington. It is perhaps surprising that her mother, a C of E vicar, who was the subject of a lot of media attention had not commented on this.'

From the BBC Archive

Will Thomas: 'I was on the eastbound Circle Line train from Paddington … I thought we had collided with the westbound train.'

Yotty Toda: 'I was in the train when the blast occurred between Edgware Road and Paddington... I was in the second carriage so I had to go through the first one in order to evacuate. When I reached the end of the first carriage, I thought I would see the driver's compartment, but it was totally blown off. I saw parts of the compartment – such as the doors and the roof – scattered around the track. I was helped down to the track by underground staff and we walked all the way to the Edgware Road station in the dark tunnel.' It is evident that Yotty Toda's frightening account is of an Eastbound train, and that its driver had almost certainly been killed.

These typical testimonies, collated by the BBC from eyewitness Edgware Road survivors, *do not localise the blast* to a single carriage; they have the blast coming from below; and they have the train windows imploding, not exploding as they would have done were the bomb inside the carriage.[27]

One would have liked to see a photograph of the floor of the coach, or even have a panel of journalists be allowed to see the floor of the coach. Instead, the coaches were hidden away, no one knows where, and then destroyed one year after the event. The primary evidence at the scene of the crime has been removed.[28] If there is an ongoing investigation, then this act of destruction of vital evidence would itself be a criminal offence.

The Edgware Road tube station has its name shared by two geographically separate stations on the London Underground. The explosion is said to have occurred in the one situated just off Edgware Road in Chapel Street, while the other station also referred to by the same name is a Bakerloo line tube station on Edgware Road. The stations are approximately 150 metres apart and on opposite sides of the Marylebone Road flyover and dual carriageway. As with events at the similarly named Aldgate and Aldgate East stations, the existence of two similarly-named tube stations may have caused much confusion on the day.

TfL have confirmed that there were no injuries or fatalities on the train passing in the opposite direction to Circle Line train 216. Could these people have been injured or killed on the platform at Edgware Road station rather than on the train, as indicated in David Minahan's comprehensive dossier? 'Bindesh' on the BBC web site appears to claim that there was an explosion on the platform: 'I was in Edgware Road train station, waiting for my friend. There was a big explosion. I was lucky to escape from that blast. I became faint and a police officer woke me up by putting water on my face. When I woke up I saw a very deadly scene which I will never forget in my life. The platform was full of blood, people were screaming and shouting to get off the platform'. (BBC News, 'London explosions: Your accounts', 19 July)

The American girls Katie and Emily Benton were sight-seeing in London that morning and were, according to early reports, intending to visit the Tower of London, and so were travelling eastwards out of Paddington — towards Edgware Road and King's Cross.

> We were only on the train for just half a minute. It wasn't — we had just sat down. The train had just taken off. We didn't have time to look around at what other people looked like or who was on there or anything. And then the explosions went off. I felt like I went into, like, the fetal position and just, like, crouched down and I felt like I was being electrocuted. And I felt like I was on fire and I was burning. I could feel my skin like, peeling off. Everything had just been, you know, ripped.

These two were kept away from the media by the drastic measure of being flown out under assumed names to Montreal, and then switched to another plane with a different crew to complete their journey home to Kentucky.[29]

CNN International were the only channel to report that the police carried out a controlled explosion at Edgware Road station, and as the reporter adds, "of course hampering the operation to collect evidence from the scene" – and, presumably, one may add, that of taking photographs. This was not reported by any newspaper, presumably because the notion of a further, unexploded bomb was incompatible with the 'suicide bomber' theory.[30]

Mortuary preparations arranged, days before

The London Mass Fatality Plan had only just been circulated when the bombings took place. This involved guidelines about cordoning off areas etc. As part of the Mass Fatality Plan, these were only issued to responders days before July 7th. (J7) This Plan had been prepared over a number of years under the aegis of a multi-agency planning group which included representatives of all the key relevant agencies. It was approved by the London Regional Resilience Forum in March 2005 and formally circulated to all stakeholders at the end of June, just days before the bombings.[31] In the event, The London Mass Fatality Plan worked well. The coroners, police, local authorities, pathologists and the London Resilience Team worked in close partnership to deliver a 'Resilience Mortuary,' which was ready to receive the deceased victims in 24 hours.

References

[1] Tony Gosling spoke to Mr Honigsbaum on August 20th, who provided these details.

[2] http://stream.guardian.co.uk:7080/ramgen/sys-audio/Guardian/audio/2005/07/07/ honigsbaum_070705.ra.

[3] www.nineeleven.co.uk/board/viewtopic.php?p=248,   www.nineeleven.co.uk/board/view topic.php?t=157.

[4] www.guardian.co.uk/uk_news/story/0,,1524554,00.html.

[5] See ref. 2.

[6] A year later, reviewing the use of his report by 'conspiracy theorists,' Honigsbaum endeavoured to detach himself from the thrust of his earlier report: 'Seeing isn't believing' *The Guardian* G2 27.06.06, pp. 6-11: www.guardian.co.uk/attackonlondon/ story/0,,1806794,00.html, but without saying what was wrong with it.

[7] http://cms.met.police.uk/news/major_operational_announcements/terrorist_attacks/ one_week_anniversary_bombings_appeal.

[8] On 24.8.06, Rachel North received a reply from Home Secretary John Reid, concerning several questions raised by survivors: http://rachelnorthlondon.blogspot. com/2006/09/77-cctv-question.html.

[9] Tulloch, *One day in July*, p.15.

[10] www.london.gov.uk/assembly/resilience/2006/77reviewmar23/minutes/transcript.pdf, 7th July Review committee 3rd session 23 March 2006.

[11] Transcript of Committee meeting, 23 March 2006, Volume 3, page 4.

[12] The Mirror, 'Tube bomber stared me straight in the eyes as he set off the explosion that blew my legs away', 24.7.05.

[13] By next January, Biddle is recalling Khan as standing up with the rucksack on his back http://www.guardian.co.uk/attackonlondon/s...1697438,00.html – a view highly incompatible with people losing their legs and feet.

[14] 4th December: www.timesonline.co.uk/article/0,,2099-1891957,00.html.

[15] *Hampstead & Highgate Express*, June 23, p.3.

[16] *Sunday Telegraph*/ Australia, 7/10/05.
John Tulloch's book *One Day in July* (June 2006) appeared more confident that he had, after all, seen Khan. http://www.team8plus.org/e107_plugins/forum/forum_ viewtopic.php?1411.

[17] News of the World, 10/9/05.

[18] Western Mail, 10/11/05 also 12th Oct. http://icwales.icnetwork.co.uk/0100news/ 0200wales/tm_objectid=16238382&method=full&siteid=50082&headline=survivor-may-have- seen-bomber-moments-before-explosion-name_page.html.

[19] http://politics.guardian.co.uk/terrorism/story/0,15935,1638843,00.html.

[20] http://bridgetdunnes.blogspot.com/

[21] www.london.gov.uk/assembly/reports/7july/report.pdf, pp.27-30, section 2.47.

[22] J.N. was travelling in from Reading and got on the Underground at Paddington. As a regular commuter she would arrive at her London office at nine o'clock: so it is hard to have her going in the other direction by mistake, as TV reconstructions have suggested. Quoting from Camden New journal, 'Jenny Nicholson – Miss Nicholson, 24, was killed in the

Edgware Road suicide blast on Thursday. Her tube carriage was going in the opposite direction to the train in which the bomber was travelling.'

John Tulloch (*One day in July*) was very concerned about the fate of Jenny Nicholson, and how come she was in an Eastbound train (p.47) – but he found, 'No one could answer my question.' www.guardian.co.uk/attackonlondon/story/0,,1725371,00.html.

[23] www.news24.com/News24/World/News/0,,2-10-1462_1733932,00.html.

[24] http://the-inquirer.net/default.aspx?article=24542.

[25] http://www.findarticles.com/p/articles/mi_qn4153/is_20050711/ai_n14719918, http://www.guardian.co.uk/attackonlondon/story/0,16132,1525969,00.html July 11th 2005.

[26] David Minahan kindly gave me a copy of his very comprehensive dossier, which is partly reprinted on the J7 site. It took him a year to compile it. I urged him to deposit a copy in some public reference library. It meticulously examines all of the evidence, indicating that there were considerably more blasts than reported in the Government's narrative. It would be essential for anyone participating in a 7/7 Inquiry to own a copy.

[27] http://news.bbc.co.uk/1/hi/talking_point/4659237.stm; http://z13.invisionfree.com/julyseventh/index.php?showtopic=12, http://news.bbc.co. uk/1/hi/uk/4662423.stm.

[28] The blasted carriages were destroyed one year after the event, I was told, by a Metronet spokesperson. Peter Zimonjic was given a great deal of information by LU for his book on July 7th, but even he, I was told, had not been allowed to view these coaches.

[29] Report 24 hours after the bombings on CNN news, but aired on 24 July http://transcripts.cnn.com/TRANSCRIPTS/0507/22/bn.03.html.

[30] www.londonprepared.gov.uk/downloads/lookingbackmovingforward.pdf.

[31] http://melbourne.indymedia.org/uploads/controlled_explosion_02.avi

Relevant Official Documents:

On March 23rd, 2006 the London Assembly heard lots of survivor-testimonies, both going West and East, as caught in the blast. On May 11th the 'Narrative' was released, the anonymous 'Official Report,' and this said nothing about which trains were involved. On June 6th, 2006, the big London Assembly's 3-volume statement appears, Vol 1 of which is called *Report of the 7 July Review Committee PDF*. Its piece on pp. 28-30, 'The First Hour, Edgware Road', only mentions the Hammersmith & City Line train as involved and no other.

III. King's Cross

Delay in announcement

The explosion on the southbound Piccadilly line between King's Cross and Russell Square was announced to the public at 10.25 am, approximately an hour and a half after this explosion. That was well after the No. 30 bus explosion in Tavistock Square had been reported. The blast time was then given as 08.56 am. For comparison, a year later, when the police were falling over themselves to say how quickly they had responded, this was the account given by Tim O'Toole of London Underground:

> I think the impressive thing about the timeline is how quickly the information came around, if you think about it. These incidents occurred at 8.51am; before 9.00am the emergency services and ambulances are on their way, by 9.02am we get a confirmation call that the LAS [London Ambulance Service] was headed there, and by 9.15am we have made a decision, that is not made very lightly, or ever before, to empty the entire system, which is itself a somewhat dangerous thing to do. [1]

The trusty clock of King's Cross here points at 09.25 am.

This begs the question, if the response had been so swift and efficient, then why could we, the public, not be told until one hour and forty minutes later? The picture shows the police and ambulance service doing a fine job of coping with the disaster, so why did another hour have to go by before it could be announced on the BBC News?

Initial accounts by Transport for London (TfL) fail to mention an explosion at King's Cross or Russell Square, reporting only explosions at Liverpool Street and Edgware Road in the first press release issued at 9.55. It is not until 10.25 that King's Cross is mentioned – with the train identified as travelling *towards* rather than *away from* King's Cross:

> Latest information confirms that there were four incidents on London's transport network this morning, three on London Underground and one on London Buses. At 09:46, the London Underground was suspended and all stations commenced evacuation following incidents at: Aldgate station heading towards Liverpool Street station on the Hammersmith & City line – Russell Square station heading *towards* King's Cross station on the Piccadilly line. (Transport for London Update at 14.25 pm)

That would have to be Aldgate East station if it were the Hammersmith and City line; thus official confusion enters the story right away; but in either case, the direction is towards King's Cross. Tube Lines also reported that the train was travelling *from* Russell Square towards King's Cross in this press release issued on the day (the Piccadilly Line is run under a Public-Private Partnership contract by Tube Lines and other consortia). The explosion on the Piccadilly Line was the most serious on that day, resulting, we were told, in 27 deaths and injuries to over 340 passengers. The train was described as being at 'crush capacity', which is approximately 133 passengers per carriage. At the moment of explosion, the tube was running along a deep-level single-track tunnel.

Fire Alert

The Piccadilly Line train which blew up, coded as being number 331, had apparently come straight from its depot and was on its first journey that day. This was what Joe Vialls claimed about the Madrid trains which blew up: that, having been specially prepared, they would have needed to be on their first journey. In addition, one would need some way of fine-tuning their timing, if the three trains had to blow up synchronously, and to look as if 'suicide bombers' had got on at King's Cross at a similar time. Here we find that the Piccadilly line was in some degree closed that morning all the way from Arnos Grove to Kings Cross – nine stops – due allegedly to a 'fire alert' at Caledonian Road, the stop immediately north of King's Cross. The exception here is Finsbury Park, where Rachel North boarded, kept open because the Victoria line also passed through.

Several people recalled that Bounds Green and Wood Green stations were closed at 08.30. Thus, 'Lorenzo' recalled, 'at a little past 8:00 was a message informing everyone that there was no service on the Piccadilly line from Cockfosters to Kings Cross as there was a suspected fire.' And Edward Cowling wrote, 'I arrived at Wood Green station at 8:30 to discover it was locked and a notice saying the service was suspended between Arnos Grove and Kings Cross.' It must have taken a while to decide to lock the station entrance. A replacement bus service was set up for passengers: 'I am a London bus driver and worked part of Thursday 7th July. I can confirm bus drivers were told just before 8.00am, via radios in their cabs, of a fire alert at Caledonian Road Tube Station on the Piccadilly Line. We were asked to carry passengers in the area and accept their tickets. This is standard procedure when tube stations close and this sort of request is very much part of our job.'[2] Dramatically, several fire engines turned up by Caledonian Road. So, were the trains still travelling through during this fire alert? Passengers seemed to have remained on the platforms.

The train leaving Arnos Grove at about 8.20 moved quite slowly through the stations,[3] which had become fairly crowded owing to the delays. At Finsbury Park, where Rachel North was getting on, the tannoy announced 'Fire at Caledonian Road,' as a cause for delays. Rachel let two trains go past because they were just too crowded to get onto and took the third, getting into the first carriage. The previous two trains may have been parked at Bounds Green or Wood Green stations, filling up with rush-hour passengers. In her book, Rachel describes how the King's Cross platform was crammed with anxious commuters, helping to make this 'the most crowded train I have ever been on.'

The bomb probably went off at 08.50, although some reports aver that this was at 08.52, so about nine minutes to nine. It is believed that the exploded train was the second in the queue once the line re-opened, and that it was running about 20 minutes late as a result of this. If train 331 had been specially prepared, then it would have needed to arrive at King's Cross at the required moment, and this delay achieved that. It was in consequence very full – as Joe Orr's testimony recalls:

> 8.50 am: Finally get into King's Cross where the platform is heaving. Only a few more people can fit into our carriage.

The 331 – 311 Mystery

Two days later, on July 9th, Transport for London was reporting on the 'Piccadilly line train number 311 travelling from King's Cross St Pancras to Russell Square southbound.' This was later claimed to be a mistake, and the train 331 averred to be the one. On the 3rd of January, 2006, the story of Tom Nairn, the driver of train 311, and Ray Wright, a tube relief driver who was his train operator passenger in the driver's cab of train 311 on July 7th, appeared in the comments on a July 7th related blog.[4] Ray Wright, who had been sitting next to Tom Nairn, wrote:

> Not wishing to denigrate any of the actions of police on the day, not ONE WORD has been said about the driver of Train 311, Tom Nairn. I joined Tom's train at King's Cross, travelling in the cab with him on my way to work as a fellow driver, based at Acton Town. I took the first couple of batches of walking wounded to Russell Square and was probably the first member of staff to meet any colleague at the station. Tom stayed behind in the first car, doing what we as drivers are paid to do, looking after his train and his passengers on it. He helped some by applying tourniquets and reassuring others. He saw things that even trained police officers found themselves unable to cope with, but most importantly had to face it on his own before help arrived probably 40 minutes later, a scene of utter devastation in almost total darkness. He has never been mentioned or praised, he has remained dignified and quiet, and has never returned to drive a train.

> Recently he applied for some compensation through his union. The response from the Met Police was "We have no knowledge of this person having been involved in this incident and therefore will not be processing his claim further." Rather odd because Tom and I were interviewed by police for around three hours after the incident. The press coverage of the other 'heroes' has left him feeling completely empty and devalued. Pity when the reaction of Police and certain members of station staff are lauded, he has been completely forgotten.

— Ray Wright, Train Operator, Acton Town Depot

Tom Nairn's name seems to have disappeared when the train number was changed from 311—his train—to 331. Gary Stevens, the Duty manager at Russell Square tube station, testified:

> I was meant to start work at 0900 that morning. I woke up early, I couldn't sleep, so I decided to start work early. If I'd have gone in at the normal time I'd have been on the affected train, train 311, and I would have been in the first car. I use that carriage every day to exit the station... I was in my office at work, and at 0854 all the lights flickered in the office... we went down to the platform, couldn't see anything at all, when we noticed there was a light in the tunnel. We hung on to see what it was and it was the driver of train 311 with about 30 or 40 injured customers, who had managed to get out and he led them down the tunnel. Some of them had quite serious head injuries, clothes blown off, things like that... (Source: BBC)

He seems in no doubt which train it was. The BBC website's graphic still cites 311 as the train number. These numbers are used as radio call signs. Train 331 had emerged fresh out of Cockfosters depot (Northern tip of the Piccadilly line) on its first trip of the day and running approx 20 minutes late due to an earlier incident at Caledonian Road. Train 311 would be travelling north, (the direction given in the first TfL press release that mentions this incident), between Earl's Court and Hyde Park Corner at the revised time of 8.50 and would have arrived at King's Cross at 9.08. Were both trains involved?[5] Was the choice of train numbers a coincidence? 311 was the date of the Madrid bombing.

Ray Wright entered the passenger carriage to assist passengers out of the carriage and towards Russell Square tube Station. He saw a "sea of blackened faces in a state of total panic. ...We were screaming, above the shouting, for everyone to calm down, that we were okay at the front and we were going to get people off." He said that, as they were helping people off the train, both he and the driver still thought it was a mechanical or electrical fault.[6] None of the three drivers of what are supposed to have been the trains that morning have *ever been interviewed in public or even named*. They remain anonymous, as if given stern ultimata to keep quiet. This story about Tom Nairn is the nearest which we get to it. I wasn't allowed to interview either Ray Wright or Tom Nairn.[7]

Andy Hayman, CBE, Assistant Commissioner Specialist Operations, the officer in charge of anti-terrorist operations, explained at an 8 July Press Conference concerning this explosion: 'The device was in the first carriage, in the standing area by the first set of double doors. It's yet to be the case for us to get near the carriage. There's the threat of the tunnel being unsafe...'

Rachel and George Remember

Initial accounts on both the Met's website and BBC state that the explosion happened by the first set of double doors (i.e., those nearest to the front) on carriage one. The centre of the explosion was later changed on the BBC web site from the first set of double doors to the second set of double doors, in the first carriage. This was presumably a consequence of Rachel North's testimony – as she was standing by the first set of double doors at the time of the incident. During this adjustment, we hear no hint that anyone could check up on this matter by inspecting the carriage and locating the large hole in the floor.

Rachel, close to the first set of double doors, claimed that initially she was unaware that a bomb had exploded in her carriage:

> When the blast went off I fell to the left into a heap of people, by the left-hand set of doors. When *I started hearing the bomb was in my carriage*, I flipped. …He (the driver) told us he was trying to have the track turned off so we could walk to the next station. We were passing the information back along the carriages. … When we got out I noticed my wrist was bleeding. All our faces were black.… (9 July, *Telegraph*)

Had a bomb indeed been placed at the end of the first carriage? A train driver and his colleague spent a heroic hour rescuing wounded passengers from the front carriage, at the end of which they believed, as we have seen, that the explosion on his train had resulted from an electromechanical fault. That is consistent with many accounts from the other wrecked tube trains that morning.

The BBC's diagram, showing blast at second set of double doors.

Initially, websites of both the BBC and the Metropolitan Police had stated that the explosion had occurred by the first set of double doors. After Rachel North's fairly high-profile expostulation, the website of the BBC — but not that of Metropolitan police — adjusted the blast site down to the second set of double doors – where the Inquest had it.[8]

Did the glass that entered Rachel's wrist come from the carriage *imploding*, causing the glass to fly into the carriage? A year later, her testimony before the London July 7th review was

> There was an immediate scraping noise as the train, I think, derailed, and then immense screaming began, as the passengers who had been rolling on the floor in the darkness struggled to find out what had happened to them.[9]

Had it indeed been derailed? That would account for the immediate halting of the train and the shock experienced by other carriages.

There is a video showing two girls blood-spattered and bandaged up, recalling how they had been in the first carriage when they experienced 'an explosion overhead' and saw the 'orange light' *outside* the train, interviewed in Brunswick Square. As soon as they had made these comments, a 'minder' appears and ushers them back towards their hotel where the wounded were being held. We see them walk back towards Russell Square. That seems to be an authentic testimony from first carriage survivors.[10]

The scene of destruction inside the first carriage looking towards the 2nd carriage: cabling can clearly be seen undamaged along the tunnel wall and there is little evidence of tunnel damage. Note that the blast appears to have affected electrical areas of the train, the lighting strips, advertising boards and central lights. This image was provided by ABC News in America, on 27th July.

As regards what was experienced in the front carriage, when PC Bryan arrived at the entrance to Russell Square tube station, he found that:

> As soon as I got into the booking hall there were five or six people that had managed to get up into the booking hall that looked like they had been involved in an explosion. Their clothes were shredded. They all had blackened faces, hair standing on end and none of them knew that they had been involved in an explosion. A few people thought they had been electrocuted.

These survivors have to be from the first carriage, because those were the only ones who evacuated to Russell Square – the rest trooped back to King's Cross (Recall how thin the single, very deep tube tunnel was, with a mere six inches between carriage and wall). It was evidently not their view that any bomb had gone off, and they had to be informed of that by a PC — most likely after the Tavistock Square bomb had exploded. Once that had detonated, it provided the idea of a bomb, which could then *explain* the terrible things that had happened on the tube.

However, some sort of blast had taken place, maybe from underneath the train as with the Edgware Road blast, as noted in the previous chapter.

The London Assembly interviewed Mr George Georgiou and their interview with him occupied some ten pages, showing how valuable they regarded his testimony to be.[11] He got on at Turnpike Lane, and, like Rachel, reports delays on the line due to the fire alert. He was likewise standing up by the first set of double doors in the first carriage – adjacent to the alleged scene of devastation. He had only a slight injury (some glass in the back of his neck), and it seemed to him that the train had crashed. He had no idea that a bomb had gone off until some time later. The train was 'packed solid' and by the time it got to King's Cross:

> I'm up against the glass partition, with my back to the double doors, facing the other double doors. The doors open, another dozen force their way on. I thought, 'That is all I want, but it is only two stops.' The doors shut. The timeframe now – other people may say different, but I'm only going from how I lived it – it was approximately 12 seconds, 12-15 seconds, and then this almighty bang.

> **Richard Barnes (Chair):** The Tube had pulled out, had it?

> **George:** The Tube was moving. The doors shut; we started to pull into the tunnel. It was approximately 12-15 seconds. I'm led to believe – again, it is all later research, people I have spoken to since – the end carriage was only about 50 metres from the end of King's Cross. This almighty bang. I said, 'What the effing hell's that?' In this millisecond, from the time that went, there was this bright, orange light opposite, and I'm facing the double doors, with my back to the doors on the platform side. In that millisecond, it went from a bright orange to nothing. What the hell was that? Of course, audibly I hear a lot – screaming, praying. We now know that 25 people around me were just outright killed; another 25 people were seriously injured. My first reaction was – I knew where I was in relation to the carriage, and I knew I was on the first carriage – I thought, 'We have hit a train.'[12]

He eventually meets the driver Tom Nairn and his colleague Ray Wright; the latter leads him with a group of others down the track. The live rail has by now been switched off, he is assured; the emergency lighting comes on, and they plod along until they reach Russell Square platform. Both George and Rachel are members of 'King's Cross United'.[13] He has seen a brilliant orange light for a very brief fraction of a second, glowing outside the double doors opposite him – and there are quite a few testimonies of this nature.

But, to continue, the survivors are sitting rather dazed outside Russell Square station, and they are discussing what on earth has just happened to them. Let's listen carefully to 'George':

> What was being bandied around by other passengers who were around – I spoke to someone and said, 'Do you know what happened down there?' 'That person over there said it was a power surge.' I said, 'Oh, right.' Again, I think I had realised by then that we hadn't hit another train, because I had actually walked out through the front of the cab, so it wasn't that, which I was pleased about. Other people had said, 'I think something dropped off the train, and it hit the tunnel wall, and that is what caused the problem.' Then I saw this guy standing over just to the left of the lifts. For some reason, I thought he was the driver, because he had a green, fluorescent jacket on. I thought he was the driver, so I

went up to this guy, and said, 'Excuse me,' I said, 'but are you a driver?' He said, 'Yes I'm actually a driver.' He said, 'I was on the train that you just came off.' I said, 'Oh.' He said, 'I'm not the driver of the train. I'm on my way to the depot. The driver of the train is still down there.' I said, 'Oh right. I have been told it was a power surge.' His words to me were, 'No, never was that a power surge. I have been involved with power surges, and with power surges you never lose the emergency lights, to start with.'

It was dawning on George that no other train has been hit, and instead the passengers together are surmising that a 'power surge' had taken place. Then Ray Wright turns up, and as a tube driver they expect him to be able to tell them – but, all he has to say is that it was not a power surge. Together, in the light of day, they are seeking explanations for what happened as an event *outside* their carriage. Such stories strongly confirm the way the perception that a bomb had exploded only develops *after* the Tavistock Square bus has blown up.

Travelling North

As the 'northbound tube carrying Zeyned Basci approaches King's Cross' on the Piccadilly line, the passengers heard a huge bang as shards of glass sprayed onto them (according to *The Independent* on Sunday, 10th July 'Attack on London: Minute by minute, the horror emerges'). "There was blood everywhere," Zeyned Basci will remember later. "People were screaming and panicking. It was pitch black and then there was smoke. I thought I was going to burn alive." Through the smoke she sees a woman lying on the floor unconscious, her face gouged and bloody. A man is beside her, writhing with agony. Ms Basci is covered with other people's blood, and the carriage fills with black, choking smoke. This is high-quality horror, but is it the wrong train? "Don't panic," said the driver, coming out of his cab into the carriage. But the passengers don't listen, they are screaming. The driver opens his own door and tells them to come through, and step down into the tunnel.

The Inquest puts Zeyned Basci right adjacent to George, whose testimony we have just heard. Somehow I doubt it ... Barrister's clerk Chris Lowry from north London, was on a Piccadilly line tube 'pulling into King's Cross' when an explosion 'ripped *through the station*', killing 21 people. He said: 'I was reading my paper when I heard a bang. I don't know if I jumped up or fell forward, but I ended up out of my seat. All the lights were off except for one in the distance. Dust started to fill the carriage and I could barely see a thing. Everyone was calm in our carriage but further up I could hear women screaming and men shouting ... When we came out I realised just how serious this was. People had hair burnt off and had deep cuts. I got out of a door that had been taken off but some had to smash windows to get out.' Mr Lowry must surely have been travelling southwards towards Holborn. But, it doesn't sound at all like the train carrying Rachel and George.[13]

'Ian' recalls electrocution: 'I remember thinking that I've never been on such a packed train. The next thing I remember was reading a paper and then getting a sharp feeling of electrocution, like I imagine anyone who has been struck by lightning gets. I was knocked unconscious either during or after the electrocution and I maybe came round about 10 minutes afterwards.' (BBC News, 16 Oct., 2005)

These accounts stubbornly refuse to gel, they will not add up to a coherent picture. In the front carriage of the southbound train, we saw how two train drivers, after rescuing passengers from a carriage that we are told a bomb went off in, believe that this explosion was the result of an electrical or mechanical fault. How could that be? At the awarding of medals, these two who probably rescued the sanity of front-coach passengers receive no award from the Queen – while a number of anonymous persons did so. Were those persons being rewarded for keeping their mouths shut? At the very least, one would like a breakdown of the number of deaths per carriage. The contradictory accounts could point to more than one train having been involved; or to deliberate exaggeration, or to confusion with Peter Power's terror-drill going on that morning. A public inquiry, required to resolve this matter, shimmers like an impossible mirage.

The Mystery

We have here tried to access the raw data of people's experience to describe the extraordinary events on the Underground that morning. Close-up, they don't quite look like the single suicide bomb stories we are given. In fact, it's quite hard to find evidence for a bomb going off inside a coach. If bombs had gone off, exploding from rucksacks on the floor, we all have a fair idea of what the holes in the floor might look like. The immediate disappearance of the damaged coaches so that nobody could examine them, could have been because they did *not* look like that. The 'huge hole' seen by PC Debnam may have been just too large to credibly resemble the effect of an exploding rucksack.

Reviewing the Aldgate blast stories, we found the accounts spread out, over three stations, over both the Circle and Hammersmith and City lines, and moreover from passengers travelling in both directions. Even when one single train becomes designated, viz a Circle Line approaching Aldgate, there still remained an unreconciled difference of opinion as to whether the blast had taken place in the second or third carriage of that train. We saw how Rachel North became embroiled in a dispute, greatly lacking in an easy resolution, as to whether the blast had taken place by the first set of double doors (where she was standing) or the second (where 'George' was standing) in the first carriage of the Piccadilly line train; and then how, a year later, she received a letter from the Home Secretary, indicating that the very same unresolved dilemma existed concerning the carriage in which the Edgware Road blast had taken place.

The phenomenon tends to appear, in each of these three cases, as too *spread out* to have emanated from a single bomb. So, what was it? Witnesses recalled an instantaneous flash of orange light, often seen outside the carriage, sometimes together with parts of the floor rushing upwards. What were all the electrical effects about, from so many witnesses?[14] Why are officials continually uncertain as to where the epicenter of the blast was located – should that not be the easiest thing to ascertain? Is there any kind of de-centred electrical field effect that could have been working here, to help us understand why officials kept alluding to a 'power surge' for several hours? There were indeed passengers with burns; however there were not, I suggest, any normal reports of burning within the carriages. We are surely compelled to accept Ahmed's view that

> the London bombs produced immense energy in the form of heat and flames in a manner entirely at odds with the properties of a putative TATP explosion.[15]

But, in the pitch darkness, do we read any accounts of the seats burning, or of light coming from fires within the carriages, or even of the smell of burning? I suggest (very tentatively) that we do not. Survivors were startled to see everyone else as soot-blackened, when a light came on. Soot from the tunnel wall seems to have entered carriages, as the implosions shattered the tube windows.[16] A hypothesis based upon military-grade explosives was given by all the top experts in the days after the event, with detonators and synchronized in their explosions. Such devices could have been either placed under the seats or under the carriages, with detonators. Was it the 'C4' explosive, as was used in the major 'Gladio' operations? That 'C4' explosive produces fires, smoke and burns. Given that the police have spent upwards of £70 million on this investigation, one could reasonably expect to have a technical report evaluating this central issue, or even some details of where their forensic labs were and what they found. Instead, we are left with a mystery.

References

[1] Tim O'Toole told the July 7 review Committee 2.34, 28 June 2006, London Assembly, July 7 Report: http://www.london.gov.uk/assembly/resilience/2006/77reviewnov22/04a-tfl. pdf, 2.72.

[2] www.advfn.com/stocks/congratulations-bush-and-blair-7-7-7-regards-illuminati_9447247. html.

[3] I interviewed Eamon Spellman, a witness who works at Harrods and who got on at Arnos Grove. He was in the second carriage. He described how passengers were held in the ticket office owing to the fire alert, then put onto a train at 08.10, then told to get out and into another train on the other side of the platform which then left at 08.20. I posted this interview 15.11.07 www.nineeleven.co.uk/board/viewtopic.php?t=11521&start =120. For whether the Piccadilly line stations were closed, see Appendix 6b.

[4] Alex Cox blog. For whether there were two trains (331 and 311) involved, see http://www.team8plus.org/print.php?plugin:forum.1914.

[5] Train 311 was scheduled to leave Cockfosters at around 6 o'clock and be on its return journey back from Uxbridge to reach King's Cross at 9 o'clock. The times of trains through King's Cross were recorded in a handwritten document, 'the Train Register', kept at Earl's Court Control Centre. That document would surely resolve the above dilemmas. When TfL were asked for a copy of this document (by J7 member Philip Dunn), they replied that they no longer possessed it.

[6] BBC 18th July 2005, http://www.officialconfusion.com/77/witnesses/180705BBCtube driverchaos.html, original http://news.bbc.co.uk/1/hi/england/london/ 4694801.stm4.

[7] My endeavours to contact the train drivers Tom Nairn and Ray Wright were firmly blocked by TfL officials, who insisted that these drivers had been too upset by the event to be prepared to be interviewed about it (which one may find difficulty believing). I received a letter from TfL's Chief Public Affairs Officer Peter MacLennan in reply to my request for interview of these drivers, stating: 'Transport for London received literally hundreds of requests to interview the members of staff who were involved – with the vast majority relating to requests to interview the drivers of the affected tube trains. In the twelve months leading up to the first anniversary of the attacks we facilitated as many filming and interview requests as possible given the widespread public interest.' Startled, I visited him at his TfL office in Victoria. He agreed to a dialogue, and I reckon he agreed that what he had meant was that *no* interviews of films whatsoever are available from *any* English-language source,

pertaining to these two drivers or indeed *any* tube workers involved directly on that morning – and moreover, that we *only* know the names of the two Piccadilly line drivers because of the above-quoted and now-deleted blog comment by Ray Wright. He did point out that comments had been made by Geoff Porter, a tube driver whose train was approaching Edgware Road at the blast-moment. (NB, At the Inquest, the driver of the Edgware Road Circle line train Ray Whitehurst was *let out,* he was allowed to speak about the event for the first time. I have argued above that his testimony definitively terminated any 'suicide bomber' theory.

[8] 'The device was in the first carriage, in the standing area near the first set of double doors.' – one week anniversary' Bombings appeal, MPS.

http://cms.met.police.uk/news/major_operational_announcements/terrorist_attacks/one_wee k_anniversary_bombings_appeal; the altered BBC story: http://news.bbc.co.uk/1/ shared/spl/hi/uk/05/london_blasts/what_happened/html/russell_sq.stm.

[9] www.london.gov.uk/assembly/resilience/2006/77reviewmar23/minutes/transcript.pdf. Neither in this testimony nor in that of her published book *Out of the Tunnel* is there any hint that Rachel or anyone else perceived 'the bomber;' however, on a web-blog (18.12.05) she wrote: 'I can vouch for the fact that Germaine Lindsay got onto my train at Kings Cross because one of the passengers who was also on carriage one with me TRIED TO GET ON BEHIND HIM and couldn't, because the carriage was rammed, so went to the next carriage. He recognised Germaine from the pictures shown on the news.' (Anything that Defies my sense of Reason, http://antagonise.blogspot.com/ 2005/11/london-77-how-to-be-good-part-1.html#c113492355563608200.) I spoke to Eamon Spellman on two occasions, the co-founder with Rachel of King's Cross United, and put the question to him as to whether he had ever come across testimony, within that group, that anyone had seen 'the bomber' at any point: he replied in the negative (I posted this 29.11.07, ref. 3 link). The witness 'George' also in the first carriage *imagined* that Mr Lindsay was near to him ('I'm out of the way, doors open and another dozen force their way on, including Jermaine Lindsay. I now know that he was approximately one metre to my left') in his testimony to the London Assembly (see ref. 9). http://www.youtube.com/watch?v=O4JD6Pnogvc &eurl= youtube.

[10] Exclusive: my leg, where's my leg? Joe, 19, tells of horror on bombed Tube *The Mirror*, By Paul Gallagher 11/07/2005.

[11]   www.london.gov.uk/assembly/reports/7july/vol3-individuals.pdf London Assembly Report of the 7 July Review Committee Volume 3: Views and information from individuals, June 2006 – Interview with 'George', pp 127-147.

[12] In Rachel North's words: 'The group of people from the Kings Cross bombed train is now 111 strong, and so we have been able to access a very great deal of information about what happened on 7th July and after, simply by sharing our stories and information for a year on our private website and by meeting up in the pub.' House of Lords' speech, 12 July 2006.

[13] Aaron Debnam, *One Morning in July*, 2007, p26.

[14] Power surge hypothesis (NB, I reckon this argument by 'The Antagonist' of J7 is quite original): http://antagonise.blogspot.com/2005/08/77-london-bus-explosion-kicker.html.

[15] Ahmed, p.33.

[16] A chemist at my college UCL, Dr A.S., who clearly had some familiarity with the case, and had advised the defence council for the 21/7 case, advised me in a definite manner that the July 7th tube explosions had not been accompanied by fire and smoke as would have resulted from the use of C4 explosive.

The rear carriages of the Piccadilly line train, blackened by soot from the blast or from the tunnel walls, being shunted into King's Cross station.

13. Magic Numbers and Synchronous Detonations

A major sequence of false-flag terror events has set the tone for this new millenium: New York's 9/11 in 2001, the Bali bomb in 2002, Madrid in 2004, 7/7 in 2005 and then the Mumbai bombs in 2006 (see Chapter 19).

I suggest that none of these were what they appeared to be — and, all in some degree have number symbolism in their timings. Thus, add one to each term of the 9/11 date, and you'll get 12.10.2002, the date of the Bali bomb. Like 7/7, 9/11 was also a fourfold event, with three fairly close together and a fourth an hour later. The first plane impact on 9/11 was at a quarter to nine, not so different from the 7/7 timings. As four planes ostensibly crashed on 9/11, so were four trains bombed in Madrid on 11.3.2004 — 911 days after 9/11 — and then again four trains in London on 7/7.

The prosecutor Olga Sanchez saw that 911-day interval as evidence of 'un factor cabalistico.'

There was also a series of four truck bombs in 2003 in Istanbul. The first two on Nov. 15th targeted synagogues and the second pair, on Nov. 20th, the HSBC bank and an empty British consulate. The second set of bombs went off at 9.10 and 9.12 GMT, that is, within one minute of 9.11 am British time, or 11.11 Turkish time. A tiny Islamic radical group claimed responsibility, but "Turkish government officials dismissed these claims, pointing out that this minor group did not have enough resources to carry out such an intricately planned and expensive attack," according to Wikipedia. That is the classic pattern of a false-flag intelligence operation.

In Appendix 3 "Numbering the dead" we see that the death toll of 52 appears to have been arbitrarily selected, with 13 at Tavistock Square, 26 at King's Cross and 13 at Aldgate and Edgware Rd. together. Fifty-two equates to seven in numerology: 5+2=7. The three tube blasts occurred 52 seconds apart. In Chapter 12 we have the mystery of the train numbers 311 and 331. 311 was the date of the Madrid bombing, and 331= 3+3+1=7. In Chapter 10 we saw that the bus blown up at Tavistock Square had the number 17758. This number contains the date of the attacks, 7/7/05 — the numerals one and the eight add to nine, which equates to zero by the rules, leaving 775 in the middle. Such 'magic numbers' are a Cabalistic or Satanist practice rather than an Islamic one.

All of the blast times on the four trains in Madrid were within three minutes of each other. The close synchrony of the Madrid bombs was evidence for remote detonation, and therefore no 'suicide bombers' were alleged.

A year after the London 7/7 event, in India at the Mumbai railway station, the bombs went off on the 11th of July — 11/7. Quoting CNN news, 'No group has claimed responsibility for the blasts, which came in a span of 11 minutes.' *Seven* trains were bombed over a period of *eleven* minutes on 11/7. Somebody seems to be playing number-games here, and is this a clue as to who is doing it? As my discerning publisher John-Paul Leonard commented: 'Their little numerology game helps these psychopaths enjoy their work and laugh at us mere mortals."

First Reports on the London Explosions

On 7/7 in London, how likely is it that three young men, in the agony of terminating their own lives, and being far apart from each other, would choose or be able to ignite their bombs at the very same moment?

One of the first experts on the scene was Vincent Cannistro, former head of the CIA's counter-terrorism centre, and he told *the Guardian* that the police had discovered 'mechanical timing devices' at the bomb scenes; likewise ABC News at first reported, 'Officials now believe that all the bombs on subway cars were detonated by timing devices' (8th July).

This original story — with military-grade explosives, timing devices and synchronous detonations — mysteriously vanished once the suicide-bomber story appeared, but it makes a lot more sense.

7/7 Synchrony (11 Minutes to 9)

Two days after July 7th , we were informed that the three Underground blasts had been synchronous, with the first one at Aldwych going off at 8.49 am. When I composed the J7 timeline (as in Ch.4 of my book) I inserted that time, because there was general agreement on it. The Circle Line train number 216 had left King's Cross at 8.42 travelling westwards, then blown up seven minutes later.

The 2010 Inquest has added a certain precision to this timing — as Hugo Keith stated on the first day:

> The Circle Line, the westbound inner rail section, tripped at 08.49.00, that is to say the inner rail — not the outer rail where the explosion occurred, but the inner rail — but it can only have been tripped by force of the explosion on the other rail. So we can say with confidence that the explosion at Aldgate occurred at that moment, 08.49.00.

> The Piccadilly Line Westbound section tripped between Holloway Road and Russell Square at 08.49.48 and, two seconds later, the indicators in the control room that indicated that the track had current in it were also extinguished. The Circle Line tripped westbound between Baker Street and Bouverie Place, incorporating the section of the track where the explosion on the westbound Circle Line occurred, but no absolute time can be computed for that explosion because there is a variant of plus or minus 30 seconds or so in the process by which the printout in the control room prints out the time stamp of the moment of the trip. But the time was somewhere around 08.49.43. (Oct 11 pm 15:1-5)

Atomic Time

The Inquest heard about how second-by-second precision was obtained, calibrating the very moments of catastrophe using atomic time:

> Using Lextranet — the Metro's data system — the times have been amended through the good offices of Transport for London to reflect a more accurate Atomic time rather than a time that the system recorded. Just after 08.49, just before 10 to 9, the Metropolitan Line controller called the eastern power desk at the London Underground power control room to report that all the lights at

Aldgate had gone off and that the station was in sheer darkness. (Oct 11 pm 71: 9-16)

At that key moment, much of East London tube power went down. Hugo Keith does NOT surmise that this crucial moment might have been chosen within a second to make the link to 9/11 — he just says, "For some unknown reason — perhaps to cause maximum devastation in the morning rush hour — it seems that the bombers intended to explode all four bombs at the same time, namely, 49 minutes past the hour." He then adds that the bus bomb went off one hour later.

11 minutes to 9: Electrical event, electrocution Of Aldgate victims and power blackout for East London line

An astonishing Inquest session on 18th October returned to this subject:

> The whole of the East London Line lost power, which affected nine stations in total from Shoreditch to New Cross." The East London Line can be seen there [Hugo Keith explained]. "This was due to the temporary loss of the following power assets." He then reads out a number of different power assets which I won't trouble my Ladyship with. "There was a complete cessation of traction current and signal supplies to the entire East London Line which caused all trains to stall with only battery-powered lighting. There was also a cessation of all lifts and 16 escalator supplies in the affected stations on the East London Line and emergency lighting only was available.' (Oct.18th pm 4:8-18)

But, just *before* the blast:

> [Damage to a feeder cable] caused the 11-kilovolt electrical feeder to trip at Moorgate substation at 08.48.40. This in turn caused the 22-kilovolt coupling transformers, which supply the Mansell Street distribution network, to trip at 08.49.02. This caused widespread power disruption to a significant area of the London Underground network. (Oct. 18th, 3:15-21)

Thus the electrical blowout occurred just *before* the bomb went off. Compare the experience of persons in the Aldgate coach which blew up, of being electrically frazzled during *and just prior to* the event. We may even wonder, if it was a part of the plan, for the bombings to go off under cover of darkness and confusion, with no CCTV cameras, or light for witnesses to see?

The Circle Line tube station at Moorgate is West of Aldgate, and there was a bit of a mystery as to how a big power cable at Moorgate had fused. At 08.50, the London Underground Network Control Centre in Broadway in Victoria received a call to say that there had been a loss of traction current at Moorgate (Oct. 18, 18: 23-25).

On Oct. 18th Mr Keith reiterated the exact blast times to within a second: "In summary, the times recorded by the power control room are 08.49 in respect of Aldgate East, 08.49.43 in respect of Edgware Road and 08.49.52 in respect of King's Cross/Russell Square." (Oct. 18 am 8:7-14)

I suggest we see reliable evidence here, most of which emerged immediately after the 7/7 events. These details did not (in contrast with much of the CCTV and mobile phone 'evidence') emerge tortuously and unconvincingly years after the event, magically supporting the final version of a repeatedly-changed Official Narrative.

Here we see the False-Flag fingerprint (11 minutes to 9) … the carefully recorded, almost synchronous, remotely-triggered explosions … a major electrical event inside and outside of the devastated Aldgate carriage … an initial diagnosis of the use of military-grade explosive and remote timing devices … every last detail contradicting the possibility of 'suicide bombers' armed with hydrogen peroxide bottles being responsible for this crime.

PART III

14. The Enigma of Mohammed Siddique Khan

Mohammed Siddique Khan (1974 – 2005) taught youngsters, and reckoned he had skills by way of getting them off drugs, as well as in conflict-resolution. Headmistress Sarah Balfour, wife of the Labour MP Jon Trickett, recalled after his death:

> He was great with the children and they all loved him … He did so much for them, helping and supporting them and running extra clubs and activities. Siddique was a real asset to the school and always showed 100% commitment.[1]

A teacher would dream of such a testimonial! Khan wrote of this professional skill of his:

> I'm energetic, I [look for a] way of bettering things … Can build up trust and rapport with disillusion, understanding and empathy... I feel patience and understanding comes through experience and maturity … I constantly analyse society and speak to people regarding current issues. I consider my ability to empathise with others and listen to their problems as well as offer viable solutions to be one of my strong assets.[2]

A graduate from Leeds Metropolitan University, he lived with his Indian-Muslim wife Hasina Patel whom he met there and married in 2001, and they had a 14-month old daughter Maryam. His wife's mother, Farida Patel, was a pillar of the community and had attended a Buckingham Palace tea party attended by the Queen, to receive an award for bilingual education, and she was one of the first Asian women to be invited there. All the locals knew Farida and Hasina from their work in Dewsbury schools. His wife Hasina is said to have held anti-Taliban, pro-feminist views, and she worked in education as a "neighbourhood enrichment officer". The Patels were known as opponents of Muslim extremism and supporters of women's rights.

Neighbours told the media: "They seemed like a really happy family. Hasina was from an Indian family and there are not often mixed Pakistani and Indian marriages but they didn't mind." They added that the family were devout, quiet and respectable. Hasina was pregnant with a second child.

At the Hillside Primary School in Beeston where he worked, Khan's task was to liaise with children's previous schools on their special needs and to assess their learning skills. On their first day at school, children would rely on Khan, who was their official "buddy". He was given the privileged position of sitting, with the head teacher, through interviews with new families to the area. Many were single mothers, fresh immigrants, refugees or victims of domestic violence. He had been a teaching assistant at this School in Leeds since 2002. "He was a good man, quiet," said one parent, speaking outside the school. "When I told my daughter she said 'no, he can't do something like that'. I had to go and buy the paper and show her." Another parent, Sharon Stevens, told the Press Association how he had been a "big supporter" of pupils and parents. During its last Ofsted inspection in 2002, the school's learning assistants had been singled out for special praise in dealing with a transient pupil population from a socially deprived area. Khan spoke about his work to the *Times Educational Supplement* at the time. "A lot of [the pupils] have said this is the best school they have been to," he said (Hillside school was profiled in the TES in 2002).[3] Khan always wore Western clothes to the school.

Each weekday morning at 8, Khan used to visit the home of Deborah Quick to pick up her two daughters, Harley and Robyn, and take them to Hillside Primary School. The two girls were members of what Mr. Khan called his "breakfast club," an early morning service to help parents on welfare get their kids to school in time for an 8:30 breakfast and 9 a.m. start. Conscientious and cheery, Mr. Khan was "brilliant," recalls the girls' mother. As word spread of his kindness, other parents in Beeston, a deprived and drug-blighted district of this Northern English town, asked Mr. Khan to pick up their children, too. Unable to fit them all into his small, navy blue Vauxhall Corsa, Mr. Khan started walking them to school. He continued to take Ms. Quick's daughters, then 6 and 4, to school until early 2005. (Mrs Quick's boyfriend recalled that Mr. Khan had urged him to take up kickboxing as a way to curb his "negative energies," and seems to have been a bit irritated by this memory; but maybe that was a psychologically insightful comment by Khan, expressing his philosophy, of helping people to fulfil their lives.)

People felt that they could rely on him. A reporter who visited the Hillside school in 2002 recalled Khan:

> He described in measured and enthusiastic terms how he would liaise with pupils' previous schools to get their records and assess their levels of maths and literacy. He gave off an air of solid dependability, depicting himself as a bridge between the education system and the cultural melting pot in the streets around. He appeared to be a successful product of multi-cultural Britain. He seemed earnest, intelligent and committed. He would sit with the head teacher in interviews with new families, many of whom had suffered domestic violence or attacks in their home countries.... At the end of the interview, he turned to me again, flashed me a white smile and patted me on the shoulder. I went away liking him, believing he was an unsung hero.[4]

Few men were more popular on the streets of Beeston than Khan, the 30-year-old family man, recognised by his sensible sweaters and neat, coiffeured hairstyle. Khan became involved in the community-run Hamara Healthy Living Centre in Beeston, and worked at its youth outreach project, the Hamara Youth Access Point on Tempest Road, a £1 million Government-funded scheme opened two years ago by Leeds MP Hilary Benn, its patron, and his father Tony—the former Labour minister—in 2003. Hamara is an Urdu term, which means "ours". Khan was given two EU grants of £4,000 to open boys-only gyms for Asian youths in the area, grants designated as supporting community groups in deprived areas. In July 2004 he was invited to the House of Commons as the guest of a local Hemsworth Labour MP Jon Trickett, and there received praise for his teaching work.[5] At this visit to Parliament, the group met the International Development secretary, Hilary Benn. Mr. Khan won respect as a social worker committed to ridding the streets of drugs, being involved in a 2001 government study on fighting drug use. He was invited to the home of Hillside Primary's head teacher, Sarah Balfour, whose husband, Jon Trickett, is a member of parliament. On a trip to London in July of 2004, Mr. Khan and his students had a tour of parliament from Mr. Trickett.

Khan used to work for the Department of Trade and Industry (DTI), helping promote British firms overseas. He also helped Leeds police deal with confrontations between rival gangs of youths. Leeds education authority's personnel file on Khan, obtained by *The Independent* under the Freedom of Information (FoI) Act, shows details of his work for the DTI's export arm in Yorkshire in the mid-1990s, when Britain was seeking more trade links with Asia. Khan left to study at Leeds Metropolitan University in September 1996, and took a 2:2 in business management, his file reveals. He clearly believed his vocation lay in steering disenchanted youths away from crime. He took paid youth and community work from Leeds Council while finishing his degree. Overall, as one acquaintance of his remarked, 'He looked like a tower of strength within the community.'[6]

He worked together with Shahzad Tanweer in getting youngsters off drugs, and they built up 'the Mullah Crew,' a group of Asian youths, to do this. It could involve forcible 'cold turkey' indoor chill-outs for several days, for the drug addicts. This would be accompanied by outdoor activities like climbing up the North Yorkshire moors and canoeing in Wales. On June 4th, 2005, Tanweer, Khan and a bunch of other youths from Beeston had a fine day out, Whitewater rafting in the Snowdonia region of Wales (see pictures, Chapter 4) It was unusual for groups of young Asian men to participate in the sport, but, thanks to Khan being in charge of the group, relaying the instructions and translating for the one or two who could not speak English, it went well. One can see Khan making the 'peace' V-sign to the photographer, and Tanweer with a broad grin at the bottom of the picture. The press had some difficulty in attributing a fiendish, sinister meaning to this outing, mere weeks before July 7th, but… they managed.[7]

He and Tanweer used to meet at the small corner-shop the Iqra Islamic Learning Bookshop (a registered charity) in Beeston where Khan was a volunteer worker. The police raided this and closed it down, its manager Naveed sent to Paddington Green. The shop sold Korans and tried to give locals somewhere to meet and get them off drugs (heroin was quite an epidemic locally, with 10-year olds on it) – and, as regards its selling 'anti-western videos,' I was told that these were probably 9/11 truth videos (by a nearby shop-owner, who knew the people).

On his school job application, he described one of his practical experiences in conflict resolution: once, when a "potentially dangerous" confrontation arose, "I have an excellent rapport with the youth [community] so … I targeted the ringleaders and spoke to them, calming them down and offering sympathy as well as empathy. We then approached the teachers and as a large group casually walked together up Beeston Hill which [defused] the situation. Associates of Khan have confirmed his role as an interlocutor between police and youths." The Independent (11 March 2006) obtained this rather vital information from Leeds Education Authority's personnel file on Khan, obtained under the Freedom of Information Act:

Lack of religious views: On his religious views, it's hard to find comments beyond a neighbour's remark: "He didn't seem to be an extremist. He was not one to talk about religion. He was generally a very nice bloke." Afzal Choudhry, a community worker who took part in the summer sessions (during summer holidays he ran workshops for kids), praises him for being "always ready to get involved. He did not recall that Mr. Khan had been particularly religious when they first met in 1997.

Mr. Khan sometimes got "what we call the Friday feeling" and would go to mosque for Friday prayers, but he otherwise didn't pray much, says Mr. Choudhry. "The other Pakistani lads would have to go mosque because their families would say 'You're going to mosque.' Recalled his old school-friend Ian Barrett, Sid wouldn't go: "He didn't seem interested in Islam and I don't ever remember him mentioning religion." Khan was, by all accounts, an exceptionally well integrated person. His anglicised name "Sid" was just one symbol of his willingness to take on a British identity. "If it wasn't for the colour of his skin, he would have been [seen as exclusively] English," says Ian. "I just thought of him as a Beeston lad – and that's what he was – a Beeston lad, born and bred." However, his religious inclinations may have developed upon doing the pilgrimage to Mecca with his wife Hasina. He took leave from Hillside to go on 'Muslim religious observation, Hajj, Pilgrimage to Saudi Arabia' from 27th January to 14th February, 2002.

Khan's anger: "You could not carry out a civilized conversation with him on Iraq," recalled Arshad Chaudhry, head of the Leeds Muslim Forum, an umbrella group of local Islamic leaders. Although Khan was a mild and gentle man, we may be glad to hear of this righteous indignation, whereby he expressed his forthright view about the war.

His mother-in-law Farida Patel became in 1998 the first Asian woman to attend a Buckingham Palace party; equally astonishing, she was in 1999 invited to Downing Street and decorated for her services to the Inner City Religious Council, at a ceremony hosted by Tony Blair. Rather graphically, the local newspaper described her as having "rubbed shoulders" on that occasion with the Queen, the Duke of Edinburgh, Prince Charles – and also the former Metropolitan Police Commissioner Sir Paul Condon. She was co-opted as a member of the British government Council of Religious Leaders from 1996 to 2000. She taught at Dewsbury's Birkdale High School until 2003 and served on the local police forum. In 2004 she appeared at a Buckingham Palace garden party with her husband, and daughter Hasina Patel.[8] It appears that at least three of Khan's extended family – his wife, his well-respected mother-in-law Farida Patel, and her husband, were all invited by the Queen for one of her exclusive summer garden parties.

A parent, Sharon Stevens, whose child went to that school, made a typical comment upon hearing the news:

> I'm just shocked. He was brilliant with the children. He went on trips with the kids and my little girl went with him on a trip to London. If you had any

problems, he used to sort them out. I'm just devastated. Just shocked. I am just totally shocked.

<u>Last sighting of Khan:</u> Some days before July 7th, Tanweer hired a car, a Nissan Micra of a blue-green colour. He and Khan were driving around in it; Arshad (Hasina Patel's brother) and his wife Kadija recall the two of them turning up at their house with it. Then on Tuesday the 5th, Hasina was in great pain from the child she was expecting from Khan, and he used the car to take her to hospital.[9] She was checked over and given a scan, and then returned to their house at Lees Holm. He then went off – and that was the last anyone ever saw of Mohammed Siddique Khan. All through Wednesday she kept trying to phone him; then on the morning of July 7th, in great pain, she suffered a miscarriage. That is a remarkable synchrony, in connection with the bombs going off in London that morning! It was an expression of her despair, at her husband being uncontactable when she really needed him.

Two months after Khan's death, the 'Khan' video was released by Al-Jazeera in Pakistan, with no explanation as to how they had come by it or the delay in releasing it. A *Guardian* journalist visited Beeston and met outright scepticism amongst those who had been acquainted with him: '...They knew Khan as a youth leader, a joker, a friend and a mentor. They had played football with him on the pitch opposite; across the main street, on the ground floor of the Hardy Street Mosque, he had supervised and encouraged them as they trained in the boys-only gym... One, who gave his name as Saj, had been on day trips quad biking with the 30-year-old youth worker... 'He never talked of terrorism to me. I just don't accept that he or the others did this. I am suspicious of what the police say, there is no proof and look how they shot that Brazilian guy who was innocent...'[10]

Summarising, in the thirty years of his life, Khan
- helped to promote Leeds business by improving exports
- liased with Parliament
- worked to get youths off drugs
- demonstrated the art of conflict-resolution
- helped educate the poor and underprivileged
- helped single mothers by getting their young kids to school
- gave local people hope by seeing their community regenerate

He had a life to look forward to. Was he indeed a model citizen, who inspired others and showed no wish to cause harm, or was there some other, darker side to his character?

Posthumous Character Assassination

After his death, a personality radically opposed to everything we had heard about in his life started to emerge: of a man bent on terror, having shadowy al-Qaeda contacts, skilled in bomb-making, secretive, deceitful and cruel to his closest family. Stories to this effect start to be leaked by British, American and Israeli intelligence services. But curiously enough, even his closest pals such as Waheed Ali and Mohammed Shakil had no inkling of this alleged dark side of his personality, as became clear in their testimony at the 2008 Kingston trial (Chapter 13).

Khan was indeed shadowed by the British police for well over a year before his death. This appears as a general feature in the lives of Muslims accused of 'terror' plots. Spook-planted tales proliferated posthumously, alleging that Khan had aided all sorts of terror-groups: 'So this guy is travelling to Israel, Pakistan, Afghanistan, Malaysia and now the Philippines – all while married with a young child and earning a teacher's salary.'[11, 12] And America, of course – don't forget America: in his *One Percent Doctrine*, Ron Susskind has Khan as 'The man who had planned attacks on US cities.'[13] Really, one has to laugh.

Khan did visit London via Luton on 28 June, with his pals Tanweer and Jamal, and was recorded on CCTV cameras at Luton and King's Cross, and at Baker Street where he was filmed eating ice-cream by Madame Tussaud's. There is a story that he was last seen on the evening of Wednesday, 6th July, in Dewsbury by his neighbour Mr. Zaman, getting into a red Mercedes;[14] but his wife last saw him on the Tuesday, when he drove her to hospital for a check-up. On 13th July, fifty police raided what had been his house, with Farida and Hasina present. This traumatised them so that they fled into hiding, and no longer live there. Hordes of journalists descended on Beeston but encountered a sullen wall of silence from locals who simply would not believe what was alleged of Khan. The BBC claimed that he had been secretly filmed and recorded by British intelligence agencies in 2004.[15] Could the film shown posthumously in September 2005 have been of Khan speaking in 2004 – with his speech adjusted? Locals who knew him seem not to have believed that it was him speaking on that video.[16] Video- and voice-morphing technology can now appear remarkably convincing.[17]

Some months after Khan's death, the radio programme 'Koran and Country, Biography of a Bomber' appeared about him (Radio 4, 18 November 2005 by Nasreen Suleaman).[18] The sinister claims there made about how he became 'radicalised' were provided by only one witness – who remained anonymous and whose voice was modulated to prevent recognition. This process allegedly happened when Khan and friends gathered to play 'paintball,' in the woods! Another interview on this programme more deserves our attention: with Ian Barrett, who had known Khan since middle-school, and who was the most-quoted witness. Let's listen carefully to how Mr Barrett found that the voice speaking on that posthumous video was not in fact that of Khan:

> I was just shocked because that's not the Sid that I went to school with. It wasn't his natural speaking rhythm, he used to be quick. You'd say something to him and he's got something witty to say back to you. You can't outdo him with sarcasm, it were a bouncing talk, he was fast, he was funny with it. That weren't him on that video.

He couldn't remember Khan mentioning religion once. He especially recalled how Khan loved America after his visit there, he wanted to *become an American* and intended to go and live there. He returned wearing an American-style hat and leather jacket and was pilloried by his Pakistani friends because the clothes didn't suit him. (Mr Susskind, please note.)

His schoolteacher friends recalled his good sense of humour and how everyone liked him, but that after returning from Mecca he had become more introvert and his manner had altered. In February 2005 he became a liason officer in another local school, after having left the Hillside school the previous December; it closed a few months later.[19]

One old friend, Rob Cardiff, bumped into Khan in Leeds in June 2005, after not having seen him for ages: Khan struck up a conversation, about having kids, nappies and being a parent, shaking hands and making full eye contact, and Mr Cardiff could not square this with what happened a few weeks later.

Details of how Khan visited a 'jihadi' training camp in Pakistan over his long 2004/5 visit there only emerged in the Kingston trial of 2008, mainly from his friend Waheed Ali. Even more doubtful here was the testimony from Mohammed Junaid Babar, who claimed to have been running an 'Al-qaeda' camp (he is now awaiting sentence in a US prison). He pleaded guilty in June 2004 to providing material support to Al-Qaeda.[20] This 'Junaid' was arrested in April 2004, then gave a secret, sealed testimony in June 2005, and then on August 10, the US government released censored parts of his testimony.[21] Junaid was originally a Pakistani citizen but became a "naturalized" American one a few years ago.

The Khan Story of July 7th

We now turn away from the real events of Khan's life, towards a nightmare dream-sequence, which *clearly could never have happened*: but which has been made to seem that way.

On the 12th of July, the Metropolitan police announced that they had found 'documents' whereby they were able to identify Khan, *both* at Edgware Road *and* at Aldgate tube station, two sites of the July 7th bombs.[22] The documents had his name on them.[23] The next day, Peter Clarke, head of the Anti-Terrorist Branch, confirmed that 'property' of Khan had been found at both stations, but that no forensic evidence had yet been found linking him to the blast: i.e., they had identified him solely from this 'property.'[24] Further documents of his then turned up at Tavistock Square.

The police have never clarified how Khan's ID could have turned up in two places at once.

Relatives of Khan were advised that his remains were stored in various separate packages, if they wanted to collect them: if the police had done all this scraping off of walls etc, how come his paper or plastic ID had remained intact? This sounds like the story of the hijacker's passport fluttering down, intact, from the raging inferno of 9/11. In reply, the relatives sensibly requested that an independent coroner be allowed to check these 'remains'.[25]

No witnesses nor any CCTV camera film could be produced to indicate Khan's presence in London on July 7th until over two months later, when Danny Biddle appeared. On the first version of his story (see previous chapter), it sounds as if 'Khan' had got on the crowded train a while before he had, as the former was sitting down while Biddle had to stand up.[26] Two months later, his story appeared in *The Sunday Times*, and we hear of Biddle getting on the Circle Line train at Liverpool Street station that morning. He does not say 'I got on at Liverpool street, then four stops later Khan got on and stood next to me,' but implies that Khan was already on the train.[27] This changeable and fragmented 'memory' cannot be relied upon.

Many claims were made about Khan in the 'Operation Crevice' trial, which appear to be based entirely on documents appearing after July 7th 2005, not one of which can be reliably dated to prior to that date. (See Chapter 11 & Appendix 10b)[28]

<u>Distress of Mrs Khan:</u> In May of 2007, four people were arrested 'on suspicion of commissioning, preparing or instigating acts of terrorism,' including Hasina Patel, her brother and her 22-year old cousin. The police came into her house, and she described how she said goodnight to her young daughter: 'I kissed her goodbye, I didn't wake her up and then when I walked out of the bedroom they handcuffed me there outside her bedroom and led me downstairs.' Then they took her to Paddington Green, '…A tiny cell, yes. I asked them, I said okay, where do I sleep at night and they said here. I thought here? The bench is narrower than a single bed, a wooden bench with a plastic mattress and a toilet bolted to the wall, no sink.'[29]

She was held but not charged. Her arrest came in the immediate wake of the secretive Crevice trial, in which diverse MI5 connections and pre-7/7 nefarious activities were alleged in regard to her husband; suggesting that this arrest with no charges was a way of indicating to her that she should keep quiet. Britain's 9/11 truth movement (of which this writer is a member) held its AGM over the weekend of 11-13th May in Leeds, and her arrest on the 9th of May lasted for six days. It is likely that members of this movement, being in Leeds, would have made an effort to contact her, which her arrest may have been designed to prevent.

Mrs Patel's solicitor, Imran Khan, said he was "shocked" at the police's handling of her arrest. 'Those in her community are incredibly angry at the way the police have approached this.' He told the BBC the police had been for some time in possession of evidence that 'unequivocally' proved she had known nothing about what her husband was planning two years ago. He added: 'To arrest her in these circumstances – a woman who lost her husband, who has been accused of the most atrocious events that have taken place in this country, has now spent seven days in isolation in Paddington Green – I wonder what she must be feeling… She's quite clearly innocent of anything, because she's been released by police having trawled through her life and possessions and caused her a tremendous amount of grief.'

Upon being released, on May 16th, Hasina Patel called for an independent, public enquiry into the events of July 7th – which is quite a remarkable response! She pertinently asked: 'Why were we arrested after two years? Why did they take such a drastic step when we have always co-operated with them?' A couple of months after her arrest, she was interviewed for Sky TV by Julie Etchingham.[30] Asked about the posthumous video, her simple comment was: *'To me that's not my husband, what I saw on TV is just a completely different person.'*

> <u>H.P.</u>: I would say he was a good Muslim, that's what I felt he was then.
>
> <u>Julie Etchingham</u>: But you didn't have any sense even at this stage, because we now know that even at this stage he was involved in something more extreme, you never had any inkling of that at all?
>
> <u>H.P.</u>: I could never have imagined in my wildest dreams, never. If we watched TV and if there was a war or you see people suffering and obviously you

comment just like anybody would, it was nothing beyond what was normal, what anybody else would say.

References

[1] 'School's shock at Dewsbury bomber' By Neil Atkinson, *The Huddersfield Daily Examiner,* 14 July 2005. (Cited on J7 site)

[2] Ian Herbert – *The Independent* March 11, 2006 'London Bomber used to work for government' http://www.propagandamatrix.com/articles/march2006/110306_b_bomber.htm (Cited on J7 site)

[3] TES 26 April 2002, Khan was the only person other than the headmistress who was quoted in this TES article.

[4] David Macaulay (Northcliffe Parliamentary Correspondent), "I interviewed suicide bomber'—reporter' 18.7.2005, www.holdthefrontpage.co.uk/news/2005/07july/050718dav.shtml.

[5] Three cities, Four killers, *The Guardian* 17.7.05 www.guardian.co.uk/attackonlondon/story/0,16132,1530338,00.html.

[6] Nick Prica, in 'My Brother the Bomber' by Shiv Malik, *Prospect,* June 2007, p.35.

[7] Kate Blyth, manager of the Whitewater rafting centre, recalls Khan as having been quite bossy: 'He was far more opinionated when he came to Wales. He was the ringleader without a doubt. He was telling the other men in the group what to do. One of them didn't speak English and he was translating what I said into their language. Khan was definitely in charge.' (Sept 14th *The Mail on a Sunday*).

[8] http://antagonise.blogspot.com/search/label/Operation%20Crevice.

[9] That story accords with the following *Guardian* report: 'As a police helicopter hovered over Mr Tanweer's home in Beeston, a hire company driver waited by a launderette. He said a car, possibly a Nissan Micra or a Renault Clio, had been rented from the First 24 Hour Hire Company in Leeds on July 1. "We have been ringing since Friday," the man said. "We kept ringing his phone number and couldn't get a reply. So we came to get the car today at 9am. We showed the police the hire sheet and they took our assistant manager and interviewed him." Thus Tanweer had hired the car days before and it would be incorrect to say that this was specifically for an event on July 7th. *The Guardian*, 13 July, 'How parents' frantic hunt ended in disbelief.' www.guardian.co.uk/attackonlondon/story/0,16132,1527437,00.html.

[10] *The Guardian,* 'Friends Claim Khan's Statement was Faked', www.guardian.co.uk/attackonlondon/story/0,16132,1561938,00.html 5 September.

[11] Israeli intelligence made this claim that Khan visited Israel on 19th April, 2003, for the purpose of arranging a bomb blast a few weeks later: 'London Bomber Helped Terrorists Bomb Tel Aviv Bar' *Arutz Sheva* Israeli News 19 July 05 (repeated in *The Sunday Times* 9.7.06 'July 7 ringleader linked to Tel Aviv suicide bombers.') His leave from Hillside school is documented as being from 27th January 2003 until 14th February, so he could not then have been abroad on the 19th. But, how interesting that Mossad should wish to fabricate this claim.

[12] Web-blog by 'soj': http://soj.weblog.ro/2005-11-02.html.

[13] Ron Suskind, *The One Percent Doctrine, Deep inside America's pursuit of its Enemies since 9/11*, 2006, p201: on Khan's *fourth* US visit, he plans to 'blow up synagogues on the East coast', etc. In his review of Suskind's book in *The Guardian*, Richard-Norton Taylor

suggests that the author muddled up Mohammed Ajmal Khan with 'Sid' – however Suskind has denied this. www.guardian.co.uk/media/2006/jun/ 20/pressandpublishing.terrorism.

[14] *Pittsburgh Post-Gazette*, How a teacher's aide evolved into a terrorist bomber, 25.7.05. www.post-gazette.com/pg/05206/543469.stm.

[15] http://weblog.ro/soj/2005-11-02.html (lost).

[16] *The Guardian* 3.9.05 'Friends claim Khan's statement was faked' www.guardian.co.uk/ attackonlondon/story/0,16132,1561938,00.html. For a 'rogue's gallery' of Al-Zawahiris from the late 90s to 2005: http://img301.imageshack.us/img301/7323/zaw0dp.jpg.

[17] http://downloads.warprecords.com/bushwhacked2.mp3.

[18] www.bbc.co.uk/radio4/koranandcountry/pip/q8q01/ (now deleted) – a copy is kept at: www.officialconfusion.com/77/themen/themen.html, scroll down.

[19] His letter of resignation to Sarah Balfour stated,

"I'm sorry I have not been in touch for a while, a lot has happened in the last few months. [Sentence deleted] there is no definite time frame as to when I will return. We are departing next week.

"Unfortunately this letter is therefore a letter of resignation from my post. It's been great working with you and I will be in touch when I return." I endeavored to contact Sarah Balfour to ascertain what that sentence may have said, and who deleted it, but to no avail. It could have been e.g. a statement to the effect that he was going to Pakistan again owing to family commitments (his remains have been buried out there, I was told by AP).

[20] http://s13.invisionfree.com/julyseventh/index.php?showtopic=34.

[21] http://weblog.ro/soj/2004-08-12.html#13748 (lost).

[22] The *Guardian*, 13 July, 'British suicide bombers carried out London attacks, say police' www.guardian.co.uk/attackonlondon/story/0,16132,1527404,00.html. They named Khan the day after, on the 13th.

[23] Metropolitan Police, July 12th, 2005, statement by Andy Hayman. http://cms.met. police.uk/news/major_operational_announcements/terrorist_attacks/press_conference_5pm_ july_12.

[24] BBC News, July 14th http://news.bbc.co.uk/1/hi/uk/4683555.stm.

[25] http://www.telegraph.co.uk/news/main.jhtml?xml=/news/2005/10/29/nterr29.xml&sSheet =/news/2005/10/29/ixnewstop.html (lost) There appears to have been, to-date, no funeral: BBC News, 'Funeral service for London bomber,' 3.11.05. But Arshad Patel told me there had been a funeral in Pakistan.

[26] *Mirror*, 24.9.05, 'Tube Bomber Stared me Straight in the Eyes as he set off the Explosion that Blew my legs away'.

[27] *The Sunday Times* 'The Survivors' 24.12.05 www.timesonline.co.uk/article/0,,2099-1891 957,00.html 4th December.

[28] Julie Hyland, 'British terror trial raises question of what MI5 knew about 2005 London bombings,' *Global Research* 9.5.07, www.globalresearch.ca/index.php? context=va&aid= 5601. Nafeez Ahmed published 'Inside the crevice, Islamist terror Networks and the 7/7 intelligence Failure' which he circulated to MPs. I challenged him on this (Appendix 10b) but he did not reply.

[29] Hasina Patel's interview with Julie Etchingham, on 27 July, 2007 Sky News: http://news.sky.com/skynews/article/0,,30100-1277315,00.html.

[30] Ibid.

<u>Document</u> – MSK's application for learning mentor post at Hillside

LEARNING MENTOR   <u>*Sidique Khan*</u>

1. Can you tell us why you have applied for this post?

   youth worker
   wants to make a difference.
   Promotes education to children.

2. What are the essential things that you would need to do as a learning mentor in your first month?

   likes challenges   rôles of C.T & L SAS.
   school policies   What is expected from him
                              + what he can expect from us
   info on current ch. Parents phone numbers etc
   a computer.

3. What sort of difficulties do you think a child would face joining a class mid-way through the year? (The child may already have had several changes of school.)

   v daunting for ch.
   Peer support befriend new ch.
   meet ch + parent to reassure + tell them what
   is expected of them.

4. What sort of system would you set up to offer support to children and families?

   detailed records — computerise for security
   meet with parents + explain rôle.
   listen to parents .. give contact no.
   liase with other agencies + a particular person
   for parent . Liase with C.T   Info management.

5. You will have to make contact with other agencies and will often be dealing with sensitive information. What is your understanding of confidentiality issues?

   → trust .
   careful —gossip.
   Pass on only specific evidence

6. Human Rights legislation now requires parents' consent for information to be shared with other agencies. How would you approach this with parents?

   Trust is impo.
   explain confidentiality
   for childs best interest
   face to face - contact .
   home visits

15. What qualities do you have that make you the best person for the job?

IT skills – databases etc

communicate with lots of diff people
good talker!

Empathy + understanding
people go to him with problems.
Good counselling skills.

Likes to try fresh approaches.
^ a challenge.

Energetic!
Wants to make a difference

15. Echoes of Phantom Terror

I. July 21st

Two weeks later, on July 21st, some bangs and pops were heard on the London Underground, but no one was hurt. Let's hear a few witnesses:[1]

Kate Reid at the Oval: 'I was sitting on the Tube, not paying much attention to anything, and I heard a pop – like a really big balloon had burst – then I saw a little bit of smoke. I saw a bag on the floor next to a young man who looked really scared. We pulled into the Oval station and he just sprinted away as soon as the doors opened. The man had a rucksack with him, but whatever had exploded had fallen out of the rucksack and onto the floor. He was about 20, I think he was black, and really young-looking. He was wearing normal sports clothing, absolutely nothing that made him stand out at all. I would not have noticed him at all if had not been for the bang. When I left the train at Oval I noticed his bag was still on the train.'

Ivan McCracken, Warren Street: The passenger told Sky News he was in the middle of a train close to Warren Street station when the door to the next carriage burst open and dozens of people rushed in. Some were falling, there was mass panic. It was difficult to get the story from any of them but when I got to ground level there was an Italian young man comforting an Italian girl who told me he had seen what had happened. He said that a man was carrying a rucksack and the rucksack suddenly exploded. It was a minor explosion but enough to blow open the rucksack. The man then made an exclamation as if something had gone wrong. At that point everyone rushed from the carriage.

Christina Sampson, Warren Street: Ms Sampson was on board the train at Warren Street. She said that overall, people had been "quite calm", and that she had not seen any injuries or damage to the train. 'In our carriage suddenly we smelt something like burning rubber and then someone pulled the emergency alarm. The sirens were going and the Tube pulled in at the station. The Tube driver then made an announcement but we couldn't quite understand. Some people rushed off the Tube at Warren Street and were kind of screaming and panicking. There were also lots of people hanging around on the platform waiting to hear what was going on.'

Guy Stock at Shoreditch: Guy Stock was near the double-decker bus in East London when there was an explosion on the upper deck. It was a Number 26 bus, on its route to Hackney Wick. There was an explosion on the top of the bus. The driver stopped the bus and got out to look around. On the back seat of the bus, on the top deck, a backpack was found. Passengers said a funny smell was coming from it, and it appeared to be split.

Paul Williamson, Shoreditch: 'The first I knew of it there were people running around in the street. I saw a blonde lady in her 20s who had been on the bus. She was quite scared and shaken and I think she was in a state of shock. She said it was a minor explosion and there were no injuries but she smelled smoke on the bus. It can't have been a very loud explosion because we didn't hear anything where we were. The police were very quick, they came in and just said for everyone to get out of the area because there was a possibility of an explosion. As I came out I saw the bus but it didn't look like there was any damage to it. I didn't see any glass in the street.'

The official line was given on that same day July 21st by Sir Ian Blair, Chief of the Metropolitan Police. "Clearly the intention must have been to kill," he said at a press conference late afternoon. "I mean, you don't do this with any other intention." The question of *what* one would not do with any other intention was buried as usual beneath Islamophobic presuppositions. The commissioner added: "The important point is that the intention of the terrorists has not been fulfilled." Like the bombings of July 7, which killed 56 people, the attacks took place at around the same time – first on three Tube trains and then on a bus. As before, all three Tube lines run through King's Cross. Thus one can see Sir Ian's point that the latest attacks had "some resonance" with the terror of two weeks ago.

It is a disturbing feature of Britain's criminal law that police officers are now allowed to arrest and seek prosecution on the basis of what they imagine a person's intentions might have been. Our society would be more stable if the definition of crime was based upon actions that have been performed. If we were to imagine a rational court, where accusations were based on logic and reason, then, given that no one had been hurt, that court would have first first sought evidence as to whether or not any bystanders on July 21st had experienced terror. Without exception, the police, media, MPs and the British public describe these four young men as 'terrorists.' Our impression is that a certain amount of fear was generated in bystanders – but not terror. We would also be interested in the question of whether anyone nearby laughed, as the flour-bombs carried by these youngsters went off.

This CCTV image shows Muktar Said-Ibrahim, on the 28 bus at Hackney, at noon on the 21st. We are perplexed to see him standing in an empty bus, with no 'bomb' visible.[2] He is standing at the back, recalling the above-quoted testimony of eye witness Guy Stock, that the exploded backpack was found 'On the back seat of the bus, on the top deck.'

The police *knew that it was going to happen* on that morning, i.e. that 'terror' was going to strike London again, as did the Government. How clever the police were, to be able to ascertain this. Here is the Mirror reporting on government precognition of the event, the day after:

THEY'LL ATTACK US THIS WEEK

Cops tipped off over blasts; Bombs will give vital clues

By Don Mackay, Oonagh Blackman and Bob Roberts (quoted with kind permission)

SCOTLAND Yard knew the Tube would be bombed yesterday after being tipped off there would be an attack this week, it emerged last night. They flooded the network with undercover armed police – while other armed officers used sniffer dogs to check passengers' rucksacks. At 9.29am an armed unit raced to Farringdon station as they closed in on one suspected bomber – but narrowly missed him. One security source revealed: "Certain information was received that pointed to another round of explosions this week, but the informant couldn't name exactly where and when. However, police chiefs deduced the attack would probably be on a Thursday, as it was two weeks ago. The source added: "After that we just knew it was going to happen and if it was going to happen it would be on Thursday." Experts believe the fact the devices did not go off properly will give detectives a "goldmine of evidence".

Barely two hours before yesterday's attacks, Home Secretary Charles Clarke warned senior cabinet colleagues the capital could face another terror onslaught. Mr Clarke gave the confidential briefing immediately after Tony Blair had chaired a full cabinet meeting in Downing Street. A senior No10 source said: "Charles Clarke made it very clear there would be further attacks and that further incidents were a strong likelihood. After officers missed nabbing the Farringdon suspect, warning memos are believed to have been sent to transport workers to be on the lookout for a tall, Middle-Eastern man. Signs of the heightened security on the London Underground network were clear yesterday morning before the bombers struck. There was a heavy, visible, armed police presence in and around stations. At Westminster station tourists were asked to take off backpacks and line them up against walls.

And in anti-suicide bomber procedures similar to those used in Iraq, sniffer dogs were brought in to smell the bags for possible explosives. One eyewitness at the station said: "I have never seen anything like that in London before, even after the July 7 bombings. There were at least eight officers, including several with machine guns, just at one underground station." At Westminster and other Government buildings the terror alert was on "amber", meaning a "substantial threat to UK interests". There is only one higher state of alert, red, which means a major target such as Parliament or the transport system is "believed to be the target of an imminent terrorist attack". In the cabinet briefing, the Home Secretary hinted at fears there could be copycat attacks in the wake of the July 7 atrocities.

Police are working on the possibility that a semi-formed terror cell unconnected with the Leeds-based suicide fanatics may have been behind yesterday's attempted atrocities. They think the terrorists may have not yet been fully trained but were sent into action anyway. Meanwhile, a former British intelligence officer who cannot be named said: "This attack is a major breakthrough. Police and security services now probably have four bombing devices which, although crude, will be a goldmine of evidence."

So a heavy police presence was in evidence that morning at the Underground station with sniffer dogs and machine guns – *before the event* – as if trying to atone for their having lowered the terror threat in the month prior to July 7th.

A huge investigation was launched. Hussain Osman, 27; Muktar Said Ibrahim, 27; Ramzi Mohamed, 24; Yassin Hassan Omar, 24; as well as Manfo Kwaku Asiedu, 32—an illegal immigrant who couldn't speak English, only Twi, a Ghanaian language—were arrested and charged with conspiracy to murder and conspiracy to cause explosions likely to endanger life or cause serious injury. None were British-born; all had come to the UK from various African countries as children of asylum-seekers. One day after that attack 'Officials refused to describe the explosives used, although they said they were investigating whether the materials were similar to those of the July 7th attacks.'[3] Three of them were arrested together and made to come out naked or only in their underpants – a humiliating procedure formerly only used in America, especially on blacks, where the persons arrested have a better chance of not being shot if they emerge naked. One of these, Asiedu, had allegedly got scared and left his 'bomb' under a bush in West London and was then apprehended the same day.

Hussain Osman ('Hamdi Isaac') had escaped under the nose of a massive police intelligence operation, by catching a Eurostar to Italy, at Waterloo station – walking past his own 'wanted' poster. He told his Italian interrogators that he and his accomplices 'had not sought to kill anyone, not even themselves'. Angry at the treatment of Muslims in Iraq and the UK, Osman described the coordinated operation as a 'demonstrative action' rather than an attempt to cause mass casualties. The British government responded by asking the Italian authorities to silence Osman, on the grounds that his statements would prejudice a forthcoming trial (in two years' time). The Italians returned Osman within two months of the UK applying for his extradition. And yet, a month after the events, the police were obfuscating the nature of the bomb material, e.g. Sir Ian Blair stated in August that:

> The devices, had they detonated properly, would have caused death and destruction on a level comparable to the July 7 attacks.

Ahmed concluded in 2006 that 'So far British authorities have refused to say exactly what the 21/7 bombs were composed of, or whether they were bombs at all.'[4] However, the ruling of the Italian panel which authorized Osman's extradition to the UK confirmed that the bombs had been created 'using plastic containers, putting flour, hair lotion, nails, nuts and bolts.' That is a somewhat muddled version of what they used, but this was not to become clear until the trial a couple of years later. The panel went on to describe 'a primitive device featuring a battery, which included a powder to act as a detonator once it had been manually attached to some electric wires.' If an explosive—the acetone and hydrogen-peroxide based TATP—was present, it was 'confined to the detonation mechanism.' 'The bombs failed to detonate' concluded Ahmed. (p.98) This is a widely held view, here rejected, because it is evident that they were not bombs, and did all that they were intended to do. But overall, Ahmed's conclusion was sound – and was, we reckon, just about the only sound and truthful account to be found on the subject:

> 'It is difficult to avoid the conclusion, in this context, that Osman's claims about the bombs are plausible. The silence of the British authorities on the bomb

components, simultaneous with their hysterical insistence that the explosives used were capable of replicating the scale of mass death, destruction and injury that occurred on 7/7, only discredits the official position further.' (p.99)

The inclusion of the bus bomb indicated that the planning was indeed supposed to mirror that of the 7/7 bombings. Further there was evidence that some of this group had attended the Finsbury Park Mosque and could thereby have come under the influence of the MI-5 controlled 'Al-Qaeda' agents there present. No such claim could ever be shown of the July 7th alleged bombers (although Ahmed has claimed this), viz. that they attended the Finsbury Park Mosque. Muktar Said Ibrahim, the alleged bus bomber, had received a full British passport in 2004, even after he had been arrested for a street robbery when he was 17, and had been jailed by Luton crown court in 1996. Ibrahim received a six-year jail sentence for carrying a knife – after which it would normally have been impossible for him to receive British citizenship. Suspicions have inevitably arisen that he had been led to believe that he would receive British nationality in return for helping to manifest the 'Al-Qaeda' terror threat.

The Court Case

22 March, 2007, Woolwich Crown Court: the public gallery is on a high level looking down on the proceedings. On the left is the judges' bench. Immediately opposite is the witness box with seats for the press behind that. The jury are not visible from the pubic gallery as they were seated immediately underneath it. There is glass between the public gallery and the court, but microphones in the ceiling made it possible to hear the proceedings, just about. There were about twenty barristers and clerks in the main area of the court, all with laptops. Behind them was another glass wall behind which sat the defendants. Behind them was a line of prison guards. On the day we were there, Ibrahim was in the witness box being cross examined by Mr Kamlish QC.

The next day, on the 23rd, the headlines were a-screaming, '21/7 BOMB PLOT WAS "BIGGER THAN 7/7"', and the like. 'The man behind the 21/7 terror plot intended it to be "bigger and better" than 7/7, a court heard this afternoon'. 'Muktar Said Ibrahim wanted to match the attacks on the transport system on 7 July, and also bring down a 12-storey block of flats in north London, it is alleged' effused the *Evening Standard*. This writer and a colleague spent the day in that court.

What we heard at Court that day did not endorse these headlines, but did endorse what Ahmed had written a year earlier, indicating a coherence of the young men's narrative even after a year of solitary confinement. The court was packed with journalists, and the big news on that day was that Manfo Asiedu (the one who couldn't speak English) had turned Queen's evidence, presumably in the hope of getting himself a lighter sentence by helping to get the other bombers convicted. Woolwich Crown Court adjoins Belmarsh Prison, which is a huge complex. It is a high security prison and terrorist suspects are held there. There is an underground passage from the prison to the courthouse, whereby suspects can be put on trial without ever really leaving the prison. I counted 16 wigs evident, a basically all-white court with only one Muslim: the man on trial. This several-month trial was estimated to have cost British taxpayers a couple of million. The charge against the four young men was 'conspiracy to murder and conspiracy to cause explosions likely to endanger life.'

MSI seemed intelligent and confident. He came from Eritrea and was a recent convert to Islam. Before the attack, Ibrahim had been to Sudan to visit relatives and had also gone to Pakistan. He denied visiting any training camps or having met any of the 7/7 suspects. He claimed that he got the information for making the explosive and the detonator off a website called 'balaclava.mac.' He had spent a while distilling the peroxide, to try and concentrate it, and had spent a while with electric wires trying to wire up the mixture.[5] As to his motive, he seemed quite clear on that. As a Muslim he was horrified by the Iraq war and wanted to give British citizens some feeling of what it was like to have bombs going off. He used words such as, 'We bought many wires for the hoax ...' and 'only for demonstration,' and 'just a bang,' clearly intending no injuries. The bombs did not 'fail', he was adamant on this. They were meant to go bang without hurting anyone, he explained, and they did. They would temporarily give the impression of a bomb scare.

As a visitor, one heard MSI repeatedly saying 'No, that's not so' to allegations from the prosecution lawyer (Mr Kamlish QC, Matrix Chambers). 'In your twisted thoughts ...,' the prosecution lawyer proclaimed, however the judge did not object. Asked about July 7th, he categorically denied approval of the means then used to protest against the Iraq war.

MSI was accused of attempted murder which he categorically rejected. He stood up moderately well for one who has been in prison for a year. The central absurdity in the prosecution's case was the claim made that hydrogen peroxide mixed with flour could bring down a block of flats in a 'ball of fire' – in addition to what they would supposedly do to the underground and a bus. It is unclear that such a mixture would explode – it would merely give off oxygen – but possibly one could get a bang out of it. The climax of the day was when the prosecution lawyer brought into the Court the very sideboard where MSI had mixed the peroxide and flour. Yes, he admitted to having done it. Then a waste-bin was produced and alleged to have contained the bomb, which MSI categorically denied. Dramatically, the prosecution put the bin into the sideboard. 'But, so what?' asked MSI – quite effectively, I thought. Basically they have no evidence that he intended to do anything more than cause a disturbance, which he did.

He has been in jail before, for a couple of years, for involvement in a mugging offence. Having come from Eritrea, he went on a holiday to the Sudan in 2004, and the prosecution continually tried to imply that he was studying rocket-launch terror strikes out there, but this remained as mere innuendo. Thrice we were told of his having fondled the breasts of a young girl when he and she were both 15 and she had filed a complaint about it. He had misread her signals he explained, and had apologised. The judge kept telling us that this indicated a predisposition to use violence.

When told that he had booby-trapped a cupboard (as brought into the Court, with traces of peroxide and flour in it) to kill a colleague with whom he shared the flat, for no very evident motive, MSI denied this vehemently, saying 'As a Muslim, I'd go to hell, especially if I killed a Muslim'. For the huge expense of this court, one would have liked to have seen one or two Muslims present, who could have made some attempt to get into the mind of this 28-year old maybe confused but surely honest young man. Everything in this day at the court confirmed what Osman Hussain (connected with the bomb at Shepherd's Bush, who had fled to Rome right after the event) had said: that there was only flour in the bombs and they were only intended to frighten people. MSI was responding to a barrage of questions about all aspects of his life over several hours, and his questions while being continually told he was lying or being deceptive by the Prosecution, maintained a fairly impressive integrity. This group *seemed* to have planned this event quite independently of the July 7th bombings.

The alleged 'fifth bomber', Manfo Asiedu, connected with a rucksack 'flour-bomb' left in a park on July 21, accused MSI of having intended to blow up the block of flats. MSI replied that the latter had changed his story because the police had bribed him, and that he would be let off if he claimed that there was a bomb in this plot, designed to kill people. Mr Kamlish, the prosecuting counsel, put to MSI that real bombs were to be exploded in London trains, and that also a 'booby-trap bomb' had been set up in the flat they were living in. 'Who told you to say that?' MSI asked; 'My client,' Kamlish replied. As *The Times* explained the next day (23rd March), Kamlish QC was counsel for Mr Asiedu – the alleged 'fifth bomber.' MSI was asked by the prosecution why he did not let the bomb off on the Underground, in the tunnel. That was because, he replied, he wanted to let it off as the train pulled into the station, as the doors opened – so he could escape. There was no remote control, i.e. he had no proper detonator switch; he would have to put two wires together. The four of them were planning to escape after the blast; they were not 'suicide bombers.'

One gathered that MSI was in some degree inspired by the event of 7/7 to go ahead with a plan which he already had. It was a non-lethal copycat act. There is no evidence that the two groups had met up together. Hussain Osman was allegedly the guy the police were trying to get when they shot Jean-Charles de Menezes the next day on 22nd July. To try and justify this outrage, they do need public belief that the 21/7 gang were really intending to let off bombs.

The peroxide

MSI had endeavoured to concentrate hair bleach peroxide in his flat, purchased at Pak Cosmetics in Finsbury Park, as the court was informed. I went there and spoke to the assistant manager, who remembered the case although he was reluctant to talk about it. He showed me the one-litre bottles of 'Tru Zone Liquid peroxide' in 20, 30 and 40 'volumes' which means 6%, 9% and 12% that they would have bought from that shop. The prosecution averred that 20% peroxide had been purchased in large quantity, and concentrated up to around 50% in a saucepan; while conceding that at least 70% was required for any explosion. You don't need a degree in chemistry to figure out that a five-volt battery connected to wires *might* get a bang out of 70% peroxide soaked into flour. The court was thus asking the wrong question. The defence should have brandished a bottle of 'Tru Zone Liquid peroxide' – which has numerous other ingredients as well as its peroxide, to obtain a gel-like consistency – and challenged anyone to get a bang by mixing it with Chapati flour. Peroxide is unstable, and I believe no one in the court commented on how far hair bleach of this kind could be concentrated by boiling it in a saucepan.

Was MSI fiddling around with a battery and wire on the underground, trying to blow up his flour bomb? On March 22nd, the QC Matrix Chambers prosecution council, wearing a wig, averred that MSI had concocted a plot that would lead to 'one block of flats, a tower going up in a ball of flames' – to quote from the *Times*. No one laughed. This was not done by sticks of dynamite attached to the stairway, but by chapati flour in some cupboard – brought into the courtroom, as proof. I would simply not have believed it, had I not personally been present.[6] The headlines the next day featured July 7th, to establish the link in everyone's mind: *The Times'* headline ran, '7/7 Suspects Held.'

On July 7th, there were four explosive events, but not much by way of visual evidence pointing to the perpetrators. On July 21st, four perpetrators were indeed visible, but there were no bombs. These two images had to fuse together in people's minds, to create a single, credible image of Muslim terrorists with bombs. It worked like a charm. Why was De Menezes shot on the 22nd? After that event, the police were no longer at liberty to discuss details of 21/7, or there was no risk that they would try to do so – viz. that the flour bombs would have been a rather dusty experience, but would soon have brushed off.

The court quietly dropped the second of the two original charges, viz. that the accused had *"maliciously conspired together"* to cause *"explosions of a nature likely to endanger life or cause serious injury to property"* and they merely pressed the mysterious charge that, between 1 Jan and 30 July, 2005, the men conspired together *"and with other persons unknown to murder other persons."* Observed 9/11 web-blogger 'Sinclair', 'The details of such facilitations were given under the cloak of secrecy by un-named individuals as a result of numerous court reporting restrictions in place throughout the trial (only to be lifted when some public-swaying headline material was required).' And that is about as far as we are likely to get concerning this bogus and racist trial of a murder charge with no murder weapon and nobody killed. Let's hope that, in the course of time, some Africans object to this.

Readers may well feel bewildered by this unfolding story which hardly makes sense. This event cannot be independent of the July 7th plot, but what is the connection? One of the 21/7 group went into the Finsbury Park Pak Cosmetics to purchase the hydrogen peroxide hair bleach, on July 5th, recorded on the CCTV camera there. In the absence of a public inquiry, we may have to settle for something like this further comment by 'Sinclair:' 'the CIA back in the 70s – 80s, used the network of the YMCAs to recruit patsies/runners for operations. Such people who are new in a country and to a highly urban area can be coerced, by perceived offers of trust/assistance, to do a range of activities... These young men do not appear to be hardened Muslim fanatics, rather tricked, lost souls.'

On the day after De Menezes was shot in a quasi-ritual execution, *The Sun* on 23rd reported a 'Suspect shot dead,' this being a 'Suicide bomb suspect' and here British papers were all singing from the same hymn-sheet. We murmur quietly that on the 21st there were in London neither bombs, nor suicides. Then on the 25th, by when the dreadful error had become apparent, *The Sun* explained that in the 'harsh reality of life in London ... we are at war,' where 'collateral damage' was inevitable and 'innocent people die.' Londoners were being introduced to Operation Kratos, whereby British police had decided unannounced to get themselves trained by the Israeli military, concerning how and when to shoot 'suspected terrorists;' Did this mean that the Met was now working with an overtly racist profile for 'terror' suspects? The pretence that the July 21st group were 'suicide bombers,' with their not being allowed to make any statements to the press themselves, was central to the new climate of fear.

Only the BBC News reported (on June 12th, 2007) that the original charge of conspiracy to cause explosions likely to endanger life in this trial, previously faced by each man, had now been left off the indictment.[7] But, if this charge has been dropped, how could the charge of 'conspiracy to murder' possibly stand? And who were the 'other persons unknown' with whom they were alleged to have conspired with? On June 28, 2007, the jury of Britain's highest profile case involving alleged terrorism, retired to consider its verdict. All of the accused denied conspiracy to murder. Let's conclude by quoting from a discerning contributor to the 'J7' site, 'Kier': 'On 21/7, no deaths occurred and no bombs exploded, yet 43 arrests were made and 17 were charged. On 7/7, 56 people died, yet no arrests have been made and to date, no one has been charged or will stand trial.'

The turncoat 'fifth man' in this case was Manfo Kwaku Asiedu, but that was not his real name. That name belonged to the son of the head of the Ghanaian Secret Services. His father had to appear on Ghanaian TV to deny that his son was a terrorist. What was going on here? Maybe we are now in a position to formulate the fundamental *purpose* of the July 7th event, using the following:

> All intelligence agencies have been, and still are, in the business of destabilising undeveloped countries to maintain their dependency and the flow of the world's natural wealth to powerful nations.[8]

Some young Africans are blamed and imprisoned for 'terror' amidst media applause for how clever our police are. At stake here were diamonds and gold, precious minerals and oil – the things that really matter to our economic masters. Something had to be done, and July 7th was it: Bush and Blair walked tall against Terror, the Summit was derailed and the hope for Africa extinguished.

None of this stopped Manfo Asiedu from being given 35 years! As he can't speak English, we are unlikely to hear his view on the matter.

Distilling peroxide

'Nigel Sweeney and flour & Peroxide Bombs: Incompetent Londonistan terrorists strike again' by George Smith, CA

Crown prosecutor Nigel Sweeney assured the court that forensic scientists had tested the mixture, and 'in every experiment this mixture has exploded', to which George Smith sagely commented, 'In the parlance, this is known as a strapped-down chicken test, a rigging. It's another way of saying that scientists are allowed to go forward and make mimic bombs from highly concentrated peroxide and flour, correcting all the intellectual deficiencies and formulations of the terrorists, using lab assets terrorists do not have, to make something work in order that the case be made more convincing in court.' One only wishes British journalists could have figured this out, it's not hard.

Hydrogen peroxide readily decomposes (when it gives off oxygen) and almost anything you do to it will make it decompose. I spoke to the chemist at UCL who turned out to have advised the defence in this case, and he believed that they could have reached 50% or so merely by boiling the peroxide. They would not have known whether they had managed that, as they lacked any means of ascertaining the concentration, he explained, but even if they had managed that it would not have been explosive. Vapour-phase hydrogen peroxide is liable to detonate. That expert opinion differs slightly from

GS's view above-quoted: "The peroxide was likely at no more than a 40% concentration when it was mixed with the flour (the remainder being water and other impurities). That level of peroxide isn't even strongly corrosive, let alone explosive."[9] From what I heard at the court trial, this seems about right. I was told that the police did have their own forensic laboratories which had done this work, and one regrets that no report of their investigations is available. The prosecution counsel Mr Sweeney averred (on 15.1.07) that several *hundred litres* of 18% peroxide had been purchased from hairdressing suppliers, and that 'scientific evidence will show' that a concentration of around 58% was achieved by means of 'two saucepans and a frying pan.' In tests this 'failed to explode' he conceded, whereas a 70% concentrate would explode. In other words, there was no case.

In despair, one can only quote Shakespeare's Richard III: 'Who is so gross That cannot see this palpable device? But who's so bold but says he sees it not?'

References

[1] http://z13.invisionfree.com/julyseventh/index.php?showforum=30.
http://z13.invisionfree.com/julyseventh/index.php?showtopic=179.

[2] The July 21 Attack: The Pictures of the Four Suspects: Where are the Other Passengers? *Global research* July 26, 2005 http://www.globalresearch.ca/index.php?context=va&aid=739.

[3] Ahmed, p.95; *Washington Post* Foreign Service 22nd July, 2005.

[4] Ahmed, *The London Bombings,* 2006, p.97.

[5] The description of the device given in court involved a battery, wires, bulb-holder, bulb, sheet of paper, TATP and flour/hydrogen peroxide dough. The bulb had a hole made in it. A piece of TATP was put in the hole. The paper was rolled up and more TATP was put inside it with the bulb at one end. This assembly was put inside the dough. The battery was wired in. To set it off one would touch the ends of the wires.

[6] Earlier, on January 15th, Prosecuting attorney Mr Sweeney had averred: 'Shrapnel was also added to the outside of the 6.25-litre plastic container by using plastic adhesive tape and tissue paper to stick large quantities of screws, tacks, washers or nuts to it in the order of 80 such items per bomb. The purpose of shrapnel is of course to increase fragmentation when the bomb explodes and thus to maximise the possibility of injury, fatal or otherwise, to those who were in the vicinity.' That was not how the 'bombs' were described by MSI on the day I visited. No press picked up on this. For the court transcripts, see: http://z13.invisionfree.com/julyseventh/index.php?showtopic=1360& st=0.

[7] BBC News, 12.6.07, 'Civil duty' of 21/7 trial expert, http://news.bbc.co.uk/1/hi/uk/6745205.stm.

[8] Dr J.W. Smith, Research Director of the Institute for Economic Democracy in California, quoted www.mediamonitors.net/mosaddeq32.html (Ahmed, *War on Freedom,* 2002, p.332, afterword by John-Paul Leonard).

[9] www.dickdestiny.com/blog/2007/01/nigel-sweeney-and-flour-peroxide-bombs.html.

II. Operation 'Crevice'

On May 1, 2007, survivors and relatives of those killed on July 7 delivered a letter to the Home Office calling for an "independent and impartial public inquiry" into the attack. That, perhaps unfortunately, synchronised with delivery of the 'Operation Crevice' judgement, the UK's longest terror case: on May 30th, the results of that highly secret trial in Court Eight of the Old Bailey had been announced, one which involved (or so we were told) 3,644 witness statements and 105 prosecution witnesses over thirteen months of hearings, where the jury took a record 27 days to deliberate their verdict. At a cost of 50 million pounds, it was the most expensive criminal trial in British history. Five African immigrants were prosecuted for 'conspiring to cause explosions likely to endanger life between January 1, 2003, and March 31, 2004,' and given sentences totalling 200 years. Nothing had actually happened; no one had been hurt. Their crime, ascertained by this huge trial, was the possession of six hundred kilograms of ammonium nitrate.[1]

We have previously examined a huge trial involving young African immigrants where no one was hurt and nothing stolen, but they were found guilty and jailed. The Operation Crevice trial was in some respects rather similar.

'Crevice' is only a codeword with no meaning. This plot was not 'discovered' by British police, but was *given to* the British Security services from America, courtesy of Fort Maryland, where lurks the NSA National Security Agency, 'Puzzle Palace' as it's called, whose Great Computer spies on everyone. The plot's existence was announced as based on eavesdropped conversations between Pakistan and the UK. Scotland Yard, MI5, etc. were given this story; soon after, half a ton of fertilizer was found in a lock up at Hanwell, near Heathrow.

The accused were alleged to have stored this material 'in a London unit in preparation for a major bomb attack in Britain.' Anyone can plant fertilizer in a storage unit and aluminium powder in someone's shed, and we are here disturbed by the degree of secrecy involved. And, by the way, a farmer's bag of fertilizer will not detonate if you whack it with a shovel.[2] *The Guardian* revealed that "restrictive limits on reporting" over the last 13 months had meant that

> the story of Operation Crevice...will come as a surprise to almost everyone outside the narrow circle of politicians and security professionals who—together with those present in court—were aware that one of the most remarkable trials in British criminal history had been underway.

Given that the Crown was not prepared to hold an open trial that the public could witness, does it merit our credulity over its findings? We may be here reminded of the explosives allegedly found in a bath in Leeds belonging to biochemist Dr El-Nashar. That was, readers will recall, the whole basis for the hunt for the July 7 perpetrators going up to Leeds, despite which it subsequently turned out that the police were neither able to tell us what the explosive was, nor even to construct a case for pursuing the biochemist in whose flat it was allegedly found.

In the case of the July 21st trial, none of the accused were allowed any media interviews in the UK – we were assured by the authorities about the threat they posed to our way of life etc., but never could we hear their point of view. Let us therefore start off by quoting two brief, prepared statements which the convicted young men wished to make. Outside the Old Bailey on 30th April, 2007, at the end of the Crevice trial, this is what their lawyer, Imran Khan, read out:

> I'm giving this statement on behalf of those defendants convicted today, that is Omar Khyam, Anthony Garcia, Waheed Mahmood, Jawad Akbar, and Salahuddin Amin. These are their words that they wish me to read out: In the name of Allah the merciful, the compassionate, we bear witness there is nothing worthy of worship except Allah, and Mohammed is his messenger. This was a prosecution driven by the security services, able to hide behind a cloak of secrecy, and eager to obtain ever greater resources and power to encroach on individual rights. There was no limit to the money, resources and underhand strategies that were used to secure convictions in this case. This case was brought in an atmosphere of hostility against Muslims, at home, and abroad. One stoked by this government throughout the course of this case. This prosecution involved extensive intrusion upon personal lives, not only ours, but our families and friends.
>
> Coached witnesses were brought forward. Forced confessions were gained through illegal detention, and torture abroad. Threats and intimidation was used to hamper the truth. All with the trial judge seemingly intent to assist the prosecution almost every step of the way. These were just some of the means used in the desperate effort to convict. Anyone looking impartially at the evidence would realise that there was no conspiracy to cause explosions in the UK, and that we did not pose any threat to the security of this country. It is not an offence to be young, Muslim and angry at the global injustices against Muslims. Allah says in the Qur'an, "Oh mankind, worship your Lord who created you, and those before you, that you may become righteous." And that's the end of the statement. Thank you.

That all sounds rather familar. And believable. Also on that same day, 30th April, on the steps of the Old Bailey, lawyer Tayab Ali read out the following statement, on behalf of Salahuddin Amin:

> This statement is provided on behalf of Salahuddin Amin: In the name of God, the most compassionate, the merciful. I am innocent. An outrageous confidence trick has been played on the jury, and against me. I was convicted by false evidence and the fruits of torture. I am innocent. I told the jury the truth. I am innocent. I told the jury I had been tortured and mistreated by the ISI, the Pakistani intelligence services, over a ten month period of illegal detention in Pakistan during 2004. I told the jury how the British security services were responsible for my illegal detention, mistreatment, and illegal transfer to the UK. Even though I am a British Citizen, the British government did not lift a finger to

protect me from abuse and torture. In fact, the British authorities made it worse by interrogating me at the same time as knowing I had been tortured. The British government have been able to hide their shameful involvement in my illegal detention and torture in secret sessions which occurred during the trial. These hearings cannot be reported to you, the public. They continue to hide behind this veil. I demand they tell the truth about what they did to me.

I demand the truth about the other people who are still in secret detention and being tortured as part of this misguided war on terror. I was illegally detained with some of these people. I know that some of them were treated far worse than I was, while British, American, and Canadian intelligence officers stood ready to benefit from the unreliable fruits of torture. I demand an apology from the head of the security services and the British government about what they did to me. I demand an explanation as to how this could have happened. My wrongful conviction has given a green light to those who carry out the heinous act of torture on behalf of civilised western governments. I will continue to fight to clear my name. Thank you.

So, this trial used the fruits of torture. A British citizen gets threatened with an electric drill, and after listening to the screams of others being tortured he finally 'confessed' to his part in the Crevice plot.[3] Alleged potential targets included the Bluewater Shopping Centre in southern England.

Omar Khyam, a gifted young cricketer with ambitions to play for England, was arrested in Crawley, West Sussex, as part of series of co-ordinated police raids. His uncle told how the security services had urged the 22-year-old student to go to Pakistan next month with his younger brother, and he had bought the tickets. (*The Times*, April 1, 2004: 'Family claims MI5 ordered teenagers to go to Pakistan') The family had contacted a solicitor who spoke to MI5 on their behalf.

The prosecution's case used an FBI informer with al-Qaida links, Mohammed Junaid Babar, 31. He told the Old Bailey on March 26th, 2007, how he met a group of about 15 to 20 young men of Pakistani descent – mostly British and mainly from London and Crawley, West Sussex – in Afghanistan who he said had "come for the jihad". Babar has pleaded guilty in a US court to being part of a British bomb plot, which seems rather peculiar. Babar is a Pakistani-born US citizen who has been given immunity from prosecution in the UK after pleading guilty to terrorism offences in a New York court. He has explained that he faced the death penalty for his role in a conspiracy to kill Pakistan's President Pervez Musharraf if he had not collaborated with the FBI.[4] What kind of witness is this?

Omar Khyam, Waheed Mahmood, Jawad Akbar, Salahuddin Amin and Anthony Garcia were jailed for life. They were not allowed to give media interviews because they or some of them had allegedly been trained by and had close links with the intelligence agencies, chiefly the Pakistani ISI, which is closely connected to (and some say controlled by) the CIA. For a lucid exposition we turn to Alex Jones' 'Prison Planet' site,[5] explaining how Omar Khyam, the leader of the so-called fertiliser bomb gang, had been trailed by MI5 for some time before being arrested in early April 2004. When his trial began in September, Khyam testified for two days, but then refused to testify further, saying that his family in Pakistan had been threatened by the Pakistani intelligence service, ISI. He was, it seemed, beginning to spill too many beans about those powers behind the global terror network: The Indian newspaper *The Hindu* reported:

> Last week, Mr. Khyam told the court that ISI was training militants and during his visit to Pakistan six years ago he trained in an ISI-supervised camp. 'The ISI was setting up camps in what we called Free Kashmir, funding it with money and weapons and people that would train people, and logistical supplies, everything,' he said. Mr. Khyam said the people who trained him in handling arms were "selected by the ISI". "The ISI works with Islamic groups," he added.

Khyam stated in court:

> I think they are worried I might reveal more about them, so right now, as much as I want to clarify matters, the priority for me has to be the safety of my family so I am going to stop... I am not going to discuss anything related to the ISI any more or the evidence.

Operation Crevice's Implications for the July 7 story

The Crevice trial produced a whole raft of accusations that the Beeston lads, 'Sid' Khan and Tanweer (of the fish and chip shop), were linked to the 'Crevice' suspects.[6] However, it would seem that this was only though retrospectively-constructed, post-7/7 data. In other words, claims made that MI5 were shadowing Khan and Tanweer and had their sights on them before 7/7 seem only to be verifiable by means of documents dateable from *after* that date. Let's hear Nafeez Ahmed on this topic:

> Richard Watson of BBC Newsnight, Vikram Dodd at the *Guardian*, and David Leppard at the *Sunday Times*, among others have obtained evidence from security sources showing that Scotland Yard and MI5 had indeed identified Khan, by name, at latest around six months prior to 7/7, via his car registration. This is also confirmed by a Crown Prosecution Service document that came up in the course of the Crevice trial...

> 'Other interesting tidbits also surfaced in that trial about what was known about Khan. Contradicting the notion that he was only believed to be a petty criminal, the Crown also wanted to produce evidence at the beginning of the trial about Khan's attendance at an al-Qaeda training camp in Pakistan, as early as 2003. In the words of the trial judge, the evidence was supposed to prove "that the purpose of the training camp was to plan and cause explosions in the UK." At this time, Khan was already under surveillance, and indeed MI5 knew that he was "fully versed in how to make bombs" by the time he returned to the UK in summer that year (*Sunday Times* 22.1.06). French security officials are insisting that the 7/7 suspects had "belonged to the same network as the Britons of Pakistani origin who were partially arrested in Great Britain in March 2004" in Operation Crevice. Out of the total number of terrorist suspects "identified by the British only eight were arrested and five escaped", according to a senior French police officer in *Liberation* (14.7.05). Among the five suspects at large, say the French, was Mohammed Siddique Khan. ...

A British security source told this author that Khan was monitored all the way through to May 2005. Further, a document disclosed by prosecution lawyers to the defence before the commencement of the crevice trial cited MI5 surveillance recordings of Tanweer "discussing bombings and using the internet to make such a bomb," as late as "two weeks before" 7th July 2005. (*Guardian*, 3.5.07)

Last year, British security sources told BBC News (30.3.06) that: "... the security services had been so concerned about him [Siddique Khan] they had *planned to put him under a higher level of investigation*. MI5 officers assigned to investigate the lead bomber in the 7 July attacks were diverted to another anti-terrorist operation sources have now told BBC News.[7]

After Khan's death, stories about him proliferate, eg concerning how his car was bugged. But there is a general problem here with the lowering of threat-level which the intelligence services made in the weeks prior to July 7th, vis-a-viz alleged foreknowledge. Was this merely to facilitate the moving of the bulk of the Metropolitan police up to Scotland for the G8 summit, to have them out of the way? Here's a comment from *Global Outlook:*[8]

Why was the threat assessment, used to estimate the likelihood of a terrorist attack, lowered just weeks prior to the bombings and kept at the reduced level during the G-8 summit of government heads of major industrial nations, which was meeting in Britain at the time of the July 7 attacks? And how much did MI5 know about the alleged bombers?

The *New York Times* reported July 19 that the decision to lower the threat level was prompted by an assessment issued by the Joint Terrorist Analysis Centre, which includes officials from Britain's main intelligence agencies, as well as police forces and customs services. "Less than a month before the London bombings, Britain's top intelligence and law enforcement officials concluded that, 'at present there is not a group with both the current intent and the capability to attack the UK,'" the *NYT* wrote.

By reducing its assessment of the threat, British officials put the possibility of a terror attack by Islamic radicals only one level higher than the current chance of a terror attack by the Irish Republican Army, now ranked as 'moderate,' the report continued.

There was every reason to expect greater vigilance from the UK's security services on July 7, given that the leaders of the eight most powerful nations, including among them the foremost proponents of the so-called "war on terrorism," were meeting in Scotland. But there has yet to be an explanation for why Britain's threat level was downgraded instead.

On their own website, MI5, have put up a 'Rumours and Reality' page to clarify their position, which is fairly cautious and minimalist:[9] the media have been blaming them for failing to identify Khan earlier from the (alleged) Crevice findings, prior to July 7th. Neither Khan nor Tanweer were involved with the fertiliser bomb plot, and they appeared in the Crevice investigation as unidentified contacts who 'were not fully identified until after 7 July'. Concerning July 7th, 'No prior warning of the attacks was received from any source.' Intelligence had been collected on Khan and Tanweer, but it 'gave no indication that they posed a terrorist threat.' Whereas some papers had averred that Omar Khyam (one of the defendants in the fertiliser plot trial) had talked to Khan over the phone about bomb-making,[10] 'The Security Service did record conversations involving an individual identified after 7 July as Khan. However there is no recording of Khyam discussing bomb-making with Khan.' Khan was quite a luminary in the Beeston area and there is nothing surprising about MI5 having some recordings of his phone-calls.

Use of Ammonium Nitrate as Explosive

Anything sold as fertiliser must pass a detonation resistance test that determines how well the product resists an explosion. In the EU, fertiliser-grade ammonium nitrate is actually manufactured to higher standards than the explosive grade, with large, dense granules to prevent them absorbing fuel oil. Stabilisers are sometimes added to prevent the granules breaking down. (19.3.04 *New Scientist*, 'Defusing fertiliser may make bomb-building harder') The IRA's 1996 bombing of London's Canary Wharf used it, causing £85 million damage.

According to Department of the Army and Air Force Technical Manual No. 9-1910, entitled Military Explosives, ANFO (ammonium nitrate and fuel oil) requires a greater than 99% purity of ammonium nitrate, as well as a specific dryness, before it can be mixed with diesel fuel to create an explosive substance. Ammonium nitrate fertilizer comes in much weaker concentrations than the 99%-plus required for explosives.

References

[1] http://www.ladlass.com/intel/archives/006824.html.

[2] The 600 kilos of ammonium nitrate, if still around, will not be explosive. We learn: 'A decision was made to ensure the explosives could not blow up', said a Scotland Yard source, who would not specify how this was achieved. 'Let's just say we did something to make it safe for the public no matter what happened', he said. 'British terror plot foiled by the spies from the Puzzle Palace', *The Times,* 7.4.04.

[3] Amin, born in London but raised in Pakistan, had earlier claimed to have only made the admissions after torture by the ISI, and that he had been tricked into returning to the UK, believing he would be free if he repeated his confessions. Counsel for Defence Sir Michael Astil QC stated, 'Amin said he had been stripped and tortured before telling ISI he would say "anything you want"'. It was claimed that Amin had obtained 'the bomb formula' 'from an Al-Qaeda contact.' What bomb formula? Surrey.Online 'Suspect 'Tortured to Confess" 15.3.07.

[4] The *Guardian,* 'FBI informer' 'met Britons on Afghan jihad' 23 March www.guardian.co.uk/terrorism/story/0,,1738592,00.html.

[5] http://infowars.net/articles/may2007/010507Terror.htm Prison Planet: 'Fertilizer Terrorists Fingered Intelligence Agencies, ISI implicated, 7/7 links exposed, terror network control by Intel beyond doubt,' Steve Watson, May 1, 2007.

[6] http://www.globalresearch.ca/index.php?context=va&aid=5601 Julie Hyland, 'British terror trial raises question of what MI5 knew about 2005 London bombings' 9.5.07, see Appendix 10b for comments.

[7] http://nafeez.blogspot.com/2007/05/inside-crevice-77-and-security-debacle.html.

[8] Mike Ingram, *Global Research*, August 8, 2005, 'Outstanding questions on July 7 bombings warrant independent inquiry' www.globalresearch.ca/index.php?context=va&aid=820.

[9] MI5 http://www.mi5.gov.uk/output/Page385.html.

[10] A *Panorama* program on Crevice, 'Real Spooks' of 30.4.07, showed Omar Khyam and Khan speaking alone at night in a car, where it may not have been evident to viewers that these were actors speaking the words, as had allegedly been recorded. Khan is being urged to abandon his family for the sake of the glory of Jihad, etc.: that does not seem very compatible with MI5's verdict on Crevice, that '...the intelligence collected on them [Khan and Tanweer] gave no indication that they posed a terrorist threat'. (www.mi5. gov.uk/output/Page385.html) Obtaining a transcript of the trial is difficult and expensive.

III. The Heathrow Liquid Bomb Hoax

"Put simply, this was intended to be mass murder on an unimaginable scale," said Deputy Commissioner Paul Stephenson from the Metropolitan Police. Nothing had actually happened, no bomb had been taken on board a plane – no one had *even made one*. So what was all the fuss about? Why all the plane cancellations at Heathrow, costing hundreds of millions in delays and lost flights, and why can't we take toothpaste in hand luggage any more? Britain's new anti-terror legislation, where you don't actually have to do anything to get arrested, had swung into action. Britain's Prime Minister Tony Blair, on holiday during these events in Barbados at Sir Cliff Richard's luxury villa, decided to stay there.

The COBRA meeting began at 9.30 pm on the 9th August, 2006, in the high-tech bunker deep below the Cabinet Office. The police raids began at midnight, with 24 suspects arrested: British-born Muslims, some of Pakistani descent, from London, Birmingham, and High Wycombe. It was an overnight operation, and their finances were frozen.Those detained included a soccer fan, cricket players, a taxi driver, an accountant and his nursery teacher wife who was expecting a baby within a few weeks, a security guard with a three-week old baby, a pizza worker, a tyre businessman and a science student.[1] British police found tins of baked beans, peanut butter, some low concentration hydrogen peroxide and a sugar solution (i.e., the latter were possibly bleach or disinfectant and a cup of tea) at the suspects' homes. These apparently normal, peaceable, well-adjusted people had all been consumed with an irresistible urge to kill themselves and were prepared to kill hundreds of others, we were told.[2] These arrests appeared to be the result of a long-standing investigation coordinated between the US, British and Pakistani governments.

On Thursday morning, thousands of holidaymakers began arriving at airports to discover total disruption and the biggest terror alert since 7/7. It was alleged that multiple commercial aircraft were intended to be targeted, maybe for the 16th August, and that their fiendish plot aimed to destroy as many as ten aircraft in mid-flight from the United Kingdom to the United States, using explosives brought on board in their hand luggage! News media reported that planned targets included American Airlines, British Airways, Continental Airlines, and United Airlines flights from London Heathrow and London Gatwick airports to Chicago, Illinois; Los Angeles, California; Miami, Florida; Orlando, Florida; Boston, Massachusetts; Newark, New Jersey; New York City; San Francisco, California; Cleveland, Ohio; and Washington, D.C. The BBC's security correspondent Gordon Corera said the plot involved a series of simultaneous attacks, targeting three planes each time. The plotters planned to use Lucozade bottles (or so *The New York Times* reported) to contain certain 'liquid explosives'. They were going to use peroxide-based explosives, the media seemed to agree, probably the dreaded triacetone triperoxide (TATP).

These arrests were *followed by* the search for evidence, as the *Financial Times* explained: "The police set about the mammoth task of gathering evidence of the alleged terrorist bomb plot yesterday" (August 12, 2006). This was an odd reversal of normal investigatory procedures, commented the French 'Voltairenet' (of Thierry Meyssan), in which arrests were only supposed to happen *after* the gathering of evidence.[3] On what basis had the arrests been made? The British government, backed by Washington (or vice versa), averred that the Pakistani government's arrest of two British-Pakistanis provided *"critical evidence"* in uncovering the plot and identifying the alleged terrorist. The Pakistani intelligence services (ISI) are notorious for use of torture in extracting 'confessions.' In this case, their evidence was based on a supposed encounter between a relative of one of the suspects and an Al-Qaeda operative on the Afghan border. The Al-Qaeda agent supposedly provided the relative and thus the accused with the bomb-making information and operative instructions. But, transmission of bomb-making information hardly required a trip half-way around the world, least of all to a frontier under military siege by US-led forces on one side and the Pakistani military on the other. Were the Al-Qaeda agents in the mountains of Afghanistan supposed to have some detailed knowledge of Heathrow Airport?

Prime Minister Tony Blair had alerted George Bush to the investigation on Sunday, 6th August, 2006, before flying out with his family to Barbados on the 8th. Bush and Blair had discussed the matter *prior to* the police arrests. On 9th August, hours before the arrests, the Home Secretary John Reid gave a major speech to *Demos* (a British think-tank) hinting at a new round of anti-terror legislation, claiming that the country was facing 'probably the most sustained period of severe threat since the end of the Second World War.'

And he decried those who "don't get it," i.e., who failed to comprehend that democratic liberties had to be surrendered to the state. He blamed *them* for the fact that "we remain unable to adapt our institutions and legal orthodoxy as fast as we need to," making it clear that the required "adaptation" meant the gutting of traditional democratic rights:

> Sometimes we may have to modify some of our own freedoms in the short term in order to prevent their misuse and abuse by those who oppose our fundamental values and would destroy all of our freedoms in the modern world.[4]

On the next day, 10th August, George Bush commented, upon his arrival in Wisconsin: "The recent arrests that our fellow citizens are now learning about are a stark reminder that this nation is at war with Islamic fascists who will use any means to destroy those of us who love freedom, to hurt our nation." Israel was brutally assaulting Lebanon as Bush slipped in that key phrase 'Islamic fascists.' Israel's July invasion led to the killing of over 1,000 people, the creation of more than a million refugees who were forced to flee their homes, and the contamination of large swathes of the countryside with lethal land-mines.

The US Homeland Security Secretary Michael Chertoff on August 10th described the (non-) event as an attack which *had the potential to kill hundreds of thousands of people.* Inevitably, he added that 'it certainly has some of the hallmarks of an al Qaeda plot,' and agreed with his interviewer that, 'this plot was the biggest terrorist threat since the attacks of September 11, 2001'. A senior congressional source claimed that the plotters planned to mix 'a sports drink with a peroxide-based paste to make an explosive cocktail that could be triggered by an MP3 player or cell phone.' Uh-huh. Meanwhile, Israeli warplanes bombed the heart of Beirut.

Seventeen of the suspects were charged with conspiracy to murder and commit acts of terrorism *or failing to disclose* information about acts of terrorism. [Citizens are obliged to report intended crimes that may come to their attention, but this civic duty becomes impossible when the definition of terrorism is so wide that no one can be sure of who among their acquaintances may fall under its catch-all categories – see next chapter.] Little did this (alleged) 'group' know that an undercover British agent had infiltrated them. On 28 August, 2006, the NYT reported that seven martyrdom tapes made by six suspects were recovered. Gigabytes of information had been confiscated from homes of dozens of suspects. Hundreds of computers and mobile phones were taken. But, that still wouldn't give the police any connection between the persons arrested who hadn't bought air tickets or made bombs; and a terror plot that never happened over the skies of America. The suspected ringleader Rashid Rauf in Pakistan will almost certainly have had 'extraordinary rendition' applied to him, i.e. been tortured, to 'confess.'

Heathrow Airport was closed down, then hand luggage was forbidden; later, liquids were forbidden in hand luggage (e.g. milk and toothpaste). The first day of delays cost the airlines over £175 million. Huge queues of passengers waited to check-in and get through the strengthened security procedures. On Sunday, 13th August, 30% of flights out of Heathrow were cancelled to reduce pressure on the screeners. British Airlines reported that 10,000 items of baggage belonging to their passengers had gone missing while Ryanair called on the British government to employ police and military reservists to speed up the full-body searches that had become mandatory. By August 12th, the owner and operator of London Heathrow ordered all airlines using the airport to make a 30 percent reduction in departing passenger flights. Carolyn Evans, head of flight safety at the British Airline Pilots Association, said that "the procedures put in place are not sustainable long term, and unless the passengers are treated more reasonably we will not have an industry left." In November 2006, BA claimed that the increased security measures since August had cost it £100 million.[5]

Amidst the madness, a word of sense was spoken by former UK Ambassador to Uzbekistan, Craig Murray:

> Many [of those arrested] did not even have passports, which given the efficiency of the UK Passport Agency would mean they couldn't be a plane bomber for quite some time … In the absence of bombs and airline tickets, and in many cases passports, it could be pretty difficult to convince a jury beyond reasonable doubt that individuals intended to go through with suicide bombings, whatever rash stuff they may have bragged in internet chat rooms….

> Then an interrogation in Pakistan revealed the details of this amazing plot to blow up multiple planes … Of course, the interrogators of the Pakistani dictator have their ways of making people sing like canaries. As I witnessed in Uzbekistan, you can get the most extraordinary information this way. The trouble is it always tends to give the interrogators all they might want, and more, in a desperate effort to stop or avert torture. What it doesn't give is the truth.[6]

Another British voice of sanity was that of political scientist Nafeez Ahmed., who expressed the view that:

> the British and American governments, for all intents and purposes, invented a terror threat in August 2006, to trigger a climate of fear and paranoia convenient for the legitimisation of a political agenda of intensifying social control at home, and escalating military repression in the Middle East.

He gave several talks together with munitions expert Lt. Colonel Wylde on the topic. Apart from these, the entire British media believed the story. It was a dream-hallucination from start to finish, with no semblance of rational evidence to link together those arrested and an alleged plot which never happened. According to Lt-Col (Ret.) Nigel Wylde, a former senior British Army Intelligence Officer with decades of anti-terror and explosives experience, the whole plot was a 'fiction' and the explosives in question could not possibly have been produced on the plane.[7] 'So who came up with the idea that a bomb could be made on board? Not Al Qaeda for sure. It would not work. Bin Laden is interested in success not deterrence by failure,' Wylde hypothesised. He suggested that the plot was an invention of the UK security services in order to justify profitable and wide-ranging new security measures that threaten to permanently curtail civil liberties and to suspend sections of the United Kingdom's Human Rights Act of 1998. Wylde added that, if there was a conspiracy, 'it did not involve manufacturing the explosives in the loo,' as this simply 'could not have worked.' The process would be quickly and easily detected. The fumes of the chemicals in the toilet 'would be smelt by anybody in the area.' They would also inevitably 'cause the alarms in the toilet and in the air change system in the aircraft to be triggered.'

Key information was supposed to have been obtained from Pakistan, but what did Pakistan have to do with it? There's no need to go to Pakistan to learn that mixing acetone, sulphuric acid and peroxide won't make a bomb, especially not in an aircraft toilet – that's only in the Hollywood movies. Those three chemicals would form a nasty mixture which would stink very badly, but they would require a freezing cabinet and a fume cupboard for the reaction to work, i.e. produce TATP – adding a drop of sulphuric acid at a time, taking several hours, then a day for the TATP to separate out. Also, what about the detonators? Without a detonator, it's not a bomb.

Had the alleged ringleader, 25-year old Rashid Rauf (born in Birmingham) invented the plot under torture in Pakistan, as Craig Murray suggested? Rauf attended a court hearing in Rawalpindi, on 22nd December, 2006:

> Head bowed and covered by a black shawl and Muslim prayer cap, the Briton named as a 'key suspect' in the alleged terror plot to blow up transatlantic airliners was escorted to a court in Pakistan yesterday… Yesterday Rauf, from Birmingham, protested his innocence of any involvement in a plot. Handcuffed and flanked by 12 armed police officers, he claimed he had been framed by the authorities. 'I have done nothing wrong but I have been framed, I am not optimistic that I will be cleared… everything against me is based on lies.'[8]

Despite his prosecutors alleging that Rauf was in possession of a number of bottles of hydrogen peroxide, the court dropped the charges, ruling that this case 'did not fall into the category of terrorism.'

An article by chemist Thomas Greene in Washington explained how the 'binary liquid munitions' story had come out of movies rather than a chemistry textbook :

> So the fabled binary liquid explosive – that is, the sudden mixing of hydrogen peroxide and acetone with sulfuric acid to create a plane-killing explosion, is out of the question. Meanwhile, making TATP ahead of time carries a risk that the mission will fail due to premature detonation, although it is the only plausible approach. Certainly, if we can imagine a group of jihadists smuggling the

necessary chemicals and equipment on board, and cooking up TATP in the lavatory, then we've passed from the realm of action blockbusters to that of situation comedy.[9]

The bomb plot hoax has caused enormous losses not only to the airlines, but also to business people, oil companies, duty-free shops, tourist agencies, resorts and hotels, not to speak of the tremendous inconvenience and health related problems of millions of stranded and stressed-out travellers. So what was the point of it? What was its *purpose*? We've already quoted Nafeez Ahmed, and let's now hear a pertinent judgement from France's Voltaire Network:

> Clearly the decision to cook up the phony bomb plot was not motivated by economic interests, but domestic political reasons. The Blair administration, already highly unpopular for supporting Bush's wars in Iraq and Afghanistan, was under attack for his unconditional support for Israel's invasion of Lebanon, his refusal to call for an immediate ceasefire and his unstinting support for Bush's servility to US Zionist lobbies. Even within the Labor party over a hundred backbenchers were speaking out against his policies ...

> The criminal frame-up of young Muslim-South Asian British citizens by the British security officials was specifically designed to cover up for the failed Anglo-American invasion of Iraq and the Anglo-American backing for Israel's destructive but failed invasion of Lebanon. Blair's *"liquid bombers"* plot sacrificed a multiplicity of British capitalist interests in order to retain political office and stave off an unceremonious early exit from power. The costs of failed militarism are borne by citizens and businesses.[10]

The liquid bomb story was soon ridiculed into obscurity, after which British Deputy Assistant Commissioner Peter Clarke merely claimed that *"bomb making equipment including chemicals and electric components had been found."*[11] Also, the Clark team claimed that they found 'martyr videotapes' in the homes of those arrested, without clarifying the fact that the videos were not made by the suspects but only viewed by them. In mid-December, the police announced that they were calling off the search at a strip of woodland where bomb-making equipment had allegedly been hidden, as none of the authorities were prepared to continue funding the operation. On May 20th, 2007 the arrested alleged plotters entered their plea of 'not guilty,' and their trial took place in 2008.

How did it begin? Some days before the arrests, on Sunday, 6th August, American Airlines flight 109 from London Heathrow to Boston boarded a family of five; after the plane left, Heathrow authorities determined that the father appeared on a British suspect list drawn up after the 7/7 London transit attacks. The pilot was instructed to fly to Boston but refused, fearing for the safety of his passengers and crew, and quickly returned to Heathrow without informing the passengers. Once on the ground, it was discovered that the male had in his carry-on baggage the combination of liquid explosive and an electronic device that was now being hyped by the British and American media. That sounds a quite unlikely combination: featuring on an alleged 'July 7th suspect' list and carrying binary liquid explosives; no wonder no one has released the name of this person. As Alex Jones' Prison Planet article concluded, 'The Israeli attack on Lebanon created a rift within Blair's Cabinet ... As a result, a suspect passenger was permitted to board an American aircraft at Heathrow with a liquid bomb to lay the groundwork for the media and travel hysteria five days later.'[12]

The police responsible need to brush up on chemistry concerning what can go bang in a bomb, for example in the 'Crevice' trial, the mere possession of bags of a *fertiliser,* ammonium nitrate was enough to put Muslims in jail, whereas fertiliser-grade ammonium nitrate is made so that it will not detonate very readily.[13] In the July 7th, July 21st, and the Heathrow liquid bomb story, TATP was featured, whereas in real life no 'terrorist' has used it for a bomb—maybe because it is too unstable and needs to be stored below 10° C.

In April 2008, the Heathrow liquid-bomb trial began at Woolwich Crown Court, with eight men accused. One of them, 27-year old Abdulla Ahmed Ali, denied any intention of boarding planes – 'We did not even think about boarding a plane' – and insisted that a device was merely intended as a demonstration of protest against Britain's foreign policy. "This whole thing has been blown up out of proportion. I'm not going to admit to something I didn't do and never intended to do." He maintained that the plastic bottle and battery explosive device he attempted to make was never intended to harm. "That's the truth," he said. "I've done something which is an offence, I'm putting my hand up to that." He claimed the charges against him had been "exaggerated", with the media being used "to ruthless effect".[14]

It would appear that Britons are prepared to pay a heavy price for their daily dose of fear, their tingle of terror, and that politicians now have to cater for this need, which has somehow spilled over from horror and action movies. No politician trying to claim that the British did not have an enemy, or did not need an enemy, could possibly hope to get elected. This writer would suggest that wolves should be re-introduced into selected woodlands. Possibly hearing the howling of wolves at night might satisfy the atavistic need for fear, and would obviate the continual need to have innocent Muslims banged up in jail on phantom terror allegations.

The 'Ricin Plot'

These phantom terror events remind one of the 'Ricin plot,' where a flat in Wood Green was raided on 5th January, 2003, by the police. They found some castor beans plus a few other ingredients. Ricin, a poison, *can be extracted* from castor beans. News reports alleging that 'traces' of ricin had been found in the flat were soon contradicted by top British experts at Porton Down – despite which, like an undead zombie, the story refused to lie down. Why not? Britain's Master of Deception held forth with one of his 'be afraid' speeches, on January 7th, 2003: Prime Minister Blair proclaimed,

> 'The arrests which were made show this danger is present and real with us now. Its potential is huge.'

'Terror on the Doorstep,' as a *Sunday Times* headline proclaimed, was ideal material for the new, pointless war which the Prime Minister was dragging Britain into. A hapless Algerian 'mastermind' was arrested, who was of course named Mohammed – the name of the Prophet is almost mandatory for these 'masterminds', e.g. Mohammed Atta (9/11), Mohammed Khan (7/7), and this disturbed loner was thrown in jail for *writing out a recipe* for making ricin.

The *purpose* of the Ricin Plot appeared a month later, when US Secretary of State Colin Powell brandished a phial of what was allegedly ricin before the United Nations on 6th February, alleging that the London 'terror cell' was part of a global network originating in Iraq. It appeared as part of his case for military intervention in Iraq.

Two years later this vacuous 'threat' could still be resurrected as a reason for Britons surrendering their democratic freedoms: Ian Blair, police superintendent, declared on the 'Breakfast with Frost' program 17.4.05 that the 'Ricin plot' demonstrated the need for new anti-terror laws; later on (5.10.05), Met police assistant Andy Hayman was citing the Ricin plot as showing the need for 90-day detentions without trial.[15] Did anyone ever apologise for all this outright mendacity, frightening the British people, dragging them into illegal war and arresting the innocent?

References

[1] On 13.8.06 The *Sunday Mirror* disclosed in 'EXCLUSIVE: BABY BOMB' story that one couple who might have been intending to take part in this plot, might also have been intending to take their new baby on board in their suicide flight, in order to be able to conceal the explosive in the baby's bottle! Mothers boarding at Heathrow with young babies were thereafter obliged to drink from their baby's bottle before boarding flights, in order to demonstrate that they were not planning to blow up the plane.

[2] 'Britain's airline terror plot: Questions that need to be answered' World Socialist Web 11.8.06, www.wsws.org/articles/2006/aug2006/lond-a11.shtml.

[3] www.voltairenet.org/article143264.html 'The Liquid Bomb hoax: The larger implications' by James Petras, on Meyssan Voltaire Network. For whether 'terror' exists in Europe, see Appendix 12. www.takeourworldback.com/short/liquidbombhoax.htm (anon).

[4] http://en.wikipedia.org/wiki/2006_transatlantic_aircraft_plot.

[5] http://en.wikipedia.org/wiki/2006_transatlantic_aircraft_plot.

[6] Craig Murray, *The Guardian,* The UK Terror plot: What's Really Going On? 15 August, 2006, archived at www.oilempire.us/blair-scare.html.

[7] http://nafeez.blogspot.com/2006/09/ex-uk-intel-official-says-liquid.html (Sept 18, 2006) Ahmed, 'August terror plot is a 'fiction' underscoring police failures'; Col. Wylde, 18 Sept www.rawstory.com/news/2006/Sources_August_Terror_Plot_Fiction_Underscoring_0918. html.

[8] *Daily Mail*, 23 Dec 2006.

[9] Appendix 9b: www.theregister.co.uk/2006/08/17/flying_toilet_terror_labs/ 'Mass murder in the skies: was the plot feasible? Let's whip up some TATP and find out', Thomas Greene (17.8.2006).

[10] Op. cit. ref. 3.

[11] BBC News, August 21, 2006.

[12] http://rense.com/general73/latest.htm 'Latest Terror Threat – More Government Foreknowledge', By Joel Skousen, World Affairs Brief, 12 August, 2006.

[13] http://en.wikipedia.org/wiki/Ammonium_nitrate.

[14] Guardian, June 3rd 2008, 'Airline accused wanted to 'cause disturbance' at airport'.

[15] Peter Osborne, *Use and Abuse of Terror,* 2006, p.25. The 'Ricin plot' was also cited in the anonymous *Official Account* of July 7th as an instance of Islamic terror: pp.30, 34.

16. A Culture of Surveillance?

'We already live in a punishment culture and we're getting perilously close to a full-blown police state. If we don't want to wake up one day and wonder where the last of our liberties went, it's time to get our skates on.'

Skating towards a police state... Richard Littlejohn, *Daily Mail* 2.8.07

On the day of July 7th, the Queen made a statement saying, 'Those who perpetrate these brutal acts against innocent people should know that they will not change our way of life.' Wouldn't they? One could paraphrase her statement as,

'This event will transform the lives of British people, catalysing their loss of liberties and leading them irreversibly into a police state of constant surveillance. It will increase acceptance of ID cards, stimulate countless arrests of innocents, and help to ensure that the people always live in fear. Through it, people will get to hear about Operation Kratos, already established, whereby senior police are at liberty to shoot civilians in the head upon mere suspicion. Britain's two million Muslims will become liable to a nightmare of racist stop-and-search, phoney arrests and police raids, and they may start to emigrate when their sense of humiliation gets too much. Soon, merely to carry toothpaste in your bag through an airport will be prohibited. We teach citizens to fear a bag left on the floor. We will ban demonstrations near Parliament and all those without a license.'

Section 58 of the *Terrorism Act* 2000 had established the thought-crime of merely collecting information about 'terror.' Thereby, a person would have committed an offence if—

(a) he collects or makes a record of information of a kind likely to be useful to a person committing or preparing an act of terrorism, or

(b) he possesses a document or record containing information of that kind.

And this section is now being used quite frequently. For example, Irfan Raja, 18, from Ilford, Essex, and 19-year-old Awaab Iqbal were accused of making a record of information 'likely to be useful' to a terrorist. Lawyers for the pair indicated both would plead not guilty, with counsel for Mr Iqbal saying the charges had "absolutely no foundation". Mr Iqbal, a first-year forensic science student studying at Bradford University, was arrested at his home in Bradford, then had his application for bail refused. Earlier, The charge against Mr Raja related to information he had allegedly collated and downloaded from his computer.

Thus even a university student of forensic science can be so charged – provided, of course, that he is Muslim. The Terrorism Act 2000 had defined 'terror' not in terms of violence, as had the UK's earlier (1996) anti-terror act, but in terms of *action,* as 'use or threat of action,' action moreover 'designed to influence the government' and 'made for the purpose of advancing a political, religious or ideological cause'. There is nothing here about killing anyone, nor even the necessity that an observer would judge that 'terror' had been produced! Further sections then explain, that this action or threat of action would have to, for example, 'seriously to disrupt an electronic system,' or involve 'serious damage to property.' This Act has been used for charging people for wearing the wrong T-shirt.

In the wake of New York's 9/11, the US and UK passed somewhat similar anti-terror laws, both of which horribly misused the key word so as to make it apply to damage, or threats to damage, of property. For the UK Act of December 2001 to be passed, the Government had to proclaim a 'state of public emergency or war.' This enabled it to derogate from Section 15 of the European Court of Human Rights, affirming that citizens cannot be jailed without a trial. The British government announced an emergency state, despite repeated confirmations from politicians that none such existed. The new Act provided for the indefinite detention, without proof, of any non-nationals whom the Home Secretary suspected might be 'terrorists.' In 2004 this clause was thrown out by the House of Lords, on the grounds of being discriminatory and ineffective. None of these anti-terror laws are at all necessary, because existing laws concerning conspiracy to commit murder are perfectly adequate.

Britain is a world leader in surveillance technology, with its citizens being the most spied-upon in the world. There are at least four million CCTV cameras in the UK, which now swivel and scan across everything in sight, being linked to automatic car number plate recognition. During the 1990s the Home Office spent 78% of its crime prevention budget – a total of £500mn – on installing these cameras, and now the average Briton is caught on camera an astonishing 300 times every day. Microphones may soon be attached to the CCTV cameras to record street conversations. No one ever voted for these millions of CCTV and speed cameras. As the surveillance society burgeons, with CCTV, biometrics, databases and tracking technologies, facial recognition databases can be constructed for everyone. One month before July 7th, a BBC website found that eighty percent of respondents opposed the scheme of national ID cards.[1] The Oyster card of a tagged individual activates the system, enabling them to be followed their entire journey. Britons may be forcefully microchipped like dogs in a few years' time, as an October 2006 report indicated.[2] Police are permitted to record the DNA of every person arrested, for whatever reason, and Britain has the largest such database in the world of four million – including one million who have never been convicted of any crime.[3]

Each year from 1997 to 2006 saw an average of 2,685 new provisions of the criminal code – a 22% increase from the average over the previous 10 years. Crime rates rise not because citizens are criminal but because the police and magistrates are losing their grip upon the meaning of the word 'crime.' British Muslims are arrested three times more frequently than non-Muslims in the UK, according to Home Office statistics. Nothing is more important to a society than a clear understanding of the word 'crime.' It needs to be defined in terms of an act, something that has been done, and preferably in public – not something which the police reckon someone might be intending to do. Britain has had a dire sequence of anti-terror laws which are highly oppressive upon its own citizens and especially Muslims, in which the key concept of 'terror' remains largely undefined. It is essential that citizens and police can agree upon the meaning and justice of laws that are in place; an ethical policeman is one who will decline to enact unjust laws, ones that have lost the proper meaning of the word 'crime' and are in effect state repression of its own citizens. At its root meaning, this word has to allude to an act, one involving unacceptable harm to others, and must not allude to a possible intention or the holding of a wrong belief.

When the police raided the Iqra learning Centre in Beeston they did so under anti-terror legislation and confiscated what they alleged were 'hate' videos. At least some of these were what we would call 'truth' videos and literature (e.g. revealing the role of the US government in constructing the event of 9/11). This is an example of the way Muslims are being victimised and of police behaviour that results from repressive legislation that is too open-ended. Thus Abu Bakr, who works in Birmingham's Maktabah bookshop, was targeted in anti-terror raids: as a PhD student in Political Islam at the city's university, he became aware of the police forcing their way into his house early in the morning when his wife started to scream. Asked how he felt about his arrest, he said: "It's a police state for Muslims. It's not a police state for everybody else because these terror laws are designed specifically for Muslims and that's quite an open fact."

On July 21st, a major meeting of the Association of Chief Police Officers was taking place at Downing Street to promote drastic new anti-terror laws, exactly synchronised with the 21/7 'bombing incidents' across London. With the Prime Minister were: MI5's director Eliza Manningham-Buller; MI6's chief John Scarlett; David Pepper, chief of GCHQ at Cheltenham; the Lord Chancellor; and Lord Goldsmith, the Attorney-General. So this was quite a top list of VIPs whose assembly had to be synchronised with the London event. They were discussing 'dealing with Al-Qaeda' etc. as the events were taking place; after they resumed, they could agree upon a drastic extension of arrest without trial for up to three months (*The Times* July 22, 'Police want more Powers to detain terrorist suspects').

British Home Secretary Charles Clarke has warned that European citizens will have to accept their civil liberties being bartered away in exchange for protection from terrorists and organised criminals. The 2005 *Prevention of Terrorism Act* gave the government the right to impose control orders on those suspected of involvement in terrorism, then the *Terrorism Act* 2006 made it a crime to 'prepare or encourage' terrorism and it included the alarmingly meaningless phrase, 'glorification of terrorism.' Warrants could then be issued enabling the police to search any property that a 'terrorist' owned. At the 2005 Labour Party conference, Tony Blair said,

> 'We know we need strict controls. They are being put in place, along with Identity Cards, also necessary in a changing world.'

Biometric scanning for passengers was introduced at Heathrow in December 2006, designed to work in conjunction with ID cards. In the weeks following July 7th, a Guardian-backed survey found that almost three-quarters of British citizens were prepared to renounce civil liberties to if that protected them against terror-attacks (source: J7 'Capitalising on terror') and favoured torture for deported terrorism suspects.

Passed in January 2006, the innocuous-sounding Legislative and Regulatory Reform Bill conferred upon ministers the power to alter any law passed by Parliament. Ministers merely have to propose an order, wait a few weeks, and, voilà, the law is changed. For ministers the advantages are obvious: no more tedious debates in which they have to answer awkward questions, no more detailed line-by-line examination in committee, no second chance at specific amendment in the Commons, and lastly no final debate and vote. Instead, the Government itself becomes able to create extra regulation and define new crimes. Carrying ID cards could suddenly be made compulsory; smoking in one's own home could be outlawed, or the definition of terrorism altered to make ordinary political protest punishable by imprisonment. In practice, ministers may protest that they do not intend to do such things, but the Bill gives them that power.[4]

The SOCRAP Act

The 2006 *Serious Organised Crime and Police* Act (SOCPA, better known as the 'Socrap Act') means that for almost any offence, the police are able, when making an arrest, to insist on taking DNA as well as photographs; and that they can now arrest one for more or less anything:

> Under the 1984 Police and Criminal Evidence Act, a balance was struck between police powers and the individual's rights. There was a clear distinction between non-arrestable offences, arrestable offences and serious arrestable offences. Everyone knew where they stood and the public was protected from officious or malevolently motivated police constables. After the SOCRAP Act there is no such distinction, every offence is arrestable: motoring infringements, dropping litter, swearing and behaving loudly in a demonstration will very likely end in arrest.[5]

There are specific tests of necessity a police officer must satisfy, yet at the end of the list come two paragraphs which allow: first, an arrest to be carried out to allow the prompt and effective investigation of the offence or of the conduct of the person in question; second, an arrest may take place 'to prevent any prosecution of the offence from being hindered by the disappearance of the person in question.'

Protests have also been severely curtailed by this Act. Demonstrators who breach the perimeter fence of "sensitive sites" can be jailed for 51 weeks or fined £5,000 for criminal trespass. For example, Helen John, 68, and Sylvia Boyes, 62, both veterans of the Greenham Common protests, were arrested under the power when they walked across the sentry line at the US base at Menwith Hill, North Yorkshire. The Home Office originally designated 10 sensitive sites, including military and nuclear bases, but another 16 government buildings and royal palaces have been added. Section 132 of the same Act requires police permission to stage demonstrations within 1km of Parliament

For all but a truly minor crime, the officer is empowered, using force if 'necessary,' to take a sample of the suspect's DNA from his mouth, to photograph and fingerprint him and even to take impressions of his footwear. Under British law, a suspect should be presumed innocent, yet he can now be forced to submit to a humiliating process as though he were about to enter prison. These new powers are in effect criminalising the public: arresting someone, photographing and forcibly taking samples from them places an individual in an entirely different relationship with the state from the one most of us have known. One-third of the DNA samples – currently at around ten thousand a week – come from Afro-Caribbean males.[6] Innocent persons can be taken away for up to 28 days without even being charged, and usually held in stations such as Paddington Green in very poor conditions. Section 23 of the Terrorism Act 2006 introduced the absurdly broad offences of Encouragement of Terrorism and Preparation of Terrorist Acts.

Taking pictures, filming or even just drawing sketches of buildings can now be considered 'hostile reconnaissance,' and one may be stopped and searched, or even arrested. Henry Porter relates how,

> Many persons who were intimidated in such circumstances by the Police emailed me, including one person who was arrested for 'sketching pictures of the Southbank,' and another for taking a picture that includes a petrol station and in 2006-08 an Iraqi was charged for filming Big Ben, the Houses of Parliament and the London Eye, eventually found not guilty, to be put under a control order. Students have been arrested after taking snapshots of Tower Bridge. Even my innocent doodles were construed by the Police as being a tube station plan.[7]

Filming or taking photographs of London tube stations without obtaining a permit in advance has been considered illegal since July 2005! Yet, ironically, we are exhorted: 'Detectives have issued an urgent appeal for any photographs, video footage or mobile phone images.' Saying or wearing the wrong words, or even wearing the wrong T-shirt, may get you arrested. The Encouragement of Terrorism section of the *Terrorism Act* 2006 is so broad as to be an incursion on freedom of speech.

The SOCRAP Act set up the Serious Organised Crime Agency (SOCA). As well as making all offences—no matter how trivial—arrestable, it grants powers to obtain DNA, intimate samples, fingerprints and photographs of those arrested, to be retained on file regardless of whether the suspect is charged with or convicted of an offence. Protestors, even a single protestor, are obliged to apply at least 24 hours (and more normally 6 days) in advance for a permit to protest within 1km of Parliament.

ID and the Web of Surveillance

The European Union has now mandated biometric identifiers on passports, visas and residence permits.[8] Just in case you forget who you are, everyone over the age of 16 applying for a passport will have their details – including fingerprints, eye or facial scans – added to a National Identity register, from 2008.

Radio Frequency Identification (RFID) chips, which can be detected and read by radio, are used in new UK passports as well as in the Oyster card system to access the London Transport network. Over the past decade, European countries have been using these chips to identify pet animals. Its use in humans has already been trialled in America, where the chips have been implanted in mentally-ill elderly people in order to track their movements. "The call for everyone to be implanted is now being seriously debated."[9] If this happens, citizens may feel that they are being reduced to mere walking barcodes.

Traditionally, National Health Service database of patient files were strictly confidential, however IT firms may gain access to these. The Health Department's IT agency states, "Patients will have data uploaded ... Patients *do not have the right* to say the information cannot be held." Some MPs have expressed concern over the fingerprinting of children in schools as contravening the Data Protection Act. In February 2007, a poll showed that as many as 3,500 schools were routinely taking pupils' fingerprints, often without parents' permission. In the wake of July 7th, is the UK descending into a police state?

If photographing of landmarks can now be classified as 'terrorist reconnaisance', then merely having a map or taking a photo is liable to be interpreted as 'terrorist reconnaissance'. Who are here being designated as 'terrorists'? And yet, when in October 2006 an ex-BNP man was arrested and bomb-making equipment was found in his flat, he was only arrested under the Victorian 'Explosive Substances Act'. Despite a huge quantity of explosive being found, the police Superintendent was able to assure residents that "It is not a bomb-making factory", and he added that it was not related to terrorism. Are there not strong racial stereotypes here at work? [10] Is it not strange, that none of the recent anti-terror acts were here invoked, but merely the century-old Explosive Substances Act?

The substances found in the raid were the "largest amount of chemical explosives of its type ever found in the country."[10] Strong racial stereotypes may here be at work.

In July 2007 the Government proposed to extend detention without charge beyond the current 28-day limit. None of the UK's European counterparts, or the US, has seen the need for a 28-day detention period. Then in September 2007 the Government gave itself the power to snoop on all phone call records. Phone companies will be compelled to keep records for up to a year and make them available to hundreds of public bodies and quangos – allegedly necessary in the fight against terror. These files can reveal where people were when they made the mobile calls. A spokesman for Liberty said: 'Hundreds of bodies have been given the power to look at this highly sensitive information. It is yet another example of how greater and greater access is being given to information on our movements with little debate and little public accountability.'[11]

New crime laws are brought in after a 'consultation exercise' rather than a vote in Parliament, as if the Government were determined to criminalise as many people as possible. The 2005 *Prevention of Terrorism Act* enables the government to impose "control orders" on anyone they suspect might be involved in "terrorism-related" activity. The person subjected to a control order does not get a trial and is not even charged with anything, and may have the evidence or accusations against them withheld from them or their lawyers. Or, if there is a trial, the court is not permitted to judge or ascertain the validity of the 'terror' accusation. The situation is becoming increasingly similar to medieval times: when a priest would damn someone as the 'Spawn of Satan,' there was nothing much the accused could say by way of defending themselves! In our view, police should not be given open-ended legislation with key terms undefined. They should be there to maintain law and order and not to 'fight terrorism.'

The *Terrorism Act* of 2006 introduced the absurd offence of glorifying terrorism, and extended the period of detention without trial – measures as were never deemed necessary during the IRA campaign from 1969 to 1997. The Government's actions in the name of "security" do nothing to ease any personal sense of vulnerability, but act *always in the enhancement of fear.* Fear is the drug whereby otherwise quite insignificant persons can get the public to listen to them.

More and more British Muslims have come to experience such things as pre-dawn raids, broken down doors, barking dogs, verbal taunts, physical abuse and fathers dragged away before their children. Life-restricting control orders set curfews, house arrest, electronic tagging and severe restrictions on use of telephones. A 'terror suspect' can become a prisoner in their own home. Arrests are carried out on grounds such as tourist photography, the study of chemistry, frequent visits to the gym, and paintballing. It has now reached the stage where British Muslims have become confused over what recreational activities they can pursue without falling under the scrutiny of the security services, and many Muslims no longer engage in public demonstrations for this reason. Others are careful of their choice of reading material on public transport. They face an almost daily barrage of news items in the mass media denigrating Muslims, which undermines confidence in relating to the wider society.[12]

Quite a lot of working-class Muslim communities are aware of the fabricated nature of the 9/11 story, and have grave suspicions about 7/7, however their spokesmen still feel obliged to maintain the polite fictions of the host community in public. It must be destructive to the confidence and self-respect of young Muslims when they see their elders/role models kowtowing in this way to the UK's 'war on terror.' The extraditions treaty now in place means that, if Muslim 9/11 activists were to start to speak out strongly, the US could concoct any evidence and there would be no necessity for a *prima facie* case to be made out in UK courts; it would be more a question of establishing identity and then off they would be sent – very possibly to Guantanamo or another torture site.

An exodus of British Muslims seems to have begun, a consequence of their systematic persecution in the wake of September 11th. Home Office statistics show over a thousand UK arrests for 'terrorism' made since then – each of which represents a harrowing tale of pain, anger and humiliation. The mere fact of having been arrested undermines their reputations, livelihoods and freedom to travel. A mere 3% of these have been convicted – and these convictions can be for something as small as wearing a badge of some proscribed organisation. Police threats instil terror and pressure Muslims to root out alleged invisible 'extremists' from their midst. Politically active Muslims find themselves being compared to Neo-Nazis by senior UK politicians.

References

[1] 'Do you support ID cards', BBC.co.uk, 30.6.05, http://newsvote.bbc.co.uk/1/hi/talking_ point/4625971.stm?display=1.

[2] *Daily Mail* 'Britons 'could be microchipped like dogs in a decade'' 30.10.06.

[3] DNA storage: Wikipedia, http://en.wikipedia.org/wiki/UK_National_DNA_Database.

[4] Quotes from 'Who wants the Abolition of Parliament Bill?' David Howarth, *The Times* 21st February 2006 http://www.timesonline.co.uk/article/0,,1072-2049791,00.html.

[5] Henry Porter 'A law the Stasi would have loved' November 6, 2005 *The Observer* http://observer.guardian.co.uk/comment/story/0,6903,1635351,00.html.

[6] *Gulf Times*, 31 Oct 2006, 'Britons may be forced to wear Microchips.'

[7] David Mery, 'Is the UK a police state?' 18.11.07 http://gizmonaut.net/bits/police_state. html.

[8] www.policestateplanning.com/abolitionofparliamentbill.htm 'The Abolition of Parliament Bill' by Michael Nield, 8th April 2006.

[9] Big Brother Britain 2006 *The Independent on Sunday*, http://news.independent.co.uk/ uk/crime/article1948209.ece, http://www.jonesreport.com/articles/021106_big_bro_britain. html 2.11.06.

[10] 'Ex-BNP man faces explosives charge www'.Burnleycitizen.co.uk 4.10.06.

[11] See www.julyseventh.co.uk/july-7-article-capitalising-on-terror.html.

[12] Fahad Ansari, 'Absorption or Exodus, The future legacy of British Anti-terror laws'. *Socialist Lawyer* April 2007. www.islamicawakening.com/viewarticle.php?articleID= 1302.

The *Magna Carta* (1225), Excerpts

38) In future no official shall place a man on trial upon his own unsupported statement, without producing credible witnesses to the truth of it.

39) No free man shall be seized or imprisoned, or stripped of his rights or possessions, or outlawed or exiled, or deprived of his standing in any other way, nor will we proceed with force against him, or send others to do so, except by the lawful judgement of his equals or by the law of the land.

40) To no one will we sell, to no one deny or delay right or justice.

45) We will appoint as justices, constables, sheriffs, or other officials, only men that know the law of the realm and are minded to keep it well.

17. The 7/7 Kingston Trial

A Strange Beginning

What has come to be called 'the July 7th trial' began on Monday, 7th April, 2008, at the Kingston Crown Court. To help select a 12-member jury for the trial, Mr Justice Gross explained to 150 potential jurors that they would first need to complete a 16-point questionnaire. Then, matter-of-factly, he told them that:

> As you know, Mohammed Siddique Khan, Shehzad Tanweer, Jermaine Lindsay and Hasib Hussain were responsible for causing a series of explosions on the London Underground and public transport system on July 7, 2005, that killed 52 people and injured hundreds of others.[1]

No one in that trial or in the media seemed inclined to doubt so evident a proposition. One would like to see that questionnaire, which assisted the jury selection. Mr Gross then explained to them what the three young men in the dock had done wrong: 'It is alleged that Waheed Ali, Sadeer Saleem and Mohammed Shakil assisted these men by, in particular, conducting reconnaissance of possible targets in December, 2004.' The twelve were selected, and the prosecution's case began the next day.

Curiously, a major international security conference also began on 7th April: *From 9/11 to 7/7: Global Terrorism Today and the Challenges of Tomorrow* in Chatham House, London. A brochure explained how,

> 'The FBI has a Legal Attaché office here in London. Our staff works every day with officials in the security services, with New Scotland Yard, and with Britain's other constabularies. FBI personnel have 20 to 30 in-person meetings every week with British intelligence and law enforcement officials. We share intelligence. We support one another's investigations.'

The FBI Director Robert Mueller was there to explain this.

Robert Mueller had been appointed to his role of head of the FBI a mere two weeks prior to 9/11. His FBI produced the list of 19 hijackers a mere 48 hours after the event, just as Colin Powell informed the American people that Osama Bin Laden was prime suspect for the event a mere two days after it. Some months later in his speech to the Commonwealth Club in San Francisco on 19 April, 2002, Mueller declared: 'In our investigation we have not uncovered a single piece of paper – either here in the United States or in the treasure trove of information that has turned up in Afghanistan and elsewhere – that mentioned any suspect of the September 11 plot.' Did that admitted complete absence of relevant evidence induce any tremor of doubt over the guilt of the swiftly-designated 19 Islamic hijackers? It did not. Could there be an analogy with the trial now commencing here in the UK?

A few days earlier, on the 3rd of April, another huge 'terror' trial opened at Woolwich Crown Court, which was the same location used for the July 21st trial a year earlier: the Heathrow liquid-bomb 'terror plot.' It shared with the July 7 trial a numinous quality in that it was hard to see how the accused had actually done anything. The case concerned what eight men might have been intending to do. Were they planning to board various trans-Atlantic aeroplanes and blow them up? Had any of them made a bomb? It ran in tandem with the July 7th trial, so the distinguished Chatham House guests could be reassured that the 'War on Terror' was being earnestly prosecuted.

To *Cause* Explosions

The first person to be arrested, in the context of the London bombings of July 7th, had been the Egyptian chemist Magdy Al-Nashar, who was released with no charges. His laptop had been confiscated and found to be full of – music. Could the British police be more successful the next time, in arresting and charging someone with regard to the dreadful crime of bombing London? In the spring of 2008, three young men were arrested who had been friends of the four alleged bombers. They were charged under a Victorian law, the *Explosive Substances Act* of 1883.

They had *conspired* to cause explosions, it was alleged: they were charged with having 'unlawfully and maliciously conspired' with the London bombers and others 'to cause explosions on the Transport for London system and/or tourist attractions in London,' between November 1, 2004, and June 29, 2005. That is indeed a vague charge: to have conspired with persons unnamed, and to cause them moreover at unspecified locations – 'tourist attractions' where it is not even clear that a bomb had gone off. No knowledge of chemistry was discerned amongst them in this trial, and the case against them hinged around an enjoyable weekend trip they made to London on December 16th-17th of December, 2004, together with the 18-year old Hasib Hussain. On that outing, did they even descend into an Underground station?

They had visited the London Eye, the Natural History Museum, the London Aquarium, and Waheed Ali's sister. My impression, as an intermittent visitor to the trial, was that there was no coherent case against these three, and that their testimonies rather tended to exonerate the four alleged bombers. The prosecution barrister Flewitt averred that the locations the group visited "bore a striking similarity" to the targets three of the bombers later identified during a 'hostile reconnaissance' two weeks before the bombings (June 28th). Comparing the Underground stations involved, the London Eye is reached via Waterloo on the Northern, Bakerloo or Waterloo & City lines, the London Aquarium the same, while the Natural History Museum is reached via South Kensington on the Circle, Central & Piccadilly lines. It is hard to see very much resemblance to the bombed Edgware Rd, Aldgate, and King's Cross/Russell Square stations. As one J7 commentator ('Numeral') drily remarked, 'The striking similarity of the 7/7 locations, the 16/17 Dec 2004 locations and the 28/6/05 locations is not yet apparent.'

In the evening of their London visit, they met Jamal Lindsay, who had driven down from Aylesbury. They then spent several hours (Ali told the Court) driving round trying to find a restaurant that did not serve alcohol, as was required for their Muslim ethics, but without much success.

The Court was given detailed accounts of exactly where the mobile phone calls were made between the friends, as they moved around. But, what did this amount to? 'We never intended to do no reconnaissance, we just had a day out' Waheed Ali explained to the Court. Such discussions of a visit to London may seem bafflingly unconnected to the Explosive Substances Act. The Prosecution Neil Flewitt conceded that the three on trial 'were not directly involved in the London bombings in the sense that they were responsible for making or transporting the bombs that were detonated with such devastating consequences (10th April).' So, although not 'directly involved' or 'responsible' for the blasts, yet they are charged with 'conspiring' to 'cause' them. Could anyone ever prove so tenuous a linkage?

When the Defence attorney for Waheed Ali began his case on 20th May, he observed that an 'outstandingly weak prosecution' had been presented, that was trying to spin out an 'invisible, nonexistent connection' with the terrible events of July 7th. On behalf of Mr Saleem, one of the three accused, Andrew Hall QC assured the jury that there was 'not a scrap of evidence that any of the defendants took one step on to the Underground' during their visit to London on that weekend. They did not visit the Tube!

The trial causes one to realise the sheer extent to which the anti-terror laws passed in the last decade have eroded that central axiom of British justice: that citizens are presumed innocent until *proved guilty*. The Prosecution's case wove tenuous webs of circumstantial evidence around the three young men, for example, that they had visited 18, Alexandra Grove in Leeds. The young men on trial had been advised not to contest the presumed guilt of the four alleged bombers, as being their best strategy if they wished to avoid hefty sentences, and neither side in the court questioned that presumption of guilt.

A Friend of the Four

Waheed Ali was in the unenviable position of having known all of the Four, quite well. His Bangladeshi parents had died when he was very young, and he had been looked after by his best friend, Shehzad Tanweer, whom he called Kaki. If some fiendish plot had been brewing up, would he not have heard about it? This seemed to be the brunt of the case against him. The most he was able to advise the Court in this respect, concerned a certain distance which Khan and Tanweer had maintained from him, upon his return from the Pakistani 'Jihad' training camp in early 2005. Earlier in December 2003 he had written a touching poem about Khan that was read out in Court:

> The Gates of Memory I will never close / How much you mean to me no one knows.

> Tears in my eyes will wipe away / But the love in my heart for you will always stay.

Later on, he was understandably distressed to realise that he was no longer part of Khan's in-crowd. But, that was all. He averred that Khan had approved of the event of 9/11, whereas he, Ali, had not. One may query this memory of Ali's, as Khan had 'spoken out against the 9/11 attacks' at his school according to the Official Report (p14). When the Prosecution asked Ali as to whether Khan had advocated any such attacks upon UK cities, he emphatically exclaimed 'No, never!' Such a defence of Khan would hardly have helped his case. Asked about 9/11, Ali replied that it was forbidden by Islam to take innocent life, or to commit suicide.

From a bugged car in 2007 on 27th February, tapes played in Court recorded Waheed Ali's laughter and sense of fun while recalling the weekend trip to London with his pals, and how 'boring' the Aquarium had been. He just didn't like fish, and preferred the Natural History Museum. One would be hard pressed to discern a sinister meaning behind his words. Waheed was careful to confess everything of possible relevance to the Court, including his descent into a cocaine habit and petty financial fraud, after 7/7:

earlier on, when first arrested, he had striven to conceal the extent of his friendship with the Four, and had made untruthful allegations in this regard. That initial concealing of his close connection with the Four, which had got him into trouble, may have been an understandable strategy of a young man concerned to stay out of jail.

In March of 2005 Ali saw Jamal (Lindsay) a bit, but 'never heard no conspiracy.' Germaine Lindsay's brother taught Arabic in the Iqra bookshop and his sister lived in the Leeds/Beeston area. Tanweer had looked after Ali very well and cared for him, and during the last cricket match they enjoyed together on Cross Flatts Park in Beeston on July 6th 2005, Ali was reassured to find Tanweer more like his old self again. 'I can never justify what he did – I'm not going to try to justify what he did, but I've got my story about Kaki,' adding 'There are two different stories.' However often he went over the events in his memory, Waheed found (I suggest) that the two different stories just would not merge together.

The Court heard that Mohammed Shakil 'had been friends with Mohammed Siddique Khan through his twenties when the pair had drunk alcohol and smoked cannabis together'. Shakil explained that he 'could not think in his wildest dreams' why his friend had gone on to become a suicide bomber. Khan had expressed resentment about the situation in Pakistan and Iraq, but not in any extreme manner, he added (8 May).

Another young man from Beeston, Khalid Khaliq, had come forward voluntarily to assist with the 7/7 investigation in July 2005, and it was probably this act of social responsibility which led to his property being searched. He was then arrested in May 2007 together with Hasina Patel and her brother Arshad, and jailed in March 2008 for possession of a CD that had been *delivered* to his flat. It comprised a web-download coming from an American CIA site about how to be an Al-Qaeda terrorist, but he had *not played* it. That sufficed to jail a young Muslim. He was subsequently let out on bail, but this case shows how arrest can be made upon the mere surmising of an intention. The three lads did take a two-day trip to London, in the company of 17-year old Hasib Hussain: but was that adequate grounds for a 4-month trial with ten barristers costing the taxpayer not much less than £50 million?

Or, was that really the point of the trial? Its purpose appeared enigmatic, as if things were not what they seemed. It was the occasion for a considerable release of 'evidence' that would tend to incriminate the Four – CCTV film releases, video footage releases, details of visits to Pakistan released, the diary of Hasina Patel released, etc. No one in the Court wished to dispute the guilt, so no critical examination of this 'evidence' took place, perhaps conveniently. As the defence attorney remarked in his opening speech (20th May), all of the CCTV released, which had been saved up – we are asked to believe – these three years, was irrelevant to the case.

Over quite a few days, I was the only member of the public in the public gallery; some other bereaved families were also there. I received a rebuke by a yellow-clad security guard upon trying to converse with one such family, while sitting outside the courtroom. Kingston seemed quite a distance from anyone likely to be interested. Was that part of the purpose of having it there? The idea of a trial is that evidence be given in public, i.e. witnessed. Who can witness a four-month process? For a visitor to the Court requiring some background information, the only way to check up on what had happened was via cursory newspaper reports: no transcripts were available, and after the trial these can only be acquired at considerable expense.

The Explosive Truth

Waheed Ali seems not to have been questioned over what happened at 18, Alexandra Grove, the alleged bomb-making factory. He did go there, as his mobile phone records testify, and (the Court was informed) some DNA of his was found there. The photographs released in the *Sun* of that flat looked as if squatters had made quite a mess there. The pictures showed plastic containers and filters, looking as if drugs had been prepared there.[2] We would have liked to have heard his view as to whether hydrogen peroxide had been left in that flat, if indeed he knew what that was? Instead we were treated at length to accounts of his faraway excursions on the Kashmir border.

If the charge against the three was that they had conspired to cause explosions, why did we never hear of any interest in chemistry amongst them, i.e. how to make things go bang? At no point were they photographed near any bomb equipment, nor were phone conversations overheard concerning how to make such. One could say the same concerning the Four, that no one ever discerned the remotest interest in chemistry amongst them. One would here like the view of Magdy al-Nashar, the Leeds University biochemistry postgraduate. After all, his flat at 18, Alexandra Grove, rented from a housing co-op, was described from the Official Account onwards as the bomb-making factory

Over the years 2005-2007, the world heard how the explosive used was TATP, allegedly found *left in the bath*. This was complicated to synthesise, and volatile, so if it had been left out anywhere for a week until the police arrival on 13th July, it would all have evaporated. The extraordinary way in which TATP detonated without heat or light had been the subject of a 2005 chemistry journal article; maybe by 2008 the gee-whiz value of this had faded away. Any TATP in the bath had quite vanished by the time *The Sun* published images of that bath on 3rd of May. Not to keep the reader in suspense, what the photos revealed was … black pepper.

Yes, black pepper. Before wasting fifty million pounds of taxpayer's money on *another* mega bogus terror trial, the Prosecution ought surely to be obliged to show that it can get a bang out of the unlikely chemicals it is alleging were used. Perhaps it should start off with 12% peroxide hair bleach, because no one attempted to show that wholesale purchase of pure hydrogen peroxide took place. Ordinary members of the public cannot purchase 70% peroxide. No one has attempted to explain how the Four would have concentrated their peroxide (e.g. by fractionally distilling it). As we learned in an earlier chapter, to produce peroxide of that strength involves advanced chemical techniques. But supposing it had been available, would it go bang with black pepper? If we are here talking about a power which ripped apart three Underground coaches like tins of sardines – a result was so awful that it could not be shown to any member of the public or journalist – then one can only say, this has to be a joke.

The jury, who were shown pictures from inside the flat, heard that containers of a mixture of black pepper and hydrogen peroxide, used as the main charge, were found sitting in the bath. Empty bags of ground black pepper were found along with ice-cube bags and ice packs in the kitchen, which the court was told were used to keep the devices cool. How did they keep a straight face? Plastic trays containing bicarbonate of soda and citric acid were also discovered (3 May, The Sun). Clifford Todd, a senior forensic investigator at Fort Halstead forensic explosives laboratory, said the devices were "unique in the UK and possibly the whole world" and it was unlikely the bombers worked alone.[3]

Ahmed's opus, *The London bombings,* discusses the incoherence of narrative as the story unfolded some days after July 7th. The powerful military-grade explosive which competent experts had first ascertained, later metamorphosed into TATP, allegedly found both in a car left in Luton car-park and in a bath in Leeds, with no explanation as to how these different judgements could be compatible. But there is a far greater incoherence in the fading away of the TATP and its replacement at the Kingston trial by black pepper. The former will at least explode.The latter has an attractive simplicity, instead of the complicated acetone, sulphuric acid, a cooling-chamber and fume-extractor required for making TATP. Attempts were even made to draw an analogy between the Chappati flour-bombs of the 21/7 episode—where the perpetrators were given forty-year sentences—and the alleged pepper bombs of 7/7. In both cases it was alleged that the 'knowledge' of how to make them had been garnered somewhere out in Pakistan.

The two big concurrent 'terror' trials of 2008—the Heathrow liquid-bomb trial and the Kingston July 7th trial—were making no allusion whatever to 'TATP,' which had featured heavily in their stories of earlier years. A comparison thus becomes of some interest here. Instead, hydrogen peroxide was invoked only in a very general way: quoting from the opening day of the former trial (3rd April, 2008):

> A sugary drink powder, Tang, would be mixed with hydrogen peroxide, used as a hair bleach, and other organic materials. Hydrogen peroxide and the other ingredients can become explosive if mixed to a specific strength.

Ah, so that was what they might have been intending to do! And put it into a lucozade bottle.[3] We observe how this report glided effortlessly from hair bleach, with a maximum 12% concentration of peroxide, to the *pure* 70% peroxide that can explode. Evaporating such hair bleach in a saucepan is not likely to concentrate the hydrogen peroxide (the reverse, its decomposition, is far more likely), yet the case continued to rest on the implication that some such method would have been used.

Reporting from the Court on 14th April, *The Express* related how the explosives used in the London bombings had been contained within large rucksacks, kept cool with ice-packs. What would the point of that have been? Nothing much will happen to peroxide and black pepper if its temperature rises a degree or two; does this not more resemble a story left over from last year's version, when TATP was in vogue? Then, a difference of a few degrees could well have affected its stability. Besides, how would the Court have come by such knowledge, from the remains of the explosion, viz. that there had been ice in the rucksacks?

Jihad Training Camps

Ali had traveled with Khan on a "gallivant" in the summer of 2001—shortly before his wedding and before the September 11 attacks, and after attending a camp on the Kashmir border where they learned to shoot Kalashnikovs, the Court heard. They hoped to go to the frontline near Bagram airbase where the Taliban were fighting the Northern Alliance, but were deemed too inexperienced to fight and stayed at a camp about a mile behind the frontline, where they became so ill with diarrhoea that they were put on drips for three or four days.

The Court was treated to an inventory of the 24-year old Waheed Ali's computer memory, full of dire scenes of Islamic nations being attacked by the West, and attempts—real or imagined—to resist and oppose this onslaught; plus photographs of the destroyed World Trade Center and the damaged Pentagon. It was surely disturbing to view such images, but was it evidence of a terrorist intent, as the prosecution alleged? Outside the courtroom I happened to meet Gareth Peirce, the renowned civil rights lawyer, who was part of the team acting on behalf of Ali. I communicated to her my suspicion that he was innocent. "Oh he is," she replied, suddenly looking me straight in the eye; "he's totally innocent." I was startled by such an emphatic answer from someone who, in my opinion, ought to know.

Waheed Ali affirmed to the Court that the practice of Jihad and terrorism were a world apart. The former was within Islamic ethics because its goal was to liberate an Islamic nation from foreign oppression, while terror against civilians is not permitted in Islam. The training camps were in Pakistan, and the goal seemed to be independence for Kashmir. [NB, I personally condemn any such resort to violence.] The ideology was shared by communities within his district of Leeds/Beeston, he explained, who collected and sent funding out to support such camps. He described how 'absolutely beautiful' were the mountains, and how they visited 'Sid's uncle' on their way out from Islamabad to the training camps. Ali went out jogging every morning, and then trained to use a Kalashnikov gun (in early 2005) where they would shoot at a tree. That visit was quite an anticlimax compared to his earlier visit in 2001 with Khan, where they had managed to get into Afghanistan – a few months before 9/11!

This story was reported in the London *Metro* of May 21st as 'At a training camp [in Pakistan], they were shown how to handle weapons such as rocket-propelled grenades.' Not having heard any such words uttered in the Court, I showed this *Metro* report the next morning to one of the barristers and he agreed with me, that no such words about 'rocket-propelled grenades' had been uttered in the courtroom. Training in how to use rocket-propelled grenades would have a clear relevance for the charge under which Ali was being tried, of conspiring to cause an explosion. In fact, Ali's court testimony on that day had described the tedium of just reloading the Kalashnikovs and shooting at a tree. Who would have wanted to put that misleading report into *The Metro*? Not many people can attend sufficient of the Court proceedings to form their own judgement, and no summary or transcript is readily available.

Ali's fairly honest (IMO) accounts were supplemented by the US 'supergrass' Junaid Babar, whose testimony was beamed over from his New York jail. Babar was quite explicitly hoping to get his jail sentence reduced by saying the right things when required, so one is perplexed that his testimony should be viewed as usable. Here is an extract from the dialogue:

'But he said he had struck a deal with the FBI including immunity from further prosecution. His wife and young child had also been brought from Pakistan to the US.

"How many years do you hope you might serve before being released?" asked Mr Bennathan.

"Well that's up to the Justice Department when they feel the co-operation is over and I go for sentencing," said Babar.

"It's possible you could be at liberty in a year or two for full co-operation," said Mr Bennathan. "That you will serve five years – rather than 70."

"Yes," replied Babar. "I hope, yes."'

See also the *Wikipedia* section on him for this 'supergrass' status. Babar had been used to incriminate the British 'Crevice' suspects in an earlier trial, and now he was being re-used to put Khan in an Al-Qaeda terror training camp.

In July 2003, Babar told the Court, a Mr 'Ibrahim' had come over to an 'Al-Qaeda' jihad training camp he was running. The Prosecution categorically assured the Court that Babar was here alluding to Khan, but I did not hear him being consulted on this issue. The reason for his visit involved 'small arms training' in order that he might fight in Afghanistan. Prior to 9/11 he had attended a training camp in Kashmir. Ibrahim asked Babar how much it would cost were his family to come over. I was not very convinced that this was Khan, and tend rather to believe what his relatives told me: that Khan's earlier visits were to his family, and only the November 2004 visit involved a military camp. As his widow commented on the Julie Etchingham interview:

> JULIE ETCHINGHAM: And you had no idea why he would be travelling to Pakistan or with whom he was travelling?
>
> HASINA PATEL: He has family in Pakistan and for people who come from those countries it is normal to travel back, you have family there, you have property, land, there are plenty of reasons you could be going there.

Would he, just after being married and while having babies and working as a school mentor, be going off to fight in Afghanistan, unknown to any of his friends in England? Was the best-known figure in Beeston secretly asking about moving his family over to live in some Pakistani mountain village? We seek for a real biography, but I suggest that the Prosecution's case is here becoming incoherent.

The Khan Home Videos

In September or October 2004, Mohammed Siddique Khan made several home videos.[4] One with his 18-month old daughter, with a mirror behind her so you could see him, reflected, taking the film; and the other of his three pals Tanweer, Hasib Hussain and Waheed Ali. He was then working as a teaching mentor at Hillside primary school. After making the video, he moved hehouse with his family. About six weeks after, he then set out on a prolonged visit to Pakistan with Tanweer. The home video as played before the Court has Khan's voice telling the baby how he is leaving forever (and, yes, he is the family breadwinner) and tough luck on his pregnant wife – for the glory of Allah, and how desperately he will miss the child and family. He won't be coming back! About six weeks later, on 18 November, he flew out to Pakistan with his pal Tanweer for nearly three months, leaving these home videos in a drawer.

The brother of Hasina Patel was Arshad, and got to hear about these videos after he and Hasina were both arrested and thrown into Paddington Green prison, solitary confinement, in May 2007. He was refusing to answer questions, as his lawyer had advised him, and then they showed him the home video. It was a shock to him because his sister had never mentioned anything to him about it. However it was clear to him that the videos had been made while the Khan-Patel family were staying in his home at Thornhill Park Avenue. They only resided there for a few weeks, before moving to a flat in Lees Holm, also in Dewsbury. From that we may with confidence date the home videos as September-October.

The existence of these home videos was first revealed on Wednesday, 9th April, at Kingston Crown Court. The prosecuting QC Neil Flewitt alleged that these tapes were handed over by Hasina to her friend Faiza Rehman, who then gave them to the police after 7/7. Arshad surmised that the police had found them when they searched the house where Hasina and her mother Farida were living, in July, 2005. In the only interview she has ever given, Hasina denied that she had ever witnessed anything that might have led her to suspect that her husband was embarking upon some program of becoming a terrorist. In one recording, Khan's wife Hasina is heard saying that the tape has almost come to an end, warning: "There are two minutes left so say your piece."

'Mariam, keep strong your Imam. Learn to fight, fighting is good.' To his one-year-old daughter? The Court was shown two parts of a home video that Khan made, dated as 26 October and 16 November 2004, before he left for Pakistan on the 18th. If these startling words were really in the video, implying a dire future, would the video really be left in a drawer, and would his wife carry on as if she had no inkling of what was to come? She has testified that she did have no such inkling, on the Sky interview with Julie Etchingham. She was innocent and there were no charges against her, the Court agreed. When she had been arrested in May 2005, no evidence had been found to implicate her over foreknowledge of a plot. As recordings can so easily be falsified, one asks if an alleged recording even be admissible in court.

Was Khan leaving forever? His actual reason for resigning from his teching job and leaving his family for a month or even more, was only disclosed at the 2011 Inquest, as follows:

> Q. Then, eventually, how did he come to leave? [his learning-mentor job at Hillside]
> A. The headmistress basically had a letter from Mr Khan stating that, due to the fact that his father was ill, he needed to return to Pakistan, he was going to go with him and, therefore, he resigned from the employment, and the deputy head confirmed this and also, later on, from one of Mr Khan's computers, there was, in fact, on the computer, a copy of a letter which was probably the same letter that was spoken about, a resignation letter. (Feb 14 am, 64-65)

It was a case of family duties and his responsibility.

Hasina's diary

Khan left the UK for over two months to visit Pakistan on 18th November, while Ali left on December 26th – hoping to meet up with them out there, but being rather disappointed. Hasina's diaries were shown to the Court, showing a record of MSK's phoning her *eight times in 10 days*, starting on the day he flew out to Pakistan. That might not sound as if he'd made a gut-wrenching decision to abandon her and Britain forever to go and fight in Afghanistan (and remember that was J. Babar's testimony given a few days earlier, that he met MSK—Aka 'Ibrahim'—in Pakistan and he had wanted to go fight in Afghanistan).

> 18 Nov Siddique leaves
> 19 Nov Siddique rang
> 20 Nov Siddique phoned
> 21 Nov Siddique rang
> 24 Nov S rang
> 25 Nov S rang. Good news.
> 26 Nov S rang. Good news. Back by Feb?
> 29 Nov Siddique rang

Let's try to summarise the plot, as the Prosecution formulated it: Khan made a farewell video, indicating that he was not intending to return, but would sacrifice his life for a holy 'Jihad' cause; he handed it over to his pregnant wife for safekeeping, then went off to Pakistan with Tanweer. He had made previous visits to fight in Afghanistan, although this seemed to be unknown to his friends. A couple of weeks later, he changed his mind and informed his wife about his coming return. While he was over there, the 'plot' to bomb London was initiated, with Hasib and Jamal making a reconnaissance mission to London. Khan returned, having learnt about bomb-making, and sets about constructing the devices. Khan's wife Hasina at no stage comprehends that unlawful matters are afoot and the police accept her claims of being wholly innocent.

This is a story that unravels rather quickly, the initial problem being that the five lads visiting London do not ever set foot inside a tube station. No one has questioned the integrity of Hasina Patel: how can she own such shocking tapes, that negate our notions of morality and advocate 'Jihad' or holy war, and then claim that she never suspected anything was amiss?

The Shadowing

UK 'Terror' trials, lasting months, have proceeded over 2006-2008, with Muslims convicted for doing rather little. Generally speaking, we find that those charged have been shadowed by the police for some while, maybe at least a year, before. There was the Old Bailey 'Crevice' trial so-called (March 2006-April 2007), where five men were given life imprisonment because they may have been intending to do something with a sack of fertiliser. Then the July 21 trial at Woolwich (January-July 2007) saw three men each given 40 years, when the sole injury they caused was an asthma attack suffered by a bystander. The Heathrow 'lucozade' or 'liquid bomb' trial started in April 2008 at Woolwich Crown Court, where eight men were charged with possibly intending to buy air tickets and blow themselves and other passengers apart with a 'binary munition' that would be synthesised in the toilet. Then the July 7 trial at Kingston Crown Court had three men charged with 'conspiring' to cause explosions, in consequence of a weekend trip to London. Really, one has to laugh. These are all phoney trials where no real guilt is ever demonstrated and instead mere tenuous webs of circumstantial evidence are woven. A little less than £200 million of taxpayer's money is spent. Muslims go to jail – of course. Three of these trials share bogus peroxide chemistry in common; it's worth comparing these.

The Court saw film of Khan, Tanweer and Waheed Ali in February, 2004, under surveillance (i.e. not just a CCTV camera image) outside a McDonald's in Crawley. They are meeting up with 'Ausman' or Omar Khayam (of Operation Crevice fame). That is more than a year before the event. This theme is no doubt of importance, and deserving of greater elucidation than can be given here, being compatible with Nafeez Ahmed's accounts of how the perceived 'Al-Qaeda' threat is sustained by British/American intelligence. The one of the Luton Four who did not have any prior police record of being 'shadowed' by intelligence was Hasib Hussain. All of the July 21 group arrested, apart from Asiedu, were under surveillance from about May, 2004.

Chemical Proof

If the Four perpetrated the terrible act, *the London bombings*, then what did they do it with? After the Kingston trial, we are in a position to comment upon the alleged murder weapon. The story we have been told, is that the Four brought their bombs to London, while traces of the explosive used were also left behind at Luton station car-park and in a flat at Beeston. We now go through the steps of the Government's evolving story, concerning what went bang that morning.

Phase 1: High Explosive

Two days after the event, on 9th July, the police announced that 'High explosives were used in the attacks and were not home-made.' Likewise, on 11th July: "All we are saying is that it is high explosives," Scotland Yard Deputy Assistant Commissioner Brian Paddick told a news conference on Saturday, "That would tend to suggest that it is not home-made explosive." Advanced bombs were so powerful that none of the dead have been identified', *World Tribune*.[5] (See Appendices 8 & 9)

Advanced and powerful bombs had been used that were not home-made, that was the immediate conclusion, and this early stage was linked to a remote-detonation scenario. They were judged to be 'C4' explosive, and that announcement is about as definite as the subject ever becomes:

> 'London explosives have military origin' – *Science Daily*. LONDON, July 13 (UPI) – Scotland Yard has asked for European cooperation in finding how last week's London subway and bus bombers obtained military plastic explosives.

> Traces of the explosive known as C4 were found at all four blast sites, and The Times of London said Scotland Yard considers it vital to determine if they were part of a terrorist stockpile. C4 is manufactured mostly in the United States, and is more deadly and efficient than commercial varieties. It is easy to hide, stable, and is often missed by traditional bomb-sniffing detection systems, the newspaper

said. Forensic scientists told the newspaper the construction of the four devices detonated in London was very technically advanced, and unlike any instructions that can be found on the Internet.

Phase II: Brewed in the Bath

On July 17th, 2005, *The Observer* reported that 22 lbs of tri-acetone tri-peroxide had been found in the bath of 18, Alexandra Grove, Leeds. A huge amount of hydrogen peroxide would have been required to make this, quite apart from the strong sulphuric acid etc. – and that was just the material left behind. How did they obtain the 70% concentration required? Jane's Terrorism & Insurgency Centre' on 22nd July averred that 'preliminary forensic testing' both at the London bomb sites and at the Leeds property' was pointing to TATP. This was, it explained, 'a powerful homemade explosive.'

Photographs of the material present in the Luton car-park appeared on 26th of July, 2005, kindly given by ABC News in America. It showed white explosive material and by this time TATP (tri-acetone tri-peroxide) was being hyped as the explosive. The TATP story did have the disadvantage that its detonation does not produce heat or light, whereas these were clearly evident to survivor-witnesses of this event.

Phase III: Black Pepper

Photographs of the material present in the bath at Alexandra Grove were shown in *The Sun,* 14 April, 2008, and revealed nothing very much: dirty water in a bath, plastic bags that could have contained anything. At Kingston, 'The jury, who were shown pictures from inside the flat, heard that containers of a mixture of black pepper and hydrogen peroxide, used as the main charge, were found sitting in the bath.... Empty bags of ground black pepper were found along with ice-cube bags and ice packs in the kitchen.'

Black pepper and peroxide, mixed together, will not really explode. The mixture would do much the same as the Chapati-flour bombs of the 21/7 crew (i.e. just go 'phut'). That decisive twist of the story at the Kingston trial argues for the innocence of the four suspects. TATP was no longer on the agenda. At no stage of this £70m enquiry 'Operation Theseus' were the public shown any authenticated forensic reports of chemical analysis, nor of explosive material left at these sites. That suggests a fictional story is here unfolding. *Something* did indeed rip apart three tube coaches, so terribly that no one was allowed to view the ruins and they had to be destroyed in secret one year after the event.

Conclusion

Now that this Kingston trial is over, the story can hardly develop any further. Of central importance has been the *incoherence* of accounts of the murder-weapon. This strongly implies that the conjecture of Islamic guilt has now to be abandoned. The incoherence is evident both in the way the alleged explosive kept changing, and in the way the several different locations had different stories attached to them. The four young men never had the faintest interest in chemistry, as far as anyone knew; neither did the three on trial at Kingston. The person to ask about all this would be Magdy El-Nashar, the Leeds Biochemistry graduate who was renting the Alexandra Grove flat; his disappearance is symptomatic of this case.

The French anti-terror chief Christophe Chaboud informed *The Times* that 'traces of military plastic explosive, more deadly and efficient than commercial varieties, are understood to have been found in the debris of the wrecked underground carriages and the bus' (*Times,* July 13th) and that seems the most credible account that anyone is likely to give us. How did the story get from there to black pepper in a bath? The most recent storytellers seem not to carry a memory of this earlier phase.

For a charge of murder to stick, there has to be a weapon. If the prosecution keeps changing its mind over what the weapon is supposed to have been, and if its story becomes more unlikely every time, we are then entitled to conclude that the case is unsound – or even worse: that it has somehow been fabricated.

The four-month trial collapsed with a hung jury unconvinced of any intent to cause explosion – then a copycat retrial began the next year! In the meantime, the BBC had to shelve its 'Conspiracy Files' 7/7 program on the grounds that it would prejudice the retrial. British law used to have a principle called 'double jeopardy,' which meant that one could not be tried twice for the same crime. That has been eroded, but even so a retrial is only supposed to be permitted if new evidence has come to light; was there any in this case? The concurrent Heathrow liquid bomb case at Woolwich likewise collapsed soon after, with a jury unconvinced of any airline-sabotage plot, and an announcement of a forthcoming retrial. Both trials started up again in the new year! On 28th April, 2009, the new jury delivered a unanimous verdict of not guilty: six months, and over a hundred thousand pounds of taxpayers' money, for three young men to be acquitted. But, two of them were still given seven years for 'plotting to attend a terrorist training camp.' It was clear, the judge said, that they were intending to do this. For example, they had purchased some camping equipment. This verdict was regarded as being the closure and termination of Operation Theseus.

CCTV release, at Kingston Trial

A reference to unshown CCTV footage from the July 7th bombings was made in October of that year, at a seminar at Preston, Lancashire, when an unnamed 'representative of the Metropolitan Police anti- terrorist branch' was reported in *Police Review* as saying:

> 'I've seen the CCTV footage of these people. They do not appear to be on their way to commit any crime at all. The Russell Square bomber [Hasib Hussain] is actually seen going into shops and bumping into people.' *The Independent,* 31st October, 2005.[6]

He had also seen Tanweer arguing with a cashier 'that he had been short-changed, after stopping at a petrol station on his way to Luton' (presumably, in the early hours of July 7th).

At the 2008 Kingston Trial, quite a lot of CCTV film was shown and released, meant to show the Four on the day of July 7th, in a manner that closely followed the Official Account. More of the June 28 CCTV has also been released, and one could hardly have a greater contrast between the two sets of data: that of 28 June is clear, crisp, properly illuminated, and sequential at one-second intervals, and always has a proper time and date stamp; whereas the alleged July 7th footage released is often dim or unrecognisable. It jumps in its sequence, typically between minute and second intervals, and mostly lacks any time and date stamp at all.

The release of these images appears as a notable feature of the Kingston Trial, possibly even its primary purpose; however it was strangely unconnected with the rest of the trial. A warning accompanied their release:

> On behalf of the prosecuting Counsel, the media is urged to ensure material released is strictly framed within the terms and context used in court when they were shown. Failure to do so could result in a breach of the Contempt of Court Act.

Not one bit short of sheer totalitarianism in the courts and media: the interpretation and context given by the Court had to be followed strictly!

Let's look at some of these icons of the 'war on terror' religion.

Tanweer at the Petrol Station

We see Tanweer filling up with petrol and a hint of Khan being in the front seat of a hired, blue Nissan Micra. Tanweer had hired this car around July 1st, and the two of them were much seen driving around in it. This image-sequence could have come from any time during that week, as there are no time or date stamps on this sequence. He is wearing a matching, all-white top and bottom, looking rather bright and cheerful for a mass-murder suicide mission.[7]

The Official Account says here: 'He buys snacks, quibbles with the cashier over his change, looks directly at the CCTV camera and leaves.' Some or maybe all of that video has now been released, at the 7/7 trial and at the Inquest.

That little car, we are asked to believe, carried three large men with large rucksacks, packed with kilos of unstable, liable-to-detonate explosive. As well as that, it was also supposed to have contained two 'primed bombs,' 14 'bomb components' and some vital 'cooling boxes' to stop the bombs from blowing up prematurely! Let's quote *The Guardian* on this matter:

A rucksack packed with two primed bombs was found under the front seat of a car used by the July 7 bombers shortly before they went to London on the day of the attacks, the officer in charge of the terrorist investigation revealed yesterday.

The bombs were made up of explosives surrounded by nails and stuffed into bottles. Mr Clarke said a bag containing "two viable devices" was found under the front passenger seat of the Nissan Micra left by the bombers at Luton station on July 7.

As well as the rucksack, 14 other bomb components were discovered in the car. Cool boxes, used to transport the highly volatile peroxide-based explosives, which detectives believe were mixed in a bath in a flat in Leeds, were also found in the boot.[8]

In addition, Tanweer carried a spare pair of trousers so he could change halfway down the M1? By the time he arrived at Luton station, he was wearing a tawdry, dark-coloured tracksuit bottom. See the image of Tanweer in Chapter 10, dressed in white, compared with the figure of him here. Some have found this all rather hard to believe.

Catching the train at Luton

We are at last shown a sequence of CCTV images of the Four arriving in Luton car-park and walking across to the station entrance, then going in and descending to the platform (although we don't see the CCTV sequence from which the single solo shot of Hasib Hussain released on July 14th, 2005, was supposedly taken). The sequence implies that their tickets had been purchased in advance, because at 07.20 they are in the car-park, at 07.21 they enter the ground-floor doorway; and by 07.22 they are swiftly passing through the ticket-barriers to descend onto the platform. That last timestamp is just barely discernable, partly concealed on one image. They would have arrived on the platform at 07.22, in plenty of time to catch the train at 07.25.

There is a problem here. For a year, police and Government spokespersons had been saying that the Four had caught either the 07.40 or maybe the 07.48 from Luton; while various web-theorists had been trying to estimate how long it would have taken them to enter the station and descend onto the platform in rush-hour: a mere two minutes is the answer now given. Had these CCTV images really been available, from say 11th July, 2005, onwards, how could official sources possibly have been and remained so greatly in error? They would surely have realised at once that the train which the four entered was the 7.25. Why would officialdom have wanted to make out, instead, that they had boarded a much later train, one that had in fact been cancelled that morning? The Official Account a year later expressed no doubt that, at 07.40, 'The London King's Cross train leaves Luton station' with them on it, and it even had *several different* witnesses on that train who recalled seeing the Four! There is a *Matrix*-type impossibility about this time-sequence.

Shadowy Figures at King's Cross

Four figures briefly walk round a corner, a now concreted-over part of the King's Cross Thameslink, leading to the underground. No faces can be seen, and certainly not recognised. Is this meant to be the sequence which gave the police their breakthrough, on Monday, 11th of July? Hussain's mother had rung them up, we were assured, and ID of Hussain including his driving license was found – which *enabled this recognition*. Can anyone recognise Hasib Hussain's face in this picture? There is only one person in this photo whose face is anywhere near visible, although not identifiable, and that is the person on the right, which 'could' be Shehzad Tanweer. That image is here shown, above; can you identify him? Here is an early account of this picture:

> At about 8pm on Monday, an officer found just what Clarke was looking for: images of four young men carrying rucksacks. They had been filmed at 8.26am on Thursday, standing together on the station concourse. Hussain's face was clearly identifiable. *Sunday Times* – July 17

The figures could not any longer be 'standing on the station concourse' once the train times for that day had been ascertained: the 07.25 arrived at 08.23, and they could not have made their way to the King's Cross station concourse by that time. Turning back to the original accounts of this pivotal moment given in Chapter 8, we recall *The Guardian's* account of how 'On Monday night came the breakthrough police were waiting for – when the CCTV at King's Cross showed the four young men setting off in different directions.' That would have to be *after* they had reached the main King's Cross concourse. So here are two contradictory accounts of the 'breakthrough' image, neither fitting the film released at Kingston.

Let's recall the account from *The Scotsman* we earlier quoted: on Monday night, 'astonished officers made an incredible discovery. Studying the footage from a camera located high above the dark, grubby station forecourt at King's Cross they noticed, at 8:30am … a man matching Hussain's description. And he was not alone.' This *Scotsman* account is of the main line station at 8.30; although they could have got there by then, our credulity is strained by the notion of Tanweer catching his Circle Line train five minutes later. In fact, *none* of the originally-published accounts of this breakthrough moment match up with the film now released at Kingston, of 'the Four' walking together along a Thameslink subway tunnel; nor could any of the figures have been recognized, as was then claimed.

The figures in this image-sequence can *only* be recognised *if* one first has the Luton station pictures. Then, we see such things as a 'Tanweer' carrying his Tesco plastic bag, rucksack straps hanging down like those at Luton, and someone with a white baseball cap. The police should be invited to explain, now that they have released this CCTV sequence, what exactly was the 'recognition' which they accomplished. They requested CCTV from Thameslink for just two stations, Luton and King's Cross. They received those on Monday, 11th July, then were up in Leeds the next day. The Kingston trial failed to produce Hussain's driving licence, which supposedly enabled this act of recognition. Would the police kindly comment upon this, given that he was receiving driving lessons from his father in the weeks before his death?

On Monday, the police were 'up working all night' and then the next morning 'Clarke applied to Bow Street magistrate's court for permission to search the men's homes [in Leeds].' That is drama, which we would be eager to believe, if only we could accept that Hasib's face was here recognisable or that he owned a driving licence. (July 17, Sunday Times, 'Web of Terror')

That image is the last we see of the four, timed to 08.26 am. No images have as yet been released of any of them in any train or bus. This brief, blurred image of the Four in London, undated, may enable us to reach some conclusion concerning the police eureka moment on Monday, 11th July at 8 pm, the turning-point of their whole investigation. Concerning the image they then beheld, we cannot say where it was, or when it was, whether the Four were standing on a platform or walking along a corridor, or whether they were splitting up or remaining together. In only one feature do the different accounts concur: that features of the four were *recognisable,* which is wholly contradicted by the image-sequence released at Kingston.

Images Released at the July 2008 Trial

Here are some comments on other images released at the 2008 'July 7th', although we're not here including the images themselves.

The Aldgate Blast

Passengers are shown entering a Circle-line train at Liverpool Street Station, with a timestamp saying 07.44 on July 7th. Moving through two-second intervals – with some sudden, one-minute gaps – onto 07.47, we see the explosion at 07.46. The Aldgate blast happened at either 08.49 or 08.50, so the timing is madly wrong. If we are being shown the blast from Liverpool Street – 'a bright flash of light is seen in the tunnel into which the train has just disappeared' (*Daily Mail*, May 2nd) – and the train has nearly reached Aldgate station, with the blast allegedly on the 2nd carriage (meaning four coaches between it and the back of the train), it must have been a very bright flash. This could not have been TATP, which explodes without heat or light.

'The Bus in Front'

CCTV footage from Tavistock Square showed not the blast of the 30 bus blowing its top off, but rather the perturbation of passengers on 'the bus in front.' We could do with some information as regards this previously-unmentioned bus. There were reports of a couple of other buses diverted that morning, crossing Tavistock Square. The film could have been from the inside of any bus, with some passengers moving around. There is a traffic cam suspended at the South end of the street pointing at where the number 30 bus was, and an image-sequence from this would clear things up by showing both buses. We've been shown *no* CCTV sequence of the astonishing detonation whereby the top of the number 30 bus was blown off.

Hasib Hussain in Boots

At 08.55, Hasib Hussain is seen outside King's Cross amidst a sea of umbrellas. Then we have a sequence of his moving across Boots the chemist in the station, looking as if his bulky rucksack should be bumping into shelves. A later-attached time and date stamp moves across from bottom left to bottom right half-way through the sequence. The single original image timestamped 09.00 released back in 2005 has notably been omitted in this sequence, as one sees by slowing it down.

30 Bus Explosion, from BMA Building

Here they show what is supposed to be the 30 bus going by, from inside the British Medical Association headquarters in Tavistock Square, followed by an explosion. The timestamp says 09.42, off by six minutes.

References

[1] J7: The Kingston Trial http://z13.invisionfree.com/julyseventh/index.php? showtopic= 2655, see also www.julyseventh.co.uk/july-7-article-the-7-7-investigation-7-arrests-part-2. html.

[2] http://news.bbc.co.uk/1/hi/england/7364628.stm.

[3] The deadly devices were made of a mixture of black pepper and hydrogen peroxide so 'unique' that the bombers must have had help designing and building them, Neil Flewitt QC, prosecuting, told the jury at Kingston Crown Court: *The Metro* 14 April, www.wikio.com/news/Pepper?wfid=53069576. 'Jurors were told the "unique" bomb mixture was made up of black pepper and hydrogen peroxide,'15.4.08, *The Telegraph.* www.telegraph.co.uk/news/main.jhtml?xml=/news/2008/04/15/nterror115.xml.

[4] http://news.bbc.co.uk/1/hi/uk/7329221.stm Airliner's plot – the allegations, BBC News.

[5] J7 Nature of the Explosions: http://z13.invisionfree.com/julyseventh/index.php? showtopic=69&st=7.

[6] Suicide bombers 'did not fit the profile' *Jane's Police Review* 28 October, 2005 p.12.

[7] The CCTV Evidence http://z13.invisionfree.com/julyseventh/index.php?s=5a8710ad467 a51a7e623c31a15523696&showtopic=97&st=126 p.19; 1st May7/7 CCTV footage released http://news.bbc.co.uk/1/hi/uk/7377649.stm, http://news.bbc.co.uk/1/hi/uk/7378468.stm. CCTV Evidence http://z13.invisionfree.com/julyseventh/ index.php?showtopic=2655 The July 7 Met CCTV sequences released at the Kingston trial were made publicly available, for a few months during the trial, at, www.met.police.uk/pressbureau/optheseus/, then withdrawn. Some have been copied onto the J7 'invisionfree' site, above.

[8] *The Guardian* on Wednesday September 21 2005 on p9
http://z13.invisionfree.com/julyseventh/index.php?showtopic=69&st=133
Nature of the Explosions, p.20.

18. A Comparison: Madrid, 2004

From War Game to Actuality

NATO's anti-terror exercise 'CMX 2004' lasted from March 4th–10th. This yearly exercise was themed as 'designed to practice crisis management procedures, including civil-military cooperation, working in national capitals.' The armies of nineteen nations were collaborating, in an exercise which war-gamed 'a widespread pattern of terrorist attacks.' The next day, the thing rehearsed then happened in real life. NATO responded with a statement:

> The terrorist atrocities in Madrid, which occurred the day after CMX 04 finished, were a deadly reminder about just how realistic such a scenario could be in the present security climate. It perhaps also served as a reminder of the importance of such scenario work for NATO's contingency planning and policy development'.[1]

Peter Power, are you listening? When the event rehearsed actually happens, it is used as an argument for enhancing the funding of the 'anti-terror' agencies. In this exercise, 'co-ordination between civil and military aspects of the crisis management procedures reportedly went well.' In other words, an unhealthy liason between domestic police and the military 'defence' establishment was developed – as required indeed, for false-flag terror to work. NATO then declared that the whole thing was 'classified' so that not a whisper of what happened over that week-long exercise went out to the press.

The Unseen Enemy

Ten bombs go off in Madrid, on 11 March, 2004, during rush-hour, on four subway trains, and then the Basque group ETA issues a statement at 10.30 denying involvement. Then at 10.50, a white van is discovered with seven detonators, a tape in Arabic and a Koran. The tape is found to consist of a chant of a Koran sura. This was three days before the elections, and Spain's Prime Minister Aznar then picks up the phone and tells a daily paper that ETA had done it: that was his arch-enemy, the Basque separatist movement, which had a history of bombs and political assassinations. He had not then heard about the white van story. Later, his government appeared unsure who to blame and Aznar urged everyone to go on the anti-terror march – which 11 million did. His government fell because of this wrong, unsupportable accusation.[2]

An 'unexploded bomb' mysteriously appears in a nearby police station in the small hours of the next morning, having a cellphone as detonator which belonged to some Morrocan Arab. Also on that day, the London-based Arab newspaper *Al-Quds Al-Arabi* said it had received an e-mail from an Al-Qaeda group, taking the credit and declaring that it was retribution for Spain's role in the Iraq war. On Saturday, 13th March, the day before the election, three Muslims were arrested as perpetrators. Then on the 14th an Arab videotape was found in a trashcan with someone claiming to be a spokesman for Al-Qaeda in Europe taking credit for the deed. This fourfold Muslim-implicating sequence of events sounds somewhat planted and contrived, reminding one of the trail of Korans etc. found after 9/11, left in hired cars and baggage of the 'hijackers.'

After unexpectedly losing the election, the Aznar government secretly paid thousands of pounds to have *all computer records* erased and all documents shredded, especially around the 11th March but more generally over the previous eight years; that is suspicious behaviour! Zapatero, as Spain's incoming Prime Minister, swiftly committed himself to the hypothesis of Islamic guilt. With his propensity to wear a Palestinian scarf, one might have expected some slight hesitation on this matter – but no! He pledged cross-party support for an international 'war on terror' and used that as his reason for not prosecuting Aznar for such outrageous conduct. Thus, when the great trial began three years later, its outcome was fore-ordained: Muslims had to be guilty.

The Muslims accused were suspended in a huge glass case in the trial-room through the five months of this rather theatrical trial. The indictment itself, for Spain's worst terror attack, was over 100,000 pages long. Halfway through it, in May of 2007, 14 of the defendants went on a week-long hunger strike, objecting to the presumption of guilt which they felt was being thrust upon them by the media. Condemning the bombings, they declared they had "lost faith" in the Spanish judicial system. After coming off their hunger strike, they issued a plea that their trial be 'extracted from the political arena.'

The Court's judgement involved a hitherto-unsuspected group of Al-Qaeda terrorists from Morocco. It ascertained, in October 2007, that: 'The March 11 suspects — both dead and alive — were mostly young Muslim men from a hodgepodge of different backgrounds who allegedly acted out of allegiance to al-Qaeda to avenge the presence of Spanish troops in Iraq and Afghanistan, although Spanish investigators say they did so without a direct order or financing from Osama bin Laden's terror network.'[3] Someone ought to have told the judge that Osama bin Laden died six years earlier. That judgement may not be fully compatible with the disclosure made by the Spanish newspaper *El Mundo* six weeks after the event, that:

> 24 of the 29 alleged perpetrators were informers and/or controlled by the Spanish Police, Civil Guard and C.N.I. (*National Centre of Intelligence*) before the attacks. (24.4.06)

All of the prosecuted appealed, protesting their innocence.

That court explained the cause of deaths:

> The blasts, from 10 backpacks filled with dynamite and nails, killed 191 people and wounded more than 1,800.[4]

An unexploded '13th bomb' contained nuts and bolts mixed together with its explosive, and clues from this rucksack pointed towards the now-jailed Muslims. Three months after that Court judgement, the medical forensic expert who oversaw the post-mortem work, Carmen Baladia, spoke out in an interview on Libertad Digital with researcher Louis del Pino (30 Jan, 2008). She affirmed that nuts and bolts of this kind had not been found in the 191 bodies. This could in some degree put a question-mark beside the grounds on which the Muslims had been prosecuted.[5]

Asturian Dynamite

The following features may not have been sufficiently considered by the Court:

* No CCTV captured images of 'bombers' and their rucksacks loading, at any railway station in Madrid.

* A story of Muslim suicide bombers carrying rucksacks, but no witnesses reported seeing Muslims with bulky rucksacks in the Alcala de Henares railway station.

* The man accused of supplying the high explosive turned out to be in possession of the private telephone number of the head of Spain's Civil Guard bomb squad, Señor Suárez Trashorras – while two other men implicated in the bombings had already been identified as police informers. The number was written on a piece of paper found in the possession of his wife Carmen Toro. (*The Times,* 21 June, 2004)

* Of the two police informants arrested as plotters, one was Mr Rafa Zhueri, who had worked for years as a police informant for a unit of the Spanish Civil Guard: 'I informed the Civil Guard that the Asturian offered me dynamite' was a headline [6, 7]

* Spanish police forensic experts concluded that the bombs were made from the highly restricted Spanish-made dynamite variant called Goma-2 Eco. This is a type of high explosive manufactured for industrial use (chiefly mining) by Unión Española de Explosivos. It is a gelatinous, nitroglycerin-based explosive widely used within Spain and exported abroad. They estimated that these Madrid attacks had been perpetrated by means of an estimated 120 kg of stolen Goma-2 Eco. This Spanish explosive was subject to tough and effective security measures that had successfully prevented ETA terrorists from getting their hands on any of it for over 20 years. The police informer who procured this explosive evidently did so despite the stringent security measures that had kept ETA from doing the same for over two decades. Surely no Moroccan al-Qaeda group could have gained access to this, nor carried such a hefty amount onto trains in the morning rush-hour and not be noticed.

* This highly-restricted military-grade explosive used was comparable to that of the earlier 'Gladio' operations. No fires broke out at any of the ten blast sites, a fingerprint of the military-grade explosive used.

* Detonations were synchronised to within a single minute, 7.38–7.39 am on the four trains, just as in London, but one hour earlier.

* Bombs may have been placed under the floorboards in at least some cases, as four trains were on 'first service' out of the night railyards after overnight servicing and cleaning. Three of the trains had come straight out of the Alcala de Henares night rail depot, according to Joe Vialls.[8]

* The alleged perpetrators are reported by the Spanish police as having committed suicide together on 3rd April – thereby rescuing the Spanish tourist industry, as Joe Vialls pointed out (see below). The remains of two 'terrorists' were subsequently found in a nearby swimming pool with bags of the requisite explosive tied round their bodies, and a third was hiding behind a mattress when killed. The bodies were apparently buried without autopsy.

* A suggested numerology in the passage of 911 days between September 11th (9-11) and March 11th (3-11).[9]

The Joe Vialls' version remains an important narrative for the Madrid bombings:

> Only a few hours later in what appeared to be a chilling and apparently stupid rerun of 9-11, police officers were tipped off by media about a suspicious white van parked near Alcala de Henares railway station, which was then found to contain a handful of detonators, and several Muslim religious tracts on a cassette tape. The names of the five Moroccan 'terror suspects' were provided to the western media by American and Israeli intelligence agencies, thus creating the illusion that Spain would never be safe until these fictional terrorists were caught.

> By doing this, America and Israel were ensuring that international fear would destroy Spain's huge tourist industry, which has already suffered tens of thousands of summer holiday cancellations since the bomb attacks in Madrid. The subliminal message to the new incoming Spanish Labour Government was therefore obvious: "Leave your troops in Iraq or we will … destroy what is left of your massive tourist industry." It must be said that the Spanish Spec Ops solution to this massive national threat was ingenious. By faking the explosive 'suicides' of the five imaginary 'terrorists' named by America and Israel, Spain completely neutered this contrived threat, because no tourist on earth is going to be frightened of 'terrorists' who have already died very publicly on international television!

The front wall of the apartment block, in a Madrid suburb, was blown out with light frame demolition charges, after which police reportedly found 200 detonators of the type used in the railway attacks. The number of blown-to-bits plotters is given as five, six, or seven, in different reports (Wikipedia cites four (5)).

The 13th bomb and Islamic guilt

We have seen how, hours after the atrocity, a 'dummy' rucksack turned up at 02.40 am in a police station. The so-called 13th or 'Vallecas' bomb, it contained *different* explosive material from that which was used in the ten bombs that exploded. Supposedly it had been brought in from the nearby train station of El Pozo along with other bits and pieces. However, there turned out to be a major problem with that story: the bomb disposal squad of the local police had earlier combed though the remains at that railway station right after the blast, at about 10 am, checking for any unexploded bombs. They had found none, especially not a heavy one weighting 24 pounds, as the '13th bomb' did.[10]

Bristling with nuts, bolts and screws, this would-be bomb had a 'SIM' card in its detonator that led directly to a group of Muslims, just in time to alter the course of the Spanish election. The rucksack was shown by X-ray not to be explodable, because its detonator-wires were not connected up. Despite this, it had a cellphone supposed to induce detonation, which had on it the fingerprints of Jamal Zougam, alleged ringleader and now in jail (with a 40,000-year jail sentence!) The phone in this backpack was one of very few types on the market that required a SIM card to operate the alarm. This led *El Mundo* to ask the question:

Why would terrorists who owned a cellphone shop and are deemed to be very technically proficient, deliberately choose to use a device that would lead the police to their door?'[11]

Madrid gave a vitally-needed affirmation to the 'war on terror' announced on September 11th, two and a half years earlier, bringing the theme of Muslim suicide-terrorists over to Europe, and thereby helping to validate and explain NATO's continued existence. There are some deep similarities with the July 7th story, and a translation into English of some of the work of Luis del Pino (e.g. his *Los Enigmas del 11-M*—the Spanish name for the event) would be a help in this direction. For example, both cases have enduring uncertainty and ambiguity over the explosives used, with experts initially agreeing that it was the hard-to-obtain military grade C3 or C4. The clearly-fabricated '13th bomb' invites comparison with those allegedly found in Luton car-park after the July 7th event, where the US-released images of 26th July, 2005, bristled with nails and shrapnel (Appendix 8), whereas no hint came from post-mortems of London July 7th bodies that they were embedded with such.

References

[1] 'Terrorists attack NATO', *Isis Europe*, 6, May 2004, p.7. The whole NATO military exercise CMX 04 was 'classified,' i.e. secret: www.isis-europe.org/pdf/2004_archives_8_nato_notes_v6n2.pdf.

[2] R. Minita, *Shadow War, 2004*.

[3] *International Herald Tribune*, Mixed Verdicts in Madrid terror bombing Trial, 30.10.07 http://iht.com/articles/ap/2007/10/31/europe/EU-GEN-Spain-Terror-Trial.php? WT.mc_id=s_europe_gg_gnrc.

[4] *The Guardian* 31.10.07 '21 Guilty, Seven Cleared over Madrid train bombings'.

[5] Wikipedia, ref. 78 (in Spanish) http://en.wikipedia.org/wiki/11_March_2004_Madrid _attacks, TV interview on Libertad Digital.

[6] *El Mundo* of 6 May, 2004; Tarpley, p.401.

[7] See Ch.14, Note 11.

[8] www.vialls.com/myahudi/madrid.html.

[9] Prosecutor Olga Sánchez discerned a Kabbalistic symbolism in the passage of 911 days, between 9/11 and 3/11, in 2001 and 2004, respectively: Un factor "cabalístico" en la elección de la fecha de la matanza en los trenes EL PAÍS – Madrid – 10/03/2005 "gran carga simbólica y cabalística para los grupos locales de Al Qaeda". Al Qaeda is (supposedly) an Arab movement, and would they have used the Kabbala? www.elpais.com/ articulo/espana/factor/cabalistico/eleccion/fecha/matanza/trenes/elpepiesp/20050310elpepin ac_2/Tes/.

[10] http://en.wikipedia.org/wiki/Controversies_about_the_2004_Madrid_train_bombings.

[11] Frank Gaffney, NRO 'Spain's Terrorgate?' 18.5.05 Report on the Madrid daily *El Mundo* 16.5.05 account of its research: www.nationalreview.com/gaffney/gaffney200505181246. asp.

19. Eternal War and False Flag Terror

We must stress the idea, unfamiliar and suppressed as it is, that the vast majority of international terrorism conducted on a spectacular scale is indeed state-sponsored terrorism. Webster Tarpley.[1]

There now exists a *main sequence* of New Millenium False-flag terror events, as follows:

Table 1: False Flag Terror

11/ 9/2001 New York

12/10/2002 Bali

20/11/2003 Istanbul

11/ 3/2004 Madrid

7/ 7/2005 London [2]

11/ 7/2006 Mumbai

- all having alleged Muslim perpetrators. For at least four of these events we can be confident that they are 'state-sponsored,' meaning set up and created by the 'Axis of Evil' CIA-Mossad-MI6. We cannot know to what extent one or another of these intelligence agencies is involved, as they are so closely interlinked. For the Istanbul and Mumbai bombings, the evidence may be less clear as yet. 9/11 established the image of Islamic terror, for a new kind of war, one 'that will not end in our lifetime' as Vice-President Cheney informed the American people – and, because this menace did not really exist, but was a mere phantom-illusion, a sequence of follow-up events was necessary to maintain its credibility. Al-Qaeda was put together in the late 1990s by the CIA, in a world where no Muslim group called themselves by that name.[3]

We enter the new millennium with the US/UK fully dedicated to Eternal War – that is the reality now facing us. We know that the question is not, "Will there be peace?" but rather, "How soon will the US/UK initiate the next war?" Israel is a creation of these two nations and is likewise just as fervently dedicated to Eternal War; indeed, it may be said to have pioneered the concept. The new millennium saw the unfolding of a new enemy image.[4] Until 1991 the Red Menace had justified the vast military budgets – Russia being one of the few sizeable countries in Europe that had never threatened or attacked Britain in its entire history.

After 1991, a decade went by with no defined enemy-image; this was awkward for the military, because during this time the US/UK military budgets continued to increase. During this interlude, some important progenitor events were taking place, examples of what remains to ordinary folk unthinkable, viz. that one's own government (or renegade elements thereof) has devised deliberate terror-events—civilian assassination programs. Why would they want to do that? The following comprises a fairly minimal, but essential, list:

Table 2: Some pre-9/11 synthetic terror ops

Bologna, railway station	1980
New York, WTC	1993
London, Israel bombs its embassy	1994
Oklahoma City, federal building	1995

Italy, 1980

The ultimate subject you never wanted to know about – you had wished to spend your life on more edifying matters – is: who plants the bombs? The solidly documented starting-point here has to be the August 1980 bombing of Bologna railway station.[5] It was successful in that, together with the kidnap and murder of the Prime Minister Aldo Moro, it stopped the Italian Communist Party from entering the government; that was the aim. It is assumed by those designing such events, that they can be blamed on left-wing groups or 'extremists' and will thereby consolidate the power of the right-wing, viz the military / politicians, those who control.[6] These, the Vampire Elite, are the Enemies of the Human Race.

Italy was about to choose to bring its own Communist Party into a coalition government. America and Britain did not wish this to happen, and were able to use secret structures of NATO to make sure it didn't. Here are three quotes:

Webster Tarpley:

> 'If the Italian left of the 1970s and the German left of the same period sympathised with the Red brigades or the Baader-Meinhof group/red army faction, they only showed their own gullibility, since both of these terrorist operations were created by and controlled by NATO intelligence.'[7] The Bologna bombing was 'the biggest terrorist attack in Europe before the Madrid train bombings of March, 2004'.

Tony Gosling:

> Hundreds of innocent people have been killed in false flag terrorist attacks, particularly in Belgium and Italy, where Prime Minister Aldo Moro was kidnapped then assassinated for inviting Communists to join the Italian Government. These attacks were blamed on leftist groups such as the Baader Meinhof, Red Brigades etc. which came out of the 1968 student uprisings.... Horrific unprovoked massacres at supermarkets and railway stations, no wonder people want to forget them. But we do so at our peril as they explain many oddities with terrorism 'spectaculars' today. 'Gladio' False Flag 'Strategy of Tension' attacks have been going on throughout Europe under the watch of NATO Intelligence's Clandestine Planning Committee (CPC) since the 1960s. It all became public with an Italian Parliamentary Enquiry in 1990 followed by one in Belgium. Make sure your local politicians, soldiers, journalists and police force are aware of Gladio, maybe by giving them a DVD copy of Allan Francovich's BBC Timewatch series.[8]

Noam Chomsky:

> Put briefly, the "stay-behind" armies of Western Europe – originally organized to fight in the event of World War III – morphed into substantial clandestine

political forces with deep roots in European police and intelligence agencies. According to parliamentary investigations, the stay-behind veterans of Gladio appear to have made and broken governments. Elsewhere, they provided channels for intelligence operations and other relationships largely unknown to the elected leaders of a half dozen democratic states. This is important stuff.

'Gladio' acted as leverage for US foreign policy. It extinguished hope,[9] ensuring that the populations of Europe would continue giving their surplus revenue to an ever-growing military, would continue to hate and fear the 'Enemy', would desire US military bases on their soil, and would not elect unduly independent governments. Let's pause awhile to reflect on how Europe might have developed, had Italy been allowed to incorporate its Communist Party into government. Italy would at last have been able to enjoy a stable government reflecting majority opinion, while the rest of Europe could have calmly seen how a 'communist' party worked, and so would no longer have needed to hate and fear it – it would no longer have been the bogeyman 'over there.' Reds under the beds could have been exorcised and Europe might even have decided that it didn't need an Enemy.

The whole story is now published as *NATO's Secret Armies*,[10] or if you can't afford the £25 for this erudite text, a DVD is available of Allan Francovich's three Timewatch 'Gladio' BBC documentaries of 1992, showing far-right NATO Special Forces gunning down and blowing up hundreds of innocent European civilians. (Francovich died suddenly of a 'heart attack' in 1997 while entering the US.) A new book, *Gladio: NATO's Dagger at the Heart of Europe* is also planned by Progressive Press. One thing remains clear: train bombings are the NATO/Gladio speciality in the false-flag terror field.

'Gladio' is the precursor to the July 7th and Madrid bombs in Europe.[11] The killers are indeed establishing a new empire of darkness in which no one will know the truth and everyone lives in fear. Orwell saw it all so clearly, in his novel *1984*:

> In some ways she was far more acute than Winston, and far less susceptible to Party propaganda. Once when he happened in some connection to mention the war against Eurasia, she startled him by saying casually that in her opinion the war was not happening. The rocket bombs which fell daily on London were probably fired by the Government of Oceana itself, "just to keep the people frightened."[12]

As British MP Michael Meacher has perceptively written,

> The "global war on terrorism" has the hallmarks of a political myth propagated to pave the way for a wholly different agenda – the US goal of world hegemony, built around securing by force command over the oil supplies required to drive the whole project. Is collusion in this myth and junior participation in this project really a proper aspiration for British foreign policy?[13]

MI5 did in effect destabilise Harold Wilson's government, when the latter refused to send British troops to Vietnam.[14] A comprehensive history of MI6 concluded that 'the modern intelligence service's prime purpose appears to be to generate fears.'[15] How true! But our intelligence services do more than that: after all, the nightmares have to incarnate now and then, taking bodily form.

9/11 was the millennium-determining phoney event, unleashing the dark moira of America's destiny, in its dedication to Eternal War.[16] Seeking out its predecessors, we turn to the 1993 World Trade centre bombing and the 1995 Oklahoma Federal Building explosions. For both of these events, the judge at the trial would only hear evidence concerning a single 'lone nut' who was accused,[17,18] and so we will always lack adequate accounts of them (There is a fine book on these precursor-events by Len Bracken).[19] The Oklahoma Federal building was demolished in the same way as the three World Trade Centre buildings six years later, through detonation of bombs placed inside it. In both cases, an outside agent was made responsible so that 'blame' could be allocated. The truck blast at Oklahoma (blamed on Timothy McVeigh)[20] could never have done more than shatter a few windows.

Table 2 includes Israel bombing its own embassy, well described in Annie Machon's book about what MI5 have been getting up to.[21] In 1994, Israel scored a propaganda victory by averring that certain Palestinian groups had attacked its London embassy.[22]

Eternal War

As regards the racist enemy-imaging that now goes on almost daily in newspapers, let's consider the list of 27 nations bombed by the US since World War II.

Table 3: *Nations bombed by the US since WW2.*[23]

Japan	1945	Lebanon	1983
China	1945-50	Grenada	1983
Korea	1950	Libya	1986-89
Guatemala	1954-1960	Iran	1987
Indonesia	1958	Panama	1989
Cuba	1959	Iraq	1991-2003
Vietnam	1961	Somalia	1992
Congo	1964	Croatia	1994
Laos	1964	Bosnia	1995
Peru	1965	Sudan	1998
Dominican Republic	1965	Former Yugoslavia	1999
Cambodia	1969	Afghanistan	1998-2001
El Salvador	1981	Pakistan	2009
Nicaragua	1981	Libya	2011

Only one of these nations was white-skinned (Bosnia). Overwhelmingly, "bombable" nations have been of a darker skin colour. The Axis of Evil US-UK is white, from Whitehall to the White House, and its holy-communion-taking leaders go about their normal business of stealing the resources, demonising and bombing nations of darker skin colour.[24] Admittedly, after Vietnam, *seven whole years* went by, without the US bombing another nation. Yes, it's hard to believe, isn't it?

Bali

The Bali bomb of 2002 was a success because it got the Aussies into the war – that was its aim. There could be a deeper purpose here involved, in that Bali had an intact and quite spiritual culture, such that its people were not generally living in fear. The New

World Order does not like that. Maybe the Balinese needed to be taught a lesson. The discerning Canadian scholar Michael Chossudovsky found that:

> like September 11th, the Kuta [Bali] bombing was probably either an American (CIA) or an Israeli (Mossad) operation (or perhaps a combined CIA/Mossad operation) ...Three days before the Bali bombings of October 1st, the Australian press published several reports pointing to an imminent terrorist attack. These reports were based on statements of the Director of the Australian Strategic Policy Institute, Mr. Aldo Borgu ... The October 1st Bali bombing occurred barely a few days after the holding of a special meeting of The Council of Australian Governments in Canberra, during which the State premiers agreed to the adoption of far-reaching antiterrorist measures.

It is the anti-terror chiefs who *enable* the event to happen. Australia, 13th October, 2005:

> Last night, the biggest fraud in the history of Australia was disclosed to the Australian people on TV. The Former President of Indonesia (who is widely known in Indonesia as the only honest Indonesian politician there) directly stated in no uncertain terms that the Indonesian police and/or military had perpetrated the infamous Bali bombing in which over 200 people were killed...about half of them Australians. To remind you, this is the blind former President who is honest and religious and beyond the possibility of being corrupted... In a one hour documentary/research/investigative program on SBS-TV Date-Line program last night, all the fabricated cover-up story about 'terrorist Moslem Organizations' in Indonesia fell apart. They do not exist! They were all created by Indonesian Military Intelligence! .... The Indonesian Generals are corrupt, they boasted on TV that they got 50 million dollars from the Americans, in order to 'fight terrorism'. In reality, they created 'terrorism' and pocketed the money.[25]

This Australian TV programme endorsed the view advocated by the late, great Joe Vialls, who had resided in Australia:

> It was late on Wednesday, 15 November, just one day before the special Hindu cleansing ceremony of the Bali bombsite in Kuta Beach, that the local Indonesian police chief thoughtfully paraded "prime suspect" Amrozi in front of the assembled media pack. The fact that Amrozi was clearly disoriented, rambling, as high as a kite on drugs and separated from western journalists by a thick glass wall, was apparently not a problem for our sacred guardians of the truth.

> Despite the obvious audio impediments and complete lack of direct access, Australian and Singaporean media outlets were nonetheless able to "accurately" interpret Amrozi's muffled and garbled mixture of Javanese and Indonesian, to mean that he confessed to killing nearly 300 people at Kuta Beach, with a minivan full of potassium chlorate detergent stolen from Java.

> Not only that, but as Amrozi peered hopefully through a thick psychedelic haze to wave cheerfully at the television cameras, we were further asked to believe he claimed to enjoy killing people, wanted to kill some more, and in particular wanted to kill lots and lots of Americans. So thick was the psychedelic fog surrounding him, Amrozi completely forgot that the punishment for "confessing" to such crimes in Indonesia is death by firing squad.

Needless to say, the entire media event was contrived rubbish, but it served the purpose for which it was mounted, i.e. to drive increased levels of Australian hatred against Amrozi, and through him against all Muslims across south east Asia.

The Bali bomb left a huge crater in the road, which IRA bombs planted in cars had never done, as Vialls pointed out. A whole lot of concrete around it was just vaporised, leaving twisted steel up to 50 feet away. That is a recurrent theme in New World Order events: special devices from the necro-technocrats.

July 7th

On 20th November, 2003, on his visit to London, Bush had become trapped in Buckingham Palace where he was staying. Anger on the streets of London prevented him from being able to even wave at a crowd. At last, tomorrow's headlines were going to be about the US President having to cancel all British engagements due to public indignation! That couldn't be allowed to happen, of course: he and Blair were rescued by a bomb – in Istanbul, in a nearly empty British embassy.[26] The next day the news was: B & B walk tall, defying terror, while foolish peace-protesters fail to apprehend, etc.

On his next visit, two years later, it was London's turn. Bush arrived on July 6th, shook hands with Blair, and then, as on the previous occasion, a day later the bombs went off. The G8 summit was aborted, the hopes of the world to 'make poverty history' successfully sidelined, and the next month a whole raft of civil liberties were successfully withdrawn from us, the British people. Terror works – state terror, that is.

Thereby, Britain has come to perceive itself as a self-bombing nation. The central issue, not easy to formulate, concerns the nature of evil. Ordinary folk can believe in desperate Muslims immolating themselves. Let's not go into why this is credible – whereas, say, Afro-Caribbeans doing so would not be very credible – and sages like Mr Galloway can tell us that this is due to their despair over our bombing their nations. This is very, very reasonable, but it happens not to be true. However hard one tries, one simply cannot find real evidence of 'suicide bombers' anywhere in London that morning, whereas, there are good reasons for believing that certain bombs were placed under the carriages (or seats) on the morning of July 7th.

Most people are just not willing to credit elements of their government with complicity in domestic terror. Let us here aspire to calm and factual exposition, and note that, on days before and after the anniversary of July 7th in 2006, Sky News and BBC News both continually presented images of three of the four alleged-bombers in their visit to London on June 28th, 2005, as recorded by CCTV cameras at Luton and King's Cross Thameslink. The time-stamps had been removed to make them look as if they had been shot on July 7th, ten days later. Three of the four suspects had indeed visited London on June 28th for a day-trip. Al-Qaeda (assuming for a moment that it did really exist) cannot do this, cannot make the BBC show fake CCTV footage for the purpose of deluding the British people. The stunt was successful, in that around half of Londoners came to believe that they had seen CCTV footage of the 'Four' in London on July 7th – whereas in reality that is highly questionable. We live in a world where discerning what is real and what is not has become rather difficult and where seeing is no longer believing.

That is partly because the notion of evil would be too awful. I mean, whoever would want to frame four Muslim youngsters who cannot defend themselves, with bogus film played and replayed in the background to … news reports? Who would? Well, let's change the subject!

A year after July 7th, the Home Secretary finally admitted to Parliament that the 7.40 am train from Luton to King's Cross had not run that morning. The Official Narrative had claimed to have CCTV coverage of the lads getting onto that train, plus witnesses in the train who noticed them, four Muslims with large rucksacks; then finally, after a year, we are told there was no such train. It happened that all the trains from Luton to London that morning were severely delayed due to an unexpected accident, which meant that there was no other train that would have transported them between the announced CCTV pictures at Luton, and King's Cross. We would all like to have a Public Enquiry, but the powers that be will make sure we do not get that. We the public cannot be allowed it, the truth cannot be allowed to come out.

By Tuesday, 12th July, 2005, police claimed to have identified the remains of altogether five bodies, either from 'forensic evidence' or I.D. remaining nearby, and this happened to include all but one of the Muslim 'bombers.' Quickly, the trail led up North to Leeds. How clever the police were! But … if there were 56 bodies altogether, that count taken on the 12th is mathematically impossible. From a mere one-eleventh of the total victims, that three of the four of the previously-unsuspected perpetrators should happen to be included? It is far too improbable. That is proof of the fabricated nature of the official July 7th story.[27]

The public are shown a doubtful, photoshopped image (of four alleged bombers entering Luton station), but have in general failed to notice this. Such a failure could result from watching too much telly, whereas it would be preferable to meet up in a group to discuss these matters. We are bombarded with untruth through our media, because journalists print what they are told, leaked from unattributed sources. They cannot spend days in listening to both or all sides' point of view, but have to commit themselves in print the next morning. We therefore live in a society where the truth that matters can be found on the Web, as an expression of the collective intelligence of the human race, whereas it is hardly to be found in a newspaper. A politician standing up on his hind legs and braying about the Islamic terror menace can be fairly confident of the ensuing news reports.

July 7th needs to be understood in the wake of 9/11, and this is primarily so in regard to the terror-drill that was going on at the time of this event, using the same tube stations, and the same morning – Peter Power's exercise. The terror-drill metamorphosed into the real thing, just as did the war-games and terror drills on the morning of 9/11: planes flying into buildings on the morning of 9/11, blips on radar screens with operators unable to tell whether they were real planes or just part of the game-simulation, as the game played out in USAF exercise-drills became real. 'Is this part of the exercise?' asked the NORAD official, at about 9.20 am, on September 11th, on hearing of the multiple hijackings. The perpetrators get the cover they need. The number 30 bus blows up on July 7th—not on its route, after having stopped, not at a bus-stop, in Tavistock Square, with all its CCTV cameras switched off—its whole top neatly lifts off.

For both events the world was informed as to who had done it soon after it had happened, before the police could possibly have reached any conclusions. Then, right after, we were assured that no public enquiry into the event would be necessary. Bin Laden had done it, as Bush told America a day or so after 9/11. Britons were told by Blair that Muslims were responsible for the July 7th event, at 6 o'clock on the very same day. Both announcements used the same script, claimaing that an enquiry would divert essential resources from the 'war on terror' that had to be fought.

Tony Gosling has slammed the BBC over its reporting:

> July 7th: Through systematic bias and a criminally complicit government the BBC, which the public is legally forced to fund, has turned on us and become an accessory to the crime. Despite the wealth of evidence to the contrary, the Corporation's misleading and partial coverage is that of the discredited Metropolitan Police and MI5 anonymous 'narrative' line of unproven but 'obvious' Islamic guilt. After London's most devastating attack since the blitz, Londoners are told there will be no enquiry and to: 'trust us, they're suicide bombers'.

> The Corporation crossed a lethal professional line when it decided to refer to the four 7/7 suspects as 'suicide bombers'. By rubber-stamping Muslim guilt here in the UK, ignoring Peter Power/Visor Consultants' parallel exercise; the Netanyahu/Scotland Yard warning and other hard facts, the Corporation has taken on a leading role in an anti-Muslim pogrom. BBC actions now fly in the face of its motto carved on Broadcasting House, 'Nation Shall Speak Peace Unto Nation', as its one-sided presentation of the facts of modern terrorism plays into a Neo-Con/Zionist case for a religious war against Islam and for Islamic oil … A professional journalistic blunder is committed with almost every new story of a 'suicide bomber'.'

A year after the event, on the anniversary, we were told that Mohammed Khan's will has mysteriously appeared, and that it declared his intention of self-martyrdom. Finally, his widow Mrs Patel was shown it.[28] Four years earlier, the will of Mohammed Atta had been allegedly found in baggage somehow prepared for the 'suicide plane' but left behind, declaring his intent to martyr himself. No one got to see it. We discern a similarity of narrative here, with the same low-credibility, B-movie scriptwriters at work. Atta wasn't on the plane; was Khan in London?

Many folk believe they have been shown pictures of the alleged 19 hijackers or at least of Mohammed Atta in one of the airports involved on 9/11 (e.g. Boston's Logan airport). They haven't—there were no pictures of any hijackers at any of the airports in question, nor evidence for any of them having been on the planes, except for the dodgy phone calls. What the public were shown instead was Atta at Portland Airport, Maine, on his way to Boston. Furthermore, analysis of the time-stamp shows the image not to have been taken that morning but probably on the previous day.[29] This is all distinctly comparable to the July 7th setup four years later, where a faked photo at Luton was all that was offered to the public, with efforts made to lull them into believing that they had seen images of the four in London on that day.

We suggest that Britain has no Muslim terror threat, or none worth speaking of.[30] It has angry Muslims, because we keep bombing their nations, but regrettably and all too often, British Muslims accept the blame and guilt they are offered. Muslims especially within the Stop the War movement should take a stand on this issue. From white, anti-war campaigners one hears the identical refrain: 'O, I'm not really into conspiracy theories' which translated means 'Shut up and take the blame.' Do you really want to take all that guilt? It may not be an integral part of the Anglo-Saxon psyche, that the Enemy is needed out there, however it works in this age as a major social control mechanism.

Thierry Meyssan,[31] manager of the French Voltaire Network intelligence service, has recently surveyed false-flag terror events in South America. Israeli agents had usually caused them, he found, while Muslims got blamed:

> It is lamentable to be able to assert that all the enquiries into the terrorist attacks imputed to Muslims are inconclusive, whether it is a case of Buenos Aires, New York, Casablanca, Madrid or London. Although that doesn't prevent the neo-conservative governments and their "experts" from drawing sweeping conclusions. The US has a habit of modifying retrospectively the perpetrators of terrorist attacks against themselves according to their real or imagined adversary of the moment. Now they are rewriting the history of other peoples' terrorist attacks. Finally, it is advisable to be vigilant with regard to warmongers who want to evoke the Buenos Aires attacks in order to categorize some or other group or government as "terrorist" and call for their eradication.

The media will print any false-flag terror story from an official source. Our last Table can be reduced to merely three items; after all, they are events which did not even happen:

Table 4: 'Foiled' false terror in UK

'Crevice' arrests	April 2004
Canary Wharf	20/11/2004
9 Planes Heathrow	10/08/2006

More Fake Terror

There are a lot of other such events, sordid packs of lies, such as the 'Ricin Plot' used to jolly up the British people for the Iraq war, but you might well not want to remember them. Britain's Foreign Office has its motto 'Any bloody lie will do' and it produces them quite frequently. These are cheap events because nothing actually happens, nobody dies, but fear is (hopefully) generated. The dastardly plot to 'blow up 9 US-bound airliners' flying out of Heathrow by fiendish Al-Qaeda terrorists was unmasked just in time (no tickets, no bombs, not even passports? Never mind, put 'em in jail) and then a *Guardian* survey showed that only 20% of the British people believed the story! Hundreds of millions of dollars were lost over airport delays etc., due to ultra-tight security that suddenly became necessary. This nine-plane episode, widely compared to 9/11, had the important function of softening up the public during Israel's act of naked aggression against Lebanon. A progenitor of this event was MI5's bland announcement two years earlier that it had foiled a sinister plot by Al-Qaeda to fly a plane out of Heathrow and crash it into Canary Wharf. MI5 did not feel obliged to produce any scrap of evidence for this slur upon British Muslims. The tale had come from 'a collusion of imaginative government lobbyists and lapdog media collaborators,' as Prison Planet correctly noted.[32]

Both Madrid and July 7th had military-grade explosive actually used, with later stories brewed up about amateur explosives which local 'terror-groups' could supposedly make. Still less credible was the liquid explosive used on 10th August, 2006 – or rather, which might have been intended to be used – to be mixed in the plane's toilet; a story well discredited by munitions expert Lt. Col. Wylde.[33] A phantom is woven together, having a mere semblance of being, to instill fear. *The people have to live in fear* – that is the fundamental axiom of modern politics. The deaths are real, the perps walk away scott-free, and the phantom of 'Muslim terror' hangs in the air.

An 'imminent' event was about to bring 'mass murder on an unbelievable scale,' according to the Deputy Chief of the Metropolitan Police in London. 10th August, 2006 and 9/11 comparisons were all over the front pages. Strangely, it appeared that Bush and Blair had been discussing the event a few days before the arrests were made. Britain's Home Secretary complained that some people still "don't get" why we had to abandon traditional liberties. Citizens were being arrested because they might nave been intending to do something. Uh-huh. 'We will now never know if any of those arrested would have gone on to make a bomb or buy a plane ticket.' – Quote from the sole sensible critique to appear in the UK media, by Craig Murray in *The Guardian*. Nafeez Ahmed posted up the definitive exposé of this fabricated tale, whose source was one Rashid Rauf in Pakistan, under torture.[34] A week or so after posting this, Ahmed's uncle was gunned down in Pakistan in front of his wife and kids. Ahmed has published a scholarly book about the July 7th bombings plus a highly regarded one about 9/11,[35] and his books contain in-depth analyses of how 'Al-Qaeda' groups have been set up and sustained by the CIA and MI6.[36] He is the only British academic to publish important material on our theme. As a Muslim daring to speak out on these vital issues, he may have had to pay a price.

All through the Cold War, the US/UK had projected its own diabolical designs upon the 'Other' beyond the Urals: whatever new megadeath weapon was to be assembled, it had to be done out of prudence, because the 'Other' was maybe already doing it. This delusion-logic mandated politicians to give ever more funding to the military, whose 'intelligence' was unaccountable and not transparent. Actually, the US/UK led more or less every step of the nuclear arms race. Old fogeys will recall how Harold Wilson was elected in 1964 on a ban-the-bomb pledge. CND-ers were ecstatic, but it didn't last long: soon after entering No.10, Harold Wilson was 'turned' by a single conversation with Lord Zuckermann, presumably about the 'realities' of power, i.e. the need for a hate-and-fear image.

Deep in the Anglo-Saxon psyche, one finds a collective reassurance, a togetherness, that is gained from that hate-and-fear image. People have been reared on films in which the enemy threatens our whole way of life, and has to be blasted to bits in the last reel, and ordinary citizens are actually grateful to their leader for telling them who to hate and fear – just as George Orwell predicted. Actually this country has got no need of an enemy. Ever wonder why all the hopes and dreams of your youth—about socialism as the sharing out of our common-wealth, whereby we could be happy together, yes that's right be happy—why none of that ever happened? Who stole your dreams away and gave you all these nightmares? Muslim terror groups? Nope, try harder.

References

[1] Webster Tarpley, *9/11 Synthetic Terror, Made in USA* 2005, p.59.

[2] The first July 7th bomb was at Aldgate station, and this went off at 8.49 am, i.e. 11 minutes to 9; Madrid was on 3/11, 911 days after 9/11.

[3] See, 'Does Al-Qaeda exist?' by Brendan O'Neill http://100777.com/doc/614 . For the evolution of 'Al-Qaeda' in the mid-90s out of US/UK use of Mujahadeen recruited to fight in Bosnia, see Ahmed, 'Al-Qaeda and Western Covert Operations after the Cold War' in The Hidden History of 9/11 Ed. Zarembaka, 2006. Originally the term was Bin Laden's name for his computer file, used while employed by the CIA in Afghanistan, to co-ordinate the 'jihad' against the Soviet Union: Thierry Meyssan, 9/11 The big Lie, 2002, p.99. As Burke pointed out, 'The US intelligence community used the term "al-Qaeda" for the first time only after the 1998 embassy bombings' of Kenya and Tanzania. James Burke, Al-Qaeda The True Story of Radical Islam, 2003, p.6.

[4] 'For several decades there has been an unrelenting demonisation of the Muslim world in the American media.' Gore Vidal, *Perpetual War for Perpetual Peace*, 2002, p.4.

[5] 'Red Bologna' had been a communist-controlled municipality.

[6] Tarpley, on the Madrid bombings: '… the terrorist attacks had failed to produce the expected effects. The Washington consensus had previously been that terrorism would infallibly stampede the voters of any country into voting for the incumbent, but this time the anti-Bush challenger was the beneficiary,' ref. 1, p.400.

[7] Tarpley (ref. 1), p.60.

[8] Or, just view it online, see Bibliography for details.

[9] In the sense of William Blum's *Killing Hope: US Military and CIA Interventions Since World War II*, 1995.

[10] Daniele Ganser , *NATO's Secret Armies, Operation Gladio and terrorism in Western Europe*.

[11] At Madrid, those who had allegedly supplied the explosives were found to have links with a senior police bomb squad: Ian Henshall, *911 Revealed*, p.188; www.vialls.com/myahudi/madrid.html.

[12] George Orwell, *1984*, p. 127.

[13] Michael Meacher, The Guardian, This War on Terrorism is bogus, 6.9.03.

[14] This did not prevent Britain from supplying intelligence help in that war, via MI6 and SAS troops, plus bomb and napalm-delivery air flights: Mark Curtis, *Web of Deceit, Britain's Real role in the World*, 2003, 105.

[15] Stephen Dorrill, *MI6 50 Years of Special Operations* p.799, quoted Curtis, p.75.

[16] As well as Tarpley's masterpiece, widely regarded as the best work on 9/11, books that will sit proudly on your shelf are: David Ray Griffin, *The New Pearl Harbour*, 2004; Thierry Meysan, *9/11 The Big Lie*, 2002; Mike Ruppert *Crossing the Rubicon*, 2004 (a British book); Ian Henshall and Rowland Morgan *9/11 Revealed*, 2005. More recently, Barry Zwicker's *Towers of deception, The media cover-up* 2006.

[17] The final word on Timothy McVeigh, executed for the Oklahoma bomb, is said to have been given in Gore *Vidal's Perpetual war for Perpetual peace, how we got to be so hated* NY, 2002.

[18] It's regarded as having been a National Security Council (NSC) operation, www.newswithviews.com/Briley/Patrick17.htm.

[19] Len Bracken, *The Shadow government, 9-11 and State Terror,* 2004 Adventures Unlimited press Ill.

[20] A Pentagon report a year after concluded that five separate bombs inside the building had caused the explosion, with McVeigh having a 'peripheral' role as a 'useful idiot:' Vidal,[17] p.120.

[21] Annie Machon, *Spies, lies and Whistleblowers MI5, MI6 and the Shayler Affair* Sussex 2005 Ch.14.

[22] Two Palestinians were convicted. They have complained that 'an unfair trial was followed, after a long wait, by an unfair appeal. This was a political trial from day one and we are totally innocent ... We were only convenient scapegoats.' www.innocent.org.uk/cases/botmehalami/index.html.

[23] These are years when bombings began, not how long they lasted. Source: William Blum, *Rogue State: A Guide to the World's Only Superpower,* 2000.

[24] A fine 'comic' here is *'Addicted to War, Why the US can't kick Militarism'* by Joel Andreas, Canada, 2003: 'Addicted to War is being used as a textbook by many high school and college teachers' (foreword).

[25] D. Leibovitz, 'There Are No Moslem Terrorist Organizations In Indonesia', Sydney, October 2005: www.rense.com/general68/NOTER.HTM Joe Vialls: www.vialls.com/nuke/bali_micro_nuke.htm.

[26] For CIA and Mossad warnings of the HSBC and British consul targetings, see:www.libertythink.com/2003/11/mi6-foreknowledge-in-istanbul-bombings.html.

[27] See Ch. 8, last section.

[28] For Ms Patel's description of the will, see her interview with Julie Etchingham on Sky News, Ch. 11.

[29] Rowland Morgan, *Flight 93 Revealed* 2006, p.95 (a companion to *9/11 Revealed, Challenging the facts behind the War on Terror*, 2005, by Ian Henshall and R. Morgan).

[30] See Appendix 11.

[31] Discerning readers may wish to have Meyssan's *9/11 The big Lie* ('L'effroyable Imposture, it sounds better in French), 2002, on their bookshelf. www.iransolidarity. endofempire.org/news.php?page=650: Thierry Meyssan, 'Argentinian judicial authority rules out Islamic lead,' Global Research 28.7.06.

[32] http://prisonplanet.com/articles/june2006/220606cookedterror.htm Cooked 'Terror Plot Recycles Politics Of Fear; plus, 'Al-Qaeda' plan to fly planes into London skyscrapers concocted by government lobbyists.'

[33] www.propagandamatrix.com/articles/September2006/180906_b_terror.htm.

[34] http://nafeez.blogspot.com/2006/08/truth-about-terror-plot-and-new-pseudo.html.

[35] Nafeez Ahmed, *The London Bombings,* 2006, *The War on Freedom*, 2003.

[36] Ahmed, 'Al-Qaeda and Western Covert operations after the Cold War' 'in The Hidden History of 9/11-2001 Ed. Zarembka 2006.

Conclusions

O you who believe, if a wicked person brings any news to you, you shall first investigate, lest you commit injustice towards some people, out of ignorance, and then become sorry and remorseful for what you have done. Holy Qu'ran, 49:6

Living in a multicultural society means that we listen to and hear the views of groups with differing sacred traditions, in order to try and find some key to integration. Most of us understand that this way forward involves some kind of path towards our happiness and collective well-being. However, that may not be the way things are going, and there is presently a very real danger that, if the thesis here argued is not accepted, the dark vision of Melanie Phillips *Londonistan, How Britain is creating a Terror State Within* (2006) will become true. Her argument represents a polar opposite to that here advocated.

Her conclusion is that 'London had become the hub of European terror networks' owing to its large fluid Muslim population (p12), and I believe that she is implicitly preaching a 'war of civilisation'. She deplores how Britain's lazy Government 'Having allowed the country to turn into a global hub of the Islamic jihad without apparently giving it a second thought' (p275) is continually 'appeasing' the Muslim menace when it ought rather to be showing 'strength' in defeating 'terror' – her message is indistinguishable from that of Ephraim Halevi published in the *Jerusalem Post* on the day of July 7th (Chapter 6). 'This is principally a war of religious ideology' – Halevi would agree. 'Britain has become Europe's terror factory,' she raves (p283). She has merely believed all the yarns put out by MI5 over the years and her book is the result.

We need improved dialogue with Muslims, especially with those courageous Muslims who are refusing to *take the blame,* as they are continually being asked to. The present work has reviewed a triad of major British fake-terror events, post-7/7, where whites found Muslims guilty after more or less nothing happened: 21/7 – some flour bombs go phut, after which Phillips' book opined that 'the British public was even more traumatised' than after July 7th (p.7); 'Crevice' – where a stash of *fertiliser* and another of aluminium powder were found in warehouses, with the convicted Muslims protesting their innocence, but were overruled by the testimony of an FBI informer in Pakistan. Then came the Heathrow liquid bomb hoax, sent courtesy of Israel via the CIA to London, where a trial was held, again with barmy chemistry alleged, and with suspects who had not even bought airline tickets, let alone constructed any bombs. The aim of such trials is that people like Melanie Phillips should have a vague memory of Islamic terror, without having to remember the details – which are plainly absurd.

How many more such bogus trial-convictions are needed? The public needs access to Muslim and other journals which dare to print sceptical critiques of these events. Finding the truth has to be the answer. Once we succumb to lies and allow them to become accepted, everything is lost. The Vampire Elite are in the business of confiscating the oil from Muslim nations, and their motto is, 'What is our oil doing under your sand?' Phillips' work implies that *not enough* Muslims are imprisoned in Belmarsh without trial and that the police should be even more vigorous in doing this. Presently, according to UK crime statistics, British Muslims are three or four times more likely to be imprisoned than non-Muslims.[1]

By way of correcting this sadly misguided vision, it would help Phillips if she could develop a historical perspective. Let's quote Webster Tarpley here:

> 'In the nineteenth century, the great headquarters of international terrorism was London. The defense of the empire required operations which the public decorum of the Victorian era could not openly avow. The main vehicle for British terrorist operations in Europe was Giusseppe Mazzini and his phalanx of organisations …Mazzini was a paid agent of the British admiralty, and received his funding through Admiralty official James Stansfield. Mazzini's terrorism was directed against what the British called 'the arbitrary powers:' Prussia, Russia and Austria. Each of these had a large population of oppressed nationalities, and Mazzini created a terrorist group for each one of them, often promising the same territory to two or more of his national sections. The important thing was that rulers and officials be assassinated, and bombs thrown. … Mazzini operated out of London during his entire career, which simply means that he was officially sanctioned…' (p.62)

Here's another historical view, this time from a study of WWII 'Special Operations':

> 'England in modern times has always been a centre of subversion – known as such to others, but not to itself… England was in the 19th century a hotbed of revolutionary conspiracy, which made London seem as horrifying to the emperors in Europe as Moscow now is to the Americans. In these matters the right hand of His Majesty's Government was careful not to know what the left hand was doing: the disposal of secret funds was one of the *arcanum imperii* … Hence the strange two-sided picture: England to the outer world was the model of intrigue, subtlety, and perfect secrecy, but of itself it seemed above all bluff, simple and well-meaning.'[2]

'Between 1995 and 1999, protests were lodged by many countries concerning the willingness of the British government to permit terror groups to operate from British territory. Among the protestors were: Israel, Algeria, Turkey, Libya, Yemen, India, Egypt, France, Peru, Germany, Nigeria, and Russia. This is a list which, if widely known, might force certain US radio commentators to change their world picture about who is soft on terrorism.'

It is distressing to hear Muslims taking the guilt and blame for these alleged events. They are supposed to search out 'extremists' in their midst. How are they supposed to do that, by spying on each other? In his humorous *Stupid White Man* Michael Moore eloquently described how it always seems to be whites who, in his experience, cause violence, whereas the TV news always seems to show a black man as caught or arrested for causing trouble.

Try to get the book by Michel Chossudovsky: *"America's 'War on Terrorism'"* (2005 2nd Edition) with a section on July 7th. Many socialists have the books of Noam Chomsky on their shelves and reckon that they know the score, however things have now changed,[3] and the political philosophers one needs to read at the dawn of this new millenium are Michel Chossudovsky and Webster Tarpley.[4]

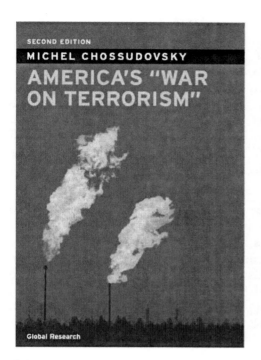

Gladio: the Dark Side of NATO

The North Atlantic Treaty defined NATO as being only defensive and not allowed to strike first, but who would ever attack the world's biggest military alliance? Year after year, did those cold warriors grow tired of doing nothing with all their shiny hardware? They tried to keep the myth of the Commie menace looming over Europe, but did the people really believe it? To help ensure that they did, an 'undercover' aspect of NATO developed, which the Italians called 'Gladio.' Europe needs a thorough, cathartic investigation of the evil perpetrated by this clandestine activity as it extinguished the bright, postwar hopes and dreams for a better world. As the 'gladiators' *buried* caches of armaments, guns, explosives, etc, it was called a 'stay-behind army,' notionally for what might be needed in case the Commies overran Europe.

Gladio was put together around 1962 by NATO's supreme Commander-in-Chief General Lyman Lemnitzer. As Chair of the US Joint Chiefs of Staff, he was also responsible for authorising the notorious 'Operation Northwoods' – a proposed series of false flag terror events including a fake 'Cuban attack' upon a US civilian airplane, which would cause civilian deaths but 'succeed' by getting the US into a war with Cuba under a bogus pretext.[5] The full story of this proposed false-flag terror program – stopped only because in March 1962 President John F. Kennedy refused to authorise it – emerged in 2001 with James Bamford's book *Body of Secrets*.[6] That book has been of enormous value in describing the perpetration of the false-flag terror that was 9/11 (and in particular the fate of flight 93 on that morning shot down in Philadelphia,[7] which considerably resembles one part of that Operation Northwoods plan). In a comparable manner, Daniele Ganser's comprehensive historical analysis on Gladio appearing in

2005 has been invaluable in the wake of July 7th, by providing a historical paradigm in terms of which that event can be interpreted.

In the lovely Italian Piazza Fontana in Milan, a bomb destroyed a bank on December 12th, 1969, killing 16 people and injuring dozens more, and *caused* a large wave of strikes to just melt away, as the police ran amuk arresting all sorts of left-wingers. Who did it, and why? This is how simple false-flag terror works. It thereby prevented the Italian Communist Party the PCI from entry into government. This dreadful new method of social control was called the 'strategy of tension' and it took 20 years before the truth came out, that the secret network of Gladio controlled by NATO intelligence was responsible. A whole series of Italian bombing incidents followed, the worst being the bombing of Bologna railway station in 1980.

The truth about 'Gladio,' as the Italians called it, began to emerge in 1990 and, as the BBC documentary pointed out, 'Britain's role in setting up stay-behinds was absolutely fundamental... Just as the Gladio sword had a double edge, there were two sides to the

story of the modern Gladio.' (pp.48-9) With its hidden supplies and arms explosives used by its mentors, Gladio was indeed used for internal subversion against the left: 'Were the agents of the state in fact responsible for an unexplained wave of terrorist killings?' the BBC asked. The Italian MP Sergio de Julio proclaimed to the camera, 'We have evidence that right from the beginning of Gladio, officers were sent to England for training.' Three excellent broadcasts by Allan Francovitch won the Best Documentary award at the Berlin film festival, disclosing the matter where the Belgian police enquiries had failed. In a 2000 investigation, the Italian Senate concluded that the 1980 Bologna train bombing, killing 85 people, was carried out by "men inside Italian state institutions and ... men linked to the structures of United States intelligence."

A full account emerged in 2005, rather providentially for our story, with Ganser's masterpiece: *NATO's Secret armies, Operation Gladio and Terrorism in Western Europe*. During the debate over whether or not to accept American Cruise missiles in 1983-85, terror was sown in Belgium: the 'Brabant terror massacres,' kicking off on 14 August, 1982, with an attack upon a food shop. There were 16 attacks altogether with very little in the way of cash stolen. A journalist commented: 'If the object was to sow terror, the terrorists chose the perfect targets. Women, children and the elderly, cut down by rapid gunfire while wheeling their trolleys through a local supermarket.' But who could want to do such a thing? Who could be so wicked? Someone called Latinus was found to have been involved and arrested, but was found hanged before he could speak in 1985. In 1990 the Belgians closed down their secret NATO army, remaining annoyed at the refusal of the CIA and MI6 to give details of the Belgian agents involved. The Belgian government concluded that the attacks had been 'the work of intelligence services working for foreigners, a terrorism aimed to destabilise democratic society.' (p.147) It was found that leading officers in the secret network had trained under the SAS in the UK. NATO had been 'involved in a whole series of terrorist operations and human rights violations that they wrongly blamed on the communists in order to discredit the left at the polls. The operations always aimed at spreading maximum fear amongst the population and ranged from bomb massacres in trains and market squares (Italy), the use of systematic torture of opponents of the regime (Turkey), the support for right-wing coup d'états (Greece and Turkey), to the smashing of opposition groups (Portugal and Spain). NATO has refused to open its files on the Gladio agents – 'the best kept and the most damaging political-military secret since WWII' as it has been called.

In 1990 there was a full Euro-debate on Gladio, and the Italian MEP Falqui urged:

> This Europe will have no future if it is not founded on truth, on the full transparency of its institutions in regard to the dark plots against democracy that have turned upside down the history, even in recent times, of many European states … There will be no future, ladies and gentlemen, if we do not remove the idea of us living in a kind of double state – one open and democratic, the other clandestine and reactionary. That is why we want to know what and how many "Gladio" networks there have been in recent years in the Member states of the European Community. (Debate over Gladio on 22 November, 1990, Ganser p.21)

Those words are as true and urgent today as they were when uttered. They should be engraved on the walls of some European ministry. An MEP from Greece spoke next, and he gravely affirmed: 'Mr President, the Gladio system has operated for four decades under various names. It had operated clandestinely, and we are entitled to attribute to it all the destabilisation, all the provocation and all the terrorism that have occurred in our countries over these four decades … In fact it was set up by the CIA and NATO which, while purporting to defend democracy were actually undermining it and using it for their own nefarious purposes.'

No democracy can hope to survive if it both runs a secret army and maintains an unaccountable intelligence service. The stay-behind network has served to spread fear amongst the population in the absence of any invasion or threat thereof. To quote Ganser, 'The secret armies in some cases functioned as an almost perfect manipulation system that transported the fears of high-ranking military officers in the Pentagon and NATO to the populations in Western Europe. .. By killing innocent citizens on market squares or in supermarkets and blaming the crime on the communists the secret armies together with convinced right-wing terrorists effectively translated the fears of Pentagon strategists into the very real fears of European citizens.' (248) Countries such as Italy and Greece have suffered more from Gladio than the UK and in consequence its work is taken more seriously there. Perhaps citizens concerned with civil liberties should turn more towards Europe. That speech by the Italian MEP represents a kind of hope for Europe.

We saw how a Gladio-type train bombing at Madrid in 2004 took place less than 24 hours after the major, yearly NATO anti-terror exercise which took place in various European capital cities. No details are available about this NATO exercise for us, the public, just as none were available concerning the US/UK Atlantic Blue exercise in London a year later. Revelations concerning the Bali bomb of 2002 (Chapter 15) suggested that it was the anti-terror chiefs who had willed and *enabled* the event to happen. Likewise, the bombing of the British Embassy in Istanbul on 20th November, 2003, happened the *day* after the annual Turkish-US Joint Defence Group meeting, 17-

19th November, 2003,[8] where Turkish and US Deputy Chiefs of Staff had met up to discuss issues pertaining to the 'war on terror': events suggesting that MEP Falqui's words concerning Gladio remain pertinent.

Britain is now second in military expenditure amongst the nations of the world, spending over thirty billion a year; this is one-twentieth of what America spends, which is around $700 billion every year,[9] including both its wars and its ongoing military expenditure. Thus what we have here called the 'Axis of Evil' are the two most militarised nations, and major arms exporters. Such a degree of military expenditure must tend to generate mythical images concerning who the enemy is, which has been the subject of this book. Britain's military expenditure remained steady through the 1990s; hovering at just over twenty billion a year; it even decreased after 1991, when the Soviet Union collapsed so that there was no longer an enemy. Then, after 9/11, it rocketed up to over thirty billion:[10] in the words of *Guardian* correspondent George Monbiot, the UK is 'sloshing out £32bn a year on a programme whose purpose is a mystery.' Continual fear is needed to justify that sum.

A new 'enemy' has now replaced the menace of Communism, so well described in the BBC's 'Power of Nightmares' trilogy. In the words of Adam Curtis, the producer of this BBC program, Al-Qaeda was imagined as:

> 'a nightmare vision of a secret, organized evil that threatens the world. A fantasy that politicians then found restored their power and authority in a disillusioned age. And those with the darkest fears became the most powerful.'[11]

This appealed to something deeply conditioned in the British people... and helped the arms exports.

The new millenium has seen a strengthening of 'strategic, military and intelligence ties between Washington and London.' To quote Chossudovsky:

> After the war in Jugoslavia, US Defence secretary William Cohen and his British counterpart Geoff Hoon, signed a 'Declaration and Principles for Defence equipment and Industrial Co-operation' so as to 'improve co-operation in procuring arms and protecting technology secrets' while at the same time 'easing the way for more joint military ventures and possible defence industry mergers.' Washington's objective was to encourage the formation of a trans-Atlantic bridge across which the DoD (the US Department of Defence) can take its globalisation policy to Europe: 'Our aim is to improve interoperability and war fighting effectiveness via closer industrial linkages between US and allied companies.' Moreover, this integration in the area of defence production has been matched by *increased co-operation between the CIA and Britain's MI5 in the sphere of intelligence and covert operation* [my emphasis] not to mention the joint operations of British and US Special Forces.[12]

July 21st, 2005, marked a step forward in the mental enslavement of America, with Bush addressing the House of Representatives over the deleting of sunset clauses from the US 'Patriot Act,' i.e. ensuring that it would be permanent. The US senate had voted it through in the immediate aftermath of 9/11, before senators had even had time to read it – and after letters containing anthrax were sent to the two key congressmen who would have been most inclined to block it. That Act demonstrated that America was violating the Biological Weapons Convention, revealed its source as a US weapons lab that made this specific type of anthrax, and oiled the passage of this Act by intimidating opposition. The anthrax letters pretended to be from an Islamic source, by containing various comments made about Allah, etc—appropriate for this Act, which was riding on the bogus 9/11-based terror threat as its basis for strangling the American Republic.

On July 21, 2005, the US House of Representatives passed HR3199, the USA Patriot and Terrorism Prevention Reauthorization Act of 2005, which removes certain sunset clauses.[13] Within hours of a second attack on the London transit system, lawmakers in the House and Senate were pushing ahead with bills to extend the controversial USA Patriot Act anti-terror law. The law made it easier for FBI agents to monitor phone calls and e-mails, to search homes and offices, and to obtain business records. It ended the distinction between foreign and domestic intelligence gathering and what had been the sacrosanct firewall between them. It compelled librarians to give details of books borrowed, and gagged them so they don't talk about it – and so forth. It was the blueprint for a police state. The senate enthusiastically voted these measures through, with the help of announcements about the new London 'terror' attacks of that day all over the morning news. Bush alluded to the London bombings in his speech to the House on that day.

Earlier on the same day back in England, a COBRA meeting of the Association of Chief police Officers just happened to be taking place at Downing Street, reportedly chaired by Tony Blair, to promote drastic new anti-terror laws, and extension of arrest without trial for up to three months. Details were hard to come by, but parts of the country were made subject to "exceptional laws and controls." Thus in both the US and UK that day, legislation was formulated, to promote fear and enhance state power. Were these events intentionally scheduled together with the London 'bombings' to facilitate their passage? Does the 'Axis of Evil' synchronise in this manner by mere accident?

Our investigation has examined several hypotheses by way of explaining the events of July 7th. My early opinion, was that there were no valid witnesses who saw any of the Four in London on that day. That view became untenable once the police released their mass of Hasib Hussain CCTV from around King's Cross that morning. The second, the 'Ripple Effect' narrative, has the four young men arrive in London, believing that they were taking part in a terror-drill game-simulation, and then three of them are shot dead at Canary Wharf. The third is that the official version is correct … and pigs can fly. Professor Rory Ridley-Duff has endorsed the second of these as being more probable than the official 'BBC Conspiracy Files' view. Our survey has modified the Ripple narrative, so that only three of the four came down into London on that terrible morning, Khan having pulled out owing to his wife's pregnancy complication. This book will have succeeded, if it encourages informed debate on the matter.

We can hardly hope to improve upon Ganser's own concluding words:

> A potential exit strategy from the spiral of fear, manipulation and violence might have to focus on the individual human being itself and a change of consciousness. With free will the individual can decide to focus on non-violent solutions of given problems and promote a dialogue of understanding and forgiveness in order to reduce extant positions. The individual can break free from fear and manipulation by considering his or her very own feelings, thoughts, words and actions, and by

focussing all of them on peaceful solutions. As more secrecy and more bloodshed are unlikely to solve the problems ahead, the new millennium seems a particularly adequate time to begin with such a shift in consciousness which can have positive effects, both for the world and for oneself.' (p249)

To help make this happen, let us try to imagine national Ministries of Peace developing around the world, and hope that responsible companies and industries would want to fund such ministries.

In conclusion, we quote Nafeez Ahmed:

If the "War on Terror" is to end, it won't be won by fighting the next futile oil war. It will be won at home: by holding the secretive structures of government to account, by prosecuting responsible officials for aiding and abetting terrorism — whether knowingly or by criminal negligence — and ultimately by restoring real democratic oversight over the conduct of covert operations which continue to foster the "enemy" we are supposed to be fighting.[14]

References

[1] Britain shelters 'terrorists': http://infowars.net/articles/february2007/140207Jihadists. htm.

[2] Chossudovsky edits the journal *Global Outlook* and the website www. globalresearch.ca 'Centre for Research on globalisation' in Montreal.

[3] Barry Zwicker, *Towers of Deception – the Media cover up of 9/11* Ch. 5, 'The Shame of Noam Chomsky & the left Gatekeepers.'

[4] W. Mackenzie, *The secret History of the SOE: Special Operations Executive 1940*-46, 2000, p.746.

[5] The story of Operation Northwoods was first published by John Elliston in *'Psywar in Cuba: The Declassified History of US anti-Castro Propaganda* in 1999, but became better known after James Bamford (former ABC newsman and Navy Intel officer) published his *Body of Secrets,* 2002.

[6] For a summary of the Northwoods plan, see Appendices C and D of Nafeez Ahmed's *The War on Freedom, How and Why America was attacked on September 11, 2001*, CA 2002.

[7] NK, www.911action.org/the-mystery-of-flight-93/.

[8] 'Turkish & US Top Military Brass meet one day before Istanbul Attacks' M.Chossudovsky22.11.03 *Global Research* http://globalresearch.ca/articles/ANA311A. html.

[9] US ¾ trillion pa: http://www.slate.com/id/2183592/pagenum/all.

[10] George Monbiot, 'Only Paranoia can justify the World's Second biggest military budget', *The Guardian,* 28.11.06.

[11] www.archive.org/details/ThePowerOfNightmares.

[12] Chossudovsky, *War and Globalisation The Truth behind September 11th* 2002 p.22.

[13] 'HR 3199 continues to violate the constitution by allowing searches and seizures of American citizens and their property without a warrant issued by an independent court upon a finding of probable cause.' *Counterpunch,* 23.7.05, www.counterpunch.org/paul07232005.html.

[14] Conclusion of unpublished paper by Ahmed, '7/7: The Inside Story of the London Bombings What do Terrorist Extremists and Western Intelligence Services Have in Common?' posted on the nineeleven.co.uk website, alluded to in Appendix 10.

Appendices

Appendix 1: No Terror in Europe?

The spectre of international terrorism is haunting Europe. The EU has declared that terrorism is a serious threat to "European security", and far-reaching measures have been initiated to deal with it, including increased police powers and mass monitoring of the population, undermining our privacy. But, does it exist?

Terrorism fatalities in Western European countries 2001-2006

Country	2001	2002	2003	2004	2005	2006
Austria	0	0	0	0	0	0
Belgium	0	0	0	0	0	0
Cyprus	0	0	0	0	0	0
Denmark	0	0	0	0	0	0
Finland	0	0	0	0	0	0
France	2	6	2	1	0	0
Germany	0	0	0	0	0	0
Greece	0	0	1	0	0	0
Iceland	0	0	0	0	0	0
Ireland	0	0	0	0	0	0
Italy	0	1	0	2	0	0
Luxembourg	0	0	0	0	0	0
Netherlands	0	1**	0	1**	0	0
Northern Ireland	9	4	1	0	0	0
Norway	0	0	0	0	0	0
Portugal	0	0	0	0	0	0
Spain	16	7	4	191*	0	0
Sweden	0	0	0	0	0	0
Switzerland	0	0	0	0	0	0
United Kingdom	0	0	0	0	56*	0

Source: MIPT Terrorism Knowledge Base

* Unsolved crimes; unclaimed crimes; anomalies in the public account. No public inquiry allowed. Suspicion of police/intelligence involvement in the crime. See specific websites dedicated to these crimes.

** Wrongly classified as terrorism. These were plain acts of murder in which the murderer intended to kill his selected victim.

To get some facts and figures on this matter, we turn to Mr Elias Davidsson, an Icelandic 9/11 activist. He comments:

> Neither the public nor legislatures have been provided with statistics on terrorism in Europe which would help constituents assess the real (as distinguished from the contrived) threat from terrorism. One is entitled to suspect that the failure to publicize these statistics is based on the fear that public awareness of these figures might undermine public support for the global "war on terror" (the figleaf behind which wars of aggression and various military interventions are hidden).[1]

He visited a string of websites about Euro-terror and was disturbed to find that none of them provided data to demonstrate the alleged threat. Eventually he found one from which he was able to derive the table of data above.[2]

This table shows that, in Europe today, the likelihood of death due to 'terror' is comparable to that of being struck by an asteroid – provided that we exclude the events of 3/11 at Madrid and 7/7 in London (and 2011 in Norway). In the year 2006 there was not a single terror-death in all Europe. It is refreshing to hear a bit of rational logic on this subject. Davidsson found that:

> 'Apart from the two unsolved "terrorist" crimes mentioned above, which are suspected to have been "false-flag" operations masterminded by Western intelligence agencies (like the events of 9/11), most terrorism fatalities between 2001 and 2006 in Western Europe occurred in Spain as a result of reported Basque terror attacks, and in Northern Ireland apparently by IRA and Unionists. Both of these cases represent local political conflicts. The effects of these terror acts on society remained marginal. They had no visible effect on "European security". The conflict in Northern Ireland is currently being solved. No terror fatalities have been recorded there since 2004. Fatalities from Basque terrorism have not been recorded since 2004 either. The remaining recorded fatalities from terrorism in Western Europe include some from simple murders which have been wrongly classified as "terrorism". In most European countries no person has died from terrorism over the period under consideration... The main unsolved cases of mass murder, designated as terrorism, are those committed in London in 2005 and Madrid in 2004. Until these crimes are fully solved, there is no factual base to consider terrorism as a real threat in Europe. But even if the crimes in London and Madrid were genuine terrorist acts committed by those who have been accused of these crimes, they would not constitute a "threat" to the security of Spain or of the United Kingdom, let alone to Europe, but merely large crimes, whose victims are not more numerous than the victims of a typical train or plane crash. While these crimes severely affected the lives and well-being of the direct victims and their relatives, they did not disrupt or undermine the operation of public institutions, economic life, defense capacity, the social fabric, or the well-being of the population. To state that terrorism constitutes a "significant threat to the security of Europe" is a monumental and most probably willful misrepresentation by the European Council.'

Mr Davidsson's conclusion is so important to us all:

International terrorism is a contrived threat, a monumental deception carried out by governments and facilitated by mass media to justify aggression, occupation, intervention and the curtailment of human rights. This deception must be exposed as an attack by colluding governments on democracy and human rights. By permitting states to engage in gross human rights violations and aggression, the contrived threat of international terrorism may itself be considered as a threat to international peace and security.

But, is his conclusion compatible with a more orthodox conclusion derived from European police statistics? Let's quote here from Europol:

Altogether 498 [terror] attacks were carried out in the EU in 2006. The vast majority of them resulted in limited material damage and were not intended to kill. However, the failed attack in Germany and the foiled London plot demonstrate that Islamist terrorists also aim at mass casualties. A total of 706 individuals suspected of terrorism offences were arrested in 15 Member States in 2006. Investigations into Islamist terrorism are clearly a priority for Member States' law enforcement as demonstrated by the number of arrested suspects reported by Member States.[3]

'Terror attacks' here include the misleading concept of damage to property. It would help if European police employed psychologists to assess whether terror was in fact generated by the crimes in question. If not, it isn't terrorism. Furthermore, the huge majority of arrests of British Muslims on 'terrorism' charges do not result in any prosecution. Less than 3.5% of those so arrested have been convicted in the UK since 9/11 – and these include individuals wearing badges for proscribed organizations.[4] Overall, the Europol report seems fairly compatible with Mr Davidsson's conclusion.[5]

On 22/7/2011, Norway did experience a major terror attack, killing 77. First a huge bomb went off by government buildings in Oslo. We should doubt whether this was an ammonium nitrate car-bomb made from garden fertilizer, as alleged. Then dozens of young leftists, on summer holiday on the island Utoya, were shot, supposedly all by one deranged right-wing fanatic 'lone gunman'. In the forthcoming book from Progressive Press, *Gladio: NATO's Dagger at the Heart of Europe*, Richard Cottrell argues that these were acts of state-sponsored terrorism, to teach Norway a lesson for its go-it-alone, pro-Palestinian stance. (See his blog 'Oslo: Down to the New World Order'.)

References

[1] http://juscogens.org/english/index.php

[2] 'MIPT Terrorism knowledge base, a comprehensive databank of global terrorist incidents and organisations' www.tkb.org: Clicking on the right column on Incident Reports by Region (Mr Davidsson explained to me), then selecting the appropriate time-frame and the region (Western Europe) in the dialogue boxes gives one the statistics.

[3] The Europol (European police) site www.europol.europa.eu/publications/.

[4] Fahasd Ansari, Ch. 12, Ref 7

[5] Home Office statistics gave two fatalities in England & Wales attributed to terrorism in 1996 and three in 2000. (www.homeoffice.gov.uk/rds/pdfs07/hosb0207.pdf) Upon inquiry, the author of this section declined to explain these figures, citing the ever-convenient pretext that such disclosure might 'impede police investigations.'

Appendix 2: Israeli Security Firms

This appendix is substantially based upon a 2007 statement put out by Tony Gosling concerning Verint Systems & ICTS.

Comverse Technology – www.cmvt.com

The world's largest maker of voice-mail software, this Israeli company is now at the centre of $8bn fraud enquiry in New York. Comverse share six directors with a wider network of linked companies also under investigation. Comverse took over Hong Kong company Multivision Intelligence Surveillance Ltd. in January 2006 but Comverse directors didn't file the financial information required by law. Delisted from NASDAQ and stock trading, suspended on 1st February, 2007, because of financial mismanagement and non-filing of essential accounting information—along with Verint Systems who are now also NASDAQ delisted—they are phone billing and mobile phone voicemail software developers.

Jacob 'Kobi' Alexander, Comverse's Chief Executive

On July 31st, 2006, Kobi Alexander, who holds Israeli citizenship, was also added to the FBI's Most Wanted List. Target of FBI, Wall Street Journal and Securities & Exchange Commission fraud enquiry in New York, he was declared a fugitive in August 2006. On August 9, 2006, the United States Securities and Exchange Commission filed a civil injunctive action in the United States District Court for the Eastern District of New York against Alexander, along with alleged co-conspirators William F. Sorin—Comverse's former Senior General Counsel—and David Kreinberg—Comverse's former Chief Financial Officer. The complaint makes nine claims of violation of the Securities Act and the Exchange Act, including fraud (First and Second Claims), and falsification of books, records or accounts (Fourth Claim). Through this action, the Commission is seeking permanent injunctive relief, disgorgement of ill-gotten gains, civil damages, and a prohibition against any of the defendants becoming officers of a securities-issuing entity under SEC jurisdiction. Wanted on 35 criminal counts, including stock option backdating, conspiracy, securities fraud, money laundering and bribery, Kobi was arrested in September 2006 after a seven-week manhunt in Namibia. Travelling via Israel, he had transferred $17m to Namibia, bought a luxury house and formed a new construction, tourism and agriculture company, now building 200 low income homes for workers at the new 'Langer Heinrich' uranium mine. Alexander's extradition hearing began in Windhoek on April 25th, 2007, and he will face up to 20 years jail in New York. He is known to be a close associate of former Chinese president Jiang Zemin.

Kobi's two brokerage accounts with $45 million have been frozen, and it appears that he transferred over $57 million to accounts in Israel in what the government asserts was a money laundering scheme "in an effort to conceal the funds from U.S. authorities." The FBI has declared him a fugitive, and is trying to extradite him from Namibia.

Verint Systems – www.verint.com

All activities of this business are directed by Comverse Technology who own 57% controlling stock. Two-thirds of Verint's business is security products used by law enforcement and intelligence services to intercept voice, video and email traffic; the other third is call centre monitoring and employee evaluation software. It has approximately 1,000 employees worldwide. Verint has hundreds of offices around the world: Kuala Lumpur airport, JFK New York, Montreal Airport, New York transit systems, etc. It is a company with several directors either in prison or under indictment or on the run in Namibia; Verint and Comverse are run by ex Shin Beth and Mossad officers. Verint CEO Daniel Bodner is a former senior Israeli army officer who gets $4m annual benefits (including salary). Verint was worth eight billion until its director, Jacob 'Kobi' Alexander, was arrested and charged in 2006.

Verint was formed in the wake of 9/11, with the surging demand for surveillance. Its 'video intelligence' products could help customers sort through hours of security videos and analyse them for potential threats. After September 11, this was a fast-growing market. In February 2002, 'Comverse Infosys,' turned into Verint Systems, with the parent company Comverse Technology retaining a majority stake. Kobi Alexander assumed the chairmanship of Verint, while Dan Bodner served as president and CEO. This happened in America; legally speaking, Verint is a US company. However, there has only ever been one press release about its use by the London Underground, and that is the one quoted in Chapter 3, by Israeli News. It began: 'An Israeli security firm has been chosen to provide security for London's Underground train network. Verint systems …' We should be concerned over the extent to which its 'video intelligence' products are prone to detect 'threats' in terms of Arab stereotypes.

It was awarded the contract for all London Underground's CCTV in September 2004 by the privatised 'Metronet Rail' (it has since gone bankrupt and is 'in receivership'); who, in turn, had a 30-year contract from the UK government to manage London Underground security. Metronet and Tube Lines Ltd are the consortia companies which have been responsible for maintaining and operating the London Underground since 2003. Northern and Piccadilly lines are maintained by Tubelines, the District, Circle and Metropolitan lines by Metronet. The latter awarded its contract without a tender in 2004 for all its CCTVs on London Underground to Verint. A Metronet spokesperson confirmed (somewhat reluctantly) that his company had a contract with Verint Systems, 'for the provision of CCTV infrastructure.' Verint provides digital recording technology. They manufacture and develop the products but don't service them. Metronet are in Holborn, Tubelines are at Canary Wharf, Transport for London is in Victoria, and Verint Systems' European base is at Leatherhead, Surrey. CCTV images are stored for two weeks by Metronet: it thus handed over (I was informed) two weeks' worth of images up to the July 7th date. Verint engineers were called back from holiday to extract well over 100,000 hours of video recording from CCTV cameras that had been requested by the Metropolitan and British Transport Police. CCTV images have a habit of disappearing when they are most needed in this story: those at Stockwell during the Jean Charles de Menezes chase and execution (Tube Lines' responsibility because it's on the Northern Line), as well as those from the four cameras of the number 30 bus, plus one in Tavistock Square on July 7th.

ICTS Europe

ICTS Europe is an Israeli security company based in the Netherlands, a subsidiary of which is Huntleigh. Huntleigh was the security contractor at Logan Airport on 9/11 that failed to provide us with CCTV evidence of hijackers. The Israeli company called

International Consultants on Targeted Security (ICTS) International N.V. is an aviation and transportation security firm headed by "former [Israeli] military commanding officers and veterans of government intelligence and security agencies." ICTS has two broad fields of operation. The first, 'Aviation Security', deals with all aspects of flight, passenger, baggage, and cargo security. The second, 'Integrated Services', consists of services and solutions specifically designed for complex, public-access environments—particularly healthcare and academic institutions, transport hubs and corporate organisations. The main UK base for ICTS is in Luton, about a mile from the Thameslink station, where it handles security for the Stansted airport. A subsidiary company ICTS UK Ltd. has its office in Tavistock Square, right in front of the spot at which the 30 bus blew up, on the first floor. When NK and TG went to interview them, they explained that they deal with airport security and had no connection with the Underground.

Secretary: Lewis, Ben Joseph MSC FCA MR; Director: Eldar, Zamir – Business Manager (Head of European operations for ICTS; Director: Golan, Ron – Marketing Director; Director: Rozanski, Techayah – Security Manager; Director: Vago, Gabriel – Computer Security Specialist (Israeli). NB, Gabriel Vago, Director of ICTS UK Ltd and Director of Fortress GB, is listed at the exact same address as Anat Eshet-Vago, Director of Fortress GB. Mortgage charges: three in the name of Bank Leumi (U.K.) PLC, the largest Israeli-owned bank in the UK, subsidiary of Bank Leumi le-Israel BM.

Huntleigh USA, a subsidiary of ICTS

Menachem Atzmon, convicted in Israel in 1996 for campaign finance fraud, and his business partner Ezra Harel, took over management of security at Boston's Logan Airport in 1999 through Huntleigh USA, a subsidiary of ICTS. ICTS also provided security at Newark airport, which was, like Boston, involved in 9/11. "Was ICTS, or one of its affiliates, involved in the July 7 terror exercise in London?" Bollyn asked ICTS spokesperson Petra Snoek at company headquarters in Amstelveen, Holland. The reply given was that ICTS International did not operate in the U.K. It does however have a subsidiary in Britain called ICTS U.K. Ltd. , located in London's Tavistock House South.[1] It has another office at Luton, about a mile from the Thameslink station.

Two months earlier, in May 2005, ICTS International reported entering into the railroad security business. This was the very company that handled security at the 9/11 airports, and in May 2005 it landed a contract for the London tube. Two of its co-chairs, Mr. Ezra Harel and Mr. Menachem Atzmon, have been arrested on charges of and subsequently released on bail in Israel by the investigative authorities of the Israeli Securities Authority in connection with a criminal investigation under Israeli law involving an unrelated company in which Mr. Harel was a former director and controlling shareholder. Atzmon and his business partner Ezra Harel are the majority owners (57%) of ICTS International Consultants on Targeted Security, run by "former [Israeli] military commanding officers and veterans of government intelligence and security agencies" according its Web site. In 1999, Atzmon's Netherlands-based firm took over management of security at Logan Airport in Boston, Massachusetts, through ICTS' subsidiary Huntleigh USA. Israeli plutocrat Menachem Atzmon was co-treasurer of the Likud, along with Jerusalem Mayor Ehud Olmert, during and after the 1988 Israeli elections. In August 1988, Atzmon worked with Olmert and two other men to collect illegal contributions for the Likud from corporations, against Israel's party funding law, by providing fictitious advertising services to the contributors. Atzmon was later convicted in that campaign finance fraud, while Olmert was acquitted.[2]

Fortress GB Ltd, 1st floor, Tavistock House, Tavistock Square

Fortress' experience with smart cards originated in the 1990's when implementations in public key cryptography (RSA) and conventional data encryptions (DES) were developed on a single chip. The revolutionary concepts in secure smart card technology reached during this period have been recognised worldwide by many blue-chip manufacturers. Fortress leveraged this thorough knowledge of chip technology and shifted its focus to top-end highly secure smart card applications such as those required for airport security, including integration to biometric applications and hardware. This experience enabled Fortress to come forward with the RFID based next generation of frequent flyer programme. The London Underground is one of Fortress GB's clients and according to their press release they provide smart card technology (personal details and biometric information) for contractors that operate in Tube stations.'

Directors: Vago Gabriel, Israeli, & Eshet-Vago, Anat; Secretary: James Rosenthal; Mortgages: two in the name of Bank Leumi (U.K.) PLC, the largest Israeli-owned bank in the UK.

In April 2003, Metronet won £8bn in contracts for revamping the tube, for the Bakerloo, Central, Victoria, Waterloo & City, Metropolitan, Circle, Hammersmith and City, District and East London – ambitious! Refurbishing track and tunnels soon overran its budgets and in 2007 the last straw came when a Central Line train was derailed. On July 18th, 2007, Metronet, the London Underground contractor, announced that it was going into administration after racking up a £2bn overspend bill.

View of Christopher Bollyn: The journalist Chrtistopher Bollyn commented: 'Fortress GB, an Israeli-run company doing business in Great Britain, is on the same floor, in the same building, as ICTS UK, which is another Israeli transportation security firm. ICTS UK Ltd. and Fortress GB Ltd. are both located on the 1st floor of Tavistock House, which is exactly where the bus blew up on July 7. An Israeli man answered the phone at Fortress GB and was noticeably reluctant to answer any questions about who ran the company although he did admit that a lot of Israelis worked there. The secretary at ICTS UK Ltd., however, quickly told me that the companies are related.'

Bollyn contacted Visor Consultants, the mayor of the City of London, Scotland Yard, and the transportation authority to ask about the identity of the partner in Visor consultant's terror exercise, whom Peter Power had declined to name. A likely candidate, he surmised, was ICTS: 'These Israeli security firms need to be investigated in light of the London bombings, because they provide "security technology" for the tube lines that were bombed. They have perfected their "security" skills in Israel and Iraq and then apply them in Britain and the U.S.A. This is a pattern. The same thing happened at Heathrow when the PanAm flight went down, the same thing occurred at Boston and Newark airports on 9/11.' (NB, when T.G. and the present writer visited the ICTS offices in Tavistock Square, they assured us they had nothing to do with the tube and were mainly concerned with airport security). Bollyn had been a writer/photographer for the *American Free Press* in Washington DC, but was fired soon after these articles appeared. He has been described as 'one of the most tenacious of false-flag terror researchers' (T.G.). He suffered an assault by the FBI in 2006.

[1]. 'Israeli Firms: Fortress GB Related to ICTS UK' *American Free Press*, August 2005, Christopher Bollyn.

[2]. See report by Tony Gosling, http://100777.com/node/1777. Also www.indymedia. org.uk/en/regions/london/2006/10/354202.html Scandal hits London Underground security/technology company. For valuable comments upon the various Israeli-related security firms, here involved, see the 10-part Youtube video: 'Montreal – the next terror target?'

Appendix 3: Numbering the Dead

We do expect an Inquest to count the dead.

As was pointed out by the intrepid J7 team, concerning the number of dead bodies identified at two of the crime scenes, Aldgate and Edgware Road, from the helpful diagrams which the Met has supplied to the Inquest:

- The Edgware Road coach had 7 dead bodies – 6 victims plus 'Khan'.
- The Aldgate coach shows 8 dead bodies – 7 victims plus 'Tanweer'.

Dr Morgan Costello told the Inquest about how he was asked to check out the crime scenes (Inquest, Nov 3rd, pm). He was known to the police because he had assisted them in 'providing medical services and medical assistance… in relation to deaths in custody.' He visited the Edgware Road crime scene at midnight 7th/8th July, where he counted **six** dead bodies. Then he went onto the Aldgate scene at 8 am that same morning – and counted altogether **seven** dead bodies. He was asked to do nothing except count the dead, he explained. For both of the sites, a police officer guided him.

When he was counting these bodies, no-one had any idea about 'suicide bombers' nor had any bodies been identified. The difficult circumstances did not prevent him from 'reaching firm conclusions,' concerning the count he was asked to perform (2:24). He was legally obliged to carry out this task properly. The numbers were too small to confuse, small enough to be literally counted on the fingers.

These counts can be reconciled, by supposing that the two 'terrorists' were not in fact present in the coaches. The only alternative is the one which the Inquest has tried to take, of assuming that Khan and Tanweer were blown into such small pieces, that Dr Costello just failed to notice them when he was counting the dead. Ah, its amazing what black pepper and peroxide will do …

We are told that Tanweer's rucksack was put down in the corner, in which case one would hardly expect him to be blown into 52 little pieces (11:7) – that is how the Inquest explained why he had been omitted from Dr Costello's count. We are told that around 'Tanweer' were found various bits of ID (such as a receipt from hydrogen peroxide he had allegedly purchased from Greenthumbs Hydroponics shop, Wakefield) – whereas his body was so blown to bits that the professional expert counting the dead for the police did not notice him…

One way of clarifying the matter would be to ask the victim-families who were given back the bodies of their young men: when the burial of Tanweer took place in Pakistan, in what form was the body?

How were 52 dead announced on July 11th?

Did the authorities have a crystal ball to tell them that the total deaths resulting from the London bombings would add up to 52, a mere four days after the event? That number was announced officially on the 11th July – although the Australian Prime Minister had come out with it on the 8th! A somewhat premature remark one feels.

The Inquest has heard about Lee Harris, in the coach at Aldgate, who died in hospital on the 15th July: 'My Lady, he remained at Royal London Hospital for just over a week and we'll hear evidence about the intensive treatment that he received there. Sadly, that treatment was to no avail and he died on 15 July 2005.' (Inquest, Oct 12 pm, 32:6-10) Being in a coma, why was he numbered amongst the dead? The Inquest did not comment upon his girlfriend's body Samantha Badham only being found on the 16th: should not the total on the 11th have been 50?

On the 11th July, names of the dead began to be released: *The Guardian* reported, "The names of two women who died in last week's London bombings were made public today, as the confirmed death toll from the attacks rose to 52." But, it also added, "Police believe all the bodies have been recovered from the Piccadilly line tube train under King's Cross, but said the confirmed number of dead could rise to 60." It seems rather strange that the final total should remain fixed at the first-announced number – especially when that number was announced the day after, on the 8th.

Can 52 be counted?

We've seen how 6 and 7 are the totals of dead bodies counted at Aldgate and Edgware Road, and there are 13 names written on the Tavistock Square plaque. So far 26, so does that mean there will be another 26 dead at Russell Square? Well not exactly …

Consulting the diagram showing the dead at Russell Square, i.e., the Piccadilly line blast, supplied by the Met for the Inquest, we notice a total of 17 dead. The diagram is entitled: 'Positions of Deceased in 1st carriage at the commencement of recovery process.' That could be a rather cryptic title.

Thus, we have no clue where the number 52 came from (unless one wishes to dabble in numerology, as its digits sum to seven, something like 7/7/2005: 5+2=7)

Mystery Death of Miriam Hyman

Myriam Hyman is listed on the plaque at Tavistock Square as amongst the 13 dead. While travelling to work at Canary Wharf on the morning of July 7th, coming in from Finchley, she was abruptly forced to get out at King's Cross, as the entire Underground began suddenly to be evacuated.[1] The evacuation order ('Amber alert') was given at 09.15, so she would have reached the concourse at around 09.30 at the earliest. She phoned home to her Father at 09.45 to explain that she was at King's Cross – two minutes before the Number 30 bus exploded – adding that she was determined to get to work despite the chaos. As a photographer, she was due to have lunch with her picture-researcher friend Sarah Dixon, who knew her from the days when she had been a student at UCL.[2]

The father of Miriam Hyman commented to the *International Herald Tribune* journalist in the wake of the tragedy:

> John Hyman, whose 32-year-old daughter, Miriam, is missing, knows a few things for certain: She was not wounded when she left the Underground. She was not on the bus because the bus exploded at about the time he was on the phone with her. Soon after, she called her workplace, and was told not to bother to come in. That was at 10 a.m., after the attacks, he said.

"I don't see how she could have got into the bus that exploded," he said. "And the route makes no sense, whether she's going to work or home." Her cellphone goes unanswered. Hyman's friends have papered the town with her image and raced to hospitals.[3]

That was published on Monday the 11th, so that statement could have been made on, say, Saturday 9th.[4] On the 11th, the family were informed that identification had been performed on a body found at Tavistock Square, as being that of M.H.

The *Jewish Journal* of 15th July described the 09.45 phone call to her Father as follows:

Other Jewish families face an agonizing wait. Miriam Hyman, 32, a freelance photo editor, called her father, John, from King's Cross Station at 9:45 a.m. Thursday to say she was all right. That was the last anyone has heard from her. After a fruitless search of London's hospitals, "we are just waiting," Hyman's mother, Mavis, told JTA.

This article, published a week after the tragedy, does not say, 'her body was found next to the number 30 bus and was readily recognized by the camera and ID' – no, it says the Mother was having an agonising wait and that she and friends of Miriam had been searching through London hospitals. Miriam's mother Mavis is quoted in the *Jewish Journal* article as saying, 'She phoned work to say she was going to be late, she was still obviously determined to get in. I think she didn't understand the seriousness of what was going on,' so it sounds as if they interviewed Miriam's mother and she confirmed the ten o'clock call into work.

A colleague of Miriam's recalled how her family had put up posters around King's Cross and St Pancras, asking if anyone knew what had happened to her, and made enquiries in London hospitals, for about a week after the event; after which they came to accept that she had died on the Number 30 bus. The total of 13 deaths at Tavistock Square was only announced some days later, whereas on the news on the morning of July 7th a total of three deaths were reported at that site. There is an obvious problem that the number 30 bus left Euston at about 09.33, and it's a ten minute walk from King's Cross to Euston. Insofar as anyone knows what the intended route of that 30 bus was, it was driving from Euston to King's Cross. That's where it would have gone to, had it not blown up. Why would MH have wanted to jump onto a bus driving back to where she had just been?

I have been roundly condemned by the media for having phoned up the father, by way of wishing to confirm with him the time and place of his daughter's last phone call to him. For researching this manuscript, I have made quite an endeavor to contact persons having authentic memories of what happened, but this was the only survivor family I contacted. For this I was censured by the 'July 7 truth' community as well as the papers. The father had given me permission to ask him a question or two, I explained, despite which they still viewed the act as unethical. I therefore here refrain from including any comments he made to me. (Sanctimoniousness and self-righteous indignation, with calls to "respect the victims" or "support the troops," are convenient forms of emotional smokescreen used to bully citizens who question the machinery of death operated by the powers that be. — Ed.)

References

[1] *The Jewish Journal,* 15.7.05, 'London's Jews Carry on After Blasts.' http://www.jewishjournal.com/home/preview.php?id=14372.

[2] International Herald Tribune – Published: Monday, July 11, 2005 http://www.iht.com/articles/2005/07/10/news/missing.php.

[3] Guy Dixon at UCL, about Miriam's lunch appointment at Canary Wharf: http://www.homepages.ucl.ac.uk/~ucyutsi/July2005UNInews.pdf.

[4] Obituary: http://news.bbc.co.uk/1/hi/england/london/4738123.stm.

Appendix 4: Terror Drills

4a. The 'Atlantic Blue' Exercise

Over four days, April 4-8, 2005, Britain, America and Canada held a joint exercise that involved simulating a terror attack on the London Underground. Before it happened, various announcements were made in the House of Commons and by the Metropolitan Police[1, 2, 3] but once it had happened there was only silence, as if a veil of secrecy had been drawn around it. One has heard of joint military manoeuvres at sea, etc, but how could the US and UK have conducted a joint role-playing simulation of a terror attack upon the London Underground?

The initiative for this shared event came from America, as indicated by its title. It was performed in conjunction with a 'TOPOFF' exercise – 'Top Officers' in US military parlance. The first TOPOFF had been solely a US exercise, while the second had been performed in collaboration with Canada. TOPOFF II was described by the Department of Homeland Security as the largest, most comprehensive terrorism response exercise ever held in the United States. It simulated the detonation of a radiological dispersal device in Seattle, Washington, and the release of the pneumonic plague in several Chicago metropolitan area locations. There was also 'pre-exercise intelligence play' (spreading rumours?), a cyber-attack, and credible terrorism threats against other locations. It involved participants from the federal government, state, local, tribal, and private sector agencies and organisations, the United Kingdom, and Canada, plus a virtual news network providing real-time reporting of the story like an actual TV network. Twenty different federal agencies collaborated in this exercise.

Then, TOPOFF 3 was held in April 2005, with the UK and Canada collaborating, described as the most comprehensive terrorism response exercise ever conducted in the United States. It had approximately 10,000 participants from more than 275 government and private sector organizations. It featured a 'Red Team' which acted as a devil's advocate, and which aimed to knowledgeably role-play the 'enemy'. This 'Red Team' simulated terrorists planning and executing weapons of mass destruction attacks in Connecticut and New Jersey. To make this realistic, TOPOFF 3 utilised a data source, the 'Universal Adversary,' that replicated actual terrorist networks down to names, photos, and drivers' license numbers.[4]

TOPOFF 3 involved

* A poison gas attack in the London subway (or at least an explosion)
* Poison gas attack in Connecticut
* A release of pneumonic plague in the New York/New Jersey area, affecting three counties in central New Jersey.

The London and Connecticut attacks may have been related, according to the exercise, with a coordinating body set up between the U.S. and British participants. *The Observer* was able to publish a bare outline account of what happened during the 'Atlantic Blue' exercise, but solely due to information it had obtained from Washington sources. It revealed that the biggest transatlantic counter-terrorism exercise since 9/11 included 'bombs' being placed on buses and explosives left on the London underground.[5] A subway attack formed a prominent element of this exercise, led in the UK by the Metropolitan Police. Visor Consultants was involved, due to a contract with the British government, in the organisation and implementation of Atlantic Blue with the assistance of Michael Chertoff's US Department of Homeland Security.[6]

Role-playing games were involved. We get a glimpse of these in a 'TOPOFF 3 after action report' produced for the Department of Homeland Security, and here is an excerpt:

'...role players (i.e., "victims"). In particular, exercise personnel did not interact with victims in the same manner as they would normal patients during an actual emergency. For example, if a role player's card indicated s/he spoke Spanish, the person interacting with him/her still addressed that person in English and did not attempt to find an interpreter. Furthermore, in some cases role players were not aware that the cards they received were supposed to reflect the type of individual they would portray (i.e., their "script"). As a result, these individuals did not "act out" the special characteristics their card may have called for (such as the example discussed above). Finally, our observers noted challenges faced by epidemiologists who were sent to the various hospitals participating in the exercise. In particular, each hospital received only one epidemiologist to assist it, even though hundreds of plague "cases" could have been or were arriving at each hospital.'[7]

The London game-simulation seems to have been quite a psycho-drama production, in which diverse actors were involved. When the July 7th Review Committee interviewed London's Mayor Ken Livingstone, (on 1 March 2006), who had been in Singapore on July 7th, having flown over to celebrate London's winning of the 2012 Olympic bid the day before, he started ruminating upon the role-playing games of a few months earlier:

'I said from Singapore that we had actually done an exercise of multiple bomb attacks on the Underground as one of the exercises and we had embellished that after the first wave. This was on a Friday afternoon, with all the Cabinet having gone back to their country estates – I think perhaps we were anticipating a different administration by then or something – but that was followed up by a second wave of attacks which destroyed New Scotland Yard and City Hall, taking out the senior management of the police and myself. The whole system was geared to work with a total decapitation, effectively, of political and police leadership, and it did.'

One would like a bit more detail of this gripping, large-scale game-cum-terror drill, somewhat casually disclosed by London's Mayor. We, the taxpayers, paid for it after all. He would here have been alluding to the Atlantic Blue exercise, though that remained unstated (possibly omitted by the Review Committee for security reasons).

The 'Strategic co-ordinator' Nikki Smith of the London Ambulance Service was in the group which wrote the script for Atlantic Blue: 'I am however, the lead for exercises and training for NHS London and do lead and direct a number of exercises annually and led the planning for Atlantic Blue,' she explained to me. The planning and writing of the script had taken at least a year. I inquired as to how nothing seemed to have been made public about that large-scale, international event since it happened. She replied: 'Atlantic Blue was not secret as you have just pointed out...it was reported internationally and nationally and we had full press coverage on the 5 days of the exercise. There is a difference between secrecy and lack of interest by the press in these matters I think!' But, in an interview she then gave to me, this appeared to be very far from the case – she could tell me *nothing,* nor even point to *any* source of information, about this enormously detailed event. At one point she did say, concerning the London Underground, 'Supposing that we had a bomb go off at, say, 9.04 am' and then her voice trailed off. My impression is that what subsequently happened was just too similar to their game-simulation, to permit a public airing, of what they had done. Clearly, the entire script for Atlantic Blue needs to be made public.

John Pullin was co-ordinator of the NHS response to a terror assault upon London, on July 7th. 'The thing that concerns me most is multi-sited bombs going off in the same time-zone' he remarked, *three days* prior to July 7th, *The Guardian* reported. He happened to be in the same London Ambulance Service office as Nikki Smith when the above-mentioned interview took place, and I remonstrated with him about this odd coincidence. 'It's not whether it will happen, but when it will happen,' Ms Smith quickly interjected, saving him from an awkward reply. Mr Pullin explained how the journalist had phoned him at 11 am on the morning of July 7th, after he had been whisked off to the strategic Gold-Command police bunker at Hendon, in order to ask him, incredulously, about these words he had uttered in an interview given three days earlier.

On the morning of July 7th, Pullin was driven to this bunker at the Hendon police college, in order to join the 'gold co-ordinating group' overseeing the crisis-management. From there the London hospitals were swiftly placed on high emergency alert. Pullin helped to organize the Atlantic Blue operation. All we are told about this is that at one point he 'killed off a nurse who, in the role-playing, had been poisoned by the chemical gas. Although she was entirely fictitious, I was quite upset by her death.'[8]

References

[1] http://press.homeoffice.gov.uk/press-releases/Atlantic_Blue_-International_Cou? version=1

[2] www.publications.parliament.uk/pa/cm200405/cmhansrd/vo041216/wmstext/ 41216m02.htm (scroll down to bottom).

[3] www.ukresilience.info/preparedness/exercises/nationalcasestudies/atlanticblue.aspx.

[4] TOPOFF 3 FAQs – http://www.dhs.gov/xprepresp/training/editorial_0603.shtm, www.dhs.gov/xprepresp/training/editorial_0603.shtm.

[5] The Observer, Anti-terror drill revealed soft targets in London, 10 July, 2005 http://observer.guardian.co.uk/uk_news/story/0,6903,1525247,00.html.

[6] Voltairenet www.voltairenet.org/article128248.html.

[7] A Review of the Top Officials III Exercise http://www.njcphp.org/pdf/topoff_afteraction_ report.pdf.

[8] *The Guardian,* 13.7.05 'A long journey to safety.'

4b. Statements by Peter Power

1. July 7th, BBC Radio 5 Live's Drivetime programme (about 7.30 pm)

> POWER: ...at half-past nine this morning we were actually running an exercise for, er, over, a company of over a thousand people in London based on *simultaneous bombs going off precisely at the railway stations where it happened this morning, so I still have the hairs on the back of my neck standing upright!*
>
> PETER ALLEN: To get this quite straight, you were running an exercise to see how you would cope with this and it happened while you were running the exercise?
>
> POWER: Precisely, and it was, er, about half-past nine this morning, we planned this for a company and for obvious reasons I don't want to reveal their name but they're listening and they'll know it.[1] And we had a room full of crisis managers for the first time they'd met and so within five minutes we made a pretty rapid decision, 'this is the real one' and so we went through the correct drills of activating crisis management procedures to jump from 'slow time' to 'quick time' thinking and so on.

Concerning his description of the 'simultaneous bombs', a pertinent comment was made by the J7 website: 'Power's fictional scenario, as explained by the man himself on the day, bears a closer resemblance to the eventual story of 7/7 than it does to the actual story that had been presented to the public by the police and authorities at the time of his interview.' His account avers that the Visor operation was *precisely* synchronized ('within five minutes...') with the real events as they began to unfold. We gain an impression of Power's 'insider' status whereby he had information like Halevi later that day of the bombs being simultaneous, not publicly reported for another two days.

2. At 20:20 on the day, ITV News:

> POWER: Today we were running an exercise for a company – bearing in mind I'm now in the private sector – and we sat everybody down, in the city – 1,000 people involved in the whole organisation – but the crisis team. And the most peculiar thing was, we based our scenario on the simultaneous attacks on an underground and mainline station. So we had to suddenly switch an exercise from 'fictional' to 'real'. And one of the first things is, get that bureau number, when you have a list of people missing, tell them. And it took a long time –
>
> INTERVIEWER: Just to get this right, you were actually working *today* on an exercise that envisioned virtually this scenario?
>
> POWER: Er, almost precisely. I was up to 2 o'clock this morning, because it's our job, my own company. Visor Consultants, we specialise in helping people to get their crisis management response. How do you jump from 'slow time' thinking to 'quick time' doing? And we chose a scenario – *with their assistance* – which is based on a terrorist attack because they're very close to, er, a property occupied by Jewish businessmen, they're in the city, and there are more American banks in the city than there are in the whole of New York – a logical thing to do. And it, I've still got the hair....

This brings in the concept of a thousand persons involved, albeit indirectly through their organizations, with the management-level exercise being run by 'Visor Consultants', and emphasizes the involvement in coping with the event in the switch from 'fictional' to 'real.' Jewish businessmen are mentioned. The Visor website emphasizes how the crisis exercises they design aspire to be 'Making the scenario come alive and be as realistic as possible. [2]

3. July 8th interview, p. 5 of the Manchester *Evening News*

> Yesterday *we were actually in the City working on an exercise involving mock broadcasts when it happened for real.* When news bulletins started coming on, people began to say how realistic our exercise was – not realising there was an attack. We then became involved in a real crisis which we had to manage for the company. Mr Power added: "During the exercise we were working on yesterday, we were looking at a situation where there had been bombs at key London Transport locations."

This concerns simulated news broadcasts, as used on the Panorama program 'London Under Attack' (see Chapter 3). It indicates that more than a mere desk exercise was involved, because participants were then obliged in some degree to 'manage' the 'real crisis.' Strangely enough this rather crucial piece of information was only made available in a local Manchester evening paper. Some later statements made by Peter Power sought to give the impression that this was 'merely' a paper exercise or just an office scenario, as if he were in some trouble and seeking to backtrack on this remarks; whereas the above statements should suffice to dispel doubts on this matter.

9/11 investigators have come to understand the mysterious process whereby the various war games and terror-drills metamorphosed into the real thing. More of these were going on during and just before 9/11 than at any other period, and it has been a key achievement of 9/11 investigators to dig these up (see below, Appendix 4d). On July 7th, there seem to have been several others, details of which are hard to come by, notably the London Ambulance Service's simulation of *four terrorist bombs going off at once across London,*" which was ongoing at 9.10 am (Chapter 8, note 7).

To what extent was Power's Visor Consultants drill out there on the street and in the tube, or to what extent was it a desk exercise? No one can presently answer that, but, the laws of probability allow us to be certain that it was causally connected to what happened that day and was not a 'mere' coincidence as Power wishes us to believe.[3] By way of analogy, the event of 9/11 did involve 'blips' appearing on radar screens for the 'wargamed' planes. Were they really there? The magician smiles – that's his secret. He only made it happen; don't expect him to explain it to you. Mike Ruppert's *Crossing the Rubicon* or Webster Tarpley's *9/11 Synthetic Terror* will give you the fullest answer you are likely to find, concerning the extent to which the multiple, ongoing wargames were 'real' on that morning.

A subsequent exercise held in Singapore, quite likely involving Visor Consultants, on January 2006 (Ch. 3), was Exercise Northstar. We get a deal more detail of its running than we ever did concerning the London exercise, showing that its aim is to be as 'actual' as possible. It 'worked' on four train stations but temporarily disrupted as many as 13 train stations. There were quite a few train stations 'temporarily disrupted' that morning with little by way of explanation as to why this should have happened.[4]

As a result of complicated public-private partnerships set up on 2003, Transport for London took over the London Underground, and subcontracted to two main tube companies, Tubelines and Metronet:[5] two artificial companies assembled as consortia of different investors.[6] These had not existed before, but were brought together for this purpose. The national government still owned London Transport, and London's Mayor Ken did not approve of this privatising process. However, he was powerless to stop it. Metronet and Tube Lines began operating in 2003 despite expensive legal challenges (of several million pounds) from Mayor Ken. The deal with these two 'consortia' companies was blueprinted for thirty years; however Metronet has now gone broke. These two companies then sub-*sub*contracted security and surveillance matters to Verint Systems, ICTS, Fortress UK and Huntleigh. These deals received no public scrutiny and indeed the awarding of their contracts was only announced in the Israeli press.

Continuing in our vein of conjecture, one could say that one of these, or possibly several, had employed Visor Consultants to go over the 'terror drill' that day, because of Peter Power's high status in Scotland Yard. He was the ideal intermediary. We may suppose that Power did not know what was going to happen, and was genuinely shocked as the synchrony between real and drill events unfolded. His sense of survival prompted him to contact Newsnight, etc. and make a public statement, which he was under no obligation to do. 'I still have the hairs on the back of my head standing up...' That was genuine shock, experienced by the maestro of terror drills. He made those public statements in order to clear himself from being approached later on and grilled with rather peculiar and hard-to-answer questions. There were things that he really did not need to know, about his clients – but, what he did need right away was an exit strategy. Those public statements were that. Later on he tried to tone down their significance *as if* the whole thing had been merely a desk exercise. PPP, the private-public partnership, has meant that nobody quite knew who was in control over the key 2005 period when Londoners were attacked.

Peter Power was taunted for refusing to divulge the name of the company he was working for that morning, and finally in September 2008 he told a forthcoming BBC 'Conspiracy files' program, on the subject of the London bombings, that its name was Reed Elsevier. This company ran the yearly ExCel Arms Fair until 2007, and why they would have wanted to run such a terror-drill remained unclear. As well as the three tube bombs, he said, his terror-drill had had a fourth one factored in as an above ground explosion, not far from the head office of the *Jewish Chronicle* magazine. That is in Holborn, not far from where the actual bomb exploded. That program was postponed, on the grounds that it would prejudice the forthcoming 'July 7th' re-trial, and instead Power announced the fact on 'Mike Rudin's blog.'

4c. Terror Drills on the Tube

For the three years leading up to 7/7, London Transport held yearly 'terror drills,' on a Sunday in order to minimize disruption:

* <u>Sunday, 7th September, 2003, at Bank Station:</u> 'Osiris II' This live exercise at Bank was designed to allow London's emergency services and health services to practice their revised response to a chemical attack on London Underground in a realistic environment. 'The exercise began shortly before midday, when the train driver reported the attack and stopped it in a tunnel 50 yards short of Bank station. About 500 firefighters, paramedics and transport workers then worked to recover and treat the 60 'casualties' on board, bringing them to street level to decontaminate them in special shower tents' ('London Undergoes Terror Test' BBC News 24). http://news.bbc.co.uk/1/hi/england/london/3086116.stm

* <u>Lambeth on Sunday, 17 Sept, 2004:</u> 'Details of the mock emergency, held at Lambeth North station in south London, were kept secret so staff will face as realistic a test as possible. Penny Hazell, general manager of the Bakerloo line, said: "With a real incident, there would be no advance warning. That is why details are not revealed, enabling London Underground and the emergency services to treat the exercise as if it were actually happening.' (http://news.bbc.co.uk/1/hi/ england/london/3745776.stm Tube suspended for emergency test)

<u>Tower Hill Sunday, 12th June, 2005:</u> Live emergency exercise at Tower Hill: 'Each year London Underground is legally required to hold an emergency exercise on the network. A different line takes turns in hosting the event.' Roland Murphy, Exercise Director, London Underground said: 'The live exercises are made as authentic as possible.' All participants including all the emergency services are unaware of the 'disaster' until the exercise starts, so that they treat it as real as possible.

No press releases for subsequent exercises have been released, nor any stations designated, however I was advised by Metronet that one had taken place at a 'station in central London' in '2006/7,' though no station had been closed to the public in order to hold it –which does not make a great deal of sense.

4d. The War Games of 9/11, a Comparison

On the day of September 11th, the scheduled war-games became hard to distinguish from the real thing, as the calamity unfolded. Here are some excerpts:

1. Federal Aviation Authority call to the North-East Air Defence sector, around 9 o'clock on the morning of September 11th:

> FAA: Hi. Boston Centre TMU [Traffic management Unit], we have a problem here. We have a hijacked aircraft headed towards New York, and we need you guys to, we need someone to scramble some F-16s or something up there, help us out.

> NEADS: [Staff Sergeant Jeremy Powell, Air national Guard] Is this real-world or exercise?

> FAA: No, this is not an exercise, not a test. (9/11 Kean Commission Report, p.20)

2. At 8.40, Deskins noticed senior technician Jeremy Powell waving his hand. Boston Centre was on the line, he said. It had a hijacked airplane. "It must be part of the exercise" Deskins thought. At first, everybody did. Then Deskins saw the glowing direct phone line to the Federal Aviation Administration. On the phone he heard the voice of a military liaison for the FAA's Boston Centre. "I have a hijacked," he told her.

Three minutes later, the drill was still a factor of confusion for Lt Deskins in the form of a simulated hijacked plane heading for JFK Airport in New York City: Deskins ran to a nearby office and phoned 1st Air Force Chief Public Affairs Officer Major Don Arias in Florida. She said NEADS had a hijacked plane – no, not the simulation likely heading for JFK. "The entire floor sensed something wrong," Chief of Operations control Lt. Col. Ian Sanderson said. "The way this unfolded, everybody had a gut sense this wasn't right."[7]

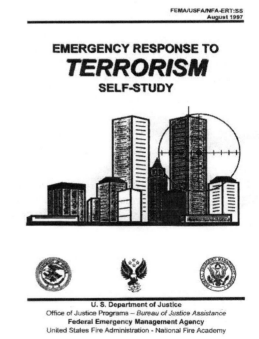

FEMA/USFA/NFA-ERT:SS
August 1997

EMERGENCY RESPONSE TO
TERRORISM
SELF-STUDY

U. S. Department of Justice
Office of Justice Programs – *Bureau of Justice Assistance*
Federal Emergency Management Agency
United States Fire Administration - National Fire Academy

3. Homeland Security conference announcement: "Agency planned exercise on September 11 built around a plane crashing into a building" was the shock announcement of an Associated Press story, in September 2002. An announcement for an upcoming Homeland Security conference in Chicago noted this exercise: in a promotion for its speaker John Fulton, a CIA officer assigned as chief of NRO's (the top-secret National Reconaissance Office) strategic gaming division, the announcement says, "On the morning of September 11th 2001, Mr Fulton and his team... were running a pre-planned

simulation to explore the emergency response issues that would be created if a plane were to strike a building. Little did they know that the scenario would come true in a dramatic way that day."[8]

4. The big FEMA vans were proud of how soon they turned up to help cope with the ruined Towers in New York on that historic morning. In fact, they turned up the previous night! Tom Kenney, spokesperson of the Federal Emergency Management Agency (FEMA) told journalist Dan Rather that his agency had been deployed in New York on Monday night, September 10, because of the drills of September 12."We're one of the first teams deployed to assist the city of New York in that disaster. We arrived in late on Monday night and we're in action on Tuesday morning." The terror-drill here involved a mock biochemical attack upon New York scheduled for 12th September.[9]

References

[1] www.visorconsultants.com/crisismanagementexercises.htm.

[2] www.julyseventh.co.uk/july-7-terror-rehearsal.html#mockbroadcasts.

[3] Chapter 7, 'Improbable Events.'

[4] Eg, Appendix 6a, 'Northern line closures.'

[5] Bollyn suggested that the company Power's firm was working for was 'Tubelines,' which operates emergency responses for the whole underground. See Appendix 6b, http://americanlibation.blogspot.com.

[6] See Ch. 3, Fn 3, also Appendix 6b.

[7] Amid crisis simulation, 'We were suddenly No-Kidding Under Attack', Newshouse News service Jan 25 2002; Tarpley 209.

[8] Mike Ruppert, *Crossing the Rubicon*, 2004, p.341.

[9] http://www.voltairenet.org/article128248.html, Simulation exercises that make attacks easier by T Meyssan.

Cover image: A FEMA 1997 document, showing the targeting of Twin Towers in a terror drill – just where the plane struck.

Appendix 5: Three Lads and a Double Agent

Letters from Mahmood Hussain, excerpts

(To the author)

3.9.05

I have received your letter today. I am very grateful for your effort to find the real truth. I do not believe that my son is responsible for this. At this time, my family life has been destroyed and one day people who are responsible for this destruction, will be standing in front of our Creator and there will be no excuse then ....

10.10.05

I or my family have no idea at all when Hasib Hussain left Leeds on 7/7/05 or night/day before. All I know is that he was seen by my family member on 6/7/05 at about 3.25 pm at home. We do not know about others...

13.2.06

Hasib was waiting to hear about his university admission. He wanted to do 3 years business advance course. He said he had applied through his college and any university will take him because his marks and achievement will be very high. He was very keen and interested to go to University. As I know he has achieved his marks and level. So any University in the U.K. will welcome him.

Yes. He was taking driving lessons from me just to learn basic things of driving. He was learning fast. About buying a car, I do not know. He was interested in cars. As I told Hasib you must have a car in this country to do any type of business. He was aware of value of his own transport and that is why he started learning.

Yes he liked the buildings of London e.g. London Eye. He used to talk to his sisters about this! Or with my grandchildren. He only told us that he is going to London with his friends.

We have no idea when they hired a car. I do not know the type of car or anything else about this matter.

No contact with other families.

Hasib never had more monies than usual. He only had his pocket money and bus fare etc. He was very wise about his money. No, he never even had extra money. He used to save some pocket money and some money from his mother just to buy clothes. That's all.

Thank you again for your letter. I hope we all will learn the truth and may get some answers. I can only hope and be patient. [Asks for Dr Naseem's phone no.]

Mahmoud's View, expressed via Imram:

From a telephone conversation that James Stewart had with Imram Hussain (brother of Hasib) N.B., James Stewart in Blackpool investigated the Luton train-times together with the present author.

* The three from Leeds did not know the Aylesbury fellow at all.

* The families of the three from Leeds had been told their lads were going up to London on Wednesday, sightseeing, so would return Thursday morning. They did not see the lads on Wednesday afternoon-evening.

* The car would have been hired Tuesday evening, to be returned on Thursday. The car-hire shop would have this info.

* Mahmoud Hussain and his son Imran: the families initially believed the police's story, but none of them do now.

* Imran: Khan looked 'stockier' in the (September) video, was obviously reading from a card by the camera, and the film had been spliced at 2 or 3 places. His voice didn't sound quite right, and was out of synch between sound and visuals.

An anniversary view: on the first anniversary of the bombings, Mahmoud Hussain was accosted on his doorstep with accusations about his son, in which spontaneous encounter he was quoted as saying: 'I don't believe Hasib did it. No one has shown me any evidence that he did it. I haven't seen nothing, no DNA, no evidence. When there is crime, you have to have evidence. There should be a public inquiry, then everyone can come and give evidence, everyone can say what they know. They could do this if there was a public inquiry.'[1]

Shehzad Tanweer, 1983-2005

The 22-year old cricket-fanatic Shehzad Tanweer had recently returned from Lahore. He was 'a God-fearing man with no interest in politics or religious fanaticism,' his uncle Bashir Ahmed stated on July 10th, and denied that his nephew had visited an extremist training camp. Shehzad was 'proud to be British' he explained, adding that: 'We simply cannot believe that he was capable of a thing like this.' Guardian, July 13th:

> "He is sound as a pound," said Azi Mohammed, a close friend. The idea that he was involved in terrorism or extremism is ridiculous. The idea that he went down to London and exploded a bomb is unbelievable. I only played cricket in the park with him around 10 days ago. He is not interested in politics." He was a sports science graduate from the University of Leeds, and hoped to play in the county cricket team. His friend Azi commented, "Shahzad went to a few mosques around here but he was more interested in his jujitsu. I trained with him all the time, he is really fit," adding "He has a great sense of humour, he is a really intelligent lad and he has loads of friends round here." A friend who did not wish to be named commented that Hasib and Shahzad were very good friends: "Shahzad was always telling kids to stay out of trouble and make something of their lives." (*The Guardian* 13 July 2005, 'From cricket-lover who enjoyed a laugh to terror suspect')

A teacher at Tanweer's school, Wortley High, commented in a reference on his 'commendable perseverance", his ability to "combat most problems", his "quick grasp of new ideas", his "natural ability" and his "quiet efficiency". On his university application form Tanweer wrote, "I am a hard working young man with a friendly personality. My main hobbies apart from sports are socialising with my friends," he wrote. "I realise that self-discipline and hard work are required to succeed. However I am more determined than ever to work at my studies and I know that I can make a contribution to university life." He mentioned winning a local sports personality of the year award, a first place in the Leeds athletic championships, (New Statesman, 2 July 2006, 'The suicide bomber in his own words') His best friend Mohammed Answar said, on hearing the news, "'It's impossible. It's not in his nature to do something like this. He's the type of guy who would condemn things like that." (13 July 2005 The Guardian)

One old friend, Shafquat Hussain, his batting partner, shared this view: describing a cricket game they were playing for their team, Shaan B, eight days before the London bombings, he recalled: "We were all just having a laugh and joking," he says incredulously. "He just said the usual things, 'good catch', that kind of thing. He was a wonderful, relaxed bloke. That's why we are all in shock. If he was a radical then he hid it from us. He would listen to everyone's point of view." (The Telegraph, 17 July 2005, 'The Path to Mass Murder')

The Tanweers' neighbour told how the man dressed in a Western way, often in designer tracksuits and trainers. "He didn't have a beard; he wore sports tops, tracksuit bottoms and trainers -like anybody else really." (14 July Independent 'Shahzad Tanweer: 'I cannot begin to explain this. He was proud to be British') Shehzad Tanweer rarely missed a Wednesday night match at the local park. "Every time I saw him, he seemed like he was enjoying life," said Tony Miller, a fellow cricket devotee from Beeston. (Washington Post July 15, 2005, 'Trail From London to Leeds Yields Portraits of 3 Bombers') This testimony was echoed by his neighbour Chris Witley, who lived across the street from the Tanweer family: "He was my best mate growing up. He couldn't go a day without playing cricket." (The Washington Post, 29 July 2005, 'Friends Describe Bomber's Political, Religious Evolution')

His friends remembered Tanweer for a remarkable virtue: "Nothing could anger him. I cannot recall the last time I heard him even raise his voice," recalled Shehzad's cousin, Safina Ahmad (The Guardian, 18 July 2005, 'The loving boy and Murderous Terrorist') Unlike Khan, Tanweer was deeply religious: "Not Mumtaz. Not his family.... it couldn't be. It's inconceivable that Mumtaz or any of his family could be involved. I've known Kaki [Shehzad] since he was two. He was always praying. He'd even get up at 4am to pray. He's a very religious lad, but a lot of his friends are white. He never put a white man down. He called me his uncle Neil. I can't believe he could be a religious fanatic. He was a good cricketer and was always watching sport on TV when he wasn't helping out at the fish and chip shop," recalled the long-time family friend Neil Kay. (Mirror, 'The Suicide Murderers', 13.7.05)

Shafquat Hussain, his batting partner, shares this view. Describing a cricket game they were playing for their team, Shaan B, eight days before the London bombings, he recalled: "We were all just having a laugh and joking," he says incredulously. "He just said the usual things, 'good catch', that kind of thing. He was a wonderful, relaxed bloke. That's why we are all in shock. If he was a radical then he hid it from us. He would listen to everyone's point of view." The Tanweers' neighbour told how the man dressed in a Western way, often in designer tracksuits and trainers. "He didn't have a beard; he wore sports tops, tracksuit bottoms and trainers -like anybody else really." (14 July, *The Independent*)

We should extend our commiserations to Shehzad's father, Mohammed Mumtaz, owner of the fish and chip shop 'South Leeds Fisheries' at Tempest road, Beeston (who has developed a heart condition after this event), to his Mother Parveen who sewed clothes – on the 14th July it was reported that she had been 'crying uncontrollably' since the news – to his sister Tabasum who managed a shoe shop, and to his younger brother Rizwan and sister Tiliat, both at university. (*The Telegraph*, July 11th)

In January 2006 the papers reported that Tanweer's 'estate' had been valued at £121,000. One could do with details of where this fabulous sum was supposed to have appeared from, for a student working part-time in a fish and chip shop who died intestate. One conjecture here is that it was the life-savings of his father, shunted into his son's account as a tax-dodge or whatever.[2] It was about this time that his father sold the South Leeds Fisheries shop – a fish and chip shop still exists there, but under a different name and owner. This may have been the proceeds of that sale.

Germaine Lindsay (1985-2005)

He was the last of the 'bombers' to be identified. On Saturday, July 16th, his wife Samantha Lewthwaite put out a statement conveying her horror at the attacks, sending condolences to the bereaved families, and remembering how 'Jamal' aged 19 had had:

'a kind, caring and calming presence about him'.

(BBC, 8 pm) A further statement by her the next day spoke of her horror, and that 'I am the wife of Germaine Lindsay, and never predicted or imagined that he was involved in such horrific activities.'

On that same day, July 16th, the front page of *The Sun* (previous page) had her expressing defiance, and insisting: 'They'll have to prove to me he did it.' Ms Lewthwaite refused to accept that Lindsay was one of the London bombers, responsible for 26 deaths. She sobbed: "He wasn't the sort of person who'd do this. I won't believe it until I see proof... Jamal (her name for him) wouldn't leave me alone to bring up his child. I want to see DNA proof." At just 22 years of age, Samantha had a 15-month-old son Abdullah Ibn-Jamal, as well as being eight months pregnant with a second child. She and Jamaican-born Jamal lived in Aylesbury, Bucks. Despite doing well in his GCSEs

Jamal dropped out of school at 16. He later worked as a carpet-fitter for a few months. For a while, he and Samantha lived in a terraced house opposite a mosque in Huddersfield. One worshipper said: "He was devout but didn't give any sign of extremist views. We just can't believe he was a suicide bomber."

The police took her away to an unknown location and sedated her. When she reappeared *two months later*, the story had changed. (Sept 23rd, *The Times*) She now claimed that, *on the 13th*, she had phoned the helpline to say her husband was missing, and soon afterwards police officers arrived and she was taken for questioning while their house was searched. She said: "The next day they showed me Jamal on CCTV and said his DNA proved he was one of the bombers. My world collapsed…"[2]

Let's recall that on the 14th July, the Met was just claiming to have identified Jamal's remains: 'We now believe that we know the identity of the fourth man who arrived in the group at King's Cross. We have just received forensic evidence which makes it very likely that he died in the explosion at Russell Square. Formal identification is of course a matter for the Coroner.'[3] Then on the 15th, Sky News announced that the police had identified the fourth bomber as Lindsay.

The doubtful picture of the four at Luton was only released on the 17th, and surely no one would claim that that was proof of Lindsay's presence? That was in Luton, not London. What had persuaded his pregnant widow?

His grieving mother, Maryam Ismaiyl, in Jamaica, said, "I can't believe it … I have so many questions, and I do not know if I will ever receive the answers. Jamal, as he would love to be called, was the best son I could have ever hoped for," she told reporters in the capital of the Caribbean island, where she was staying for the summer with her husband's family. "I am still in shock and know not how to grieve for my son. Therefore, I grieve first for the victims." (*Boston Globe* July 22nd)

By the age of 17, Lindsay had developed a markedly more serious attitude towards life; friends commented how he stopped chasing girls and play-fighting in the halls of Rawthorpe High School and turned his attention to academics and athletics, where by all accounts he shone. He broke records in track and scored some of the highest marks in the school on exams. Other youngsters would write a few paragraphs for a history essay, but he would lay out his argument all afternoon, in page after page after page, recalled Chris John, 17, a high school classmate and neighborhood friend from Lindsay's youth. He would tend to give credit to the Deity when making his comments. He had moved up to Bradford, where he became a regular at the Hamara Youth Centre in Leeds, then moved down to Aylesbury in 2005.

His friend Maz Milenovic had known him for seven years, and recalled: 'The last time I spoke to him was only last month. He seemed happy and just the same old Germaine I had always known… I was planning on going to visit him and see his baby. I still can't believe it is him.' Had Lindsay been somehow brainwashed? To this question, Maz replied: 'I find that hard to believe because he was so strong-minded.'[5]

MI-6 Double Agent from Dewsbury, Leeds

From time to time the press alleges that some 'mastermind' of the July 7th events has been identified, and the unlikely character Haroon Rashid Aswat tends to crop up here. A British citizen, he comes from the same town in West Yorkshire, Dewsbury in which two of the alleged bombers lived (Hasib Hussain and Tanweer lived in Beeston, in the Leeds inner-city area, and about twelve miles away 'Sid' Khan lived in Dewsbury, where Jamal had also gone to school). Fox News presented Aswat as the "mastermind" and also points to Aswat's relationship to British and US intelligence, through a British based Islamic organization Al-Muhajiroun. In an interview with Fox News on 29 July 2005, intelligence expert John Loftus revealed that Haroon Rashid Aswat had connections to the British Secret Service MI-6:

> "the entire British police are out chasing him, and one wing of the British government, MI-6 or the British Secret Service, has been hiding him... Absolutely. Now we knew about this guy Aswat. Back in 1999 he came to America. The Justice Department wanted to indict him in Seattle because him and his buddy were trying to set up a terrorist training school in Oregon.
>
> JERRICK: So they indicted his buddy, right? But why didn't they indict him?
>
> LOFTUS: Well it comes out, we've just learned that the headquarters of the US Justice Department ordered the Seattle prosecutors not to touch Aswat.
>
> JERRICK: Hello? Now hold on, why?
>
> LOFTUS: Well, apparently Aswat was working for British intelligence... Pakistanis arrest him. They jail him. He's released within 24 hours. Back to Southern Africa, goes to Zimbabwe and is arrested in Zambia. Now the US--... [6]

A *New York Times* report of July 31 stated, citing as its source a British security official, that investigators had decided, "For now, this man [Aswat] or any role he may have does not figure, to any degree of importance, in our inquiry," adding that, initial reports that Aswat had made 20 calls to the suicide bombers in Britain were not true. "Investigators also found that calls had been made from his cell phone to West Yorkshire, where three of the July 7 bombers lived. But investigators said they now had determined that no calls were to the bombers," the article states.

Many of the allegations from the 'Crevice' trial (Chapter 11 & Appendix 10b) alleging connections with Khan and Tanweer, revolve around this shadowy figure. All of these allegations seem to derive from documents appearing after July 7th (while the Crevice trial started in 2004), i.e. there existed no testimony on record, dateable prior to July 7th 2005, indicating some connection of the lads from Leeds with the Crevice alleged plot. It is unlikely that Tanweer and Khan knew anything about the 'Crevice plot, which probably never even existed. The Holborn-based lawyer Imran Khan spoke out in protest against the frame-up of Muslims here involved.

For an intelligence character who may have played a rather key role one could turn to a Mr Martin McDaid, an ex-SBS (Special Boat Service) who 'converted' to Islam, becoming Martin Abdulla McDaid, and who ran the Iqra bookshop in Beeston from

2000 onwards. Thus an ex-anti-terror agent had a co-ordinating role in the charity-bookshop where Siddique Khan worked.

References

[1] *The Mirror,* 'Your Son killed my girlfriend' and *The Independent* 'Father of the bus bomber reveals his anguish' both covered this story on 6 July, 2006. The latter alluded to the 'extraordinary half-hour conversation' on Hussain's doorstep, but neglected to give its readers the above quotation, and explained that Mr Hussain was 'in a state of profound denial.'

[2] This came from Arshad Patel's wife, Kadija.

[3] *The Times* 23.9.05 'Bomber's widow says extremists twisted his mind' http://www.timesonline.co.uk/article/0,,22989-1793594,00.html. Rai's *7/7 The London bombings* has this change of heart happen 'after seeing the CCTV footage of her husband in King's Cross station' (p39), but it is doubtful whether he has any evidence for that statement.

[4] On the afternoon of the 14th, the Met DAC Peter Clarke stated this: http://cms.met.police.uk/met/layout/set/print/content/view/full/1320.

[5] *Huddersfield Daily Examiner,* 'Friends of Germaine Linday remember him as normal caring person', 18.7.05.

[6] Michel Chossudovsky, 'London 7/7 Terror Suspect Linked to British Intelligence?' *Global Research*, August 1, 2005 www.globalresearch.ca/index.php?context=va& aid=782 . Hear this interview live at http://infowars.net/Pages/Aug05/020805Aswat. html 'Terror Expert: 7/7 Mastermind was working for British Intelligence'

Appendix 6: Line Closures.

Northern line Incidents on the Morning of July 7th

At 07.10 am on the Northern line that morning, a tube train halted in a tunnel for 15 minutes between Tooting Bec and Balham, and passengers finally had to disembark at Balham, exiting via the driver's carriage in front. They saw many firemen on the platform, scrutinising the bottom of another train which was already in the station. Here is the official log for the incident:

Northern line log for Balham incident:

06.25 Balham – train became defective in service

06.30 T/Op confirms that the axle is glowing.

06.50 NA100 introduced with Station Supervisor made Silver Control.

08.54 Traction current switched on South Wimbledon to Balham northbound, Balham to Clapham Common northbound

09.00 A special train service was in operation due to the defective train at Balham. Seven stations were closed due to loss of power supply

09.05 Northbound service restored. 160 minute delay

Here is an anonymous web-testimony of this closure:

I was due to pick a work colleague up from Balham at 7:15am, but when I got there I was greeted with Tube emergency vans, police and hoards of people being turned away from a closed station. All very strange they must have known something was going to happen, they surely had a tip off. As I drove along the road, (which also follows the tubes) they were all shut and hundreds of people were queuing for buses. When I reached Oval, which was open there were two armed policemen in a road next to the station, which for a quiet area like that is extremely rare. The northern line was shut from Morden to Stockwell.

'Kirsty K.' recalled on the web: 'I got to Clapham North tube (on the Northern line) and the whole line was down – at 8:15am! Usually there are problems with this line, but in my 4 years in London I cannot last remember when the entire line was shut down.' Numerous Northern line stations closed down due to loss of power supply at 08.51 when the bombs went off, including: Angel, Kentish Town, Bank, Kings Cross, Camden Town and Old Street stations, and the City branch was suspended due to these closures. Earlier, at 07.05, Bank station had closed for 22 minutes due to security alert.

At Euston Station, David Gibbs, who just moved to London from the West Country, said:

At first we all thought it was just a routine fire drill when they told us to evacuate the Underground (Euston) and there were the usual grumbles of irritation. But then when the announcer told us to leave the main station, his voice sounded much tenser and there was a definite sense all was not alright. "Just as I got outside there was a thudding explosion from somewhere nearby, which sent my heart rate soaring. Minutes later the streets were in chaos. People were going in all directions. Some people were in tears but there was no panic, just general bewilderment.

This indicates an evacuation taking place before the bomb went off at or near King's Cross.

Piccadilly line closures

Were eight stations closed on the Piccadilly line between 08.00–08.30, from Arnos Grove to Caledonian Road, or not? Rachel North in her book describes how she waited at Finsbury park station, when 'it had gone half past eight' and the tannoy announced that 'Fire at Caledonian road' was causing delays. Two trains passed by, but they were just too crowded for her to get on. They were crowded *as a consequence* of the delays further up the line. More and more people got on at each stop until she decided 'This is the most crowded train I have ever been on.' By the time it got to King's Cross, the crowds were six or seven persons deep, indeed one marvels at the perseverance of the alleged suicide bomber wearing a large backpack in being able to force his way onto such a crowded train.

By way of confirming Rachel's testimony, let us quote from the official log of the Piccadilly line, re the fire alert:

> At 07.54hrs, E270 was delayed at Caledonian Road when a passenger alarm was operated [NB, E270 means that this was an Eastbound train, i.e travelling away from King's Cross up towards Cockfosters]. On investigation, the train operator found that there was an unusual smell in the 4th car of the train. Train services were suspended between Kings Cross and Arnos Grove. The Kings Cross Train Maintainer, ERU staff and LFB personnel attended. The traction motors and brakes were isolated and the train was worked empty to Cockfosters depot for further investigation. Initial indications are that brakes were hanging on in car 4. A 32 minute delay was booked. The train service was severely delayed as a result of the incident, particularly westbound from Arnos Grove with headways up to 12 minutes between trains.

This makes it sound as if Piccadilly line trains were still travelling towards King's Cross, albeit somewhat delayed and slowed down. It is not easy to reconcile this with buses carrying the tube passengers owing to line closure, notices up announcing line closure, and fire engines turning up at Caledonian road. Bus driver Paul Brandon recalled how buses were instructed to honour train tickets after the closure of this line. In rush hour, it takes 27 minutes for a train from Arnos Grove to reach the explosion-point between King's Cross and Russell Square, and the train in question left King's Cross at 08.48. If there had been a fire alert, over nine adjacent stations on one line, one would rather expect passengers to be upstairs outside the tube and not allowed downstairs on the platform.

Mr Spellman told me that he and others got onto a train at Arnos Grove at 08.10 and sat waiting for ten minutes, then were all told to move across the platform and get into another train, which then departed at 08.20. He confirmed Rachel's story of how extremely crowded it became. Both these trains had come from the Cockfosters depot.

Here is the testimony of 'Joe Orr':

8.15 am: Tube arrives. Arnos Grove is one of the first stops on the Piccadilly so I always get a seat.

8.22 am: End up waiting for several minutes at each Tube stop as there has been a fire alert at Caledonian Road. Our train is packed because of the delays holding people up.

8.50 am: Finally get into King's Cross where the platform is heaving. Only a few more people can fit into our carriage.

Again, this does not indicate any closure of the line.

A suspicious commuter, Edward Cowling, comments: 'I arrived at Wood Green station at 8:30 to discover it was locked and a notice saying the service was suspended between Arnos Grove and Kings Cross. Yet the Piccadilly line bomb was at 08:50?! I received a text alert from TfL at 08:25 announcing services were badly disrupted due to a train failure at Caledonian Road. If they had suspected that was the case I'm pretty sure they would have suspended the whole service.' (web link inserted in 1st edition no longer working)

Compare a delay on the Bakerloo line, also reported before the explosions:

> Bakerloo line – suspended between Paddington and Elephant and Castle in both directions from 08:07 due to a defective train in Piccadilly Circus northbound platform. Services resumed with severe delays. www.julyseventh.co.uk/7-7-kings-cross-russell-square.html

(The Bakerloo line crosses over the Piccadilly line at Piccadilly Circus)

Tube Lines: 'New Civil Engineer' Report

From an interview with Stephen Peat, Tubeline Director of Operations, in *the New civil Engineer*: 'Tubelines and Metronet are the Underground's maintenance and upgrade contractors[1], but unlike Metronet, Tube Lines operates the emergency response teams for the whole underground network. As such its staff were responsible for everything from assessing damage to evacuating those caught up in the blasts. Tube Lines repaired the damage, to track components plus cables carrying signalling information, communications and power. Parts of the track were replaced and extensive repairs carried out to cables and signals. Tube Lines is also responsible for providing a range of services to London Underground and Metronet across the entire network, including the Emergency Response Unit. The latter ensures that the network is kept safe and that services are restored as quickly as possible after emergencies.[2]

'At Russell Square our engineers went in to check the tunnel before any of the police forensic teams could start. The police couldn't and wouldn't put any of their people inside until we had checked that it was safe,' said Peat.[3] He is here claiming that Tube Lines told the police when they could enter and check the site. 'Tube Lines established a rebuild and recovery team at its headquarters at Canary Wharf. After 26th July: 'We had three people looking to see if anything had moved or cracked and were checking the torque on all the bolts,' says Peat. 'Next we got the track boys in and they replaced about 30ft of damaged track. The signal team also came in to repair the broken cables, several hundred metres worth. We also had to repair a 22,000V power cable and both the phone and radio systems were wrecked.' The police found that of the wrecked

Piccadilly line train's 6 carriages, 'Four were unaffected by the blast, and could be towed out as soon as the police had inspected them using a battery powered train.'[4]

Metronet manages the District and Circle and Metropolitan lines, Tube Lines manages the Northern and Piccadilly lines.

Bechtel Corporation runs Tube Lines, along with two other private companies. Bechtel's Jim Haynes is its Director of Projects. Bechtel has established a reputation around the world for being rather ruthless, wolf-like and involved in military enterprises. A report, 'Bechtel: Profiting from Destruction' by TruthOut stated: "Bechtel has demonstrated brazen moral corruption by first contributing to the development of Iraq's weapons, then pushing for a war against Iraq, and finally profiting from the tragedy and destruction wrought by that war." Andrea Buffa, peace campaign coordinator at Global Exchange (San Francisco): 'It is a textbook example of what war profiteering looks like.' However, Tube Lines has survived, whereas Metronet is (to-date) in receivership.

References:

[1] See Ch.3, Note 6.

[2] *New Civil Engineer*, 28.8.05, 'Righting the Damage' by B.Redfern.

[3] This somewhat contradicts PC Aaron Debnam's account *One Morning in July* whereby he arrived at 10 am and commenced rescue work on the front Piccadilly-line carriage.

[4] http://www.tubelines.com/news/releases/200602/20050803.aspx 3.8.05, 'Back in business – Tube Lines completes repairs on Piccadilly line after bomb.'

Appendix 7: Fake Terror in Birmingham

On Saturday, July 9th, 2005, the whole of central Birmingham was evacuated, with thousands having to sleep on park benches etc, due to a 'credible and specific threat,' according to Chief Superintendent Peter Goodman. Helicopters circled, ambulances lined the streets, police flooded the centre, and roadblocks were athwart every road from the centre. Some 80,000 people were evacuated from the town centre (*The Telegraph*, 10th July). West Midlands Police threw an exclusion cordon around the A38 inner-city ring road, blocking off the city's Broad Street entertainment district and the city's Chinese quarter, an area full of pubs, theatres, restaurants, flats and hotels. Four 'controlled explosions' were carried out on a bus on Corporation Street, but then officers said the item destroyed (whatever it was) had not posed a threat. Birmingham city centre was thus transformed into a ghost town, as a major security alert forced its Saturday night revellers to the outskirts (BBC News, Sunday, 10th July).

Birmingham city centre had faced "a real and very credible threat," West Midlands Chief Constable Paul Scott Lee said. But, what was it? Emergency accommodation was provided by Aston University, with blankets and pillows, but most citizens were too nervous to sleep, as they were joined by hundreds more residents, hotel guests and hospitality workers flooding onto the streets, heading out of the city. The next day the police are performing 'controlled explosions' here and there, but one can't avoid the sense of anticlimax. A firework is found in the Premier Travel Inn; that was about all. But … the story you didn't hear was only told in Urdu, in the *Daily Jang* (Britain's Pakistani newspaper) of the 12th.

In January of 2005, an Irishman and a Spaniard booked into the Waqar Hotel in Birmingham, to rent a twin room. The Spaniard informed the hotel proprietor that he was working for a US company located in Spain, and that it would be sending him rent cheques on a bimonthly basis. Over the following six months the room was rented, and three of the cheques duly arrived; however, the proprietor Mr Barki noticed that the two tenants were never there. Then, on 9th July, they suddenly turned up and took away nine heavy bags, which they would not allow anyone else to carry.

Here we note that Tuesday, 12th July, was the date when police claimed to have found a bath full of 'several kilos' of explosives in a Leeds house, owned by Mahmood el-Nashar (who had recently completed his PhD at Leeds biochemistry Department), a tenuous link thereby being made to the 'Leeds bombers.' The day before, on the 11th of July, central Birmingham (the Broad Street area) was sealed off by the police due to a 'credible' terror alert – and some 'controlled explosions' were set off by the police.

At last, on 11th July, the hotel proprietor decided to take a look inside the room. In it he found:

* two black bags containing a large amount of British currency;

* a 'Bin Laden' tape;

* 'Al Qaeda' manuals on "How to make bombs" and " How to blow up an air-liner";

* a knife with bloodstains on it, in one of the bags.

The proprietor called the police, and two or three local uniformed officers soon arrived. When they saw the room and its contents, they became excited and called colleagues, saying "We've found a Bin Laden cell here!" Mr Barki also called his good friend Mr Appas Malik, reporter of the local *Daily Jang,* a Pakistani newspaper, and told him his extraordinary news.

A short while later, non-uniformed officers (who did not identify themselves) arrived on the scene. They rebuked the others for having phoned their colleagues, and turned them out of the hotel. Having inspected the room, they then went down into the hotel-lobby, evicted everyone from the hotel, including the staff and the manager, and confiscated the film from the CCTV cameras. They then asked the hotel proprietor to sign a blank sheet of paper. He strongly objected to doing any such thing, but eventually he complied. They instructed him not to talk to anyone outside, from then on.

The story was reported in the *Daily Jang,* as well as being aired on the British Pakistani TV channel 'GEO' (which has the same proprietership as the Jang). On that same day, the 17th, Mr Malik told the story to Dr Naseem, the sage Chair of the Birmingham Mosque.[1] Dr Naseem then endeavoured to obtain confirmation of this story from the hotel owner – who, initially, would not speak. The Deputy Chief constable of Birmingham was visiting the Mosque, and, in response to Dr Naseem's queries about this incident, he declared that he had never heard about it – however, he assured Dr Naseem that the Area Superintendent of the Birmingham police would call him to clarify the matter: this never happened. Dr Naseem had a forthcoming appointment to visit the Chief Constable of Birmingham, by way of liasing and maintaining community relations: so, worried about the safety of the hotel owner, Dr Naseem questioned him about the incident – and gained the impression that he genuinely didn't know anything at all about it.

Four weeks after the event, the hotel proprietor Mr Barki was finally prepared talk to Dr Naseem about it. The story then told was identical to that which Dr Naseem had heard earlier from his journalist friend. Dr Naseem related it to a group of us members of the London 9/11 Sceptics movement, two of whom went up to this hotel and stayed the night there (this writer and 'Dr Jazz'). Mr Barki's hotel business has slumped since the incident, even though officially nothing has happened, being totally unreported in the local or national press (except for the *Daily Jang*). The Birmingham town Council had helped supply the hotel with lodgers, but this seems to have dried up. Left unresolved is the question of the tracking down of the two persons who rented the room, which would surely have been quite easy: no one seems inclined to do this.

We may count up to seven phantom terror events, and they were *centered* upon the date of July 7th. These took the form of bomb scares accompanied by city-centre evacuations, where no cause for fear existed, as far as could be ascertained. They happened over the nine days, 3rd – 12th July: Cardiff on the 3rd; in Sheffield, Nottingham and Auchterarder on the 5th; then Birmingham on 9th-10th; Sheffield on the 11th; and Leeds on the 12th (see Ch. 3, last section, and Ch. 8, 2nd page for July 12th, plus penultimate section).

References

[1] www.centralmosque.org.uk/. His view on the events of 7/7, were expressed in the August issue of the Birmingham Mosque newsletter, 'Dawn.'

Appendix 8: The Luton 'bombs' and the ABC Pictures

On Tuesday, 12th July, the police sealed off Luton station and car park. The *Luton News* reported on the 13th that 'A 200-metre cordon was put around the area by Bedfordshire police "on the grounds of public safety," so that three controlled explosions could be carried out on a car.' It quoted police spokeswoman Jo Hobbs as saying that the suspect car 'will be examined in the car park for safety reasons before being taken away to a secure location by the Met police.' That was the first report of this event by the local newspaper, and it seems fairly credible. The Channel Four news of that day also confirmed that *three* controlled explosions had been performed.[1]

Soon after, the number of 'controlled explosions' that had been performed went up to nine, while 'up to nine bombs' were deemed to have been left in the car.[2] Nowhere did the local paper reports say what kind of car it was, although the national papers soon assured us that it was the small Nissan Micra, which had been driven down from Leeds. A day later, on the 14th, The *Herald and Post* interviewed a local pub owner Alice Grayson, who explained what the police were doing: 'They'd found some stuff in the car, but they didn't know what it was so they would have to blow it up.' That becomes the canonical story. However, cars in Luton car park are tightly packed together on weekdays and police could hardly blow up a car containing explosives under such circumstances. Ms Grayson heard the first two explosions and then the police told her and others with her to go inside and stay there.

Flocks of journalists descended on the town, many from Europe and America, but what had really happened? We let the *Daily Mail* continue the narrative, six days later on the 18th:

> 'Police are investigating the possibility that up to nine bombs, primed and ready to use, could have been left in the hired Nissan Micra used by the gang. Forensic experts will today continue to examine the remains of the car left outside Luton station when the men caught a train to King's Cross. Bomb disposal teams carried out nine controlled explosions on the vehicle using, it is believed, a procedure for dealing with bombs already fitted with detonators.[3]

So, the 'remains' of the little hired Micra, blown to bits on the 12th, were being examined on the 17th, with police surmising that 'up to nine' bombs left behind in the car went off when the 'controlled explosions' were performed. Thus they are not claiming to have any of these bombs, or to have seen them. If there were ever an inquiry into this matter, one would want to ask: did the police take photographs of this exciting, detonative moment? If the police are asking us to believe that this really happened, then they can hardly also ask us to believe that they found in the Micra vital evidence such as the name and address of the car hire shop in Leeds. We may be fairly confident that no such event ever happened, because none of the three local papers covering the Luton area reported a police-engineered explosion of a car carrying bombs, nor likely protests from incensed locals. The cars in Luton car-park are packed like sardines in the daytime.

On Tuesday, 26 July, 2005, ABC News in America 'leaked' pictures both of train damage and of bombs allegedly left in Luton car park,[4] after the Metropolitan Police had asked them not to. The next day, the Met sent e-mail messages asking news organizations "in the strongest possible terms" not to replay the images "because they may prejudice both the ongoing investigation and any future prosecutions," calling the

images "unauthorized," and despite this – or maybe because of it – the story made dramatic headlines. A police spokeswoman commented: "Obviously they made their own decision. We asked them to be responsible and they were not."

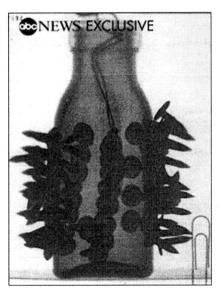

The pictures had been leaked to ABC news 'by US law enforcement sources,' *The Times* explained. ABC News reported on 27th that *altogether 16 bombs* had been found in the boot of the car, rented by Tanweer, viz. the Micra. Scotland Yard *disagreed* however, and 'dismissed the idea that a cache of bombs had been found in the Luton car park'.[5] 'Senior police sources continued to dispute the US reports yesterday, saying that a number of *components for* bombs were found in the car'. In other words, on Wednesday, *The Times'* journalist had been told that the Met disapproved of the US release of these pictures, and disputed the notion that bombs had been found in the car.

If a car had been blown up by controlled explosions, how could anyone claim to have pictures of the bombs inside it, or, even more unlikely, how could anyone claim to have discovered another dozen or so bombs that had been in it? The stories were entirely incommensurate. On the 27th, the *Luton News* carried a new story about a 'terror alert,' with mass evacuation due to a bag that had been left at a bus-stop: 'Controlled explosions were carried out on a bag in the bus station in what turned out to be a false alarm, on Monday', and 'A car containing explosives was discovered at Luton railway station, left by the four July 7 London bombers.' This was not explained, however the train and bus stations and nearby university flats were evacuated and a cordon put around the area. This Luton non-event was evidently synchronised with the big US news release.

On July 28th, *The Times* tried to reconcile the new ABC photos of alleged bomb components taken from the car plus the larger number of bombs, with the earlier report of its having been a mere wreck after the nine explosions around it on July 12th:

'According to ABC's report, 16 bombs were found in the boot of a hire car …The American report contradicts information provided by Scotland Yard. They dismissed the idea that a cache of bombs had been found in the Luton car park. Senior police sources continued to dispute the US reports yesterday.' A hiatus appeared in the narrative, with an American story wholly incompatible with earlier-reported events.

Here we cannot do better than quote the bewilderment of Mr Ahmed:

> How many bombs had been discovered? Nine? 12? 16? And why such discrepancies? In perhaps the most bizarre report of all, the *Daily Mail* described how, 'Police are investigating the possibility that up to nine bombs, primed and ready to use, could have been left in the hired Nissan Micra used by the gang.' Still investigating? A possibility? Up to nine? Could have been? Were bombs found or not? (p.44)

Surely not. That has to be the simple answer. A Nissan Micra is one of the smallest cars that can be hired (shown), and it would be absurd to believe that three large young men, with rucksacks (maybe also with refrigerating equipment to cool the TATP), plus between 9 and 16 unstable nail-bombs, could have fitted into one of these, and that it be then driven from Leeds to Luton.

The Times had to admit, concerning the explosives used: 'The description of the explosive material recovered in Luton and Leeds varied, but sources have admitted that they cannot definitively identify it.' With copious amounts supposedly found in a bath in Leeds and bombs in Luton, and its effects seen in several Underground stations, how could they have failed to identify it? Tens of millions were being spent on 'Operation Theseus', the largest-ever UK police operation, and they could not manage a simple chemical analysis? Even assuming that there never were any such bombs, as here suggested, why could not the police put together a coherent story?

Three of the nine images released by ABC News were genuine, if rather unhelpful, showing the inside of the three exploded coaches, on unknown dates. Coach walls had been removed, and the one at Russell Square avoided showing the floor of the carriage, which could have been crucial. Nonetheless, that is an important picture (shown in Chapter 9), as appearing to show frazzled electrical systems and wires hanging down from the roof, as if the blast had been somehow electrical in nature. The pictures shown come from America, together with the story of bombs left at Luton also in large degree from America, despite doubts being expressed by Scotland Yard. The discerning web-commentator 'Kier' made an analogy:

> The finding of the bombs in the cars curiously echoes the way in which a trail was similarly found to incriminate the suspected 9/11 hijackers and the Madrid bombing suspects. The 9/11 suspects apparently left their car in the *car park* of Logan airport, which contained an Arabic flight manual for a 767, a copy of the Qu'ran and a fuel consumption calculator. The Madrid suspects were traced through their apparently careless abandoning of a van near the train station *car park* which contained spare detonators and an Arabic tape of Qu'ranic quotes.
>
> Perpetrators of any kind of crime, let alone one of this magnitude, tend not to leave such an easy trail straight to them and their possible associates.[6]

This story indicates an American dimension to the plot. We may therefore note that a November 2004 *Newsweek* article described how the FBI, but not other US agencies, were avoiding the London Underground; FBI agents were turning up late to cross-town meetings because they insisted on using London taxis.

References

[1] 12.7.05 Breakthrough in bomb enquiry Channel 4 News. NB this Channel 4 news announced that the car park at Luton station had been emptied, implying that 100 or so cars had been removed; contradicting local news reports whereby commuters were merely delayed from accessing their cars in the car park (Luton News, July 13th). This is important as regards the lack of credibility of the official narrative whereby controlled explosions were performed around the suspect car. www.learning.channel4.co.uk/news/articles/uk/break through %20in%20bomb%20enquiry/108865

[2] 'Nine controlled explosions were performed upon the Micra on 12th July', *Report of the Official Account*, p.10.

[3] *Daily Mail* 18 July "'Primed bombs' could point to more suicide cells" www.dailymail. co.uk/pages/live/articles/news/news.html?in_article_id=356180&in_page_id=1770

[4] http://news.bbc.co.uk/1/hi/in_pictures/4722775.stm.

[5] The *Times*, 'Deadly device image Leaked to US' Thursday, July 28th www.timesonline. co.uk/article/0,,22989-1711360,00.html.

[6] www.julyseventh.co.uk/july-7-mind-the-gaps-part-1.html#lethalbombs.

Appendix 9: Explosives

Military or Home-made?

In the days after the event, police and intelligence officials soon confirmed that military-grade explosives had been used, together with detonators that had been synchronised. On the very day of the attacks, investigators stated that 'the three bombs used in the subway apparently were detonated by timers';[1] and, on the 8th, Vincent Cannistro, former head of the CIA's counter-terrorism centre, told the Guardian that the police had discovered 'mechanical timing devices' at the bomb scenes.[2]

On July 8th, British security officials confirmed to *ABC News* that:

> Police have recovered what they believe are the remnants of timing devices on the subway explosions, leading them to believe they were not suicide bombs but explosives planted in packages or bags and left behind. Officials now believe that all the bombs on subway cars were detonated by timing devices.'[3]

That would establish an analogy with the Madrid bombers, where timers detonated the bombs synchronously and no perpetrators died.

On the 9th there came the statement that the blasts were synchronous, and not spread out over half an hour or so – leading to puzzlement as to why it took them two days to ascertain this fact. Here is the statement: 'The police say the Tube explosions took place at 8.50am – and the synchronisation could suggest bombs used in the attack were triggered by timing devices. High explosives were used in the attacks and were not home-made, say the police'.[4] That seemed fairly definite.

France's anti-terror chief Christophe Chaboud was in London assisting Scotland Yard, and he confirmed to *The Times* that 'The nature of the explosives appears to be military, which is very worrying.'[5] A Europe-wide search was set up 'to uncover the source of the military explosives used in the bombings.' This was because traces of 'military plastic explosive, more deadly and efficient than commercial varieties, are understood to have been found in the debris of the wrecked underground carriages and the bus.' (*Times*, July 13th) Moreover, the trigger device was 'almost identical' to that used in the Madrid bombings in March of 2004. This would not be the first time that high-quality plastic explosive had been used by Al-Qaeda, military sources noted.

The Gladio operatives set up by NATO used C4, a substance then viewed as 'the most powerful explosive available' and moreover 'an explosive exclusively used by the US forces, which has never been used in any of the anarchist bombings' – the verdict of the Italian judge Salvini, in evidence given before the Gladio-related inquiry in 1997.[6]

Then, on July 15th, everything began to change, with no explanation given. Suddenly, it was home-brewed explosives. On the 17th, *The Observer* reported that 22 lbs of TATP had been found, in a bath, in Alexandra Grove in the Burley area of Leeds. The flat was empty, but was being rented by a Leeds University biochemistry student, Dr Magdy El-Nashar. To prepare this substance requires cooling to below 10° C – which begs the question as to how that was possible in a bath. Why would a chemist have wanted to leave it in a bath during hot summer days rather than keep it in the fridge? TATP needs to be kept sealed up because if left out it will evaporate, so it may well have tended to disappear over such a period.

Chemically speaking, the remarkable feature of TATP is that its products of detonation differ from its products of combustion. When burnt, it turns into water vapour and carbon dioxide and emits heat; on detonation, one molecule of TATP turns into four molecules of acetone (vapour) and ozone, but gives no heat. TATP isn't a thermochemical explosive that burns, but rather it releases sudden, large amounts of gas that should not leave people with burns or leave charred remains. That bizarre, unexpected decomposition of a solid into gas was only shown in 2004, published in the 2005 edition of the *Journal of the American Chemical Society*. Also, TATP lacks nitrogen, unlike nearly all other explosives: gunpowder, TNT (trinitrotoluene), 'C4' etc. Detectors of explosives normally search for nitrate radicals. For these reasons TATP had a certain gee-whiz value in the summer of 2005. Its products should have been straightforward to detect on the tube, but that detection would have had to have been within a day or so, because its products of explosion are gaseous.

On the 22nd of July, 'Jane's Terrorism & Insurgency Centre' was alleging that 'preliminary forensic testing' at the Leeds property as well as at 'the scenes of the 7 July terrorist attacks in London have identified traces of Triacetonetriperoxide (TATP), a powerful homemade explosive.'[7] The Jane's report added, 'Further testing by explosives forensic experts will still be necessary to confirm the presence of TATP.' That surely has to be nonsense, because the gaseous products of its explosion would not still be around two weeks later.

Similarly, the police source who told the *Daily Mail* that TATP was found in Leeds, added that 'police were still carrying out tests to establish its exact make-up and to see whether there was any link to the substance used by the four London bombers.' Tests had not confirmed whether the substance was indeed TATP, or that the substance was the same as that detected at the London blast sites.

Three days before July 7th, El-Nashar traveled to Egypt. A chemist went to Egypt knowing that highly unstable explosive was in his bath in Leeds? The story is here becoming absurd. The four young lads are now dead, and in their lives had had no discernable interest in making high-tech explosives. So it appears that the truth briefly blossomed, *before* the Leeds connection and the suicide bomber story kicked in.[8]

Concerning the need for detonation devices, Lt. Colonel Wylde noted, in relation to the criminal investigation into the 7th July terrorist attacks in London, that police and government sources had maintained "total silence" about the detonation devices used in the bombs on the London Underground and the bus at Tavistock Square. "Whatever the nature of the primary explosive materials, even if it was home-made TATP, the detonator that must be used to trigger an explosion is an extremely dangerous device to make, requiring a high level of expertise that cannot be simply self-taught or picked-up over the internet." The government's silence on the detonation device used in the attacks is "disturbing," he said, as the creation of the devices requires the involvement of trained explosives experts. Wylde surmised that such individuals would have to be present either inside the country or outside, perhaps in Eastern Europe, where they would be active participants in an international supply-chain to UK operatives. "In either case, we are talking about something far more dangerous than home-grown radicals here."[9]

Is TATP a 'Binary' explosive?

'Mass murder in the skies: was the plot feasible?
Let's whip up some TATP and find out.'[10]

For the remainder of this Appendix, I hand over the floor to Thomas C. Greene, reproducing his article on the subject with kind permission. The issue here discussed relates to Chapter 11, part 3:

Binary liquid explosives are a sexy staple of Hollywood thrillers. It would be tedious to enumerate the movie terrorists who've employed relatively harmless liquids that, when mixed, immediately rain destruction upon an innocent populace, like the seven angels of God's wrath pouring out their bowls full of pestilence and pain.

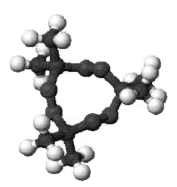

The funny thing about these movies is, we never learn just which two chemicals can be handled safely when separate, yet instantly blow us all to kingdom-come when combined. Nevertheless, we maintain a great eagerness to believe in these substances, chiefly because action movies wouldn't be as much fun if we didn't.

Now we have news of the recent, supposedly real-world, terrorist plot to destroy commercial airplanes by smuggling onboard the benign precursors to a deadly explosive, and mixing up a batch of liquid death in the lavatories. So, *The Register* has got to ask, were these guys for real, or have they, and the counterterrorist officials supposedly protecting us, been watching too many action movies?

We're told that the suspects were planning to use TATP, or triacetone triperoxide, a high explosive that supposedly can be made from common household chemicals unlikely to be caught by airport screeners. A little hair dye, drain cleaner, and paint thinner – all easily concealed in drinks bottles – and the forces of evil have effectively smuggled a deadly bomb onboard your plane.

Or at least that's what we're hearing, and loudly, through the mainstream media and its legions of so-called "terrorism experts." But what do these experts know about chemistry? Less than they know about lobbying for Homeland Security pork, which is what most of them do for a living. But they've seen the same movies that you and I have seen, and so the myth of binary liquid explosives dies hard.

Making a quantity of TATP sufficient to bring down an airplane is not quite as simple as ducking into the toilet and mixing two harmless liquids together.

First, you've got to get adequately concentrated hydrogen peroxide. This is hard to come by, so a large quantity of the 3% solution sold in pharmacies might have to be concentrated by boiling off the water.[11] Only this is risky, and can lead to mission failure by means of burning down your makeshift lab before a single infidel has been harmed.

But let's assume that you can obtain it in the required concentration, or cook it from a dilute solution without ruining your operation. Fine. The remaining ingredients, acetone and sulfuric acid, are far easier to obtain, and we can assume that you've got them on hand.

Now for the fun part. Take your hydrogen peroxide, acetone, and sulfuric acid, measure them very carefully, and put them into drinks bottles for convenient smuggling onto a plane. It's all right to mix the peroxide and acetone in one container, so long as it remains cool. Don't forget to bring several frozen gel-packs (preferably in a Styrofoam chiller deceptively marked "perishable foods"), a thermometer, a large beaker, a stirring rod, and a medicine dropper. You're going to need them.

Once the plane is over the ocean, very discreetly bring all of your gear into the toilet. You might need to make several trips to avoid drawing attention. Once your kit is in place, put a beaker containing the peroxide / acetone mixture into the ice water bath (Champagne bucket), and start adding the acid, drop by drop, while stirring constantly. Watch the reaction temperature carefully. The mixture will heat, and if it gets too hot, you'll end up with a weak explosive. In fact, if it gets really hot, you'll get a premature explosion possibly sufficient to kill you, but probably no one else.

After a few hours – assuming, by some miracle, that the fumes haven't overcome you or alerted passengers or the flight crew to your activities – you'll have a quantity of TATP with which to carry out your mission. Now all you need to do is dry it for an hour or two. But where are the fume vents and the drier? And where to plug this stuff in?

The genius of this scheme is that TATP is relatively easy to detonate. But you must make enough of it to crash the plane, and you must make it with care to assure potency. One needs quality stuff to commit "mass murder on an unimaginable scale," as Deputy Police Commissioner Paul Stephenson put it. While it's true that a slapdash concoction will explode, it's unlikely to do more than blow out a few windows. At best, an infidel or two might be killed by the blast, and one or two others by flying debris as the cabin suddenly depressurizes, but that's about all you're likely to manage under the most favorable conditions possible.

We believe this because a peer-reviewed 2004 study in the Journal of the American Chemical Society (JACS) entitled "Decomposition of Triacetone Triperoxide in an Entropic Explosion" tells us that the explosive force of TATP comes from the sudden decomposition of a solid into gases. There's no rapid oxidizing of fuel, as there is with many other explosives: rather, the substance changes state suddenly through an entropic process, and quickly releases a respectable amount of energy when it does. (Thus the lack of ingredients typically associated with explosives makes TATP, a white crystalline powder resembling sugar, difficult to detect with conventional bomb sniffing gear.)

By now you'll be asking why these jihadist wannabes didn't conspire simply to bring TATP onto planes, colored with a bit of vegetable dye, and disguised as, say, a powdered fruit-flavored drink. The reason is that they would be afraid of failing: TATP is notoriously sensitive and unstable. Mainstream journalists like to tell us that terrorists like to call it "the mother of Satan." (Whether this reputation is deserved, or is a consequence of homebrewing by unqualified hacks, remains open to debate.)

It's been claimed that the 7/7 bombers used it, but this has not been positively confirmed. Some sources claim that they used C-4, and others that they used RDX. Nevertheless, the belief that they used TATP has stuck with the media, although going about in a crowded city at rush hour with an unstable homebrew explosive in a backpack is not the brightest of all possible moves. It's surprising that none of the attackers enjoyed an unscheduled launch into Paradise.

So, assuming that the homebrew variety of TATP is highly sensitive and unstable – or at least that our inept jihadists would believe that – to avoid getting blown up in the taxi on the way to the airport, one might, if one were educated in terror tactics primarily by Hollywood movies, prefer simply to dump the precursors into an airplane toilet bowl and let the mother of Satan work her magic. Indeed, the mixture will heat rapidly as TATP begins to form, and it will soon explode. But this won't happen with much force, because little TATP will have formed by the time the explosion occurs.

We asked University of Rhode Island Chemistry Professor Jimmie C. Oxley, who has actual, practical experience with TATP, if this is a reasonable assumption, and he told us that merely dumping the precursors together would create "a violent reaction," but not a detonation. To release the energy needed to bring down a plane (far more difficult to do than many imagine, as Aloha Airlines flight 243 neatly illustrates), it's necessary to synthesize a good amount of TATP with care.

So the fabled binary liquid explosive – that is, the sudden mixing of hydrogen peroxide and acetone with sulfuric acid to create a plane-killing explosion, is out of the question. Meanwhile, making TATP ahead of time carries a risk that the mission will fail due to premature detonation, although it is the only plausible approach. Certainly, if we can imagine a group of jihadists smuggling the necessary chemicals and equipment on board, and cooking up TATP in the lavatory ('tis a lavatory, not a laboratory), then we've passed from the realm of action blockbusters to that of situation comedy.

It should be small comfort that the security establishments of the UK and the USA – and the "terrorism experts" who inform them and wheedle billions of dollars out of them for bomb puffers and face recognition gizmos and remote gait analyzers and similar hi-tech phrenology gear – have bought the Hollywood binary liquid explosive myth, and have even acted upon it.

But the Hollywood myth of binary liquid explosives now moves governments and drives public policy. We have reacted to a movie plot. Liquids are now banned in aircraft cabins (while crystalline white powders would be banned instead, if anyone in charge were serious about security). Nearly everything must now go into the hold, where adequate amounts of explosives can easily be detonated from the cabin with cell phones, which are generally not banned.

It's a pity that our security rests in the hands of government officials who understand as little about terrorism as the Florida clowns who needed their informant to suggest attack scenarios, as the 21/7 London bombers who injured no one, as lunatic "shoe bomber" Richard Reid,[8] as the Forest Gate nerve gas attackers who had no nerve gas, as the British nitwits who tried to acquire "red mercury," and as the recent binary liquid bomb attackers who had no binary liquid bombs.

References

[1] 'Timers used in Blasts, police say' *NY Times,* 7.7.05.

[2] The *Guardian,* 8 July, 'Four bombs in 50 minutes.'

[3] ABC News, 8 July, 'Officials: London Bus Body could be bomber'
Tube bombs 'almost simultaneous' http://news.bbc.co.uk/1/hi/uk/4666591.stm

[4] See Appendix 8; also, http://otukungu.blogspot.com/2005/07/terror-propaganda-for-war-on-islam.html.

[5] *The Times* 12th July, Terror Gang 'Used military explosives.'

[6] Ganser, p.3, 122.

[7] Ahmed, p. 31

[8] 'Shoe-bomber' Richard Reid, the Briton who allegedly tried to blow up an airliner in December 2001, used TATP for his device, this being found in his shoe-heel. This seems an odd plan, as it is readily detonated by friction. Reid was quite retarded mentally, and for Webster Tarpley's view of him as a patsy groomed for the job, see *Synthetic Terror* p.74.

[9] Nafeez Ahmed, 'August Terror Plot Is A 'Fiction,' British Army expert casts doubt on 'liquid explosives' threat', 18.9.06 http://www.scoop.co.nz/stories/HL0609/S00297.htm (many versions of this article are posted, the original is in *New Criminologist,* a subscription-only web-journal.

[10] *The Register,* www.theregister.co.uk/2006/08/17/flying_toilet_terror_labs/.

[11] That 3% figure pertains to America: hair bleach containing 12% hydrogen peroxide is purchasable in the UK.

Appendix 10: Comments on Ahmed

The London Bombings – A Review

7/7: The Inside Story of the London Bombings was the bold title of Mr Nafeez Ahmed's public address given on August 16th, 2006, in a London Muslim centre. It was ambitious, and indeed some were heard to murmur at the end that he had not really given any definite answers. Over central issues he remains agnostic. He summarised main themes of his book, which combines devastating critique of police obfuscation over the 'clues' and the incoherence of the story they have given, with a belief that somewhere out there, in Europe or maybe Pakistan, 'Al-Qaeda' elements plotted and masterminded the event.

But surely, one wants to cry out, if the bombs really were placed under the carriage, as he more than half suggests, and if the police have been telling us absolute baloney for a year over the trains which the four lads are alleged to have caught from Luton, then does not this argue for a source more within British intelligence for the event? He has clearly shown any discerning reader that all the competent bomb-experts in Europe and America first proclaimed (a) that remote-control detonators were used, and then (b) that military-grade explosives were used; then in mid-July, the story changed with no detonators and a home-made explosive called TATP brewed up in a bath, etc. as if all the former conclusions were simply 'inoperative.' We surely expect Nafeez to conclude that someone is just making up the script on the hoof. He doesn't.

Nafeez uses the big words like 'Truth' in his book titles, and I sometimes feel he writes his books a bit too quickly. Is he avoiding such conclusions merely because they would lose him his publisher? Surely not. He told Keith Mothersson that he had wanted to put 'alleged bombers' in his book, but had been told by his publisher that this would make the book unpublishable. So the four accused became simply 'the bombers. Thankfully, in his book the July 21st suspects do remain, 'the alleged bus bomber,' etc.

A member of our 9/11 group in the audience asked him, afterwards, about the terror-drill rehearsal conducted by Peter Power: his talk had not mentioned it and neither had his book! We are there treated to a hundred pages about terror-networks around the world (by brown-skinned persons), but nothing about the centrally-relevant terror-drill performed on the morning of July 7th (by white-skinned persons) relating to the very same railway-stations as were attacked.

I'm tempted to say that Nafeez needs to read Mike Ruppert or Webster Tarpley on how the war-games and terror drills of September 11th metamorphosed into the real thing. If the talk he gave did not quite satisfy anyone, he remains the one figure in the great debate who is respected by all the different sides. 'Even minor details of the official account remain absurdly impossible' (i.e. that released in May of this year) – but tell us, Nafeez, why would they have mudded up all these details if the truth is to be found in these far-flung international 'terror' networks?

Public Inquiry

The most significant feature of his book may be its clear call for a public inquiry. We do here appreciate hearing the view of a Muslim intellectual. His presence at the CAMPAAC (Campaign Against Criminalizing Communities) group working towards a public enquiry—on which several members of our group are present—will surely help it to succeed. Persons with radically incompatible views are sitting round the same table, and Nafeez' urbane presence helps to reassure the organisers that a balanced and scholarly view may prevail over invective.

After discussing the official reports from anonymous government sources released this summer, his book concludes: 'These two documents are little more than an insult to the intelligence of the British people. More than ever, it proves beyond doubt that an independent public enquiry into the London bombings and the events surrounding them is absolutely essential to discovering precisely whet happened on 7/7, how and why; and to ensure that the fundamental reforms necessary to rehabilitate the British national security systems are implemented.' Hear, hear! Let us hope that momentum towards such a non-partisan public enquiry can continue to develop, and it surely can, provided that the factions with differing views can have the humility to acknowledge, like Nafeez, that none of us know exactly what happened on that day.

The Fiendish Threat

We learn about Muslim 'terrorists' dedicated to a 'Jihad' in which civilians, including women and children, are fair game, and who expected an event in the summer of 2005; though strangely they were not arrested by the police after their quite public proclamations. The trouble here is that they did not have much to do with Leeds, and their connection was rather with the Finsbury Park mosque. The author assures us rather casually that Mohammed Khan 'is known to have frequented' this mosque. The dates of this are not made clear, but (p.82) a period prior to January 2003 seems indicated. Khan was then working full-time at Hillside Primary school, had just got married, was known as a very public figure in terms of his work for Hamara Healthy Living Centre (which Tony Benn had come up to visit not long before, to inaugurate), and with his pal Tanweer their 'Mullah group' was acquiring a local reputation for getting youngsters off narcotic-addiction, which involved organising outdoor expeditions such as boating and mountain-climbing. Is Nafeez sure that Khan would really have had the time or inclination to drive all the way down to Finsbury Park to listen to some ranting mullah? Can he reconcile that with one of the most marked characteristics of Khan as recalled by the many who knew him, namely his lack of interest in religion? The Radio 4 program 'Biography of a Bomber' was the most detailed investigation of Khan's life we are likely to hear about, and none of the persons there interviewed gave any hint that Khan had commuted down to Finsbury Park. We require more corroboration than the mere word of a journalist, which is all that Nafeez offers us, before we will accept that the Leeds suspects were ever sitting in the Finsbury Park mosque.

Nafeez treats the 'Al Qaeda terror network' characters in great detail – the longest section of his book – and continually comes back to how they are employed by the MI5 or CIA: 'Every leading member of al'Qaeda's Finsbury division – Omar Bakri, Abu Hamza, Abu Qatada – has according to credible reports, a close relationship to Britain's security services'.[1] A lot of this is of interest, but rather doubtful relevance, as we have seen. Al-Zawahiri is the character who features on the Mohammed Khan video of September 2005, widely hyped as Bin Laden's second-in-command. He was involved in the assassination of the Egyptian premier, Anwar Sadat, in 1981, after which he escaped safely to London, where the authorities refused pleas by Sadat's family to have him extradited. He was recruited by the CIA in 1997 (Ahmed, p. 203), appropriate for someone on the FBI's Most Wanted terror list.

Last year Blair justified the assault on Fallujah by explaining that 'Zawahiri is operating there,' i.e. his name had become a convenient one to conjure with. It's a hall of mirrors. In the analysis of far-flung terrorist groups we learn of certain persons who are even in touch with (gasp) Osama bin Laden. That ambiguous millionaire died in December 2001 in the Tora Bora Mountains, and we do expect Nafeez to recognise lousy, fake, ISI-produced posthumous videos when he sees them.

The Joint Terrorism Analysis Centre of MI5 did respond to any such assorted threats, by (three weeks before 7/7) lowering their threat-risk assessment, because 'At present there is not a group with both the current intent and the capability to attack the UK.' This was necessary *in order that* (the language of intent is mine, not Nafeez's) London would be left 'virtually undefended as police officers were extracted out of London to Gleneagles for the G-8 summit.' (Ahmed, p. 142). The perps didn't want ordinary bobbies snooping around. Intelligence expert Crispin Black asked, 'What kind of pressure was at work on the JTAC when it lowered... Its threat level on 2 June'? He, as Nafeez put it, unfortunately failed to answer that 'critical question.'

I had to laugh at Ahmed's account of how 'Hasib Hussain boarded the bus in a panicked last-minute decision when the pre-planning was foiled by the suspension of the Northern line that morning.'[2] Not a word about the mysterious re-routing of this 30 bus to Tavistock Square as the only one so diverted, nor how a London bus driver stopped his bus in order to ask someone the way (and was then startled to look round, and see its top blow off), nor all that marvellous theatrical blood spattered around the BMA's door, nor that 'Outright Terror, Bold and Brilliant' for all to see. No, all that constructed theatre somehow slides out of his view, and instead what he sees is a phantom: the image of 'the bomber,' unseen by a single credible witness.

Police Prescience

Nafeez does an excellent job of comparing the 21/7 and 7/7 events, with the Home Secretary Clarke warning about the 21/7 events a mere two hours before they happened, warning senior colleagues of 'another terror onslaught' in a confidential briefing. Why, how clever of him. Also Scotland Yard somehow knew that the next event would also be on a Thursday: police chiefs independently 'deduced the attack would probably be on a Thursday.' On the morning of the 21st, just before the event, armed police raced to Farringdon Station to close in on a suspected bomber but 'alas' narrowly missed – i.e. they knew where it would happen, as well as when. As Nafeez comments, if they had such detailed foreknowledge as to where and when the event would happen, why was the public not warned? Benjamin Netanyahu's well-publicised foreknowledge (by six minutes) of the 7/7 event is here ascribed to a tip by Scotland Yard, so the police apparently knew when both events were going to happen. One feels they should be invited to say a bit more about this remarkable prescience.

Posted 20.8.06 at www.nineeleven.co.uk/board/viewtopic.php?t=3341&highlight= ahmed

Islamist Terror Networks and the 7/7 Intelligence Failure, 2007, some queries

Nafeez Ahmed sent a briefing paper to British MPs on the threat posed by Al-Qaeda to British security,[3] in 2007. Most journalists would agree with its position as regards what has been shown by the 'Crevice' trial concerning two of the 7/7 suspects, Tanweer and Khan.

His new publication may have exerted considerable influence upon British MPs, especially with its Introduction by former head of CID Desmond Thomas. We can surely agree with this Intro, which declared:

> "It never pays to underestimate your opponent. It seems that this atrocity was the product of a mind that understood both British politics and the culture of the security services. The principal and political purpose of the 7/7 attacks may have been to facilitate the introduction of repressive legislation and oppressive policing resulting in the frightening and alienation of the Muslim community".

Ahmed's position expressed inhis book 'The London bombings' remained somewhat ambiguous, so we welcome the clarification that appeared with his new text, which one might summarise as follows:

1. The suspected four young Muslims did perpetrate the deed of 7/7;

2. There exists an extended network of Al-Qaeda terrorist agents in Britain and abroad, with whom these four young men were in touch.

3. Because of this, the UK intelligence community had been monitoring the suspected four, especially Khan and Tanweer, for some while before 7/7, despite initial proclamations that the young men were 'clean skins.'

He argued that MI5 and MI6 have for long nourished and helped to sustain Al-Qaeda cells, for their own reasons, and even conferred upon them immunity from prosecution, and that MPs need to become aware of this. 'Potential terrorist cells' in the UK are in fact interlinked with an interconnected al-Qaeda network, he argued.

One wonders, what evidence is there for claiming that the four lads suspected of the bombing had connections with 'Al-Qaeda' agents, and that various sources were therefore monitoring them? His paper here relied greatly upon documents and stories generated after the event of 7/7, averring:.

* Mobile phone calls confirm Haroon Aswat's regular contact with the 7/7 cell, especially Khan' (pp.16). He had spoken to Khan on the morning of 7/7.

* A Saudi Arabian warning was issued to Britain in December 2004 ('specifically dismissed by the House of Commons Intel & Security Report March 2006') stating 'that a cell of four British Muslims was planning a terrorist attack upon the London Underground within 6 months'(p.1).

* Khan and Tanweer were arrested in March 2004 as part of Operation Crevice, who 'appeared as petty fraudsters in loose contact with members of the plot' (p.23). They came under surveillance, but were not arrested.

* Khan met Bluewater plot ringleader (Omar Kyyam) five times in February and March 2004, with Tanweer attending 3 meetings, 'each time tracked and photographed by MI5' (p.2) – yes, this is true.

* In the context of this Crevice trial, *The Sunday Times* has a tape recording of Khan 'talking about how to build the device and then leave the country' (p.29). Can anyone hear this tape, or is there even anyone claiming to have listened to it who can be asked about it?[4]

* Khan and Tanweer did visit a military camp in Pakistan -, but, you can't show that this involved intent to conduct an attack inside Britain.

* That Omar Bakri Muhammed was proclaiming the inevitability of an attack upon London in 2004 (p.3) – I checked out the article (*The Times* 17 Jan, 2005) and it had Bakri denying that he was calling for violent action and saying that Muslims should consider emigrating to their homelands because of the oppression they experienced in the UK, as if they were under siege.

* Khan was linked to 'the Luton cell' which is a 'focus of terror' in the UK (p.40). Is there a 'focus of terror' in Luton? There is a branch of ICTS there, the Israeli security firm.

Any evidence for these doubtful assertions that does not involve retrospective claims by UK police and Intelligence would be of value here.

For Ahmed's comments on Crevice, similar to above, see http://nafeez.blogspot.com/ 2007/05/inside-crevice-77-and-security-debacle.html

For MI5's comments on the 'Crevice' trial vs July 7th suspects, especially Khan, see www.mi5.gov.uk/output/Page385.html

For *Global Outlook's* comments on the Crevice trial, see www.globalresearch.ca/index.php?context=va&aid=5601

References

[1] p.175 of *The London Bombs*; see also *Defending the Realm, Inside MI5 and the War on Terrorism,* Mark Hollingsworth and Nick Fielding, 2003, p 169.

[2] There was no suspension as such of the Northern Line that morning, although some stations were closed: See Appendix 6a.

[3] Ahmed, *Inside the crevice Islamist terror Networks and the 7/7 intelligence Failure*, August 2007 www.campacc.org.uk/Library/071003_iprd_press_release.doc.

[4] The article alluded to (Leppard and Woods, 'Spies Hid bomber tape from *MPs' The Sunday Times* 14.5.06) said, 'Transcripts of the tapes were never shown to the parliamentary intelligence and security committee…A committee member, who asked not to be named, admitted that it had not seen transcripts of MI5's recordings of Khan.' etc, suggesting that no such tapes were seen by the *Sunday Times* – or, one assumes, anyone else.

Select Bibliography

Nafeez Ahmed, *The London bombings, an Independent Inquiry*, 2006
— 'Al-Qaeda and Western Covert operations after the Cold War' in *The hidden History of 9/11-2001* Ed. Paul Zarembka 2006, pp. 149-188.
Crispin Black, *7/7 – The London bombings, What went wrong*, 2006
Michel Chossudowsky, *America's 'War on Terrorism'* 2002, 2005 2nd Ed.
Len Bracken, *The Shadow Government: 9-11 And State Terror*, 2002
Mark Curtis, *Web of Deceit, Britain's Real role in the World*, 2003
N.Davies, *Flat Earth News, An Award-winning Reporter Exposes Falsehood, Distortion and Propaganda in the Global Media*, 2008
Aaron Debnam, *One Morning in July – The Man Who Was First on the Scene Tells His Story*, 2007
Daniele Ganser, *NATO's Secret Armies, Operation Gladio and Terrorism in Western Europe*, 2005
Gill Hicks, *One Unknown, A powerful account of survival*, 2007
Annie Machon, *Spies, Lies and Whistleblowers, MI5, MI6 and the Shayler Affair* 2005
Neil Mackay, *The War on Truth,* Sunday Herald Books (concerning the Iraq war), 2006
Benjamin Netanyahu, *Terrorism: How the West Can Win*
Rachel North, *Out of the Tunnel, Before & After 7/7: One Woman's Extraordinary Story* 2007
Daniel Obachike, *The 4th Bomb, Inside London's Terror Storm*, 2007
Peter Osborne, *The Use & Abuse of Terror, the Construction of a False Narrative on the Domestic Terror Threat,'* 2006
Milan Rai, *77 The London Bombings, Islam and the Iraq War*, 2006
Michael Ruppert, *Crossing the Rubicon, The Decline of the American Empire at the End of the Age of Oil*, 2005
Webster Tarpley, *9/11 Synthetic Terror: Made in USA*, 2005, 2006
John Tulloch, *One Day in July Experiencing 7/7*, 2006; *Risk and Everyday Life*, 2003
Peter Zimonjic, *Into the Darkness: The story of 7/7*, 2008
Anon, *Report of the Official Account of the bombings in London on 7th July 2005*, HMSO, 2006

Journals

Prospect, June 2007: 'My Brother the Bomber' pp.30-41, by Shiv Malik
New Civil Engineer, 'Righting the Damage' *18/25 August 2005, pp. 14-15,* by B. Redfern

DVDs

Terrorstorm, Alex Jones
Ludicrous Diversions released anonymously in September 2006, via Google video
Mind the Gap by Adrian Connock and David Shayler
The Homefront, Thomas Ikimi, Director Anthony Fatayi-Williams
7/7 the Ripple Effect by Muad'Dib
(www.officialconfusion.com/77/mindthegap/Google/mindthegap.html

http://video.google.com/videoplay?docid=-4943675105275097719&q=ludicrous
www.thehomefrontmovie.net , http://jforjustice.co.uk/77/)
The DVDs and videos are concerned with the *truth* of what happened that day, whereas the published books are, generally speaking, promoting an *illusion*. The 'survivor testimonies' are no doubt honestly described but they accept the establishment view. These testimonies do not spend a moment in wondering who was responsible for the event, still less in presenting the reader with evidence as to why we should believe that the four young men were guilty of so frightful a crime. To his credit, Nafeez Ahmed does spend a while pondering this matter in 'The London Bombings', and his text does retain vestiges of doubt concerning their guilt.

Websites

July 7th collective: www.julyseventh.co.uk   The premier July 7th website. It has a forum: www.invisionfree.com/julyseventh/

Team 8plus: www.team8plus.org/e107_plugins/forum/forum.php. An early, pioneer site, presently inactive.

Official Confusion: www.officialconfusion.com/77. Adrian Connock's valuable collection of articles and data sources.

9/11 Truth: www.911forum.co.uk/board/viewforum.php?f=9 News and discussion.

'Physics9/11' site: http://physics911.net/karinbrothers

London Assembly: www.london.gov.uk/assembly/reports/general.jsp#7july

Global Research: www.globalresearch.ca/index.php?context=newsHighlights&newsId= 26

Wikipedia sections are helpful, e.g. July 7th, Crevice, Heathrow bomb, Mohammed Khan, July 21st, False Flag terror and Operation Gladio, TATP etc.

July 7th orbituaries: http://news.bbc.co.uk/1/shared/spl/hi/uk/05/london_blasts/victims/default.stm

'The Report on the Official Account of the Bombings in London on the 7th July 2005' This 'Narrative' was published on June 5th, 2006 (36 pages, no author or editor) obtainable at 'The Stationary Office' (used to be HMSO but it got privatised) – opposite Holborn tube, cost £8.50, ISBN 0102-937-745; it is a printout of the web version that emerged on May 11: www.officialconfusion.com/77/Reports%20Narratives.zip

'The final report of the 7th July Review Committee' a 3-volume report by the London Assembly was web-published on 5 June, 2006, synchronously with the printed 'Official Account'. This runs to several hundred pages. Volume 1, pp.28-30 has a summary of Edgware Road evidence. Volume 3 just has a reprint of the witnesses statements, somewhat abridged, that the London assembly heard earlier, 23rd March: www.london.gov.uk/assembly/reports/general.jsp#7july that had appeared as a web-text a month earlier. (Or see www.julyseventh.co.uk/, link on the top right hand section to download these.)

Allan Francovich's legendary three-part BBC 'Timewatch' series (1992) concerning 'Gladio': The Ringmasters http://11syyskuu.net/video/Gladio-1.wmv; The Puppeteers http://11syyskuu. net/video/Gladio-2.wmv; The Foot-Soldiers http://11syyskuu.net/ video/Gladio-3.wmvAdam Curtis' 3-part BBC series, 'The Power of Nightmares': www.archive.org/ details/ThePowerOfNightmares. [Also available from Progressive Press.]

Index

Conspiracy, NWO

Top sellers by F. Wm. Engdahl, *Gods of Money:* The banksters stop at nothing: setting world wars, nuking cities, keeping our world in chaos and corruption. *Full Spectrum Dominance.* Total control: land, sea, air, space, outer space, cyberspace, media, movements, money. *Seeds of Destruction: The Hidden Agenda of Genetic Manipulation.* A corporate gang is out for complete control of the world by patenting our food. A world of organized crime inside the boardrooms and science labs. Sale price just $14.95 each:

Corporatism: the Secret Government of the New World Order by Prof. Jeffrey Grupp. Corporations control all world resources. Their New World Order is the "prison planet" that Hitler aimed for. 408 pp, on sale: $11.99.

Three by Henry Makow PhD, all on sale $13.95 ea. *Illuminati: Cult that Hijacked the World* tackles taboos like Zionism, British Empire, Holocaust denial. How international bankers stole a monopoly on government credit, and took over the world. They run it all: wars, schools, media. 249 pp. *Illuminati 2: Deception & Seduction* , 285 pp., more hidden history. *Cruel Hoax: Feminism and the New World Order. The Attack on Your Human Identity.* Insights on social and sexual aspects of the conspiracy to enslave humanity. 232 pp.

Dope Inc.: Britain's Opium War against the United States. "The Book that Drove Kissinger Crazy." New edition of the Underground Classic. 320 pp, $14.95.
Final Warning: A History of the New World Order by D. A. Rivera. In-depth research the Great Conspiracy: the Fed, the CFR, Trilateral Commission, Illuminati. 360 pp, $14.95.
The Globalization of Poverty and the New World Order. M. Chossudovsky. How corporatism feeds on poverty, destroying the environment, apartheid, racism, sexism, and ethnic strife. 401 pp., $17.89.
How the World Really Works by A.B. Jones. Crash course in conspiracy; digests of 11 classics. 336 pp., $9.45.

The Triumph of Consciousness. The real Global Warming agenda: more hegemony by the NWO. 347 pp, $14.95.

Conspiracy: 9/11 False Flag

9/11 Synthetic Terror: Made in USA. W G Tarpley. The network of moles, patsies, and killers, corrupt politicians and media. The MIHOP bible: authoritative account of 9/11. "Strongest of the 770+ books I have reviewed" – R. Steele, #1 Amazon non-fiction reviewer. 4th ed, 512 pp., just $10.
In Spanish: *11-S Falso Terrorismo.* 408 pp, $14.98.
9/11 on Trial: The W T C Collapse. 20 proofs the WTC went down by a controlled demolition. 192 pp, only $6.
America's "War on Terrorism" Concise, wide-reaching, hard-hitting study on 9/11 in geopolitical context, by Prof. Chossudovsky. 387 pp, $22.95, on sale, $13.95.
Conspiracies, Conspiracy Theories and the Secrets of 9/11, Fascinating German best-seller explores conspiracy in history before tackling 9/11. 274 pp, just $9.
The War on Freedom. The classic exposé of 9/11. "Far and away the best and most balanced analysis of September 11th." – Gore Vidal. 400 pp, $16.95, on sale: only $6.95.
Terror on the Tube: Behind the Veil of 7/7, an Investigation, by Nick Kollerstrom. Only book with the glaring evidence that all four Muslim scapegoats were completely innocent. Third ed., 329 pp, $14.77.
9/11 Truth Novel *Instruments of the State,* sale price $11.95.

Modern History

1,000 Americans Who Rule the USA (1947, 324 pp, $12.95) and *Facts and Fascism* (1943, 292 pp., $11.95) by the great muckraking journalist George Seldes – whistleblower on the American plutocrats who keep the media in lockstep, and finance fascism.
Witness in Palestine: A Jewish American Woman in the Occupied Territories. The nuts and bolts of everyday oppression. Packed with color photos. 400 pp, $14.95.
Enemies by Design: Inventing the War on Terrorism. A century of imperialism in the Middle East. Bio of Osama bin Ladeen; Zionization of America; PNAC, Afghanistan, Palestine, Iraq; 416 pp, $17.95, on sale, $10.

Inside the Gestapo: Hitler's Shadow over the World. Intimate, fascinating Nazi defector's tale of ruthlessness, intrigue, and geopolitics. 287 pp, $13.95.

Two by by S. H. Ross. *Propaganda for War: How the US was Conditioned to Fight the Great War* Britain and her agents like Teddy Roosevelt sucked the USA into the war to smash the old world order. *Global Predator: US Wars for Empire.* The atrocities committed by US armed forces over two centuries. Each about 350 pages, $18.95, on sale: $14.95.

The Nazi Hydra in America: Suppressed History of a Century by Glen Yeadon. US plutocrats launched Hitler, then recouped Nazi assets to erect today's police state. Fascists won WWII because they ran both sides. 700 pp, $19.95, on sale: $11.99.

Terrorism and the Illuminati, A 3000-Year History, by David Livingstone. "Islamic" terrorists are tentacles of the Illuminati. 2nd edition, Nov. 2011. On sale $13.95.

Psychology: Brainwashing

The Telescreen: An Empirical Study of the Destruction of Consciousness, by Grupp. How mass media brainwash us with consumerism and war propaganda. Fake history, news, issues, and reality to steal our souls. 199 pp, $9.99.

The Rape of the Mind: The Psychology of Thought Control, Menticide and Brainwashing. Conditioning in open and closed societies; tools for self-defense against torture or social pressure. 320 pp, $11.95.

Biography, New World Oligarchy

Barack H. Obama: the Unauthorized Biography W. G. Tarpley. Obama's doings in the trough of graft and corruption of the Chicago Combine, his plans for brutal austerity to finance Wall Street bailouts, and confrontation with Russia and China. 595 pp, $19.95, on sale, $11.99.

George Bush: The Unauthorized Biography Vivid X-ray of the oligarchy dominating U.S. politics. 700 pp, $10.95.

Obama – The Postmodern Coup: Making of a Manchurian Candidate. Tarpley reveals that the Obama puppet's advisors are even more radical reactionaries than the neo-cons. A crash course in political science, it distills

decades of political insight and astute analysis. 320 pp, $15.95, on sale: $10.95.

Economics, Financier Oligarchy

Surviving the Cataclysm, Your Guide through the Greatest Financial Crisis in Human History, by W.G. Tarpley. The unwinding of the hedge funds and derivatives bubble, and with them, life as we knew it in the USA. Richly detailed history of the financier oligarchy, how they plunder our nation. Plus, How to cope with the crisis. 668 pp, $15.95.

The Global Economic Crisis: The Great Depression of the XXI Century. by Prof. Michel Chossudovsky and a dozen other experts. 416 pp., $25.95, sale price $16.95.

DVDs

DVD hits by BBC director Adam Curtis:
(1) Power of Nightmares, how governments sell terror. All 3 parts, 3 hours, $7.50. In Amaray case, $11.99.
(2) The Century of Self, an expose of mass-market brainwashing techniques, and the Freud dynasty. All four hours on one disc, $7.95. Best quality version on two discs: in Amaray box case, $15.95.
(3) The Trap. This highly intelligent film exposes the dire effects of materialist behaviorist ideas like game theory and shock "therapy" on society, health, education. Worth looking up on Wikipedia. 3 hours, $7.50.
Adam Curtis Trilogy: All 3 programs, on 4 discs (Century of Self on 2 discs), or, all 4 Adam Curtis single DVDs, including The Living Dead: in Amaray box case, $24.
(4) The Living Dead Curtis explores how history is manipulated to control us in the present. $7.95.
(5) The Mayfair Set. Four stories about the rise of business and the decline of political power. Asset strippers reducing Britain and the US to playthings of "market forces" — i.e., speculators. $7.95.
(6) Pandora's Box. 6 episodes, 3 discs, on societies gone awry when leaders make science a religion. **$12.**
(7) All Watched Over by Machines of Loving Grace. The folly of humans imitating machines. **$7.95**

~ ProgressivePress.com ~
More details at info@progressivepress.com

CPSIA information can be obtained at www.ICGtesting.com
Printed in the USA
LVOW050628160212

268961LV00003B/1/P